TRAVELLERS' TALES

Stories of adventure in far lands, told by
Marco Polo, Columbus, Hernando Cortes, Sir
Walter Raleigh, Captain Cook, and other
famous explorers of an unknown world.

Arranged by JAY Du BOIS

EVERYBODY'S VACATION PUBLISHING CO.

New York

41401

Contents

Introduction

When Marco Polo returned from the Far East with glowing accounts of the fabulous treasures to be found there, he blazed the trail for countless adventurers eager to get their share of these riches. His colorful exaggerations were a lure in that continuous search for a shorter route to Cathay which would inflame the minds of men for centuries.

The accounts in journal form which appear here were all written by actual participants in these hazardous voyages, who were in addition blessed with the ability to recount their adventures in vivid detail. Few leaders of these expeditions possessed the gift of writing, nor did scholars appear to venture on the high seas; but among the intrepid explorers and navigators who made history there was always someone to write a record of such eloquent wonder that it must become a part of world literature. Representative selections in this book will acquaint the reader with the flavor, as well as the fact, of the awful hardships endured—and the gratifying joy of the discoveries made.

"The Letter of Columbus on the Discovery of America," edited by Wilberforce Eames, is here reprinted by courteous permission of the New York Public Library, Astor, Lenox and Tilden Foundations.

Jay Du Bois

CHAPTER I

Marco Polo—1254–1324

Of all the remarkable tales of travel handed down through the ages, there is none to equal the amazing journey of Marco Polo. Marco Polo was a Venetian who, in 1271, at the age of 15, accompanied his father and uncle, Nicolo and Maffeo Polo, to Peking, the capital of the Tartar empire. Nicolo and Maffeo had already been well received by the great conqueror, Kublai Khan, and were on a mission for him as the result of a journey started by them in 1260. They had started out as merchants, but were imperial envoys of the great Khan when the young Marco set forth. Their travels, truly one of the greatest expeditions in history, lasted from 1260 to 1295. Although they were the first Europeans to cross Asia, their stories of the fabulous wealth of the East were scarcely believed—in fact, they were laughed at.

The manner in which the book was written is in itself astonishing. Here was a man who had travelled unharmed over half the face of the globe; but in the year 1298 Marco Polo found himself in a Genoese jail, a prisoner of a war between Venice and Genoa. Luckily, a professional writer named Rusticiano was also in jail, and to him Marco Polo dictated a full account of the magnificent wonders of the East.

PROLOGUE

GREAT Princes, Emperors and Kings, Dukes and Marquises, Counts, Knights, and Burgesses! and People of all degrees who desire to get knowledge of the various races of mankind and of the diversities of the sundry regions of the World, take this Book and cause it to be read to you. For ye shall find therein all kinds of wonderful things, and the divers histories of the Great Armenia, and of Persia, and of the Land of the Tartars, and of India, and of many another country of which our Book doth speak, particularly and in regular succession, according to the description of Messer Marco Polo, a wise and noble citizen of Venice, as he saw them with his own eyes. Some things indeed there be therein which he beheld not; but these he heard from men of credit and veracity. And we shall set down things seen as seen, and things heard as heard only, so that no jot of falsehood may mar the truth of our Book, and that all who shall read it or hear it read may put full faith in the truth of all its contents.

For let me tell you that since our Lord God did mould with His hands our first Father Adam, even until this day, never hath there been Christian, or Pagan, or Tartar, or Indian, or any man of any nation, who in his own person hath had so much knowledge and experience of the divers parts of the World and its Wonders as hath had this Messer Marco! And for that reason he bethought himself that it would be a very great pity did he not cause to be put in writing all the great marvels that he had seen, or on sure information heard of, so that other people who had not these advantages might, by his Book, get such knowledge. And I may tell you that in acquiring this knowledge he spent in those various parts of the World good six-and-twenty years. Now, being thereafter an inmate of the Prison at Genoa, he caused Messer Rusticiano of Pisa, who was in the said Prison likewise, to reduce the whole to writing; and this befell in the year 1298 from the birth of Jesus.

How the Two Brothers Polo set forth from Constantinople to traverse the World

It came to pass in the year of Christ 1260, when Baldwin was reigning at Constantinople, that Messer Nicolas Polo, the father of my lord Mark, and Messer Maffeo Polo, the brother of Messer Nicolas, were at the said city of Constantinople, whither they had gone from Venice with their merchants' wares. Now these two Brethren, men singularly noble, wise, and provident, took counsel together to cross the Greater Sea on a venture of trade; so they laid in a store of jewels and set forth from Constantinople, crossing the Sea to Soldaia.

How the Two Brothers went on beyond Soldaia

Having stayed a while at Soldaia, they considered the matter, and thought it well to extend their journey further. So they set forth from Soldaia and travelled till they came to the Court of a certain Tartar Prince, Barka Khan by name, whose residences were at Sarai and at Bolgara [and who was esteemed one of the most liberal and courteous Princes that ever was among the Tartars]. This Barka was delighted at the arrival of the Two Brothers, and treated them with great honour; so they presented to him the whole of the jewels that they had brought with them. The Prince was highly pleased with these, and accepted the offering most graciously, causing the Brothers to receive at least twice its value.

After they had spent a twelvemonth at the court of this Prince there broke out a great war between Barka and Hulagu, the Lord of the Tartars of the Levant, and great hosts were mustered on either side.

But in the end Barka, the Lord of the Tartars of the Ponent, was defeated, though on both sides there was great slaughter. And by reason of this war no one could travel without peril of being taken; thus it was at least on the road by which the Brothers had come, though there was no obstacle to their travelling forward. So the Brothers, finding they could not retrace their steps, determined to go forward. Quitting Bolgara, therefore, they proceeded to a city called UKEK, which was at the extremity of the kingdom of the Lord of the Ponent; and thence departing again, and passing the great River Tigris, they travelled across a Desert which extended for seventeen days' journey, and wherein they found neither town nor village, falling in only with the tents of Tartars occupied with their cattle at pasture.

How THE TWO BROTHERS, AFTER CROSSING A DESERT, CAME TO THE CITY OF BOKHARA, AND FELL IN WITH CERTAIN ENVOYS THERE

AFTER they had passed the desert, they arrived at a very great and noble city called BOKHARA, the territory of which belonged to a king whose name was Borrak, and is also called Bokhara. The city is the best in all Persia. And when they had got thither, they found they could neither proceed further forward nor yet turn back again; wherefore they abode in that city of Bokhara for three years. And whilst they were sojourning in that city, there came from Hulagu, Lord of the Levant, Envoys on their way to the Court of the Great Khan, the Lord of all the Tartars in the world. And when the Envoys beheld the Two Brothers they were amazed, for they had never before seen Latins in that part of the world. And they said to the Brothers: "Gentlemen, if ye will take our counsel, ye will find great honour and profit shall come thereof." So they replied that they would be right glad to learn how. "In truth," said the Envoys, "the Great Khan hath never seen any Latins, and he hath a great desire so to do. Wherefore, if ye will keep us company to his Court, ye may depend upon it that he will be right glad to see you, and will treat you with great honour and liberality; whilst in our company ye shall travel with perfect security, and need fear to be molested by nobody."

How THE TWO BROTHERS TOOK THE ENVOYS' COUNSEL, AND WENT TO THE COURT OF THE GREAT KHAN

So when the Two Brothers had made their arrangements, they set out on their travels, in company with the Envoys, and journeyed for a whole year, going northward and north-eastward, before they reached the Court of that Prince. And on their journey they saw many marvels of divers and sundry kinds, but of these we shall say nothing at present, because Messer Mark, who has likewise seen them all, will give you a full account of them in the Book which follows.

How THE TWO BROTHERS ARRIVED AT THE COURT OF THE GREAT KHAN

WHEN the Two Brothers got to the Great Khan, he received them with great honour and hospitality, and showed much pleasure at their visit, asking them a great number of questions. First, he asked about the emperors,

how they maintained their dignity, and administered justice in their dominions; and how they went forth to battle, and so forth. And then he asked the
like questions about the kings and princes and other potentates.

How the Great Khan asked all about the manners of the Christians, and particularly about the Pope of Rome

AND then he inquired about the Pope and the Church, and about all that is
done at Rome, and all the customs of the Latins. And the Two Brothers
told him the truth in all its particulars, with order and good sense, like sensible men as they were; and this they were able to do as they knew the
Tartar language well.

How the Great Khan sent the Two Brothers as his Envoys to the Pope

WHEN that Prince, whose name was KUBLAI KHAN, Lord of the Tartars all
over the earth, and of all the kingdoms and provinces and territories of that
vast quarter of the world, had heard all that the Brothers had to tell him
about the ways of the Latins, he was greatly pleased, and he took it into his
head that he would send them on an Embassy to the Pope. So he urgently
desired them to undertake this mission along with one of his Barons; and they
replied that they would gladly execute all his commands as those of their
Sovereign Lord. Then the Prince sent to summon to his presence one of his
Barons whose name was COGATAL, and desired him to get ready, for it was
proposed to send him to the Pope along with the Two Brothers. The Baron
replied that he would execute the Lord's commands to the best of his ability.

After this the Prince caused letters from himself to the Pope to be indited
in the Tartar tongue, and committed them to the Two Brothers and to that
Baron of his own, and charged them with what he wished them to say to
the Pope. Now the contents of the letter were to this purport: He begged
that the Pope would send as many as an hundred persons of our Christian
faith; intelligent men, acquainted with the Seven Arts, well qualified to enter
into controversy, and able clearly to prove by force of argument to idolaters
and other kinds of folk, that the Law of Christ was best, and that all other
religions were false and naught; and that if they would prove this, he and
all under him would become Christians and the Church's liegemen. Finally he
charged his Envoys to bring back to him some Oil of the Lamp which burns
on the Sepulchre of our Lord at Jerusalem.

How the Great Khan gave them a Tablet of Gold, bearing his orders in their behalf

WHEN the Prince had charged them with all his commission, he caused to be
given them a Tablet of Gold, on which was inscribed that the three Ambassadors should be supplied with everything needful in all the countries
through which they should pass—with horses, with escorts, and, in short,
with whatever they should require. And when they had made all needful

preparations, the three Ambassadors took their leave of the Emperor and set out.

When they had travelled I know not how many days, the Tartar Baron fell sick, so that he could not ride, and being very ill, and unable to proceed further, he halted at a certain city. So the Two Brothers judged it best that they should leave him behind and proceed to carry out their commission; and, as he was well content that they should do so, they continued their journey. And I can assure you, that whithersoever they went they were honourably provided with whatever they stood in need of, or chose to command. And this was owing to that Tablet of Authority from the Lord which they carried with them.

So they travelled on and on until they arrived at Ayas in Armenia, a journey which occupied them, I assure you, for three years. It took them so long because they could not always proceed, being stopped sometimes by snow, or by heavy rains falling, or by great torrents which they found in an impassable state.

How the Two Brothers came to the city of Acre

They departed from Ayas and came to Acre, arriving there in the month of April, in the year of Christ 1269, and then they learned that the Pope was dead. And when they found that the Pope was dead (his name was Pope Clement IV), they went to a certain wise Churchman who was Legate for the whole kingdom of Egypt, and a man of great authority, by name Theobald of Piacenza, and told him of the mission on which they were come. When the Legate heard their story, he was greatly surprised, and deemed the thing to be of great honour and advantage for the whole of Christendom. So his answer to the two Ambassador Brothers was this: "Gentlemen, ye see that the Pope is dead; wherefore ye must needs have patience until a new Pope be made, and then shall ye be able to execute your charge." Seeing well enough that what the Legate said was just, they observed: "But while the Pope is a-making, we may as well go to Venice and visit our households." So they departed from Acre and went to Negropont, and from Negropont they continued their voyage to Venice. On their arrival there, Messer Nicolas found that his wife was dead, and that she had left behind her a son of fifteen years of age, whose name was Marco; and 'tis of him that this Book tells. The Two Brothers abode at Venice a couple of years, tarrying until a Pope should be made.

How the Two Brothers again Departed from Venice, on their way back to the Great Khan, and took with them Mark, the son of Messer Nicolas

When the Two Brothers had tarried as long as I have told you, and saw that never a Pope was made, they said that their return to the Great Khan must be put off no longer. So they set out from Venice, taking Mark along with them, and went straight back to Acre, where they found the Legate of whom we have spoken. They had a good deal of discourse with him concerning the matter, and asked his permission to go to JERUSALEM to get some Oil from the Lamp on the Sepulchre, to carry with them to the Great Khan, as he had enjoined. The Legate giving them leave, they went from Acre to Jerusalem and got some of the Oil, and then returned to Acre, and went to the Legate and said to him: "As we see no sign of a Pope's being made, we desire to return to the Great Khan; for we have already tarried long, and there has been more than enough delay." To which the Legate replied: "Since 'tis your wish to go back, I am well content." Wherefore he caused letters to be written for delivery to the Great Khan, bearing testimony that the Two Brothers had come in all good faith to accomplish his charge, but that as there was no Pope they had been unable to do so.

How the Two Brothers set out from Acre, and Mark along with them

WHEN the Two Brothers had received the Legate's letters, they set forth from Acre to return to the Great Khan, and got as far as Ayas. But shortly after their arrival there they had news that the Legate aforesaid was chosen Pope, taking the name of Pope Gregory of Piacenza; news which the Two Brothers were very glad indeed to hear. And presently there reached them at Ayas a message from the Legate, now the Pope, desiring them, on the part of the Apostolic See, not to proceed further on their journey, but to return to him incontinently. And what shall I tell you? The King of Armenia caused a galley to be got ready for the Two Ambassador Brothers, and despatched them to the Pope at Acre.

How the Two Brothers presented themselves before the new Pope

AND when they had been thus honourably conducted to Acre they proceeded to the presence of the Pope, and paid their respects to him with humble reverence. He received them with great honour and satisfaction, and gave them his blessing. He then appointed two Friars of the Order of Preachers to accompany them to the Great Khan, and to do whatever might be required of them. These were unquestionably as learned Churchmen as were to be found in the Province at that day—one being called Friar Nicolas of Vicenza, and the other Friar William of Tripoli. He delivered to them also proper credentials, and letters in reply to the Great Khan's messages [and gave them authority to ordain priests and bishops, and to bestow every kind of absolution, as if given by himself in proper person; sending by them also many fine vessels of crystal as presents to the Great Khan]. So when they had got all that was needful, they took leave of the Pope, receiving his benediction; and the four set out together from Acre, and went to Ayas, accompanied always by Messer Nicolas's son Marco.

Now, about the time that they reached Ayas, Bundakdar, the Sultan of Babylon, invaded Armenia with a great host of Saracens, and ravaged the country, so that our Envoys ran a great peril of being taken or slain. And when the Preaching Friars saw this they were greatly frightened, and said that go they never would. So they made over to Messer Nicolas and Messer Maffeo all their credentials and documents, and took their leave, departing in company with the Master of the Temple.

How Messer Nicolo and Messer Maffeo Polo, accompanied by Mark, travelled to the Court of the Great Khan

So the Two Brothers, and Mark along with them, proceeded on their way, and journeying on, summer and winter, came at length to the Great Khan, who was then at a certain rich and great city, called Kaiminfu. As to what they met with on the road, whether in going or coming, we shall give no particulars at present, because we are going to tell you all those details in regular order in the after part of this Book. Their journey back to the Khan occupied a good three years and a half, owing to the bad weather and severe cold that they encountered. And let me tell you in good sooth that when the Great Khan heard that Messers Nicolo and Maffeo Polo were on their way back, he sent people a journey of full 40 days to meet them; and on this journey, as on their former one, they were honourably entertained upon the road, and supplied with all that they required.

How Messer Nicolo and Messer Maffeo Polo and Marco presented themselves before the Great Khan

And what shall I tell you? when the Two Brothers and Mark had arrived at that great city, they went to the Imperial Palace, and there they found the Sovereign attended by a great company of Barons. So they bent the knee before him, and paid their respects to him, with all possible reverence [prostrating themselves on the ground]. Then the Lord bade them stand up, and treated them with great honour, showing great pleasure at their coming, and asked many questions as to their welfare, and how they had sped. They replied that they had in verity sped well, seeing that they found the Khan well and safe. Then they presented the credentials and letters which they had received from the Pope, which pleased him right well; and after that they produced the Oil from the Sepulchre, and at that also he was very glad, for he set great store thereby. And next, spying Mark, who was then a young gallant, he asked who was that in their company? "Sire," said his father, Messer Nicolo, " 'tis my son and your liegeman." "Welcome is he too," quoth the Emperor. And why should I make a long story? There was great rejoicing at the Court because of their arrival; and they met with attention and honour from everybody.

So there they abode at the Court with the other Barons.

How the Emperor sent Mark on an Embassy of his

Now it came to pass that Marco, the son of Messer Nicolo, sped wondrously in learning the customs of the Tartars, as well as their language, their manner of writing, and their practice of war; in fact he came in brief space to know several languages, and four sundry written characters. And he was discreet and prudent in every way, insomuch that the Emperor held him in great esteem. And so when he discerned Mark to have so much sense, and to conduct himself so well and beseemingly, he sent him on an ambassage of his, to a country which was a good six months' journey distant. The young gallant executed his commission well and with discretion. Now he had taken note on several occasions that when the Prince's ambassadors returned from different parts of the world, they were able to tell him about nothing except the business on which they had gone, and that the Prince in consequence held them for no better than fools and dolts, and would say: "I had far liever hearken about the strange things, and the manners of the different countries you have seen, than merely be told of the business you went upon"; —for he took great delight in hearing of the affairs of strange countries. Mark therefore, as he went and returned, took great pains to learn about all kinds of different matters in the countries which he visited, in order to be able to tell about them to the Great Khan.

How Mark returned from the Mission whereon he had been sent

When Mark returned from his ambassage he presented himself before the Emperor, and after making his report of the business with which he was charged, and its successful accomplishment, he went on to give an account in a pleasant and intelligent manner of all the novelties and strange things that he had seen and heard; insomuch that the Emperor and all such as heard his story were surprised, and said: "If this young man live, he will assuredly come to be a person of great worth and ability." And so from that time forward he was always entitled Messer Marco Polo, and thus we shall style him henceforth in this Book of ours, as is but right.

Thereafter Messer Marco abode in the Khan's employment some seventeen years, continually going and coming, hither and thither, on the missions that were entrusted to him by the Lord [and sometimes, with the permission and authority of the Great Khan, on his own private affairs]. And, as he knew all the sovereign's ways, like a sensible man he always took much pains to gather knowledge of anything that would be likely to interest him, and then on his return to Court he would relate everything in regular order, and thus the Emperor came to hold him in great love and favour. And for this reason also he would employ him the oftener on the most weighty and most distant of his missions. These Messer Marco ever carried out with discretion and success, God be thanked. So the Emperor became ever more partial to him, and treated him with the greater distinction, and kept him so close to his person that some of the Barons waxed very envious thereat. And thus it came about that Messer Marco Polo had knowledge of, or had actually visited, a greater number of the different countries of the World than any other man; the more that he was always giving his mind to get knowledge, and to spy out and enquire into everything in order to have matter to relate to the Lord.

How Messer Nicolo, Messer Maffeo, and Messer Marco asked leave of the Great Kahn to go their way

When the Two Brothers and Mark had abode with the Lord all that time that you have been told [having meanwhile acquired great wealth in jewels and gold], they began among themselves to have thoughts about returning to their own country; and indeed it was time. [For, to say nothing of the length and infinite perils of the way, when they considered the Khan's great age, they doubted whether, in the event of his death before their departure, they would ever be able to get home.] They applied to him several times for leave to go, presenting their request with great respect, but he had such a partiality for them, and liked so much to have them about him, that nothing on earth would persuade him to let them go.

Now it came to pass in those days that the Queen Bulughan, wife of Arghun, Lord of the Levant, departed this life. And in her Will she had desired that no Lady should take her place, or succeed her as Arghun's wife, except one of her own family [which existed in Cathay]. Arghun therefore despatched three of his Barons, by name respectively Uladai, Apushka, and Koja, as ambassadors to the Great Khan, attended by a very gallant company, in order to bring back as his bride a lady of the family of Queen Bulughan, his late wife.

When these three Barons had reached the Court of the Great Khan, they delivered their message, explaining wherefore they were come. The Khan received them with all honour and hospitality, and then sent for a lady whose name was Kukachin, who was of the family of the deceased Queen Bulughan. She was a maiden of 17, a very beautiful and charming person, and on her arrival at Court she was presented to the three Barons as the Lady chosen in compliance with their demand. They declared that the Lady pleased them well.

Meanwhile Messer Marco chanced to return from India, whither he had gone as the Lord's ambassador, and made his report of all the different things that he had seen in his travels, and of the sundry seas over which he had voyaged. And the three Barons, having seen that Messer Nicolo, Messer Maffeo, and Messer Marco were not only Latins, but men of marvellous good sense withal, took thought among themselves to get the three to travel with them, their intention being to return to their country by sea, on account of the great fatigue of that long land journey for a Lady. And the ambassadors were the more desirous to have their company, as being aware that those three had great knowledge and experience of the Indian Sea and the countries by which they would have to pass, and especially Messer Marco. So they went to the Great Khan, and begged as a favour that he would send the three Latins with them, as it was their desire to return home by sea.

The Lord, having that great regard that I have mentioned for those three Latins, was very loath to do so [and his countenance showed great dissatisfaction]. But at last he did give them permission to depart, enjoining them to accompany the three Barons and the Lady.

How the Two Brothers and Messer Marco took leave of the Great Kahn, and returned to their own Country

And when the Prince saw that the Two Brothers and Messer Marco were ready to set forth, he called them all three to his presence, and gave them two golden Tablets of Authority, which should secure them liberty of passage through all his dominions, and by means of which, whithersoever they should go, all necessaries would be provided for them, and for all their company, and whatever they might choose to order. He charged them also with messages to the King of France, the King of England, the King of Spain, and the other kings of Christendom. He then caused thirteen ships to be equipt, each of which had four masts, and often spread twelve sails. And I could easily give you all particulars about these, but as it would be so long an affair I will not enter upon this now, but hereafter, when time and place are suitable. [Among the said ships were at least four or five that carried crews of 250 or 260 men.]

And when the ships had been equipt, the Three Barons and the Lady, and the Two Brothers and Messer Marco, took leave of the Great Khan, and went on board their ships with a great company of people, and with all necessaries provided for two years by the Emperor. They put forth to sea, and after sailing for some three months they arrived at a certain Island towards the South, which is called Java, and in which there are many wonderful things which we shall tell you all about by-and-bye. Quitting this Island they continued to navigate the Sea of India for eighteen months more before they arrived whither they were bound, meeting on their way also with many marvels, of which we shall tell hereafter.

And when they got thither they found that Arghun was dead, so the Lady was delivered to Ghazan, his son.

But I should have told you that it is a fact that, when they embarked, they were in number some 600 persons, without counting the mariners; but nearly all died by the way, so that only eight survived.

The sovereignty when they arrived was held by Kaikhatu, so they commended the Lady to him, and executed all their commission. And when the Two Brothers and Messer Marco had executed their charge in full, and done all that the Great Khan had enjoined on them in regard to the Lady, they took their leave and set out upon their journey. And before their departure, Kaikhatu gave them four golden tablets of authority, two of which bore gerfalcons, one bore lions, whilst the fourth was plain, and having on them inscriptions which directed that the three Ambassadors should receive honour and service all through the land as if rendered to the Prince in person, and that horses and all provisions, and everything necessary, should be supplied to them. And so they found in fact; for throughout the country they received ample and excellent supplies of everything needful;

and many a time indeed, as I may tell you, they were furnished with 200 horsemen, more or less, to escort them on their way in safety. And this was all the more needful because Kaikhatu was not the legitimate Lord, and therefore the people had less scruple to do mischief than if they had had a lawful prince.

Another thing too must be mentioned, which does credit to those three Ambassadors, and shows for what great personages they were held. The Great Khan regarded them with such trust and affection, that he had confided to their charge the Queen Kukachin, as well as the daughter of the King of Manzi, to conduct to Arghun the Lord of all the Levant. And those two great ladies who were thus entrusted to them they watched over and guarded as if they had been daughters of their own, until they had transferred them to the hands of their Lord; whilst the ladies, young and fair as they were, looked on each of those three as a father, and obeyed them accordingly. Indeed, both Ghazan, who is now the reigning prince, and the Queen Kukachin his wife, have such a regard for the Envoys that there is nothing they would not do for them. And when the three Ambassadors took leave of that Lady to return to their own country, she wept for sorrow at the parting.

What more shall I say? Having left Kaikhatu they travelled day by day till they came to Trebizond, and thence to Constantinople, from Constantinople to Negropont, and from Negropont to Venice. And this was in the year 1295 of Christ's Incarnation.

And now that I have rehearsed all the Prologue as you have heard, we shall begin the Book of the Description of the Divers Things that Messer Marco met with in his Travels.

Here the Book begins; and first it speaks of the Lesser Armenia

There are two Armenias, the Greater and the Less. The Lesser Armenia is governed by a certain King, who maintans a just rule in his dominions, but is himself subject to the Tartar. The country contains numerous towns and villages, and has everything in plenty; moreover, it is a great country for sport in the chase of all manner of beasts and birds. It is, however, by no means a healthy region, but grievously the reverse. In days of old the nobles there were valiant men, and did doughty deeds of arms; but nowadays they are poor creatures, and good at nought, unless it be at boozing; they are great at that. Howbeit, they have a city upon the sea, which is called Ayas, at which there is a great trade. For you must know that all the spicery, and the cloths of silk and gold, and the other valuable wares that come from the interior, are brought to that city. And the merchants of Venice and Genoa, and other countries, come thither to sell their goods, and to buy what they lack. And whatsoever persons would travel to the interior (of the East), merchants or others, they take their way by this city of Ayas.

DESCRIPTION OF THE GREATER ARMENIA

THIS is a great country. It begins at a city called ERZINJAN, at which they weave the best buckrams in the world. It possesses also the best baths from natural springs that are anywhere to be found. The people of the country are Armenians, and are subject to the Tartar. There are many towns and villages in the country, but the noblest of their cities is Erzinjan, which is the See of an Archbishop, and then ERZERUM and ARJISH.

The country is indeed a passing great one, and in the summer it is frequented by the whole host of the Tartars of the Levant, because it then furnishes them with such excellent pasture for their cattle. But in winter the cold is past all bounds, so in that season they quit this country and go to a warmer region, where they find other good pastures. [At a castle called BAIBURT, that you pass in going from Trebizond to Tauris, there is a very good silver mine.]

And you must know that it is in this country of Armenia that the Ark of Noah exists on the top of a certain great mountain [on the summit of which snow is so constant that no one can ascend; for the snow never melts, and is constantly added to by new falls. Below, however, the snow does melt, and runs down, producing such rich and abundant herbage that in summer cattle are sent to pasture from a long way round about, and it never fails them. The melting snow also causes a great amount of mud on the mountain].

The country is bounded on the south by a kingdom called Mosul, the people of which are Jacobite and Nestorian Christians, of whom I shall have more to tell you presently. On the north it is bounded by the Land of the Georgians, of whom also I shall speak. On the confines towards Georgia there is a fountain from which oil springs in great abundance, insomuch that a hundred shiploads might be taken from it at one time. This oil is not good to use with food, but 'tis good to burn, and is also used to anoint camels that have the mange. People come from vast distances to fetch it, for in all the countries round about they have no other oil.

Now, having done with Great Armenia, we will tell you of Georgia.

OF GEORGIA AND THE KINGS THEREOF

IN GEORGIA there is a King called David Melic, which is as much as to say "David King"; he is subject to the Tartar. In old times all the kings were born with the figure of an eagle upon the right shoulder. The people are very handsome, capital archers, and most valiant soldiers. They are Christians of the Greek Rite, and have a fashion of wearing their hair cropped, like Churchmen.

This is the country beyond which Alexander could not pass when he wished to penetrate to the region of the Ponent, because that the defile was so narrow and perilous, the sea lying on the one hand, and on the other lofty mountains impassable to horsemen. The strait extends like this for four leagues, and a handful of people might hold it against all the world. Alexander caused a very strong tower to be built there, to prevent the people beyond from passing to attack him, and this got the name of the IRON GATE. This is the place that the Book of Alexander speaks of, when it tells us how he shut up the Tartars between two mountains; not that they were really Tartars, however, for there were no Tartars in those days, but they consisted of a race of people called COMANIANS and many besides.

[In this province all the forests are of box-wood.] There are numerous towns and villages, and silk is produced in great abundance. They also weave cloths of gold, and all kinds of very fine silk stuffs. The country produces the best goshawks in the world [which are called *Avigi*]. It has indeed no lack of anything, and the people live by trade and handicrafts. 'Tis a very mountainous region, and full of strait defiles and of fortresses, insomuch that the Tartars have never been able to subdue it out and out.

There is in this country a certain Convent of Nuns called St. Leonard's, about which I have to tell you a very wonderful circumstance. Near the church in question there is a great lake at the foot of a mountain, and in this lake are found no fish, great or small, throughout the year till Lent come. On the first day of Lent they find in it the finest fish in the world, and great store too thereof; and these continue to be found till Easter Eve. After that they are found no more till Lent come round again; and so 'tis every year. 'Tis really a passing great miracle!

That sea whereof I spoke as coming so near the mountains is called the SEA of GHEL or GHELAN, and extends about 700 miles. It is twelve days' journey distant from any other sea, and into it flows the great River Euphrates and many others, whilst it is surrounded by mountains. Of late the merchants of Genoa have begun to navigate this sea, carrying ships across and launching them thereon. It is from the country on this sea also that the silk called *Ghella* is brought. [The said sea produces quantities of fish, especially sturgeon, at the river-mouths salmon, and other big kinds of fish.]

OF THE KINGDOM OF MOSUL

ON the frontier of Armenia towards the south-east is the kingdom of MOSUL. It is a very great kingdom, and inhabited by several different kinds of people whom we shall now describe.

First there is a kind of people called ARABS, and these worship Mahomet. Then there is another description of people who are NESTORIAN and JACOBITE Christians. These have a Patriarch, whom they call the JATOLIC, and this Patriarch creates Archbishops, and Abbots, and Prelates of all other degrees, and sends them into every quarter, as to India, to Bagdad, or to Cathay, just as the Pope of Rome does in the Latin countries. For you must know that though there is a very great number of Christians in those countries, they are all Jacobites and Nestorians; Christians indeed, but not in the fashion enjoined by the Pope of Rome, for they come short in several points of the Faith.

All the cloths of gold and silk that are called *Mosolins* are made in this country; and those great Merchants called *Mosolins*, who carry for sale such quantities of spicery and pearls and cloths of silk and gold, are also from this kingdom.

There is yet another race of people who inhabit the mountains in that quarter, and are called KURDS. Some of them are Christians, and some of them are Saracens; but they are an evil generation, whose delight it is to plunder merchants.

[Near this province is another called MUSH and MARDIN, producing an immense quantity of cotton, from which they make a great deal of buckram and other cloth. The people are craftsmen and traders, and are all subject to the Tartar King.]

OF THE GREAT CITY OF BAGDAD, AND HOW IT WAS TAKEN

BAGDAD is a great city, which used to be the seat of the Calif of all the Saracens in the world, just as Rome is the seat of the Pope of all the Christians. A very great river flows through the city, and by this you can descend to the Sea of India. There is a great traffic of merchants with their goods this way; they descend some eighteen days from Bagdad, and then come to a certain city called KISH, where they enter the Sea of India. There is also on the river, as you go from Bagdad to Kish, a great city called BASRA, surrounded by woods, in which grow the best dates in the world.

In Bagdad they weave many different kinds of silk stuffs and gold brocades, such as *nasich,* and *nac,* and *cræmoisy,* and many another beautiful tissue richly wrought with figures of beasts and birds. It is the noblest and greatest city in all those regions.

Now it came to pass on a day in the year of Christ 1255, that the Lord of the Tartars of the Levant, whose name was Hulagu, brother to the Great Kahn now reigning, gathered a mighty host and came up against Bagdad and took it by storm. It was a great enterprise! for in Bagdad there were more than 100,000 horse, besides foot soldiers. And when Hulagu had taken the place he found therein a tower of the Calif's, which was full of gold and silver and other treasure; in fact the greatest accumulation of treasure in one spot that ever was known. When he beheld that great heap of treasure he was astonished, and, summoning the Calif to his presence, he said to him: "Calif, tell me now why thou hast gathered such a huge treasure? What didst thou mean to do therewith? Knewest thou not that I was thine enemy, and that I was coming against thee with so great an host to cast thee forth of thine heritage? Wherefore didst thou not take of thy gear and employ it in paying knights and soldiers to defend thee and thy city?"

The Calif wist not what to answer, and said never a word. So the Prince continued, "Now then, Calif, since I see what a love thou hast borne thy treasure, I will e'en give it thee to eat!" So he shut the Calif up in the Treasure Tower, and bade that neither meat nor drink should be given him, saying, "Now, Calif, eat of thy treasure as much as thou wilt, since thou art so fond of it; for never shalt thou have aught else to eat!"

So the Calif lingered in the tower four days, and then died like a dog. Truly his treasure would have been of more service to him had he bestowed it upon men who would have defended his kingdom and his people, rather than let himself be taken and deposed and put to death as he was. Howbeit, since that time, there has been never another Calif, either at Bagdad or anywhere else.

Now I will tell you of a great miracle that befell at Bagdad, wrought by God on behalf of the Christians.

How the Calif of Bagdad took counsel to slay all the Christians in his Land

I will tell you then this great marvel that occurred between Bagdad and Mosul.

It was in the year of Christ . . . that there was a Calif at Bagdad who bore a great hatred to Christians, and was taken up day and night with the thought how he might either bring those that were in his kingdom over to his own faith, or might procure them all to be slain. And he used daily to take counsel about this with the devotees and priests of his faith, for they all bore the Christians like malice. And, indeed, it is a fact, that the whole body of Saracens throughout the world are always most malignantly disposed towards the whole body of Christians.

Now it happened that the Calif, with those shrewd priests of his, got hold of that passage in our Gospel which says, that if a Christian had faith as a grain of mustard seed, and should bid a mountain be removed, it would be removed. And such indeed is the truth. But when they had got hold of this text they were delighted, for it seemed to them the very thing whereby either to force all the Christians to change their faith, or to bring destruction upon them all. The Calif therefore called together all the Christians in his territories, who were extremely numerous. And when they had come before him, he showed them the Gospel, and made them read the text which I have mentioned. And when they had read it he asked them if that was the truth? The Christians answered that it assuredly was so. "Well," said the Calif, "since you say that it is the truth, I will give you a choice. Among such a number of you there must needs surely be this small amount of faith; so you must either move that mountain there," —and he pointed to a mountain in the neighbourhood—"or you shall die an ill death; unless you choose to eschew death by all becoming Saracens and adopting our Holy Law. To this end I give you a respite of ten days; if the thing be not done by that time, ye shall die or become Saracens." And when he had said this he dismissed them, to consider what was to be done in this strait wherein they were.

How the Christians were in great dismay because of what the Calif had said

THE Christians on hearing what the Calif had said were in great dismay, but they lifted all their hopes to God, their Creator, that He would help them in this their strait. All the wisest of the Christians took counsel together, and among them were a number of bishops and priests, but they had no resource except to turn to Him from whom all good things do come, beseeching Him to protect them from the cruel hands of the Calif. So they were all gathered together in prayer, both men and women, for eight days and eight nights. And whilst they were thus engaged in prayer it was revealed in a vision by a Holy Angel of Heaven to a certain Bishop who was a very good Christian, that he should desire a certain Christian Cobbler, who had but one eye, to pray to God; and that God in His goodness would grant such prayer because of the Cobbler's holy life.

Now I must tell you what manner of man this Cobbler was. He was one who led a life of great uprightness and chastity, and who fasted and kept from all sin, and went daily to church to hear Mass, and gave daily a portion of his gains to God. And the way how he came to have but one eye was this. It happened one day that a certain woman came to him to have a pair of shoes made, and she showed him her foot that he might take her measure. Now she had a very beautiful foot and leg; and the Cobbler in taking her measure was conscious of sinful thoughts. And he had often heard it said in the Holy Evangel, that if thine eye offend thee, pluck it out and cast it from thee, rather than sin. So, as soon as the woman had departed, he took the awl that he used in stitching, and drove it into his eye and destroyed it. And this is the way he came to lose his eye. So you can judge what a holy, just, and righteous man he was.

How the One-eyed Cobbler was desired to pray for the Christians

Now when this vision had visited the Bishop several times, he related the whole matter to the Christians, and they agreed with one consent to call the Cobbler before them. And when he had come they told him it was their wish that he should pray, and that God had promised to accomplish the matter by his means. On hearing their request he made many excuses, declaring that he was not at all so good a man as they represented. But they persisted in their request with so much sweetness, that at last he said he would not tarry, but do what they desired.

How the Prayer of the One-eyed Cobbler caused the Mountain to move

AND when the appointed day was come, all the Christians got up early, men and women, small and great, more than 100,000 persons, and went to church, and heard the Holy Mass. And after Mass had been sung, they all went forth together in a great procession to the plain in front of the mountain, carrying the precious cross before them, loudly singing and greatly weeping as they went. And when they arrived at the spot, there they found the Calif with all his Saracen host armed to slay them if they would not change their faith; for the Saracens believed not in the least that God would grant such favour to the Christians. These latter stood indeed in great fear and doubt, but nevertheless they rested their hope on their God Jesus Christ.

So the Cobbler received the Bishop's benison, and then threw himself on his knees before the Holy Cross, and stretched out his hands towards Heaven, and made this prayer: "Blessed LORD GOD ALMIGHTY, I pray Thee by Thy goodness that Thou wilt grant this grace unto Thy people, insomuch that they perish not, nor Thy faith be cast down, nor abused nor flouted. Not that I am in the least worthy to prefer such request unto Thee; but for Thy great power and mercy I beseech Thee to hear this prayer from me Thy servant full of sin."

And when he had ended this his prayer to God the Sovereign Father and Giver of all grace, and whilst the Calif and all the Saracens, and other people there, were looking on, the mountain rose out of its place and moved to the spot which the Calif had pointed out! And when the Calif and all his Saracens beheld, they stood amazed at the wonderful miracle that God had wrought for the Christians, insomuch that a great number of the Saracens became Christians. And even the Calif caused himself to be baptised in the name of the Father and of the Son and of the Holy Ghost, Amen, and became a Christian, but in secret. Howbeit, when he died they found a little cross hung round his neck; and therefore the Saracens would not bury him with the other Califs, but put him in a place apart. The Christians exulted greatly at this most holy miracle, and returned to their homes full of joy, giving thanks to their Creator for that which He had done.

And now you have heard in what wise took place this great miracle. And marvel not that the Saracens hate the Christians; for the accursed law that Mahomet gave them commands them to do all the mischief in their power to all other descriptions of people, and especially to Christians; to strip such of their goods, and do them all manner of evil, because they belong not to their law. See then what an evil law and what naughty commandments they have! But in such fashion the Saracens act, throughout the world.

Now I have told you something of Bagdad. I could easily indeed have told you first of the affairs and the customs of the people there. But it would be too long a business, looking to the great and strange things that I have got to tell you, as you will find detailed in this Book.

OF THE GREAT COUNTRY OF PERSIA; WITH SOME ACCOUNT OF THE THREE KINGS

PERSIA is a great country, which was in old times very illustrious and powerful; but now the Tartars have wasted and destroyed it.

In Persia is the city of SABA, from which the Three Magi set out when they went to worship Jesus Christ; and in this city they are buried, in three very large and beautiful monuments, side by side. And above them there is a square building, carefully kept. The bodies are still entire, with the hair and beard remaining. One of these was called Gaspar, the second Melchior, and the third Balthasar. Messer Marco Polo asked a great many questions of the people of that city as to these Three Magi, but never one could he find that knew aught of the matter, except that these were three kings who were buried there in days of old. However, at a place three days' journey distant he heard of what I am going to tell you. He found a village there which goes by the name of CALA ATAPERISTAN, which is as much as to say, "The Castle of the Fire-worshippers." And the name is rightly applied, for the people there do worship fire, and I will tell you why.

They relate that in old times three kings of that country went away to worship a Prophet that was born, and they carried with them three manner of offerings, Gold, and Frankincense, and Myrrh; in order to ascertain whether that Prophet were God, or an earthly King, or a Physician. For, said they, if he take the Gold, then he is an earthly King; if he take the Incense he is God; if he take the Myrrh he is a Physician.

So it came to pass when they had come to the place where the Child was born, the youngest of the Three Kings went in first, and found the Child apparently just of his own age; so he went forth again marvelling greatly. The middle one entered next, and like the first he found the Child seemingly of his own age; so he also went forth again and marvelled greatly. Lastly, the eldest went in, and as it had befallen the other two, so it befell him. And he went forth very pensive. And when the three had rejoined one another, each told what he had seen; and then they all marvelled the more. So they agreed to go in all three together, and on doing so they beheld the Child with the appearance of its actual age, to wit, some thirteen days. Then they adored, and presented their Gold and Incense and Myrrh. And the Child took all the three offerings, and then gave them a small closed box; whereupon the Kings departed to return into their own land.

WHAT BEFELL WHEN THE THREE KINGS RETURNED TO THEIR OWN COUNTRY

AND when they had ridden many days they said they would see what the Child had given them. So they opened the little box, and inside it they found a stone. On seeing this they began to wonder what this might be that the Child had given them, and what was the import thereof. Now the signification was this: when they presented their offerings, the Child had accepted all three, and when they saw that they had said within themselves that He was the True God, and the True King, and the True Physician. And what the gift of the stone implied was that this Faith which had begun in them should abide firm as a rock. For He well knew what was in their thoughts. Howbeit, they had no understanding at all of this signification of the gift of the stone; so they cast it into a well. Then straightway a fire from Heaven descended into that well wherein the stone had been cast.

And when the Three Kings beheld this marvel they were sore amazed, and it greatly repented them that they had cast away the stone; for well they then perceived that it had a great and holy meaning. So they took of that fire, and carried it into their own country, and placed it in a rich and beautiful church. And there the people keep it continually burning, and worship it as a god, and all the sacrifices they offer are kindled with that fire. And if ever the fire becomes extinct they go to other cities round about where the same faith is held, and obtain of that fire from them, and carry it to the church. And this is the reason why the people of this country worship fire. They will often go ten days' journey to get of that fire.

Such then was the story told by the people of that Castle to Messer Marco Polo; they declared to him for a truth that such was their history, and that one of the three kings was of the city called SABA, and the second of AVA, and the third of that very Castle where they still worship fire, with the people of all the country round about.

Having related this story, I will now tell you of the different provinces of Persia, and their peculiarities.

OF THE EIGHT KINGDOMS OF PERSIA, AND HOW THEY ARE NAMED

Now you must know that Persia is a very great country, and contains eight kingdoms.

In this country of Persia there is a great supply of fine horses; and people take them to India for sale, for they are horses of great price, a single one being worth as much of their money as is equal to 200 livres Tournois; some will be more, some less, according to the quality. Here also are the finest asses in the world, one of them being worth full 30 marks of silver, for they are very large and fast, and acquire a capital amble. Dealers carry their horses to Kish and Ormuz, two cities on the shores of the Sea of India, and there they meet with merchants who take the horses on to India for sale.

In this country there are many cruel and murderous people, so that no day passes but there is some homicide among them. Were it not for the Government, which is that of the Tartars of the Levant, they would do great mischief to merchants; and indeed, maugre the Government, they often succeed in doing such mischief. Unless merchants be well armed they run the risk of being murdered, or at least robbed of everything; and it sometimes happens that a whole party perishes in this way when not on their guard. The people are all Saracens, *i.e.* followers of the Law of Mahomet.

In the cities there are traders and artizans who live by their labour and crafts, weaving cloths of gold, and silk stuffs of sundry kinds. They have plenty of cotton produced in the country; and abundance of wheat, barley, millet, panick, and wine, with fruits of all kinds.

[Some one may say, "But the Saracens don't drink wine, which is pro-hibited by their law." The answer is that they gloss their text in this way, that if the wine be boiled, so that a part is dissipated and the rest becomes sweet, they may drink without breach of the commandment; for it is then no longer called wine, the name being changed with the change of flavour.]

Concerning the Old Man of the Mountain

MULEHET is a country in which the Old Man of the Mountain dwelt in former days; and the name means "*Place of the Aram*." I will tell you his whole history as related by Messer Marco Polo, who heard it from several natives of that region.

The Old Man was called in their language ALADDIN. He had caused a certain valley between two mountains to be enclosed, and had turned it into a garden, the largest and most beautiful that ever was seen, filled with every variety of fruit. In it were erected pavilions and palaces the most elegant that can be imagined, all covered with gilding and exquisite paint-ing. And there were runnels too, flowing freely with wine and milk and honey and water; and numbers of ladies and of the most beautiful damsels in the world, who could play on all manner of instruments, and sung most sweetly, and danced in a manner that it was charming to behold. For the Old Man desired to make his people believe that this was actually Paradise. So he had fashioned it after the description that Mahomet gave of his Paradise, to wit, that it should be a beautiful garden running with conduits of wine and milk and honey and water, and full of lovely women for the delectation of all its inmates. And sure enough the Saracens of those parts believed that it *was* Paradise!

Now no man was allowed to enter the Garden save those whom he in-tended to be his ASSASSINS. There was a Fortress at the entrance to the Garden, strong enough to resist all the world, and there was no other way to get in. He kept at his Court a number of the youths of the country, from 12 to 20 years of age, such as had a taste for soldiering, and to these he used to tell tales about Paradise, just as Mahomet had been wont to do, and they believed in him just as the Saracens believed in Mahomet. Then he would introduce them into his garden, some four, or six, or ten at a time, having first made them drink a certain potion which cast them into a deep sleep, and then causing them to be lifted and carried in. So when they awoke, they found themselves in the Garden.

How the Old Man used to train his Assassins

WHEN therefore they awoke, and found themselves in a place so charming, they deemed that it was Paradise in very truth. And the ladies and damsels dallied with them to their hearts' content, so that they had what young men would have; and with their own good will they never would have quitted the place.

Now this Prince whom we call the Old One kept his Court in grand and noble style, and made those simple hill-folks about him believe firmly that he was a great Prophet. And when he wanted one of his *Assassins* to send on any mission, he would cause that potion whereof I spoke to be given to one of the youths in the garden, and then had him carried into his Palace. So when the young man awoke, he found himself in the Castle, and no longer in that Paradise; whereat he was not over well pleased. He was then conducted to the Old Man's presence, and bowed before him with great veneration as believing himself to be in the presence of a true Prophet. The Prince would then ask whence he came, and he would reply that he came from Paradise! and that it was exactly such as Mahomet had described it in the Law. This of course gave the others who stood by, and who had not been admitted, the greatest desire to enter therein.

So when the Old Man would have any Prince slain, he would say to such a youth: "Go thou and slay So and So; and when thou returnest my Angels shall bear thee into Paradise. And shouldst thou die, natheless even so will I send my Angels to carry thee back into Paradise." So he caused them to believe; and thus there was no order of his that they would not affront any peril to execute, for the great desire they had to get back into that Paradise of his. And in this manner the Old One got his people to murder any one whom he desired to get rid of. Thus, too, the great dread that he inspired all Princes withal, made them become his tributaries in order that he might abide at peace and amity with them.

I should also tell you that the Old Man had certain others under him, who copied his proceedings and acted exactly in the same manner. One of these was sent into the territory of Damascus, and the other into Kurdistan.

How the Old Man came by His End

Now it came to pass, in the year of Christ's Incarnation, 1252, that Hulagu, Lord of the Tartars of the Levant, heard tell of these great crimes of the Old Man, and resolved to make an end of him. So he took and sent one of his Barons with a great Army to that Castle, and they besieged it for three years, but they could not take it, so strong was it. And indeed if they had had food within it never would have been taken. But after being besieged those three years they ran short of victual, and were taken. The Old Man was put to death with all his men [and the Castle with its Garden of Paradise was levelled with the ground]. And since that time he has had no successor; and there was an end to all his villainies.

Now let us go back to our journey.

Of those who did Reign after Jengis Khan, and of the Customs of the Tartars

Now the next that reigned after Jengis Khan, their first Lord, was KUYUK KHAN, and the third Prince was BATU KHAN, and the fourth was HULAGU

KHAN, the fifth MANGU KHAN, the sixth KUBLAI KHAN, who is the sovereign now reigning, and is more potent than any of the five who went before him; in fact, if you were to take all those five together, they would not be so powerful as he is. Nay, I will say yet more; for if you were to put together all the Christians in the world, with their Emperors and their Kings, the whole of these Christians,—aye, and throw in the Saracens to boot,—would not have such power, or be able to do so much as this Kublai, who is the Lord of all the Tartars in the world, those of the Levant and of the Ponent included; for these are all his liegemen and subjects. I mean to show you all about this great power of his in this Book of ours.

You should be told also that all the Grand Khans, and all the descendants of Jengis their first Lord, are carried to a mountain that is called ALTAY to be interred. Wheresoever the Sovereign may die, he is carried to his burial in that mountain with his predecessors; no matter if the place of his death were 100 days' journey distant, thither must he be carried to his burial.

Let me tell you a strange thing too. When they are carrying the body of any Emperor to be buried with the others, the convoy that goes with the body doth put to the sword all whom they fall in with on the road, saying: "Go and wait upon your Lord in the other world!" For they do in sooth believe that all such as they slay in this manner do go to serve their Lord in the other world. They do the same too with horses; for when the Emperor dies, they kill all his best horses, in order that he may have the use of them in the other world, as they believe. And I tell you as a certain truth, that when Mangu Khan died, more than 20,000 persons, who chanced to meet the body on its way, were slain in the manner I have told.

CONCERNING THE CUSTOMS OF THE TARTARS

Now that we have begun to speak of the Tartars, I have plenty to tell you on that subject. The Tartar custom is to spend the winter in warm plains, where they find good pasture for their cattle, whilst in summer they betake themselves to a cool climate among the mountains and valleys, where water is to be found as well as woods and pastures.

Their houses are circular, and are made of wands covered with felts. These are carried along with them whithersoever they go; for the wands are so strongly bound together, and likewise so well combined, that the frame can be made very light. Whenever they erect these huts the door is always to the south. They also have waggons covered with black felt so efficaciously that no rain can get in. These are drawn by oxen and camels, and the women and children travel in them. The women do the buying and selling, and whatever is necessary to provide for the husband and household; for the men all lead the life of gentlemen, troubling themselves about nothing but hunting and hawking, and looking after their goshawks and falcons, unless it be the practice of warlike exercises.

They live on the milk and meat which their herds supply, and on the produce of the chase; and they eat all kinds of flesh, including that of horses and dogs, and Pharaoh's rats, of which last there are great numbers in burrows on those plains. Their drink is mare's milk.

They are very careful not to meddle with each other's wives, and will not do so on any account, holding that to be an evil and abominable thing. The women too are very good and loyal to their husbands, and notable housewives withal. [Ten or twenty of them will dwell together in charming peace and unity, nor shall you ever hear an ill word among them.]

The marriage customs of Tartars are as follows. Any man may take a hundred wives an he so please, and if he be able to keep them. But the first wife is ever held most in honour, and as the most legitimate [and the same applies to the sons whom she may bear]. The husband gives a marriage payment to his wife's mother, and the wife brings nothing to her husband. They have more children than other people, because they have so many wives. They may marry their cousins, and if a father dies, his son may take any of the wives, his own mother always excepted; that is to say the eldest son may do this, but no other. A man may also take the wife of his own brother after the latter's death. Their weddings are celebrated with great ado.

Concerning the God of the Tartars

This is the fashion of their religion. [They say there is a Most High God of Heaven, whom they worship daily with thurible and incense, but they pray to Him only for health of mind and body. But] they have [also] a certain [other] god of theirs called Natigay, and they say he is the god of the Earth, who watches over their children, cattle, and crops. They show him great worship and honour, and every man hath a figure of him in his house, made of felt and cloth; and they also make in the same manner images of his wife and children. The wife they put on the left hand, and the children in front. And when they eat, they take the fat of the meat and grease the god's mouth withal, as well as the mouths of his wife and children. Then they take of the broth and sprinkle it before the door of the house; and that done, they deem that their god and his family have had their share of the dinner.

Their drink is mare's milk, prepared in such a way that you would take it for white wine; and a right good drink it is, called by them *Kumiz*.

The clothes of the wealthy Tartars are for the most part of gold and silk stuffs, lined with costly furs, such as sable and ermine, vair and fox-skin, in the richest fashion.

Concerning the Tartar Customs of War

All their harness of war is excellent and costly. Their arms are bows and arrows, sword and mace; but above all the bow, for they are capital archers, indeed the best that are known. On their backs they wear armour of cuirbouly, prepared from buffalo and other hides, which is very strong.

They are excellent soldiers, and passing valiant in battle. They are also more capable of hardships than other nations; for many a time, if need be, they will go for a month without any supply of food, living only on the milk of their mares and on such game as their bows may win them. Their horses also will subsist entirely on the grass of the plains, so that there is no need to carry store of barley or straw or oats; and they are very docile to their riders. These, in case of need, will abide on horseback the livelong night, armed at all points, while the horse will be continually grazing.

Of all troops in the world these are they which endure the greatest hardship and fatigue, and which cost the least; and they are the best of all for making wide conquests of country. And this you will perceive from what you have heard and shall hear in this book; and (as a fact) there can be no manner of doubt that now they are the masters of the biggest half of the world. Their troops are admirably ordered in the manner that I shall now relate.

You see, when a Tartar prince goes forth to war, he takes with him say, 100,000 horse. Well, he appoints an officer to every ten men, one to every hundred, one to every thousand, and one to every ten thousand, so that his own orders have to be given to ten persons only, and each of these ten persons has to pass the orders only to other ten, and so on; no one having to give orders to more than ten. And every one in turn is responsible only to the officer immediately over him; and the discipline and order that comes of this method is marvellous, for they are a people very obedient to their chiefs. Further, they call the corps of 100,000 men a *Tuc;* that of 10,000 they call a *Toman;* the thousand they call . . . . ; the hundred *Guz;* the ten. . . . And when the army is on the march they have always 200 horsemen, very well mounted, who are sent a distance of two marches in advance to reconnoitre, and these always keep ahead. They have a similar party detached in the rear, and on either flank, so that there is a good look-out kept on all sides against a surpise. When they are going on a distant expedition they take no gear with them except two leather bottles for milk; a little earthenware pot to cook their meat in, and a little tent to shelter them from rain. And in case of great urgency they will ride ten days on end without lighting a fire or taking a meal. On such an occasion they will sustain themselves on the blood of their horses, opening a vein and letting the blood jet into their mouths, drinking till they have had enough, and then staunching it.

They also have milk dried into a kind of paste to carry with them; and when they need food they put this in water, and beat it up till it dissolves, and then drink it. [It is prepared in this way; they boil the milk, and when the rich part floats on the top they skim it into another vessel, and of that they make butter; for the milk will not become solid till this is removed. Then they put the milk in the sun to dry. And when they go on an expedition, every man takes some ten pounds of this dried milk with him. And of a morning he will take a half pound of it and put it in his leather bottle, with as much water as he pleases. So, as he rides along, the milk-paste and the water in the bottle get well churned together into a kind of pap, and that makes his dinner.]

When they come to an engagement with the enemy, they will gain the victory in this fashion. [They never let themselves get into a regular medley, but keep perpetually riding round and shooting into the enemy. And] as they do not count it any shame to run away in battle, they will [sometimes pretend to] do so, and in running away they turn in the saddle and shoot hard and strong at the foe, and in this way make great havoc. Their horses are trained so perfectly that they will double hither and thither, just like a dog, in a way that is quite astonishing. Thus they fight to as good purpose in running away as if they stood and faced the enemy, because of the vast volleys of arrows that they shoot in this way, turning round upon their pursuers, who are fancying that they have won the battle. But when the Tartars see that they have killed and wounded a good many horses and men, they wheel round bodily, and return to the charge in perfect order and with loud cries: and in a very short time the enemy are routed. In truth they are stout and valiant soldiers, and inured to war. And you perceive that it is just when the enemy sees them run, and imagines that he has gained the battle, that he has in reality lost it; for the Tartars wheel round in a moment when they judge the right time has come. And after this fashion they have won many a fight.

All this that I have been telling you is true of the manners and customs of the genuine Tartars. But I must add also that in these days they are greatly degenerated; for those who are settled in Cathay have taken up the practices of the Idolaters of the country, and have abandoned their own institutions; whilst those who have settled in the Levant have adopted the customs of the Saracens.

CONCERNING THE ADMINISTERING OF JUSTICE AMONG THE TARTARS

THE way they administer justice is this. When any one has committed a petty theft, they give him, under the orders of authority, seven blows of a stick, or seventeen, or twenty-seven, or thirty-seven, or forty-seven, and so forth, always increasing by tens in proportion to the injury done, and running up to one hundred and seven. Of these beatings sometimes they die. But if the offence be horse-stealing, or some other great matter, they cut the thief in two with a sword. Howbeit, if he be able to ransom himself by paying nine times the value of the thing stolen, he is let off. Every Lord or other person who possesses beasts has them marked with his peculiar brand, be they horses, mares, camels, oxen, cows, or other great cattle, and then they are sent abroad to graze over the plains without any keeper. They get all mixt together, but eventually every beast is recovered by means of its owner's brand, which is known. For their sheep and goats they have shepherds. All their cattle are remarkably fine, big, and in good condition.

They have another notable custom, which is this. If any man have a daughter who dies before marriage, and another man have had a son also die before marriage, the parents of the two arrange a grand wedding between the dead lad and lass. And marry them they do, making a regular contract! And when the contract papers are made out they put them in the fire, in order (as they will have it) that the parties in the other world may know the fact, and so look on each other as man and wife. And the parents thenceforward consider themselves sib to each other, just as if their children had lived and married. Whatever may be agreed on between the parties as dowry, those who have to pay it cause to be painted on pieces of paper and then put these in the fire, saying that in that way the dead person will get all the real articles in the other world.

Now I have told you all about the manners and customs of the Tartars; but you have heard nothing yet of the great state of the Grand Khan, who is the Lord of all the Tartars and of the Supreme Imperial Court. All that I will tell you in this Book in proper time and place, but meanwhile I must return to my story which I left off in that great plain when we began to speak of the Tartars.

THE KHAN, HIS COURT AND CAPITAL

Of Kublai Khan, the Great Khan now Reigning, and of his Great Puissance

Now am I come to that part of our Book in which I shall tell you of the great and wonderful magnificence of the Great Khan now reigning, by name Kublai Khan; Khan being a title which signifyeth "The Great Lord of Lords," or Emperor. And of a surety he hath good right to such a title, for all men know for a certain truth that he is the most potent man, as regards forces and lands and treasure, that existeth in the world, or ever hath existed from the time of our First Father Adam until this day. All this I will make clear to you for truth, in this book of ours, so that every one shall be fain to acknowledge that he is the greatest Lord that is now in the world, or ever hath been. And now ye shall hear how and wherefore.

Concerning the Person of the Great Khan

The personal appearance of the Great Khan, Lord of Lords, whose name is Kublai, is such as I shall now tell you. He is of a good stature, neither tall nor short, but of a middle height. He has a becoming amount of flesh, and is very shapely in all his limbs. His complexion is white and red, the eyes black and fine, the nose well formed and well set on. He has four wives, whom he retains permanently as his legitimate consorts; and the eldest of his sons by those four wives ought by rights to be emperor;—I mean when his father dies. Those four ladies are called empresses, but each is distinguished also by her proper name. And each of them has a special court of her own, very grand and ample; no one of them having fewer than 300 fair and charming damsels. They have also many pages and eunuchs, and a number of other attendants of both sexes; so that each of these ladies has not less than 10,000 persons attached to her court.

When the Emperor desires the society of one of these four consorts, he will sometimes send for the lady to his apartment and sometimes visit her at her own. He has also a great number of concubines, and I will tell you how he obtains them.

You must know that there is a tribe of Tartars called KUNGURAT, who are noted for their beauty. [The Great Khan sends his commissioners to the Province to select four or five hundred, or whatever number may be ordered, of the most beautiful young women, according to the scale of beauty enjoined upon them. And they set a value upon the comparative beauty of the damsels in this way. The commissioners on arriving assemble all the girls of the province, in presence of appraisers appointed for the purpose. These carefully survey the points of each girl in succession, as (for example) her hair, her complexion, eyebrows, mouth, lips, and the proportion of all her limbs. They will then set down some as estimated at 16 points, some at 17, 18, 20, or more or less, according to the sum of the beauties or defects of each. And whatever standard the Great Khan may have fixed for those that are to be brought to him, whether it be 20 points or 21, the commissioners select the required number from those who have attained that standard, and bring them to him. And when they reach his presence he has them appraised anew by other parties, and has a selection made of 30 or 40 of those, who then get the highest valuation.] Now every year an hundred of the most beautiful maidens of this tribe are sent to the Great Khan, who commits them to the charge of certain elderly ladies dwelling in his palace. And these old ladies make the girls sleep with them, in order to ascertain if they have sweet breath [and do not snore], and are sound in all their limbs. Then such of them as are of approved beauty, and are good and sound in all respects, are appointed to attend on the Emperor by turns. Thus six of these damsels take their turn for three days and nights, and wait on him when he is in his chamber and when he is in his bed, to serve him in any way, and to be entirely at his orders. At the end of the three days and nights they are relieved by other six. And so throughout the year, there are reliefs of maidens by six and six, changing every three days and nights.

CONCERNING THE GREAT KHAN'S SONS

THE Emperor hath, by those four wives of his, twenty-two male children; the eldest of whom was called CHIMKIN for the love of the good Jengis

Khan, the first Lord of the Tartars. And this Chimkin, as the Eldest Son
of the Khan, was to have reigned after his father's death; but, as it came
to pass, he died. He left a son behind him, however, whose name is TEMUR,
and he is to be the Great Khan and Emperor after the death of his Grandfather, as is but right; he being the child of the Great Khan's eldest son.
And this Temur is an able and brave man, as he hath already proven on
many occasions.

The Great Khan hath also twenty-five other sons by his concubines;
and these are good and valiant soldiers, and each of them is a great chief.
I tell you moreover that of his children by his four lawful wives there are
seven who are kings of vast realms or provinces, and govern them well;
being all able and gallant men, as might be expected. For the Great Khan
their sire is, I tell you, the wisest and most accomplished man, the greatest
Captain, the best to govern men and rule an Empire, as well as the most
valiant, that ever has existed among all the Tribes of Tartars.

CONCERNING THE PALACE OF THE GREAT KHAN

You must know that for three months of the year, to wit December,
January, and February, the Great Khan resides in the capital city of Cathay,
which is called CAMBALUC, [and which is at the north-eastern extremity
of the country]. In that city stands his great Palace, and now I will tell
you what it is like.

It is enclosed all round by a great wall forming a square, each side of
which is a mile in length; that is to say, the whole compass thereof is four
miles. This you may depend on; it is also very thick, and a good ten paces
in height, whitewashed and loop-holed all round. At each angle of the
wall there is a very fine and rich palace in which the war-harness of the
Emperor is kept, such as bows and quivers, saddles and bridles, and bow-
strings, and everything needful for an army. Also midway between every
two of these Corner Palaces there is another of the like; so that taking the
whole compass of the enclosure you find eight vast Palaces stored with
the Great Lord's harness of war. And you must understand that each Palace
is assigned to only one kind of article; thus one is stored with bows, a
second with saddles, a third with bridles, and so on in succession right round.

The great wall has five gates on its southern face, the middle one being the great gate which is never opened on any occasion except when the
Great Khan himself goes forth or enters. Close on either side of this great
gate is a smaller one by which all other people pass; and then towards
each angle is another great gate, also open to people in general; so that
on that side there are five gates in all.

Inside of this wall there is a second, enclosing a space that is somewhat
greater in length than in breadth. This enclosure also has eight palaces
corresponding to those of the outer wall, and stored like them with the
Lord's harness of war. This wall also hath five gates on the southern face,
corresponding to those in the outer wall, and hath one gate on each of the

other faces, as the outer wall hath also. In the middle of the second enclosure is the Lord's Great Palace, and I will tell you what it is like.

You must know that it is the greatest Palace that ever was. [Towards the
north it is in contact with the outer wall, whilst towards the south there is a
vacant space which the Barons and the soldiers are constantly traversing.
The Palace itself] hath no upper story, but is all on the ground floor, only
the basement is raised some ten palms above the surrounding soil [and this
elevation is retained by a wall of marble raised to the level of the pavement,
two paces in width and projecting beyond the base of the Palace so as to
form a kind of terrace-walk, by which people can pass round the building,
and which is exposed to view, whilst on the outer edge of the wall there is
a very fine pillared balustrade; and up to this the people are allowed to
come]. The roof is very lofty, and the walls of the Palace are all covered
with gold and silver. They are also adorned with representations of dragons
[sculptured and gilt], beasts and birds, knights and idols, and sundry other
subjects. And on the ceiling too you see nothing but gold and silver and
painting. [On each of the four sides there is a great marble staircase leading
to the top of the marble wall, and forming the approach to the Palace.]

The Hall of the Palace is so large that it could easily dine 6000 people; and
it is quite a marvel to see how many rooms there are besides. The building
is altogether so vast, so rich, and so beautiful, that no man on earth could
design anything superior to it. The outside of the roof also is all coloured
with vermilion and yellow and green and blue and other hues, which are
fixed with a varnish so fine and exquisite that they shine like crystal, and
lend a resplendent lustre to the Palace as seen for a great way round. This
roof is made too with such strength and solidity that it is fit to last for ever.

[On the interior side of the Palace are large buildings with halls and
chambers, where the Emperor's private property is placed, such as his treasures of gold, silver, gems, pearls, and gold plate, and in which reside the
ladies and concubines. There he occupies himself at his own convenience,
and no one else has access.]

Between the two walls of the enclosure which I have described, there
are fine parks and beautiful trees bearing a variety of fruits. There are beasts
also of sundry kinds, such as white stags and fallow deer, gazelles and roebucks, and fine squirrels of various sorts, with numbers also of the animal
that gives the musk, and all manner of other beautiful creatures, insomuch
that the whole place is full of them, and no spot remains void except where
there is traffic of people going and coming. [The parks are covered with
abundant grass; and the roads through them being all paved and raised
two cubits above the surface, they never become muddy, nor does the rain
lodge on them, but flows off into the meadows, quickening the soil and
producing that abundance of herbage.]

From that corner of the enclosure which is towards the north-west there
extends a fine Lake, containing foison of fish of different kinds which the
Emperor hath caused to be put in there, so that whenever he desires any
he can have them at his pleasure. A river enters this lake and issues from it,

but there is a grating of iron or brass put up so that the fish cannot escape in that way.

Moreover on the north side of the Palace, about a bow-shot off, there is a hill which has been made by art [from the earth dug out of the lake]; it is a good hundred paces in height and a mile in compass. This hill is entirely covered with trees that never lose their leaves, but remain ever green. And I assure you that wherever a beautiful tree may exist, and the Emperor gets news of it, he sends for it and has it transported bodily with all its roots and the earth attached to them, and planted on that hill of his. No matter how big the tree may be, he gets it carried by his elephants; and in this way he has got together the most beautiful collection of trees in all the world. And he has also caused the whole hill to be covered with the ore of azure, which is very green. And thus not only are the trees all green, but the hill itself is all green likewise; and there is nothing to be seen on it that is not green; and hence it is called the GREEN MOUNT; and in good sooth 'tis named well.

On the top of the hill again there is a fine big palace which is all green inside and out; and thus the hill, and the trees, and the palace form together a charming spectacle; and it is marvellous to see their uniformity of colour! Everybody who sees them is delighted. And the Great Khan had caused this beautiful prospect to be formed for the comfort and solace and delectation of his heart.

You must know that beside the Palace (that we have been describing), *i.e.* the Great Palace, the Emperor has caused another to be built just like his own in every respect, and this he hath done for his son when he shall reign and be Emperor after him. Hence it is made just in the same fashion and of the same size, so that everything can be carried on in the same manner after his own death. [It stands on the other side of the lake from the Great Khan's Palace, and there is a bridge crossing the water from one to the other.] The Prince in question holds now a Seal of Empire, but not with such complete authority as the Great Khan, who remains supreme as long as he lives.

Now I am going to tell you of the chief city of Cathay, in which these Palaces stand; and why it was built, and how.

CONCERNING THE CITY OF CAMBALUC

Now there was on that spot in old times a great and noble city called CAMBALUC, which is as much as to say in our tongue "The city of the Emperor." But the Great Khan was informed by his Astrologers that this city would prove rebellious, and raise great disorders against his imperial authority. So he caused the present city to be built close beside the old one, with only a river between them. And he caused the people of the old city to be removed to the new town that he had founded; and this is called TAIDU. [However, he allowed a portion of the people which he did not suspect to remain in the old city, because the new one could not hold the whole of them, big as it is.]

As regards the size of this (new) city you must know that it has a compass of 24 miles, for each side of it hath a length of 6 miles, and it is four-square. And it is all walled round with walls of earth which have a thickness of full ten paces at bottom, and a height of more than 10 paces; but they are not so thick at top, for they diminish in thickness as they rise, so that at top they are only about 3 paces thick. And they are provided throughout with loop-holed battlements, which are all whitewashed.

There are 12 gates, and over each gate there is a great and handsome palace, so that there are on each side of the square three gates and five palaces; for (I ought to mention) there is at each angle also a great and handsome palace. In those palaces are vast halls in which are kept the arms of the city garrison.

The streets are so straight and wide that you can see right along them from end to end and from one gate to the other. And up and down the city there are beautiful palaces, and many great and fine hostelries, and fine houses in great numbers. [All the plots of ground on which the houses of the city are built are four-square, and laid out with straight lines; all the plots being occupied by great and spacious palaces, with courts and gardens of proportionate size. All these plots were assigned to different heads of families. Each square plot is encompassed by handsome streets for traffic; and thus the whole city is arranged in squares just like a chessboard, and disposed in a manner so perfect and masterly that it is impossible to give a description that should do it justice.]

Moreover, in the middle of the city there is a great clock—that is to say, a bell—which is struck at night. And after it has struck three times no one must go out in the city, unless it be for the needs of a woman in labour, or of the sick. And those who go about on such errands are bound to carry lanterns with them. Moreover, the established guard at each gate of the city is 1000 armed men; not that you are to imagine this guard is kept up for fear of any attack, but only as a guard of honour for the Sovereign, who resides there, and to prevent thieves from doing mischief in the town.

How the Great Khan Maintains a Guard of Twelve Thousand Horse, which are called Keshikten

You must know that the Great Khan, to maintain his state, hath a guard of twelve thousand horsemen, who are styled KESHIKTEN, which is as much as to say "Knights devoted to their Lord." Not that he keeps these for fear of any man whatever, but merely because of his own exalted dignity. These 12,000 men have four captains, each of whom is in command of 3000; and each body of 3000 takes a turn of three days and nights to guard the palace, where they also take their meals. After the expiration of three days and nights they are relieved by another 3000, who mount guard for the same space of time, and then another body takes its turn, so that there are always 3000 on guard. Thus it goes until the whole 12,000, who are styled (as I said) Keshikten, have been on duty; and then the tour begins again, and so runs on from year's end to year's end.

The Fashion of the Great Khan's Table at his High Feasts

And when the Great Khan sits at table on any great court occasion, it is in this fashion. His table is elevated a good deal above the others, and he sits at the north end of the hall, looking towards the south, with his chief wife beside him on the left. On his right sit his sons and his nephews, and other kinsmen of the Blood Imperial, but lower, so that their heads are on a level with the Emperor's feet. And then the other Barons sit at other tables lower still. So also with the women; for all the wives of the Lord's sons, and of his nephews and other kinsmen, sit at the lower table to his right; and below them again the ladies of the other Barons and Knights, each in the place assigned by the Lord's orders. The tables are so disposed that the Emperor can see the whole of them from end to end, many as they are. [Further, you are not to suppose that everybody sits at table; on the contrary, the greater part of the soldiers and their officers sit at their meal in the hall on the carpets.] Outside the hall will be found more than 40,000 people; for there is a great concourse of folk bringing presents to the Lord, or come from foreign countries with curiosities.

In a certain part of the hall near where the Great Khan holds his table, there [is set a large and very beautiful piece of workmanship in the form of a square coffer, or buffet, about three paces each way, exquisitely wrought with figures of animals, finely carved and gilt. The middle is hollow, and in it] stands a great vessel of pure gold, holding as much as an ordinary butt; and at each corner of the great vessel is one of smaller size [of the capacity of a firkin], and from the former the wine or beverage flavoured with fine and costly spices is drawn off into the latter. [And on the buffet aforesaid are set all the Lord's drinking vessels, among which are certain pitchers of the finest gold], which are called *verniques,* and are big enough to hold drink for eight or ten persons. And one of these is put between every two persons, besides a couple of golden cups with handles, so that every man helps himself from the pitcher that stands between him and his neighbour. And the ladies are supplied in the same way. The value of these pitchers and cups is something immense; in fact, the Great Khan has such a quantity of this kind of plate, and of gold and silver in other shapes, as no one ever before saw or heard tell of, or could believe.

[There are certain Barons specially deputed to see that foreigners, who do not know the customs of the Court, are provided with places suited to their rank; and these Barons are continually moving to and fro in the hall, looking to the wants of the guests at table, and causing the servants to supply them promptly with wine, milk, meat, or whatever they lack. At every door of the hall (or, indeed, wherever the Emperor may be) there stand a couple of big men like giants, one on each side, armed with staves. Their business is to see that no one steps upon the threshold in entering, and if this does happen, they strip the offender of his clothes, and he must pay a forfeit to have them back again; or in lieu of taking his clothes, they give him a certain number of blows. If they are foreigners ignorant of the order, then there are Barons appointed to introduce them, and explain it to them. They think, in fact, that it brings bad luck if any one touches the threshold. Howbeit, they are not expected to stick at this in going forth again, for at that time some are like to be the worse for liquor, and incapable of looking to their steps.]

And you must know that those who wait upon the Great Khan with his dishes and his drink are some of the great Barons. They have the mouth and nose muffled with fine napkins of silk and gold, so that no breath nor odour from their persons should taint the dish or the goblet presented to the Lord. And when the Emperor is going to drink, all the musical instruments, of which he has vast store of every kind, begin to play. And when he takes the cup all the Barons and the rest of the company drop on their knees and make the deepest obeisance before him, and then the Emperor doth drink. But each time that he does so the whole ceremony is repeated.

I will say nought about the dishes, as you may easily conceive that there is a great plenty of every possible kind. But you should know that in every case where a Baron or Knight dines at those tables, their wives also dine there with the other ladies. And when all have dined and the tables have been removed, then come in a great number of players and jugglers, adepts at all sorts of wonderful feats, and perform before the Emperor and the rest of the company, creating great diversion and mirth, so that everybody is full of laughter and enjoyment. And when the performance is over, the company breaks up and every one goes to his quarters.

CONCERNING THE GREAT FEAST HELD BY THE GRAND KHAN EVERY YEAR ON HIS BIRTHDAY

YOU must know that the Tartars keep high festival yearly on their birthdays. And the Great Khan was born on the 28th day of the September moon, so on that day is held the greatest feast of the year at the Khan's Court, always excepting that which he holds on New Year's Day, of which I shall tell you afterwards.

Now, on his birthday, the Great Khan dresses in the best of his robes, all wrought with beaten gold; and full 12,000 Barons and Knights on that day come forth dressed in robes of the same colour, and precisely like those of the Great Khan, except that they are not so costly; but still they are all of the same colour as his, and are also of silk and gold. Every man so clothed has also a girdle of gold; and this as well as the dress is given him by the Sovereign. And I will aver that there are some of these suits decked with so many pearls and precious stones that a single suit shall be worth full 10,000 golden bezants.

And of such raiment there are several sets. For you must know that the Great Khan, thirteen times in the year, presents to his Barons and Knights such suits of raiment as I am speaking of. And on each occasion they wear the same colour that he does, a different colour being assigned to each festival. Hence you may see what a huge business it is, and that there is no prince in the world but he alone who could keep up such customs as these.

On his birthday also, all the Tartars in the world, and all the countries and governments that owe allegiance to the Khan, offer him great presents according to their several abilities, and as prescription or orders have fixed the amount. And many other persons also come with great presents to the Khan, in order to beg for some employment from him. And the Great Khan has chosen twelve Barons on whom is laid the charge of assigning to each of these supplicants a suitable answer.

On this day likewise all the Idolaters, all the Saracens, and all the Christians and other descriptions of people make great and solemn devotions, with much chaunting and lighting of lamps and burning of incense, each to the God whom he doth worship, praying that He would save the Emperor, and grant him long life and health and happiness.

And thus, as I have related, is celebrated the joyous feast of the Khan's birthday.

How the Great Khan enjoineth his People to supply him with Game

The three months of December, January, and February, during which the Emperor resides at his Capital City, are assigned for hunting and fowling, to the extent of some 40 days' journey round the city; and it is ordained that the larger game taken be sent to the Court. To be more particular: of all the larger beasts of the chase, such as boars, roebucks, bucks, stags, lions, bears, etc., the greater part of what is taken has to be sent, and feathered game likewise. The animals are gutted and despatched to the Court on carts. This is done by all the people within 20 or 30 days' journey, and the quantity so despatched is immense. Those at a greater distance cannot send the game, but they have to send the skins after tanning them, and these are employed in the making of equipments for the Emperor's army.

Concerning the City of Cambaluc, and its Great Traffic and Population

You must know that the city of Cambaluc hath such a multitude of houses, and such a vast population inside the walls and outside, that it seems quite past all possibility. There is a suburb outside each of the gates, which are twelve in number; and these suburbs are so great that they contain more people than the city itself [for the suburb of one gate spreads in width till it meets the suburb of the next, whilst they extend in length some three or four miles]. In those suburbs lodge the foreign merchants and travellers, of whom there are always great numbers who have come to bring presents to the Emperor, or to sell articles at Court, or because the city affords so good a mart to attract traders. [There are in each of the suburbs, to a distance of a mile from the city, numerous fine hostelries for the lodgment of merchants from different parts of the world, and a special hostelry is assigned to each description of people, as if we should say there is one for the Lombards, another for the Germans, and a third for the Frenchmen.] And thus there are as many good houses outside of the city as inside, without counting those that belong to the great lords and barons, which are very numerous.

You must know that it is forbidden to bury any dead body inside the city. If the body be that of an Idolater it is carried out beyond the city and suburbs to a remote place assigned for the purpose, to be burnt. And if it be of one belonging to a religion the custom of which is to bury, such as the Christian, the Saracen, or what not, it is also carried out beyond the suburbs to a distant place assigned for the purpose. And thus the city is preserved in a better and more healthy state.

Moreover, no public woman resides inside the city, but all such abide outside in the suburbs. And 'tis wonderful what a vast number of these there are for the foreigners; it is a certain fact that there are more than 20,000 of them living by prostitution. And that so many can live in this way will show you how vast is the population.

[Guards patrol the city every night in parties of 30 or 40, looking out for any persons who may be abroad at unseasonable hours, *i.e.* after the great bell hath stricken thrice. If they find any such person he is immediately taken to prison, and examined next morning by the proper officers. If these find him guilty of any misdemeanour they order him a proportionate beating with the stick. Under this punishment people sometimes die; but they adopt it in order to eschew bloodshed; for their *Bakshis* say that it is an evil thing to shed man's blood.]

To this city also are brought articles of greater cost and rarity, and in greater abundance of all kinds, than to any other city in the world. For people of every description, and from every region, bring things (including all the costly wares of India, as well as the fine and precious goods of Cathay itself with its provinces), some for the sovereign, some for the court, some for the city which is so great, some for the crowds of Barons and Knights, some for the great hosts of the Emperor which are quartered round about; and thus between court and city the quantity brought in is endless.

As a sample, I tell you, no day in the year passes that there do not enter the city 1000 cart-loads of silk alone, from which are made quantities of cloth of silk and gold, and of other goods. And this is not to be wondered at; for in all the countries round about there is no flax, so that everything has to be made of silk. It is true, indeed, that in some parts of the country there is cotton and hemp, but not sufficient for their wants. This, however, is not of much consequence, because silk is so abundant and cheap, and is a more valuable substance than either flax or cotton.

Round about this great city of Cambaluc there are some 200 other cities at various distances, from which traders come to sell their goods and buy others for their lords; and all find means to make their sales and purchases, so that the traffic of the city is passing great.

How the Great Khan causeth the Bark of Trees, made into something
like Paper, to pass for Money over all his Country

Now that I have told you in detail of the splendour of this City of the Emperor's, I shall proceed to tell you of the Mint which he hath in the same
city, in the which he hath his money coined and struck, as I shall relate to
you. And in doing so I shall make manifest to you how it is that the Great
Lord may well be able to accomplish even much more than I have told you,
or am going to tell you, in this Book. For, tell it how I might, you never
would be satisfied that I was keeping within truth and reason!

The Emperor's Mint then is in this same City of Cambaluc, and the way
it is wrought is such that you might say he hath the Secret of Alchemy in
perfection, and you would be right! For he makes his money after this
fashion.

He makes them take of the bark of a certain tree, in fact of the Mulberry
Tree, the leaves of which are the food of the silkworms,—these trees being
so numerous that whole districts are full of them. What they take is a certain fine white bast or skin which lies between the wood of the tree and the
thick outer bark, and this they make into something resembling sheets of
paper, but black. When these sheets have been prepared they are cut up into
pieces of different sizes. The smallest of these sizes is worth a half tornesel;
the next, a little larger, one tornesel; one, a little larger still, is worth half a
silver groat of Venice; another a whole groat; others yet two groats, five
groats, and ten groats. There is also a kind worth one Bezant of gold, and
others of three Bezants, and so up to ten. All these pieces of paper are
[issued with as much solemnity and authority as if they were of pure gold
or silver; and on every piece a variety of officials, whose duty it is, have to
write their names, and to put their seals. And when all is prepared duly, the
chief officer deputed by the Khan smears the Seal entrusted to him with
vermilion, and impresses it on the paper, so that the form of the Seal remains
printed upon it in red; the Money is then authentic. Any one forging it
would be punished with death.] And the Khan causes every year to be made
such a vast quantity of this money, which costs him nothing, that it must
equal in amount all the treasure in the world.

With these pieces of paper, made as I have described, he causes all pay-
ments on his own account to be made; and he makes them to pass current
universally over all his kingdoms and provinces and territories, and whithersoever his power and sovereignty extends. And nobody, however important
he may think himself, dares to refuse them on pain of death. And indeed
everybody takes them readily, for wheresoever a person may go throughout
the Great Khan's dominions he shall find these pieces of paper current, and
shall be able to transact all sales and purchases of goods by means of them
just as well as if they were coins of pure gold. And all the while they are so
light that ten bezants' worth does not weigh one golden bezant.

Furthermore all merchants arriving from India or other countries, and bringing with them gold or silver or gems and pearls, are prohibited from selling to any one but the Emperor. He has twelve experts chosen for this business, men of shrewdness and experience in such affairs; these appraise the articles, and the Emperor then pays a liberal price for them in those pieces of paper. The merchants accept his price readily, for in the first place they would not get so good an one from anybody else, and secondly they are paid without any delay. And with this paper-money they can buy what they like anywhere over the Empire, whilst it is also vastly lighter to carry about on their journeys. And it is a truth that the merchants will several times in the year bring wares to the amount of 400,000 bezants, and the Grand Sire pays for all in that paper. So he buys such a quantity of those precious things every year that his treasure is endless, whilst all the time the money he pays away costs him nothing at all. Moreover, several times in the year proclamation is made through the city that any one who may have gold or silver or gems or pearls, by taking them to the Mint shall get a handsome price for them. And the owners are glad to do this, because they would find no other purchaser give so large a price. Thus the quantity they bring in is marvellous, though these who do not choose to do so may let it alone. Still, in this way, nearly all the valuables in the country come into the Khan's possession.

When any of those pieces of paper are spoilt—not that they are so very flimsy neither—the owner carries them to the Mint, and by paying three per cent. on the value he gets new pieces in exchange. And if any Baron, or any one else soever, hath need of gold or silver or gems or pearls, in order to make plate, or girdles, or the like, he goes to the Mint and buys as much as he list, paying in this paper-money.

How the Emperor bestows Help on his People, when they are afflicted with Dearth or Murrain

Now you must know that the Emperor sends his Messengers over all his Lands and Kingdoms and Provinces, to ascertain from his officers if the people are afflicted by any dearth through unfavourable seasons, or storms or locusts, or other like calamity; and from those who have suffered in this way no taxes are exacted for that year; nay more, he causes them to be supplied with grain of his own for food and seed. Now this is undoubtedly a great bounty on his part. And when winter comes, he causes inquiry to be made as to those who have lost their cattle, whether by murrain or other mishap, and such persons not only go scot free, but get presents of cattle. And thus, as I tell you, the Lord every year helps and fosters the people subject to him.

[There is another trait of the Great Khan I should tell you; and that is, that if a chance shot from his bow strike any herd or flock, whether belonging to one person or to many, and however big the flock may be, he takes no tithe thereof for three years. In like manner, if the arrow strike a boat full of goods, that boat-load pays no duty; for it is thought unlucky that an arrow strike any one's property; and the Great Khan says it would be an abomination before God, were such property, that has been struck by the divine wrath, to enter into his Treasury.]

How the Great Khan causes Trees to be Planted by the Highways

The Emperor moreover hath taken order that all the highways travelled by his messengers and the people generally should be planted with rows of great trees a few paces apart; and thus these trees are visible a long way off, and no one can miss the way by day or night. Even the roads through uninhabited tracts are thus planted, and it is the greatest possible solace to travellers. And this is done on all the ways, where it can be of service. [The Great Khan plants these trees all the more readily, because his astrologers and diviners tell him that he who plants trees lives long.

But where the ground is so sandy and desert that trees will not grow, he causes other landmarks, pillars or stones, to be set up to show the way.]

Concerning the Rice-Wine drunk by the people of Cathay

Most of the people of Cathay drink wine of the kind that I shall now describe. It is a liquor which they brew of rice with a quantity of excellent spice, in such fashion that it makes better drink than any other kind of wine; it is not only good, but clear and pleasing to the eye. And being very hot stuff, it makes one drunk sooner than any other wine.

Concerning the Black Stones that are dug in Cathay, and are Burnt for Fuel

It is a fact that all over the country of Cathay there is a kind of black stones existing in beds in the mountains, which they dig out and burn like firewood. If you supply the fire with them at night, and see that they are well kindled, you will find them still alight in the morning; and they make such capital fuel that no other is used throughout the country. It is true that they have plenty of wood also, but they do not burn it, because those stones burn better and cost less.

[Moreover with that vast number of people, and the number of hot baths that they maintain—for every one has such a bath at least three times a week, and in winter if possible every day, whilst every nobleman and man of wealth has a private bath for his own use—the wood would not suffice for the purpose.]

How the Great Khan causes Stores of Grain to be made, to help his People withal in time of Dearth

You must know that when the Emperor sees that grain is cheap and abundant, he buys up large quantities, and has it stored in all his provinces in great granaries, where it is so well looked after that it will keep for three or four years.

And this applies, let me tell you, to all kinds of grain, whether wheat, barley, millet, rice, panick, or what not, and when there is any scarcity of a particular kind of grain, he causes that to be issued. And if the price of the grain is at one bezant the measure, he lets them have it at a bezant for four measures, or at whatever price will produce general cheapness; and every one can have food in this way. And by this providence of the Emperor's, his people can never suffer from dearth. He does the same over his whole Empire; causing these supplies to be stored everywhere according to calculation of the wants and necessities of the people.

OF THE CHARITY OF THE EMPEROR TO THE POOR

I HAVE told you how the Great Khan provides for the distribution of necessaries to his people in time of dearth, by making store in time of cheapness. Now I will tell you of his alms and great charity to the poor of his city of Cambaluc.

You see he causes selection to be made of a number of families in the city which are in a state of indigence, and of such families some may consist of six in the house, some of eight, some of ten, more or fewer in each as it may hap, but the whole number being very great. And each family he causes annually to be supplied with wheat and other grain sufficient for the whole year. And this he never fails to do every year. Moreover, all those who choose to go to the daily dole at the Court receive a great loaf apiece, hot from the baking, and nobody is denied; for so the Lord hath ordered. And so some 30,000 people go for it every day from year's end to year's end. Now this is a great goodness in the Emperor to take pity of his poor people thus! And they benefit so much by it that they worship him as he were God.

[He also provides the poor with clothes. For he lays a tithe upon all wool, silk, hemp, and the like, from which clothing can be made; and he has these woven and laid up in a building set apart for the purpose; and as all artizans are bound to give a day's labour weekly, in this way the Khan has these stuffs made into clothing for those poor families, suitable for summer or winter, according to the time of year. He also provides the clothing for his troops, and has woollens woven for them in every city, the material for which is furnished by the tithe aforesaid. You should know that the Tartars, before they were converted to the religion of the Idolaters, never practised almsgiving. Indeed, when any poor man begged of them they would tell him, "Go with God's curse, for if He loved you as He loves me, He would have provided for you." But the sages of the Idolaters, and especially the *Bakshis* mentioned before, told the Great Khan that it was a good work to provide for the poor, and that his idols would be greatly pleased if he did so. And since then he has taken to do for the poor so much as you have heard.]

CONCERNING THE ASTROLOGERS IN THE CITY OF CAMBALUC

[THERE are in the city of Cambaluc, what with Christians, Saracens, and Cathayans, some five thousand astrologers and soothsayers, whom the Great

Khan provides with annual maintenance and clothing, just as he provides the poor of whom we have spoken, and they are in the constant exercise of their art in this city.

They have a kind of astrolabe on which are inscribed the planetary signs, the hours and critical points of the whole year. And every year these Christian, Saracen, and Cathayan astrologers, each sect apart, investigate by means of this astrolabe the course and character of the whole year, according to the indications of each of its Moons, in order to discover by the natural course and disposition of the planets, and the other circumstances of the heavens, what shall be the nature of the weather, and what peculiarities shall be produced by each Moon of the year; as, for example, under which Moon there shall be thunderstorms and tempests, under which there shall be disease, murrain, wars, disorders, and treasons, and so on, according to the indications of each; but always adding that it lies with God to do less or more according to His pleasure. And they write down the results of their examination in certain little pamphlets for the year, which are called *Tacuin*, and these are sold for a groat to all who desire to know what is coming. Those of the astrologers, of course whose predictions are found to be most exact, are held to be the greatest adepts in their art, and get the greater fame.

And if any one having some great matter in hand, or proposing to make a long journey for traffic or other business, desires to know what will be the upshot, he goes to one of these astrologers and says: "Turn up your books and see what is the present aspect of the heavens, for I am going away on such and such a business." Then the astrologer will reply that the applicant must also tell the year, month, and hour of his birth; and when he has got that information he will see how the horoscope of his nativity combines with the indications of the time when the question is put, and then he predicts the result, good or bad, according to the aspect of the heavens.

You must know, too, that the Tartars reckon their years by twelves; the sign of the first year being the Lion, of the second the Ox, of the third the Dragon, of the fourth the Dog, and so forth up to the twelfth; so that when one is asked the year of his birth he answers that it was in the year of the Lion (let us say), on such a day or night, at such an hour, and such a moment. And the father of a child always takes care to write these particulars down in a book. When the twelve yearly symbols have been gone through, then they come back to the first, and go through with them again in the same succession.]

CONCERNING THE RELIGION OF THE CATHAYANS; THEIR VIEWS AS TO THE SOUL; AND THEIR CUSTOMS

As we have said before, these people are Idolaters, and as regards their gods, each has a tablet fixed high up on the wall of his chamber, on which is inscribed a name which represents the Most High and Heavenly God; and before this they pay daily worship, offering incense from a thurible, raising their hands aloft, and gnashing their teeth three times, praying Him to grant them health of mind and body; but of Him they ask nought else. And below on the ground there is a figure which they call *Natigai*, which is the god of things terrestrial. To him they give a wife and children, and they worship him in the same manner, with incense, and gnashing of teeth, and lifting up of hands; and of him they ask seasonable weather, and the fruits of the earth, children, and so forth.

Their view of the immortality of the soul is after this fashion. They believe that as soon as a man dies, his soul enters into another body, going from a good to a better, or from a bad to a worse, according as he hath conducted himself well or ill. That is to say, a poor man, if he have passed through life good and sober, shall be born again of a gentlewoman, and shall be a gentleman; and on a second occasion shall be born of a princess and shall be a prince, and so on, always rising, till he be absorbed into the Deity. But if he have borne himself ill, he who was the son of a gentleman shall be reborn as the son of a boor, and from a boor shall become a dog, always going down lower and lower.

The people have an ornate style of speech; they salute each other with a cheerful countenance, and with great politeness; they behave like gentlemen, and eat with great propriety. They show great respect to their parents; and should there be any son who offends his parents, or fails to minister to their necessities, there is a public office which has no other charge but that of punishing unnatural children, who are proved to have acted with ingratitude towards their parents.

Criminals of sundry kinds who have been imprisoned, are released at a time fixed by the Great Khan (which occurs every three years), but on leaving prison they are branded on one cheek that they may be recognized.

The Great Khan hath prohibited all gambling and sharping, things more prevalent there than in any other part of the world. In doing this, he said: "I have conquered you by force of arms, and all that you have is mine; if, therefore, you gamble away your property, it is in fact my property that you are gambling away." Not that he took anything from them however.

I must not omit to tell you of the orderly way in which the Khan's Barons and others conduct themselves in coming to his presence. In the first place, within a half mile of the place where he is, out of reverence for his exalted majesty, everybody preserves a mien of the greatest meekness and quiet, so that no noise of shrill voices or loud talk shall be heard. And every one of the chiefs and nobles carries always with him a handsome little vessel to spit in whilst he remain in the Hall of Audience—for no one dares spit on the floor of the hall,—and when he hath spitten he covers it up and puts it aside. So also they all have certain handsome buskins of white leather, which they carry with them, and, when summoned by the sovereign, on arriving at the entrance to the hall, they put on these white buskins, and give their others in charge to the servants, in order that they may not foul the fine carpets of silk and gold and divers colours.

Concerning the Province of Tibet

AFTER those five days' march that I spoke of, you enter a province which has been sorely ravaged; and this was done in the wars of Mangu Khan. There are indeed towns and villages and hamlets, but all harried and destroyed.

You ride for 20 days without finding any inhabited spot, so that travellers are obliged to carry all their provisions with them, and are constantly falling in with those wild beasts which are so numerous and so dangerous. After that you come at length to a tract where there are towns and villages in considerable numbers. The people of those towns have a strange custom in regard to marriage which I will now relate.

No man of that country would on any consideration take to wife a girl who was a maid; for they say a wife is nothing worth unless she has been used to consort with men. And their custom is this, that when travellers come that way, the old women of the place get ready, and take their unmarried daughters or other girls related to them, and go to the strangers who are passing, and make over the young women to whomsoever will accept them; and the travellers take them accordingly and do their pleasure; after which the girls are restored to the old women who brought them, for they are not allowed to follow the strangers away from their home. In this manner people travelling that way, when they reach a village or hamlet or other inhabited place, shall find perhaps 20 or 30 girls at their disposal. And if the travellers lodge with those people they shall have as many young women as they could wish coming to court them! You must know too that the traveller is expected to give the girl who has been with him a ring or some other trifle, something in fact that she can show as a lover's token when she comes to be married. And it is for this in truth and for this alone that they follow that custom; for every girl is expected to obtain at least 20 such tokens in the way I have described before she can be married. And those who have most tokens, and so can show they have been most run after, are in the highest esteem, and most sought in marriage, because they say the charms of such an one are greatest. But after marriage these people hold their wives very dear, and would consider it a great villainy for a man to meddle with another's wife; and thus though the wives have before marriage acted as you have heard, they are kept with great care from light conduct afterwards.

Now I have related to you this marriage custom as a good story to tell, and to show what a fine country that is for young fellows to go to!

Conclusion

AND now ye have heard all that we can tell you about the Tartars and the Saracens and their customs, and likewise about the other countries of the world as far as our researches and information extend. . . .

Of the manner in which we took our departure from the Court of the Great Khan you have heard at the beginning of the Book, and in the same chapter is related the lucky chance that led to our departure. And you may be sure that but for that lucky chance, we should never have got away in spite of all our trouble, and never have got back to our country again. But I believe it was God's pleasure that we should get back in order that people might learn about the things that the world contains. For according to what has been said in the introduction at the beginning of the Book, there never was a man, be he Christian or Saracen or Tartar or Heathen, who ever travelled over so much of the world as did that noble and illustrious citizen of the City of Venice, Messer Marco the son of Messer Nicolas Polo.

Thanks be to God! Amen! Amen!

CHAPTER II

Christopher Columbus

Very little is actually known of the birth or bithplace of Columbus, but the weight of evidence points to about 1446 as the time, and Genoa, Italy, as the place.

It required the utmost perseverance and tenacity on the part of Columbus to secure the support, first of the Portuguese, and finally of the Spanish sovereigns for his proposal to reach the fabulous riches of the Indies by way of the West. After many weary years of discouragement, he finally set sail on August 3, 1492, under the sponsorship of Ferdinand and Isabella. It seems incredible that such a small fleet of fragile ships as the "Pinta," the "Nina," and the "Santa Maria" ever survived the terrible journey. He encountered much dissatisfaction and fear among his crew, who dreaded this voyage into uncharted seas. It was indeed a monument to his character and skill as a navigator that he persisted in his course and reached what he assumed to be his goal. For the Admiral died in 1506, still under the impression that he had reached the western parts of India or Asia, and the new islands were consequently referred to everywhere as the West Indies, or the New World.

His momentous voyage of discovery is related in his own words in the following letter.

DISCOVERY OF AMERICA—1492

Letter of Christopher Columbus, to whom our age owes much, concerning the islands recently discovered in the Indian sea. For the search of which, eight months before, he was sent under the auspices and at the cost of the most invincible Ferdinand, king of Spain. Addressed to the magnificent lord Raphael Sanxis, treasurer of the same most illustrious king, and which the noble and learned man Leander de Cosco has translated from the Spanish language into Latin, on the third of the kalends of May, 1493, the first year of the pontificate of Alexander the Sixth.

BECAUSE my undertakings have attained success, I know that it will be pleasing to you: these I have determined to relate, so that you may be made acquainted with everything done and discovered in this our voyage. On the thirty-third day after I departed from Cadiz,[1] I came to the Indian sea, where I found many islands inhabited by men without number, of all which I took possession for our most fortunate king, with proclaiming heralds and flying standards, no one objecting. To the first of these I gave the name of the Blessed Saviour,[2] on whose aid relying I had reached this as well as the other islands. But the Indians call it Guanahany. I also called each one of the others by a new name. For I ordered one island to be called Santa Maria of the Conception, another Fernandina, another Isabella, another Juana,[3] and so on with the rest.

As soon as we had arrived at that island which I have just now said was called Juana, I proceeded along its coast towards the west for some distance; I found it so large and without perceptible end, that I believed it to be not an island, but the continental country of Cathay;[4] seeing, however, no towns or cities situated on the sea-coast, but only some villages and rude farms, with whose inhabitants I was unable to converse, because as soon as they saw us they took flight. I proceeded farther, thinking that I would discover some city or large residences. At length, perceiving that we had gone far enough, that nothing new appeared, and that this way was leading us to the north, which I wished to avoid, because it was winter on the land, and it was my intention to go to the south, moreover the winds were becoming violent, I therefore determined that no other plans were practicable, and so, going back, I returned to a certain bay that I had noticed, from which I sent two of our men to the land, that they might find out whether there was a king in this country, or any cities. These men traveled for three days, and they found people and houses without number, but they were small and without any government, therefore they returned.

Now in the meantime I had learned from certain Indians, whom I had seized there, that this country was indeed an island, and therefore I proceeded towards the east, keeping all the time near the coast, for 322 miles, to the extreme ends of this island. From this place I saw another island to the east, distant from this Juana 54 miles, which I called forthwith Hispana;[5] and I sailed to it; and I steered along the northern coast, as at Juana, towards the east, 564 miles. And the said Juana and the other islands there appear very fertile. This island is surrounded by many very safe and wide harbors, not excelled by any others that I have ever seen. Many great and salubrious rivers flow through it. There are also many very high mountains there. All these islands are very beautiful, and distinguished by various qualities; they are accessible, and full of a great variety of trees stretching

---

[1] A mistake of the Latin translator. Columbus sailed from Palos on the 3d of August, 1492; on the 8th of September he left the Canaries, and on the 11th of October, or thirty-three days later, he reached the Bahamas.

[2] In Spanish, San Salvador, one of the Bahama islands.

[3] The island of Cuba.

[4] China.

[5] Hispaniola, or Hayti.

up to the stars; the leaves of which I believe are never shed, for I saw them as green and flourishing as they are usually in Spain in the month of May; some of them were blossoming, some were bearing fruit, some were in other conditions; each one was thriving in its own way. The nightingale and various other birds without number were singing, in the month of November, when I was exploring them. There are besides in the said island Juana seven or eight kinds of palm trees, which far excel ours in height and beauty, just as all the other trees, herbs, and fruits do. There are also excellent pine trees, vast plains and meadows, a variety of birds, a variety of honey, and a variety of metals, excepting iron. In the one which was called Hispana, as we said above, there are great and beautiful mountains, vast fields, groves, fertile plains, very suitable for planting and cultivating, and for the building of houses. The convenience of the harbors in this island, and the remarkable number of rivers contributing to the healthfulness of man, exceed belief, unless one has seen them. The trees, pasturage, and fruits of this island differ greatly from those of Juana. This Hispana, moreover, abounds in different kinds of spices, in gold, and in metals.

On this island, indeed, and on all the others which I have seen, and of which I have knowledge, the inhabitants of both sexes go always naked, just as they came into the world, except some of the women, who use a covering of a leaf or some foliage, or a cotton cloth, which they make themselves for that purpose. All these people lack, as I said above, every kind of iron; they are also without weapons, which indeed are unknown; nor are they competent to use them, not on account of deformity of body, for they are well formed, but because they are timid and full of fear. They carry for weapons, however, reeds baked in the sun, on the lower ends of which they fasten some shafts of dried wood rubbed down to a point; and indeed they do not venture to use these always; for it frequently happened when I sent two or three of my men to some of the villages, that they might speak with the natives, a compact troop of the Indians would march out, and as soon as they saw our men approaching, they would quickly take flight, children being pushed aside by their fathers, and fathers by their children. And this was not because any hurt or injury had been inflicted on any one of them, for to every one whom I visited and with whom I was able to converse, I distributed whatever I had, cloth and many other things, no return being made to me; but they are by nature fearful and timid. Yet when they perceive that they are safe, putting aside all fear, they are of simple manners and trustworthy, and very liberal with everything they have, refusing no one who asks for anything they may possess, and even themselves inviting us to ask for things. They show greater love for all others than for themselves; they give valuable things for trifles, being satisfied even with a very small return, or with nothing; however, I forbade that things so small and of no value should be given to them, such as pieces of plates, dishes and glass, likewise keys and shoe-straps; although if they were able to obtain these, it seemed to them like getting the most beautiful jewels in the world. It happened, indeed, that a certain sailor obtained in exchange for a shoe-strap as much worth of gold as would equal three golden coins; and likewise other things for articles of very little value, especially for new silver coins, and for some gold coins, to obtain which they gave whatever the seller desired, as for instance an ounce and a half and two ounces of gold, or thirty and forty pounds of cotton, with which they were already acquainted. They also traded cotton and gold for pieces of bows, bottles, jugs and jars, like persons without reason, which I forbade because it was very wrong; and I gave to them many beautiful and pleasing things that I had brought with me, no value being taken in exchange, in order that I might the more easily make them friendly to me, that they might be made worshippers of Christ, and that they might be full of love towards our king, queen, and prince, and the whole Spanish nation; also that they might be zealous to search out and collect, and deliver to us those things of which they had plenty, and which we greatly needed.

These people practice no kind of idolatry; on the contrary they firmly believe that all strength and power, and in fact all good things are in heaven, and that I had come down from thence with these ships and sailors; and in this belief I was received there after they had put aside fear. Nor are they slow or unskilled, but of excellent and acute understanding; and the men who have navigated that sea give an account of everything in an admirable manner; but they never saw people clothed, nor these kind of ships. As soon as I reached that sea, I seized by force several Indians on the first island, in order that they might learn from us, and in like manner tell us about those things in these lands of which they themselves had knowledge; and the plan succeeded, for in a short time we understood them and they us, sometimes by gestures and signs, sometimes by words; and it was a great advantage to us. They are coming with me now, yet always believing that I descended from heaven, although they have been living with us for a long time, and are living with us to-day. And these men were the first who announced it wherever we landed, continually proclaiming to the others in a loud voice, "Come, come, and you will see the celestial people." Whereupon both women and men, both children and adults, both young men and old men, laying aside the fear caused a little before, visited us eagerly, filling the road with a great crowd, some bringing food, and some drink, with great love and extraordinary good will. On every island there are many canoes of a single piece of wood; and though narrow, yet in length and shape similar to our row-boats, but swifter in movement. They steer only by oars. Some of these boats are large, some small, some of medium size. Yet they row many of the larger row-boats with eighteen cross-benches, with which they cross to all those islands, which are innumerable, and with these boats they perform their trading, and carry on commerce among them. I saw some of these row-boats or canoes which were carrying seventy and eighty rowers. In all these islands there is no difference in the appearance of the people, nor in the manners and language, but all understand each other mutually; a fact that is very important for the end which I suppose to be earnestly desired by our most illustrious king, that is, their conversion to the holy religion of Christ, to which in truth, as far as I can perceive, they are very ready and favorably inclined.

I said before how I proceeded along the island Juana in a straight line from west to east 322 miles, according to which course and the length of the way, I am able to say that this Juana is larger than England and Scotland together; for besides the said 322 thousand paces, there are two more provinces in that part which lies towards the west, which I did not visit; one of these the Indians called Anan, whose inhabitants are born with tails. They extend to 180 miles in length, as I have learned from those Indians I have with me, who are all acquainted with these islands. But the circumference of Hispana is greater than all Spain from Colonia to Fontarabia. This is easily proved, because its fourth side, which I myself passed along in a straight line from west to east, extends 540 miles. This island is to be desired and is very desirable, and not to be despised; in which, although as I have said, I solemnly took possession of all the others for our most invincible king, and their government is entirely committed to the said king, yet I especially took possession of a certain large town, in a very convenient location, and adapted to all kinds of gain and commerce, to which we gave the name of our Lord of the Nativity. And I commanded a fort to be built there forthwith, which must be completed by this time; in which I left as many men as seemed necessary, with all kinds of arms, and plenty of food for more than a year. Likewise one caravel, and for the construction of others men skilled in this trade and in other professions; and also the extraordinary good will and friendship of the king of this island towards us. For those people are very amiable and kind, to such a degree that the said king gloried in calling me his brother. And if they should change their minds, and should wish to hurt those who remained in the fort, they would not be able, because they lack weapons, they go naked, and are too cowardly. For that reason those who hold the said fort are at least able to resist easily this whole island, without any imminent danger to themselves, so long as they do not transgress the regulations and command which we gave. In all these islands, as I have understood, each man is content with only one wife, except the princes or kings, who are permitted to have twenty. The women appear to work more than the men. I was not able to find out surely whether they have individual property, for I saw that one man had the duty of distributing to the others, especially refreshments, food, and things of that kind. I found no monstrosities among them, as very many supposed, but men of great reverence, and friendly. Nor are they black like the Ethiopians. They have straight hair, hanging down. They do not remain where the solar rays send out the heat, for the strength of the sun is very great here, because it is distant from the equinoctial line, as it seems, only twenty-six degrees. On the tops of the mountains too the cold is severe, but the Indians, however, moderate it, partly by being accustomed to the place, and partly by the help of very hot victuals, of which they eat frequently and immoderately.

And so I did not see any monstrosity, nor did I have knowledge of them any where, excepting a certain island named Charis,[6] which is the second in passing from Hispana to India. This island is inhabited by a certain people who are considered very warlike by their neighbors. These eat human flesh. The said people have many kinds of row-boats, in which they cross over to all the other Indian islands, and seize and carry away everything that they can. They differ in no way from the others, only that they wear long hair like the women. They use bows and darts made of reeds, with sharpened shafts fastened to the larger ends, as we have described. On this account they are considered warlike, wherefore the other Indians are afflicted with continual fear, but I regard them as of no more account than the others. These are the people who visit certain women, who alone inhabit the island Mateunin,[7] which is the first in passing from Hispana to India. These women, moreover, perform no kind of work of their sex, for they use bows and darts, like those I have described of their husbands; they protect themselves with sheets of copper, of which there is great abundance among them. They tell me of another island greater than the aforesaid Hispana, whose inhabitants are without hair, and which abounds in gold above all the others. I am bringing with me men of this island and of the others that I have seen, who give proof of the things that I have described.

Finally, that I may compress in few words the brief account of our departure and quick return, and the gain, I promise this, that if I am supported by our most invincible sovereigns with a little of their help, as much gold can be supplied as they will need, indeed as much of spices, of cotton, of chewing gum (which is only found in Chios), also as much of aloes wood, and as many slaves for the navy, as their majesties will wish to demand. Likewise rhubarb and other kinds of spices, which I suppose these men whom I left in the said fort have already found, and will continue to find; since I remained in no place longer than the winds forced me, except in the town of the Nativity, while I provided for the building of the fort, and for the safety of all. Which things, although they are very great and remarkable, yet they would have been much greater, if I had been aided by as many ships as the occasion required. Truly great and wonderful is this, and not corresponding to our merits, but to the holy Christian religion, and to the piety and religion of our sovereigns, because what the human understanding could not attain, that the divine will has granted to human efforts. For God is wont to listen to his servants who love his precepts, even in impossibilities, as has happened to us on the present occasion, who have attained that which hitherto mortal men have never reached. For if any one has written or said anything about these islands, it was all with obscurities and conjectures; no one claims that he had seen them; from which they seemed like fables. Therefore let the king and queen, the princes and their most fortunate kingdoms, and all other countries of Christendom give thanks to our Lord and Saviour Jesus Christ, who has bestowed upon

[6]Identified with Dominica.
[7]Supposed to be Martinique.

us so great a victory and gift. Let religious processions be solemnized; let sacred festivals be given; let the churches be covered with festive garlands. Let Christ rejoice on earth, as he rejoices in heaven, when he foresees coming to salvation so many souls of people hitherto lost. Let us be glad also, as well on account of the exaltation of our faith, as on account of the increase of our temporal affairs, of which not only Spain, but universal Christendom will be partaker. These things that have been done are thus briefly related. Farewell. Lisbon, the day before the ides of March.[8]

Christopher Columbus, admiral of the Ocean fleet.

[8]March 14th, 1493.

CHAPTER III

Fernando Magellan—1480?—1521

The exact date of Magellan's birth remains obscure, but it is known that he was a small boy when Columbus returned from his discovery of the West Indies. He was a Portuguese of good birth, who was as well trained in the art of navigation and cosmography as the times permitted, and lived in a day when the imagination of everyone was fired by great adventures.

Because of an insult by the Portuguese government, who refused his just claim for services rendered in war, he renounced his citizenship and became a Spanish subject. Thus it came about that he set sail in 1519 under the Spanish flag, bringing renown to that monarch and himself by accomplishing what Columbus had failed to do—reaching the East by way of the West.

He sailed from Seville on August 10th, 1519, magnificently outfitted, in sad contrast to the poor fleet which Columbus had. He reached Rio de Janeiro on the 13th of December, continuing southward until the 21st of October, 1520, when he discovered the Straits which now bear his name. The hazardous passage through these Straits is eloquently recounted by Pigafetta, a fellow voyager.

DISCOVERY OF THE STRAITS OF MAGELLAN—1520

NARRATED BY ANTONIO PIGAFETTA, A FELLOW VOYAGER

We crossed as far as a country named Verzin,[1] which is in twenty-four degrees and a half of the antarctic sky. This country is from the cape St. Augustine, which is in eight degrees in the antarctic sky. At this place we had refreshments of victuals, like fowls and meat of calves, also a variety of fruits, called battate, pigne (pine-apple), sweet, of singular goodness, and many other things, which I have omitted mentioning, not to be too long. The people of the said place gave, in order to have a knife, or a hook for catching fish, five or six fowls, and for a comb they gave two geese, and for a small mirror, or a pair of scissors, they gave so much fish that ten men could have eaten of it. And for a hawk's-bell they gave a full basket of the fruit named battate; this has the taste of a chestnut, and is of the

[1]Brazil, at Rio de Janeiro.

length of a shuttle. For a king of cards, of that kind which they used to play with in Italy, they gave me five fowls, and thought they had cheated me. We entered into this port the day of Saint Lucy [13th December], before Christmas, on which day we had the sun on the zenith, which is a term of astrology. This zenith is a point in the sky, according to astrologers, and only in imagination, and it answers to over our head in a straight line, as may be seen by the treatise of the sphere, and by Aristotle, in the first book, *De Cœlo et Mondo*. On the day that we had the sun in the zenith we felt greater heat, as much as when we were on the equinoctial line.

The said country of Verzin is very abundant in all good things, and is larger than France, Spain, and Italy together. It is one of the countries which the King of Portugal has conquered. Its inhabitants are not Christians, and adore nothing, but live according to the usage of nature, rather bestially than otherwise. Some of these people live a hundred, or a hundred and twenty, or a hundred and forty years, and more; they go naked, both men and women. Their dwellings are houses that are rather long, and which they call "boy"; they sleep upon cotton nets, which they call, in their language, "amache." These nets are fastened to large timbers from one end of their house to the other. They make the fire to warm themselves right under their bed. It is to be known that in each of these houses, which they call "boy," there dwells a family of a hundred persons, who make a great noise. In this place they have boats, which are made of a tree, all in one piece, which they call "canoo." These are not made with iron instruments, for they have not got any, but with stones, like pebbles, and with these they plane and dig out these boats. Into these thirty or forty men enter, and their oars are made like iron shovels: and those who row these oars are black people, quite naked and shaven, and look like enemies of hell. The men and women of this said place are well made in their bodies. They eat the flesh of their enemies, not as good meat, but because they have adopted this custom. Now this custom arose as follows: an old woman of this place of Verzin had an only son, who was killed by his enemies, and, some days afterwards, the friends of this woman captured one of the said enemies who had put her son to death, and brought him to where she was. Immediately the said old women, seeing the man who was captured, and recollecting the death of her child, rushed upon him like a mad dog, and bit him on the shoulder. However, this man who had been taken prisoner found means to run away, and told how they had wished to eat him, showing the bite which the said old woman had made in his shoulder. After that those who were caught on one side or other were eaten. Through that arose this custom in this place of eating the enemies of each other. But they do not eat up the whole body of the man whom they take prisoner; they eat him bit by bit, and for fear that he should be spoiled, they cut him up into pieces, which they set to dry in the chimney, and every day they cut a small piece, and eat it with their ordinary victuals in memory of their enemies. I was assured that this custom was true by a pilot, named John Carvagio, who was in our company, and had remained four years in this place; it is also to be observed that the inhabitants of this place, both men and women, are accustomed to paint themselves with fire, all over the body, and also the face. The men are shaven, and wear no beard, because they pluck it out themselves, and for all clothing they wear a circle surrounded with the largest feathers of parrots, and they only cover their posterior parts, which is a cause of laughter and mockery. The people of this place, almost all, excepting women and children, have three holes in the lower lip, and carry, hanging in them, small round stones, about a finger in length. These kind of people, both men and women, are not very black, but rather brown, and they openly show their shame, and have no hair on the whole of their bodies. The king of this country is called Cacich, and there are here an infinite number of parrots, of which they give eight or ten for a looking-glass; there are also some little cat-monkeys having almost the appearance of a lion; they are yellow, and handsome, and agreeable to look at. The people of this place make bread, which is of a round shape, and they take the marrow of certain trees which are there, between the bark and the tree, but it is not at all good, and resembles fresh cheese. There are also some pigs which have their navel on the back, and large birds which have their beak like a spoon, and they have no tongue. For a hatchet or for a knife they used to give us one or two of their daughters as slaves, but their wives they would not give up for anything in the world. According to what they say the women of this place never render duty to their husbands by day, but only at night; they attend to business out of doors, and carry all that they require for their husbands' victuals inside small baskets on their heads, or fastened to their heads. Their husbands go with them, and carry a bow of verzin, or of black palm, with a handful of arrows of cane. They do this because they are very jealous of their wives. These carry their children fastened to their neck, and they are inside a thing made of cotton in the manner of a net. I omit relating many other strange things, not to be too prolix; however, I will not forget to say that mass was said twice on shore, where there were many people of the said country, who remained on their knees, and their hands joined in great reverence, during the mass, so that it was a pleasure and a subject of compassion to see them. In a short time they built a house for us, as they imagined that we should remain a long time with them, and, at our departure thence, they gave us a large quantity of verzin. It is a colour which proceeds from the trees which are in this country, and they are in such quantity that the country is called from it Verzin.

It is to be known that it happened that it had not rained for two months before we came there, and the day that we arrived it began to rain, on which account the people of the said place said that we came from heaven, and had brought the rain with us, which was great simplicity, and these people were easily converted to the Christian faith. Besides the above-mentioned things which were rather simple, the people of this country showed us another, very simple; for they imagined that the small ships' boats were the children of the ships, and that the said ships brought them forth when the boats were hoisted out to send the men hither and thither; and when the boats were alongside the ship they thought that the ships were giving them suck.

A beautiful young girl came one day inside the ship of our captain, where I was, and did not come except to seek for her luck: however, she directed her looks to the cabin of the master, and saw a nail of a finger's length, and went and took it as something valuable and new, and hid it in her hair, for otherwise she would not have been able to conceal it, because she was naked, and, bending forwards, she went away; and the captain and I saw this mystery.

We remained thirteen days in this country of Verzin, and, departing from it and following our course, we went as far as thirty-four degrees and a third towards the antarctic pole; there we found, near a river, men whom they call "cannibals," who eat human flesh, and one of these men, great as a giant, came to the captain's ship to ascertain and ask if the others might come. This man had a voice like a bull, and whilst this man was at the ship his companions carried off all their goods which they had to a castle further off, from fear of us. Seeing that, we landed a hundred men from the ships, and went after them to try and catch some others; however they gained in running away. This kind of people did more with one step than we could do at a bound. In this same river there were seven little islands, and in the largest of them precious stones are found. This place was formerly called the Cape of St. Mary, and it was thought there that from thence there was a passage to the Sea of Sur; that is to say, the South Sea. And it is not found that any ship has ever discovered anything more, having passed beyond the said cape. And now it is no longer a cape, but it is a river which has a mouth seventeen leagues in width, by which it enters into the sea. In past time, in this river, these great men named Canibali ate a Spanish captain, named John de Sola, and sixty men who had gone to discover land, as we were doing, and trusted too much to them.

Afterwards following the same course towards the antarctic pole, going along the land, we found two islands full of geese and goslings, and sea wolves, of which geese the large number could not be reckoned; for we loaded all the five ships with them in an hour. These geese are black, and have their feathers all over the body of the same size and shape, and they do not fly, and live upon fish; and they were so fat that they did not pluck them, but skinned them. They have beaks like that of a crow. The sea wolves of these two islands are of many colours, and of the size and thickness of a calf, and have a head like that of a calf, and the ears small and round. They have large teeth, and have no legs, but feet joining close on to the body, which resemble a human hand; they have small nails to their feet, and skin between the fingers like geese. If these animals could run they would be very bad and cruel, but they do not stir from the water, and swim and live upon fish. In this place we endured a great storm, and thought we should have been lost, but the three holy bodies, that is to say, St. Anselmo, St. Nicolas, and Sta. Clara, appeared to us, and immediately the storm ceased.

Departing thence as far as forty-nine degrees and a half in the antarctic heavens (as we were in the winter), we entered into a port to pass the winter, and remained there two whole months without ever seeing anybody. However, one day, without anyone expecting it, we saw a giant, who was on the shore of the sea, quite naked, and was dancing and leaping, and singing, and whilst singing he put the sand and dust on his head. Our captain sent one of his men towards him, whom he charged to sing and leap like the other to reassure him, and show him friendship. This he did, and immediately the sailor led this giant to a little island where the captain was waiting for him; and when he was before us he began to be astonished, and to be afraid, and he raised one finger on high, thinking that we came from heaven. He was so tall that the tallest of us only came up to his waist; however he was well built. He had a large face, painted red all round, and his eyes also were painted yellow around them, and he had two hearts painted on his cheeks; he had but little hair on his head, and it was painted white. When he was brought before the captain he was clothed with the skin of a certain beast, which skin was very skilfully sewed. This beast has its head and ears of the size of a mule, and the neck and body of the fashion of a camel, the legs of a deer, and the tail like that of a horse, and its neigh like a horse. There is a great quantity of these animals in this same place. This giant had his feet covered with the skin of this animal in the form of shoes, and he carried in his hand a short and thick bow, with a thick cord made of the gut of the said beast, with a bundle of cane arrows, which were not very long, and were feathered like ours, but they had no iron at the end, though they had at the end some small white and black cut stones, and these arrows were like those which the Turks use. The captain caused food and drink to be given to this giant, then they showed him some things, amongst others, a steel mirror. When the giant saw his likeness in it, he was greatly terrified, leaping backwards, and made three or four of our men fall down.

After that the captain gave him two bells, a mirror, a comb, and a chaplet of beads, and sent him back on shore, having him accompanied by four armed men. One of the companions of this giant, who would never come to the ship on seeing the other coming back with our people, came forward and ran to where the other giants dwelled. These came one after the other all naked, and began to leap and sing, raising one finger to heaven, and showing to our people a certain white powder made of the roots of herbs, which they kept in earthen pots, and they made signs that they lived on that, and that they had nothing else to eat than this powder. Therefore our people made them signs to come to the ship and that they would help them to carry their bundles. Then these men came, who carried only their bows in their hands; but their wives came after them laden like donkeys, and carried their goods. These women are not as tall as the men, but they

are very sufficiently large. When we saw them we were all amazed and astonished, for they had the breasts half an ell long, and had their faces painted
and were dressed like the men. But they wore a small skin before them to
cover themselves. They brought with them four of those little beasts of
which they make their clothing, and they led them with a cord in the
manner of dogs coupled together. When these people wish to catch these
animals with which they clothe themselves, they fasten one of the young
ones to a bush, and afterwards the large ones come to play with the little
one, and the giants are hid behind some hedge, and by shooting their arrows
they kill the large ones. Our men brought eighteen of these giants, both
men and women, whom they placed in two divisions, half on one side of
the port, and the other half at the other, to hunt the said animals. Six days
after, our people on going to cut wood, saw another giant, with his face
painted and clothed like the above-mentioned, he had in his hand a bow
and arrows, and approaching our people he made some touches on his head
and on his body, and afterwards did the same to our people. And this being done he raised both his hands to heaven. When the captain-general
knew all this, he sent to fetch him with his ship's boat, and brought him to
one of the little islands which are in the port, where the ships were. In
this island the captain had caused a house to be made for putting some of
the ships' things in whilst he remained there. This giant was of a still better
disposition than the others, and was a gracious and amiable person, who
liked to dance and leap. When he leapt he caused the earth to sink in a
palm depth at the place where his feet touched. He was a long time with
us, and at the end we baptised him, and gave him the name of John. This
giant pronounced the name of Jesus, the Pater noster, Ave Maria, and his
name as clearly as we did: but he had a terribly strong and loud voice.
The captain gave him a shirt and a tunic of cloth, and seaman's breeches,
a cap, a comb, some bells, and other things, and sent him back to where
he had come from. He went away very joyous and satisfied. The next day
this giant returned, and brought one of those large animals before mentioned, for which the captain gave him some other things, so that he should
bring more. But afterwards he did not return, and it is to be presumed
that the other giants killed him because he had come to us.

Fifteen days later we saw four other giants, who carried no arrows, for
they had hid them in the bushes, as two of them showed us, for we took
them all four, and each of them was painted in a different way. The captain
retained the two younger ones to take them to Spain on his return; but
it was done by gentle and cunning means, for otherwise they would have
done a hurt to some of our men. The manner in which he retained them
was that he gave them many knives, forks, mirrors, bells, and glass, and
they held all these things in their hands. Then the captain had some irons
brought, such as are put on the feet of malefactors: these giants took pleasure in seeing the irons, but they did not know where to put them, and it
grieved them that they could not take them with their hands, because they
were hindered by the other things which they held in them. The other

wo giants were there, and were desirous of helping the other two, but he captain would not let them, and made a sign to the two whom he vished to detain that they would put those irons on their feet, and then hey would go away: at this they made a sign with their heads that they vere content. Immediately the captain had the irons put on the feet of oth of them, and when they saw that they were striking with a hammer n the bolt which crosses the said irons to rivet them, and prevent them rom being opened, these giants were afraid, but the captain made them a ign not to doubt of anything. Nevertheless when they saw the trick which ad been played them, they began to be enraged, and to foam like bulls, rying out very loud Setebos, that is to say, the great devil, that he should elp them. The hands of the other two giants were bound, but it was with reat difficulty; then the captain sent them back on shore, with nine of his nen to conduct them, and to bring the wife of one of those who had re- nained in irons, because he regretted her greatly, as we saw by signs. But n going away one of those two who were sent away, untied his hands and scaped, running with such lightness that our men lost sight of him, and e went away where his companions were staying; but he found nobody f those that he had left with the women because they had gone to hunt. However he went to look for them, and found them, and related to them ll that had been done to them. The other giant whose hands were tied truggled as much as he could to unfasten himself, and to prevent his doing o, one of our men struck him, and hurt him on the head, at which he got very angry; however he led our people there where their wives were. Then John Carvagio, the pilot who was the chief conductor of these two giants, would not bring away the wife of one of the giants who had re- nained in irons on that evening, but was of opinion that they should sleep here, because it was almost night. During this time the one of the giants vho had untied his hands came back from where he had been, with an- other giant, and they seeing their companion wounded on the head, said nothing at that moment, but next morning they spoke in their language o the women, and immediately all ran away together, and the smallest an faster than the biggest, and they left all their chattels. Two of these giants being rather a long way off shot arrows at our men, and fighting hus, one of the giants pierced with an arrow the thigh of one of our men, f which he died immediately. Then seeing that he was dead, all ran away. Our men had crossbows and guns, but they never could hit one of these giants, because they did not stand still in one place, but leaped hither and hither. After that, our men buried the man who had been killed, and set ire to the place where those giants had left their chattels. Certainly these giants run faster than a horse, and they are very jealous of their wives.

* * * * * *

We remained in this port, which was called the port of St. Julian, about ive months, during which there happened to us many strange things, of which I will tell a part. One was, that immediately that we entered into this port, the masters of the other four ships plotted treason against the captain-general, in order to put him to death. These were thus named: John of Carthagine, conductor of the fleet; the treasurer, Loys de Mendoza the conductor, Anthony Cocha; and Gaspar de Casada. However, the treason was discovered, for which the treasurer was killed with stabs of a dagger, and then quartered. This Gaspar de Casada had his head cut off, and afterwards was cut into quarters; and the conductor having a few days later attempted another treason, was banished with a priest, and was put in that country called Pattagonia. The captain-general would not put this conductor to death, because the Emperor Charles had made him captain of one of the ships. One of our ships, named St. James, was lost in going to discover the coast; all the men, however, were saved by a miracle, for they were hardly wet at all. Two men of these, who were saved, came to us and told us all that had passed and happened, on which the captain at once sent some men with sacks full of biscuit for two months. So, each day we found something of the ship of the other men who had escaped from the ship which was lost; and the place where these men were was twenty-five leagues from us, and the road bad and full of thorns, and it required four days to go there, and no water to drink was to be found on the road, but only ice, and of that little. In this port of St. Julian there were a great quantity of long capres, called missiglione; these had pearls in the midst In this place they found incense, and ostriches, foxes, sparrows, and rabbit a good deal smaller than ours. We set up at the top of the highest mountain which was there a very large cross, as a sign that this country belonged to the King of Spain; and we gave to this mountain the name of Mount of Christ.

* * * * * *

After going and taking the course to the fifty-second degree of the said antarctic sky, on the day of the Eleven Thousand Virgins [October 21] we found, by a miracle, a strait which we called the Cape of the Eleven Thousand Virgins,[2] this strait is a hundred and ten leagues long, which are four hundred and forty miles, and almost as wide as less than half a league, and it issues in another sea, which is called the peaceful sea; it is surrounded by very great and high mountains covered with snow. In this place it was not possible to anchor with the anchors, because no bottom was found, on which account they were forced to put the moorings of twenty-five or thirty fathoms length on shore. This strait was a round place surrounded by mountains, as I have said, and the greater number of the sailors thought that there was no place by which to go out thence to enter into the peaceful sea. But the captain-general said that there was another strait for going out, and said that he knew it well, because he had seen it by a marine chart of the King of Portugal, which map had been made by a great pilot and mariner named Martin of Bohemia. The captain sent on

[2] Afterwards named the Straits of Magellan.

before two of his ships, one named *St. Anthony* and the other the *Conception*, to seek for and discover the outlet of this strait, which was called the Cape de la Baya. And we, with the other two ships, that is to say, the flagship named *Trinitate*, and the other the *Victory*, remained waiting for them within the bay, where in the night we had a great storm, which lasted till the next day at midday, and during which we were forced to weigh the anchors and let the ships go hither and thither about the bay. The other two ships met with such a head wind that they could not weather a cape which the bay made almost at its extremity; wishing to come to us, they were near being driven to beach the ships. But, on approaching the extremity of the bay, and whilst expecting to be lost, they saw a small mouth, which did not resemble a mouth but a corner, and (like people giving up hope) they threw themselves into it, so that by force they discovered the strait. Seeing that it was not a corner, but a strait of land, they went further on and found a bay, then going still further they found another strait and another bay larger than the first two, at which, being very joyous, they suddenly returned backwards to tell it to the captain-general. Amongst us we thought that they had perished: first, because of the great storm; next, because two days had passed that we had not seen them. And being thus in doubt we saw the two ships under all sail, with ensigns spread, come towards us: these, when near us, suddenly discharged much artillery, at which we, very joyous, saluted them with artillery and shouts. Afterwards, all together, thanking God and the Virgin Mary, we went to seek further on.

After having entered inside this strait we found that there were two mouths, of which one trended to the Sirocco (S.E.), and the other to the Garbin (S.W.). On that account the captain again sent the two ships, *St. Anthony* and *Conception*, to see if the mouth which was towards Sirocco had an outlet beyond into the said peaceful sea. One of these two ships, named *St. Anthony*, would not wait for the other ship, because those who were inside wished to return to Spain; this they did, and the principal reason was on account of the pilot of the said ship being previously discontented with the said captain-general, because that before this armament was made, this pilot had gone to the Emperor to talk about having some ships to discover countries. But, on account of the arrival of the captain-general, the Emperor did not give them to this pilot, on account of which he agreed with some Spaniards, and the following night they took prisoner the captain of their ship, who was a brother of the captain-general, and who was named Alvar de Meschite; they wounded him, and put him in irons. So they carried him off to Spain. And in this ship, which went away and returned, was one of the two above-mentioned giants whom we had taken, and when he felt the heat he died. The other ship, named the *Conception*, not being able to follow that one, was always waiting for it, and fluttered hither and thither. But it lost its time, for the other took the road by night for returning. When this happened, at night the ship of the captain and the other ship went together to discover the other mouth to Garbin (S.W.), where, on always holding on our course, we found the same strait. But at the end we arrived at a river which we named the River of Sardines, because we found a great quantity of them. So we remained there four days to wait for the other two ships. A short time after we sent a boat well supplied with men and provisions to discover the cape of the other sea: these remained three days in going and coming. They told us that they had found the cape, and the sea great and wide. At the joy which the captain-general had at this he began to cry, and he gave the name of Cape of Desire to this cape, as a thing which had been much desired for a long time. Having done that we turned back to find the two ships which were at the other side, but we only found the *Conception*, of which ship we asked what had become of her companion. To this the captain of the said ship, named John Serrano (who was pilot of the first ship which was lost, as has been related), replied that he knew nothing of her, and that he had never seen her since she entered the mouth. However, we sought for her through all the strait, as far as the said mouth, by which she had taken her course to return. Besides that, the captain-general sent back the ship named the *Victory* as far as the entrance of the strait to see if the ship was there, and he told the people of this ship that if they did not find the ship they were looking for, they were to place an ensign on the summit of a small hill, with a letter inside a pot placed in the ground near the ensign, so that if the ship should by chance return, it might see that ensign, and also find the letter which would give information of the course which the captain was holding. This manner of acting had been ordained by the captain from the commencement, in order to effect the junction of any ship which might be separated from the others. So the people of the said ship did what the captain had commanded them, and more, for they set two ensigns with letters; one of the ensigns was placed on a small hill at the first bay, the other on an islet in the third bay, where there were many sea wolves and large birds. The captain-general waited for them with the other ship near the river named Isles: and he caused a cross to be set upon a small island in front of that river, which was between high mountains covered with snow. This river comes and falls into the sea near the other river of the Sardines.

If we had not found this strait the captain-general had made up his mind to go as far as seventy-five degrees towards the antarctic pole; where at that height in the summer time there is no night, or very little: in a similar manner in the winter there is no daylight, or very little, and so that every one may believe this, when we were in this strait the night lasted only three hours, and this was in the month of October.

The land of this strait on the left hand side looked towards the Sirocco wind, which is the wind collateral to the Levant and South; we called this strait Pathagonico. In it we found at every half league a good port and place for anchoring, good waters, wood all of cedar, and fish like sardines, missiglione, and a very sweet herb named appio (celery). There is also some of the same kind which is bitter. This herb grows near the springs, and from not finding anything else we ate of it for several days. I think that there is not in the world a more beautiful country, or better strait than this one.

* * * * * *

Wednesday, the 28th of November, 1520, we came forth out of the said strait, and entered into the Pacific sea, where we remained three months and twenty days without taking in provisions or other refreshments, and we only ate old biscuit reduced to powder, and full of grubs, and stinking from the dirt which the rats had made on it when eating the good biscuit, and we drank water that was yellow and stinking. We also ate the ox hides which were under the main-yard, so that the yard should not break the rigging: they were very hard on account of the sun, rain, and wind, and we left them for four or five days in the sea, and then we put them a little on the embers, and so ate them; also the sawdust of wood, and rats which cost half-a-crown each, moreover enough of them were not to be got. Besides the above-named evils, this misfortune which I will mention was the worst, it was that the upper and lower gums of most of our men grew so much that they could not eat, and in this way so many suffered, that nineteen died, and the other giant, and an Indian from the country of Verzin. Besides those who died, twenty-five or thirty fell ill of divers sicknesses, both in the arms and legs, and other places, in such manner that very few remained healthy. However, thanks be to the Lord, I had no sickness. During those three months and twenty days we went in an open sea, while we ran fully four thousand leagues in the Pacific sea. This was well named Pacific, for during this same time we met with no storm, and saw no land except two small uninhabited islands, in which we found only birds and trees. We named them the Unfortunate Islands; they are two hundred leagues apart from one another, and there is no place to anchor, as there is no bottom. There we saw many sharks, which are a kind of large fish which they call Tiburoni. The first isle is in fifteen degrees of austral latitude, and the other is in nine degrees. With the said wind we ran each day fifty or sixty leagues, or more; now with the wind astern, sometimes on a wind or otherwise. And if our Lord and his Mother had not aided us in giving us good weather to refresh ourselves with provisions and other things, we should all have died of hunger in this very vast sea, and I think that never man will undertake to perform such a voyage.

When we had gone out of this strait, if we had always navigated to the west we should have gone without finding any land except the Cape of the Eleven Thousand Virgins, which is at the eastern head of the strait in the ocean sea, with the Cape of Desire at the west in the Pacific sea. These two capes are exactly in fifty-two degrees of latitude of the antarctic pole.

The antarctic pole is not so covered with stars as the arctic, for there are to be seen there many small stars congregated together, which are like to two clouds a little separated from one another, and a little dimmed, in the midst of which are two stars, not very large, nor very brilliant, and they move but little: these two stars are the antarctic pole. Our compass needle still pointed a little to its arctic pole; nevertheless it had not as much power as on its own side and region. Yet when we were in the open sea, the captain-general asked of all the pilots, whilst still going under sail, in what direction they were navigating and pointing the charts. They all replied, by the course he had given, punctually [pricked in]; then he answered, that they were pointing falsely (which was so), and that it was fitting to arrange the needle of navigation, because it did not receive so much force as in its own quarter. When we were in the middle of this open sea we saw a cross of five stars, very bright, straight, in the west, and they are straight with one another.

* * * * * *

The Monday of Passion week, the 25th of March, and feast of our Lady, in the afternoon, and being ready to depart from this place [Zamal], I went to the side of our ship to fish, and putting my feet on a spar to go down to the store room, my feet slipped, because it had rained, and I fell into the sea without any one seeing me, and being near drowning by luck I found at my left hand the sheet of the large sail which was in the sea, I caught hold of it and began to cry out till they came to help and pick me up with the boat. I was assisted not by my merits, but by the mercy and grace of the fountain of pity. That same day we took the course between west and southwest, and passed amidst four small islands, that is to say, Cenalo, Huinanghar, Ibusson, and Abarien.

Thursday, the 28th of March, having seen the night before fire upon an island, at the morning we came to anchor at this island; where we saw a small boat which they call Boloto, with eight men inside, which approached the ship of the captain-general. Then a slave of the captain's, who was from Sumatra, otherwise named Traprobana, spoke from afar to these people, who understood his talk, and came near to the side of the ship, but they withdrew immediately, and would not enter the ship from fear of us. So the captain seeing that they would not trust to us showed them a red cap, and other things, which he had tied and placed on a little plank, and the people in the boat took them immediately and joyously, and then returned to advise their king. Two hours afterwards, or thereabouts, we saw come two long boats, which they call balangai, full of men. In the largest of them was their king sitting under an awning of mats; when they were near the ship of the captain-general, the said slave spoke to the king, who understood him well, because in these countries the kings know more languages than the common people. Then the king ordered some of his people to go to the captain's ship, whilst he would not move from his boat, which was near enough to us. This was done, and when his people returned to the boat, he went away at once. The captain gave good entertainment to the men who came to his ship, and gave them all sorts of things, on which account the king wished to give the captain a rather large bar of solid gold, and a chest full of ginger. However, the captain thanked him very much but would not accept the present. After that, when it was late, we went with the ships near to the houses and abode of the king.

The next day, which was Good Friday, the captain sent on shore the before-mentioned slave, who was our interpreter, to the king to beg him to give him for money some provisions for his ships, sending him word that he had not come to his country as an enemy, but as a friend. The king on hearing this came with seven or eight men in a boat, and entered the ship, and embraced the captain, and gave him three china dishes covered with leaves full of rice, and two *dorades*, which are rather large fish, and of the sort above-mentioned, and he gave him several other things. The captain gave this king a robe of red and yellow cloth, made in the Turkish fashion, and a very fine red cap, and to his people he gave to some of them knives, and to others mirrors. After that refreshments were served up to them. The captain told the king, through the said interpreter, that he wished to be with him, *cassi cassi*, that is to say, brothers. To which the king answered that he desired to be the same towards him. After that the captain showed him cloths of different colours, linen, coral, and much other merchandise, and all the artillery, of which he had some pieces fired before him, at which the king was much astonished; after that the captain had one of his soldiers armed with white armour, and placed him in the midst of three comrades, who struck him with swords and daggers. The king thought this very strange, and the captain told him, through the interpreter, that a man thus in white armour was worth a hundred of his men; he answered that it was true; he was further informed that there were in each ship two hundred like that man. After that the captain showed him a great number of swords, cuirasses, and helmets, and made two of the men play with their swords before the king; he then showed him the sea chart and the ship compass, and informed him how he had found the strait to come there, and of the time which he had spent in coming; also of the time he had been without seeing any land, at which the king was astonished. At the end the captain asked if he would be pleased that two of his people should go with him to the places where they lived, to see some of the things of his country. This the king granted, and I went with another.

When I had landed, the king raised his hands to the sky, and turned to us two, and we did the same as he did; after that he took me by the hand, and one of his principal people took my companion, and led us under a place covered with canes, where there was a balangai, that is to say, a boat, eighty feet long or thereabouts, resembling a fusta. We sat with the king upon its poop, always conversing with him by signs, and his people stood up around us, with their swords, spears, and bucklers. Then the king ordered to be brought a dish of pig's flesh and wine. Their fashion of drinking is in this wise, they first raise their hands to heaven, then take the drinking vessel in their right hand, and extend the left hand closed towards the people. This the king did, and presented to me his fist, so that I thought that he wanted to strike me; I did the same thing towards him; so with this ceremony, and other signs of friendship, we banqueted, and afterwards supped with him.

* * * * * *

Sunday, the 7th of April, about midday, we entered the port of Zzubu, having passed by many villages. There we saw many houses which were built on trees. On approaching the principal town the captain-general commanded all his ships to hang out their flags. Then we lowered the sails in the fashion in which they are struck when going to fight, and he had all the artillery fired, at which the people of this place were greatly frightened. The captain sent a young man whom he had brought up, with the interpreter to the king of this island Zzubu. These having come to the town, found a great number of people and their king with them, all alarmed by the artillery which had been fired. But the interpreter reassured them, saying that it was the fashion and custom to fire artillery when they arrived at ports, to show signs of peace and friendship; and also, to do more honour to the king of the country, they had fired all the artillery. The king and all his people were reassured. He then bade one of his principal men ask what we were seeking. The interpreter answered him that his master was captain of the greatest king in the world, and that he was going by the command of the said sovereign to discover the Molucca islands. However, on account of what he had heard where he had passed, and especially from the King of Mazzava, of his courtesy and good fame, he had wished to pass by his country to visit him, and also to obtain some refreshment of victuals for his merchandise. The king answered him that he was welcome, but that the custom was that all ships which arrived at his country or port paid tribute, and it was only four days since that a ship called the Junk of Ciama, laden with gold and slaves, had paid him his tribute, and, to verify what he said, he showed them a merchant of the said Ciama, who had remained there to trade with the gold and slaves. The interpreter said to him that this captain, on account of being captain of so great a king as his was, would not pay tribute to any sovereign in the world; and that if he wished for peace he would have peace, and if he wished for war he would have war. Then the merchant above-mentioned replied to the king in his own language, "Look well, oh king, what you will do, for these people are of those who have conquered Calicut, Malacca, and all greater India; if you entertain them well and treat them well you will find yourself the better for it, and if ill, it will be so much the worse for you as they have done at Calicut and Malacca." The interpreter, who understood all this discourse, said to them that the king, his master, was a good deal more powerful in ships and by land than the King of Portugal, and declared to him that he was the King of Spain and Emperor of all Christendom, wherefore, if he would not be his friend and treat his subjects well, he would another time send against him so many men as to destroy him. Then the king answered that he would speak to his council, and give an answer the next day. Afterwards the king ordered a collation to be brought of several viands, all of meat, in porcelain dishes, with a great many vessels of wine. When the repast was over, our people returned, and related all to the captain; and the King of Mazzabua, who was on board the captain's ship, and who was the first king after him of Zzubu, and the lord of several isles, wished to go on shore to relate to the king the politeness and courtesy of our captain.

Monday morning our clerk went with the interpreter to the town of Zzubu, and the king, accompanied by the principal men of his kingdom, came to the open space, where we made our people sit down near him, and he asked whether there was more than one captain in all those ships, and whether he wished that the king should pay tribute to the emperor, his master, to which our people answered, no, but that the captain only wished to trade with the things which he had brought with the people of his country, and not with others. Then the king said that he was content, and as a greater sign of affection he sent him a little of his blood from his right arm, and wished he should do the like. Our people answered that he would do it. Besides that, he said that all the captains who came to his country had been accustomed to make a present to him, and he to them, and therefore they should ask their captain if he would observe the custom. Our people answered that he would; but as the king wished to keep up the custom, let him begin and make a present, and then the captain would do his duty.

Tuesday morning following the King of Mazzava, with the Moor, came to the ship, and saluted the captain on behalf of the King of Zzubu, and said that the king was preparing a quantity of provisions, as much as he could, to make a present of to him, and that after dinner he would send two of his nephews, with others of his principal people, to make peace with him. Then the captain had one of his men armed with his own armour, and told him that all of us would fight armed in that manner, at which the Moorish merchant was rather astonished; but the captain told him not to be afraid, and that our arms were soft to our friends and rough to our enemies; and that as a cloth wipes away the sweat from a man, so our arms destroy the enemies of our faith. The captain said this to the Moor, because he was more intelligent than the others, and for him to relate it all to the King of Zzubu.

After dinner, the nephew of this king, who was a prince, with the King of Mazzava, the Moor, the governor, and the chief of police, and eight of the principal men, came to the ship to make peace with us. The captain-general was sitting in a chair of red velvet, and near him were the principal men of the ships sitting in leather chairs, and the others on the ground on mats. Then the captain bade the interpreter ask the above-mentioned persons if it was their custom to speak in secret or in public, and whether the prince who was come with them had power to conclude peace. They answered yes, that they would speak in public, and that they had the power to conclude peace. The captain spoke at length on the subject of peace, and prayed God to confirm it in heaven. These people replied that they had never heard such words as these which the captain had spoken to them, and they took great pleasure in hearing them. The captain, seeing then that those people listened willingly to what was said to them, and that they gave good answers, began to say a great many more good things to induce them to become Christians. After many other subjects, the captain asked them who would succeed the king in their country after his death. They answered that the king had no son, but several daughters, and that this prince was his nephew, and had for a wife the king's eldest daughter, and for the sake of that they called him prince. They also said that when the father and mother were old they took no further account of them, but their children commanded them. Upon which the captain told them how God had made heaven and earth and all other things in the world, and that He had commanded that everyone should render honour and obedience to his father and mother, and that whoever did otherwise was condemned to eternal fire. He then pointed out to them many other things concerning our faith. The people heard these things willingly, and besought the captain to leave them two men to teach and show them the Christian faith, and they would entertain them well with great honour. To this the captain answered that for the moment he could not leave them any of his people, but that if they wished to be Christians that his priest would baptise them, and that another time he would bring priests and preachers to teach them the faith. They then answered that they wished first to speak to their king, and then would become Christians. Each of us wept for the joy which we felt at the goodwill of these people, and the captain told them not to become Christians from fear of us, or to please us, but that if they wished to become Christian they must do it willingly, and for the love of God, for even though they should not become Christian, no displeasure would be done them, but those who became Christian would be more loved and better treated than the others. Then they all cried out with one voice, that they did not wish to become Christians from fear, nor from complaisance, but of their free will. The captain then said that if they became Christians he would leave them the arms which the Christians use, and that his king had commanded him so to do. At last they said they did not know what more to answer to so many good and beautiful words which he spoke to them, but that they placed themselves in his hands, and that he should do with them as with his own servants. Then the captain, with tears in his eyes, embraced them, and, taking the hand of the prince and that of the king, said to him that by the faith he had in God, and to his master the emperor, and by the habit of St. James which he wore, he promised them to cause them to have perpetual peace with the King of Spain, at which the prince and the others promised him the same. After peace had been concluded, the captain had refreshments served to them. The prince and the King of Mazzava, who was with him, presented to the captain on behalf of his king large baskets full of rice, pigs, goats, and fowls, and desired the captain to be told he should pardon them that their present was not as fine as was fitting for him. The captain gave to the prince some very fine cloth and a red cap, and a quantity of glass and a cup of gilt glass. Glasses are much prized in this country. To the other people belonging to the Prince he gave various things. Then he sent by me and another person to the King of Zzubu a robe of yellow and violet silk in the fashion of a Turkish jubbeh, a red cap, very fine, and certain pieces of glass, and had all of them put in a silver dish, and two gilt glasses.

When we came to the town we found the King of Zzubu at his palace, sitting on the ground on a mat made of palm, with many people about him. He was quite naked, except that he had a cloth round his middle, and a loose wrapper round his head, worked with silk by the needle. He had a very heavy chain round his neck, and two gold rings hung in his ears with precious stones. He was a small and fat man, and his face was painted with fire in different ways. He was eating on the ground on another palm mat, and was then eating tortoise eggs in two china dishes, and he had four vessels full of palm wine, which he drank with a cane pipe. We made our obeisance, and presented to him what the captain had sent him, and told him through the interpreter that it was not as a return for his present which he had sent to the captain, but for the affection which he bore him. That done, his people told him all the good words and explanations of peace and religion which he had spoken to them. The king wished to detain us to supper, but we made our excuses and took leave of him. The prince, nephew of the king, conducted us to his house, and showed us four girls who played on four instruments, which were strange and very soft, and their manner of playing is rather musical. Afterwards he made us dance with them. These girls were naked except from the waist to the knees, where they wore a wrap made of the palm tree cloth, which covered their middles, and some were quite naked. There we made a repast, and then returned to the ships.

Wednesday morning, because the night before one of our men had died, the interpreter and I, by order of the captain, went to ask the king for a place where we might bury the deceased. We found the king accompanied by a good many people, and, after paying him due honour, we told him of the death of our man, and that the captain prayed him that he might be put into the ground. He replied that if he and his people were ready to obey our master, still more reason was there for his land and country being subject to him. After that we said we wished to consecrate the grave in our fashion and place a cross on it. The sovereign said that he was content, and that he would worship that cross as we did. The deceased was buried in the middle of the open space of the town, as decently as possible, and performing the above-mentioned ceremonies to set them a good example, and in the evening we buried another. This done, we brought a good quantity of merchandise into the town of this king, and placed it in a house, and he took it under his charge and promised that no one would do harm or injury to the king. Four of our men were chosen to despatch and sell this merchandise. These people live with justice, and good weight and measure, loving peace, and are people who love ease and pleasure. They have wooden scales, after the fashion of those of north of the Loire, for weighing their merchandise. Their houses are made of wood and beams and canes, founded on piles, and are very high, and must be entered by means of ladders; their rooms are like ours, and underneath they keep their cattle, such as pigs, goats, and fowls. The young people sound bagpipes, made like ours, and call them Subin.

In this island of the king's there is a kind of animal carrying a shell called carniolle, fine to look at, which causes the whale to die. For the whale swallows them alive; then, when they are inside its body, they come out of their shell and go and eat the whale's heart: and the people of this country find this animal alive inside the whale. These animals, the carniolles, have the teeth and skin black, and their shell is white. Their flesh is good to eat, and they call them Laghan.

The following Friday we showed them a shop full of our merchandise, which was of various strange sorts, at which they were surprised. For metal, iron, and other big goods they gave us gold, and for the other small and sundry goods they gave us rice, pigs, goats, and other provisions. They gave us ten weights of gold for fourteen pounds of iron; each weight is a ducat and a half. The captain-general would not allow a large quantity of gold to be taken, so that the sailors should not sell what belonged to them too cheap from thirst for gold, and lest by that means he might be constrained to do likewise with his merchandise, for he wished to sell it better.

Saturday following a scaffolding was made in the open space, fitted with tapestry and palm branches, because the king had promised our captain to become Christian on Sunday. He told him not to be afraid when our artillery fired on that day, for it was the custom to load it on those feasts without firing stones or other balls.

Sunday morning, the fourteenth day of April, we went on shore, forty men, of whom two were armed, who marched before us, following the standard of our king emperor. When we landed the ships discharged all their artillery, and from fear of it the people ran away in all directions. The captain and the king embraced one another, and then joyously we went near the scaffolding, where the captain and the king sat on two chairs, one covered with red, the other with violet velvet. The principal men sat on cushions, and the others on mats, after the fashion of the country. Then the captain began to speak to the king through the interpreter to incite him to the faith of Jesus Christ, and told him that if he wished to be a good Christian, as he had said the day before, that he must burn all the idols of his country, and, instead of them, place a cross, and that everyone should worship it every day on their knees, and their hands joined to heaven: and he showed him how he ought every day to make the sign of the cross. To that the king and all his people answered that they would obey the commands of the captain and do all that he told them. The captain took the king by the hand, and they walked about on the scaffolding, and when he was baptised he said that he would name him Don Charles, as the emperor his sovereign was named; and he named the prince Don Fernand, after the brother of the emperor, and the King of Mazzava Jehan: to the Moor he gave the name of Christopher, and to the others each a name of his fancy. Thus, before mass, there were fifty men baptised. After mass had been heard the captain invited the king and his other principal men to dine with him, but he would not. He accompanied the captain, however, to the beach, and on his arrival there the ships fired all their artillery. Then, embracing one another, they took leave.

After dinner our chaplain and some of us went on shore to baptise the queen. She came with forty ladies, and we conducted them on to the scaffolding; then made her sit down on a cushion, and her women around her, until the priest was ready. During that time they showed her an image of our Lady, of wood, holding her little child, which was very well made, and a cross. When she saw it, she had a greater desire to be a Christian, and, asking for baptism, she was baptised and named Jehanne, like the mother of the emperor. The wife of the prince, daughter of this queen, had the name of Catherine, the Queen of Mazzava Isabella, and the others each their name. That day we baptised eight hundred persons of men, women, and children. The queen was young and handsome, covered with a black and white sheet; she had the mouth and nails very red, and wore on her head a large hat made of leaves of palm, with a crown over it made of the same leaves, like that of the Pope. After that she begged us to give her the little wooden boy to put in the place of the idols. This we did, and she went away. In the evening the king and queen, with several of their people, came to the sea beach, where the captain had some of the large artillery fired, in which they took great pleasure. The captain and the king called one another brother.

At last, in eight days, all the inhabitants of this island were baptised, and some belonging to the neighbouring islands. In one of these we burned a village because the inhabitants would not obey either the king or us. There we planted a cross because the people were Gentiles: if they had been Moors, we should have erected a column, as a sign of their hardness of heart, because the Moors are more difficult to convert than the Gentiles. The captain-general went ashore every day to hear mass, to which there came many of the new Christians, to whom he explained various points of our religion. One day the queen came with all her state. She was preceded by three damsels, who carried in their hands three of her hats: she was dressed in black and white, with a large silk veil with gold stripes, which covered her head and shoulders. Very many women followed her, with their heads covered with a small veil, and a hat above that: the rest of their bodies and feet were naked, except a small wrapper of palm cloth which covered their natural parts. Their hair fell flowing over their shoulders. The queen, after making a bow to the altar, sat upon a cushion of embroidered silk, and the captain sprinkled over her and over some of her ladies rose water and musk, a perfume which pleases the ladies of this country very much. The captain on that occasion approved of the gift which I had made to the queen of the image of the Infant Jesus, and recommended her to put it in the place of her idols, because it was a remembrancer of the Son of God. She promised to do all this, and to keep it with much care.

In order that the king might be more respected and obeyed, the captain-general got him to come one day at the hour of mass with his silk robe, and summoned his two brothers, one named Bondara, who was the father of the prince, and the other named Cadaro, and some of his chief men, whose names were Simiut, Sibuaia, Sisacai, Magalibe, and others whom it is unnecessary to name separately; and he made them all swear to be obedient to their king, whose hand they all of them kissed. He then asked the king to swear that he would always be obedient and faithful to the King of Spain, and he took the oath. Then the captain drew a sword before the image of the Virgin Mary, and said to the king that when such an oath had been taken by anyone, he should rather die than be wanting to his oath. After that he himself promised to be always faithful to him, swearing by the image of our Lady, by the life of the emperor his sovereign, and by the habit which he wore. He then made a present to the king of a velvet chair, and told him that wherever he went he should always have it carried before him by some of his attendants, and showed him the way in which it should be carried. The king told the captain that he would do all this on account of the affection which he bore him, of which he wished to give him a token, preparing for that purpose some jewels to present to him; these were two rather large gold rings for the ears, two others for the arms, and two for the ancles, all of them adorned with precious stones. The finest ornaments of the kings of these countries consist in these rings, for otherwise they go naked and barefooted, with only a piece of cloth from the waist to the knees.

The captain-general, who had informed the king and all those who had been baptised of the obligation they were under of burning their idols, which they had promised to do, seeing that they retained them and made them offerings of meat, reproved them severely for it. They thought to excuse themselves sufficiently by saying that they did not do that now on their own account, but for a sick person, for the idols to restore him his health. This sick man was a brother of the prince, and was reputed to be the most valiant and wise man in the island, and his illness was so severe that for four days he had not spoken. Having heard this, the captain, seized with zeal for religion, said that if they had a true faith in Jesus Christ, they should burn all the idols, and the sick man should be baptised, and he would be immediately cured, of which he was so certain that he consented to lose his head if the miracle did not take place. The king promised that all this should be done, because he truly believed in Jesus Christ. Then we arranged, with all the pomp that was possible, a procession from the place to the house of the sick man. We went there, and indeed found him unable to speak or to move. We baptised him, with two of his wives and ten girls. The captain then asked him how he felt, and he at once spoke, and said that by the grace of our Lord he was well enough. This great miracle was done under our eyes. The captain, on hearing him speak, gave great thanks to God.

* * * * * *

When our people went on shore by day or by night, they always met with some one who invited them to eat and drink. They only half cook their victuals, and salt them very much, which makes them drink a great deal; and they drink much with reeds, sucking the wine from the vessels. Their repasts always last from five to six hours.

When one of their chiefs dies they always use the following funeral ceremonies, of which I was witness. The most respected women of the country came to the house of the deceased, in the midst of which lay the corpse in a chest; round which were stretched cords after the manner of an enclosure, and many branches of trees were tied to these cords: a strip of cotton was fastened to each of these branches like a pennant. Under these the women I have mentioned sat down covered with white cotton cloth. Each of them had a damsel who fanned her with a palm fan. The other women sat sadly round the room. Meanwhile a woman cut off by degrees the hair of the dead man with a knife: another who had been his principal wife, lay extended on him, with her mouth, hands and feet on the mouth, hands and feet of the dead man. When the first woman cut off the hair, she wept, and when she stopped cutting, she sang. Round the room there were many vases of porcelain, with embers in them, on which, from time to time, they threw myrrh, storax, and benzoin, which gave out a good and strong smell in the room. These ceremonies last for five or six days, during which the corpse is kept in the house, and I believe that they anoint it with oil of camphor to preserve it. They afterwards put it in a chest, closed with wooden bolts, and place it in an enclosed place covered with logs of wood.

The islanders told us that every evening towards midnight, there used to come to the city, a black bird of the size of a crow, which perching on the houses whistled, and caused all the dogs to howl, and these double cries lasted four or five hours. They would never tell us the cause of that phenomenon, of which we also were witnesses.

Friday, the 26th of April, Zula, who was one cf the principal men or chiefs of the island of Matan, sent to the captain a son of his with two goats to make a present of them, and to say that if he did not do all that he had promised, the cause of that was another chief named Cilapulapu, who would not in any way obey the King of Spain, and had prevented him from doing so: but that if the captain would send him the following night one boat full of men to give him assistance, he would fight and subdue his rival. On the receipt of this message, the captain decided to go himself with three boats. We entreated him much not to go to this enterprise in person, but he as a good shepherd would not abandon his flock.

We set out from Zzubu at midnight, we were sixty men armed with corslets and helmets; there were with us the Christian king, the prince, and some of the chief men, and many others divided among twenty or thirty balangai. We arrived at Matan three hours before daylight. The captain before attacking wished to attempt gentle means, and sent on shore the Moorish merchant to tell those islanders who were of the party of Cilapulapu, that if they would recognize the Christian king as their sovereign, and obey the King of Spain, and pay us the tribute which had been asked, the captain would become their friend, otherwise we should prove how our lances wounded. The islanders were not terrified, they replied that if we had lances, so also had they, although only of reeds, and wood hardened with fire. They asked however that we should not attack them by night, but wait for daylight, because they were expecting reinforcements, and would be in greater number. This they said with cunning, to excite us to attack them by night, supposing that we were ready; but they wished this because they had dug ditches between their houses and the beach, and they hoped that we should fall into them.

We however waited for daylight; we then leaped into the water up to our thighs, for on account of the shallow water and the rocks the boats could not come close to the beach, and we had to cross two good crossbow shots through the water before reaching it. We were forty-nine in number, the other eleven remained in charge of the boats. When we reached land we found the islanders fifteen hundred in number, drawn up in three squadrons; they came down upon us with terrible shouts, two squadrons attacking us on the flank, and the third in front. The captain then divided his men in two bands. Our musketeers and crossbow-men fired for half an hour from a distance, but did nothing, since the bullets and arrows, though they passed through their shields made of thin wood, and perhaps wounded their arms, yet did not stop them. The captain shouted not to fire, but he was not listened to. The islanders seeing that the shots of our guns did them little or no harm would not retire, but shouted more loudly, and springing from one side to the other to avoid our shots, they at the same time drew nearer to us, throwing arrows, javelins, spears hardened in fire, stones, and even mud, so that we could hardly defend ourselves. Some of them cast lances pointed with iron at the captain-general.

He then, in order to disperse this multitude and to terrify them, sent some of our men to set fire to their houses, but this rendered them more ferocious. Some of them ran to the fire, which consumed twenty or thirty houses, and there killed two of our men. The rest came down upon us with greater fury; they perceived that our bodies were defended, but that the legs were exposed, and they aimed at them principally. The captain had his right leg pierced by a poisoned arrow, on which account he gave orders to retreat by degrees; but almost all our men took to precipitate flight, so that there remained hardly six or eight of us with him. We were oppressed by the lances and stones which the enemy hurled at us, and we could make no more resistance. The bombards which we had in the boats were of no assistance to us, for the shoal water kept them too far from the beach. We went thither, retreating little by little, and still fighting, and we had already got to the distance of a crossbow shot from the shore, having the water up to our knees, the islanders following and picking up again the spears which they had already cast, and they threw the same spear five or six times; as they knew the captain they aimed specially at him, and twice they knocked the helmet off his head. He, with a few of us, like a good knight, remained at his spot without choosing to retreat further. Thus we fought for more than an hour, until an Indian succeeded in thrusting a cane lance into the captain's face. He then, being irritated, pierced the Indian's breast with his lance, and left it in his body, and trying to draw his sword he was unable to draw it more than half way, on account of a javelin wound which he had received in the right arm. The enemies seeing this all rushed against him, and one of them with a great sword, like a great scimitar gave him a great blow on the left leg, which brought the captain down on his face, then the Indians threw themselves upon him, and ran him through with lances and scimitars, and all the other arms which they had, so that they deprived of life our mirror, light, comfort, and true guide. Whilst the Indians were thus overpowering him, several times he turned round towards us to see if we were all in safety, as though his obstinate fight had no other object than to give an opportunity for the retreat of his men. We who fought to extremity, and who were covered with wounds, seeing that he was dead, proceeded to the boats which were on the point of going away. This fatal battle was fought on the 27th of April of 1521, on a Saturday; a day which the captain had chosen himself, because he had a special devotion to it. There perished with him eight of our men, and four of the Indians, who had become Christians; we had also many wounded, amongst whom I must reckon myself. The enemy lost only fifteen men.

He died; but I hope that your illustrious Highness will not allow his memory to be lost, so much the more since I see revived in you the virtue of so great a captain, since one of his principal virtues was constance in the most adverse fortune. In the midst of the sea he was able to endure hunger better than we. Most versed in nautical charts, he knew better than any other the true art of navigation, of which it is certain proof that he knew by his genius, and his intrepidity, without any one having given him the example, how to attempt the circuit of the globe, which he had almost completed.

CHAPTER IV

Hernando Cortes—1485–1547

Hernando Cortes was born in Spain. He made his first voyage to the New World in 1504 in company with Velasquez, the conqueror of Cuba, and was well versed in the cruel Spanish method of conquest.

In charge of an expedition for the exploration and acquisition of Mexico, on February 10th, 1519, he set sail from Cuba with seven hundred men and eleven ships. For sheer audacity and ingenuity, there has never been anyone to equal Cortes and the methods he employed to conquer the rich and magnificent Aztec civilization. By a ruse, Cortes succeeded in getting the great Montezuma (Muteczuma) to place himself in his hands as hostage. How Montezuma was finally slain by his own people, and how the City of Mexico was besieged for nine months and finally surrendered, makes one of the most brilliant and gory tales of conquest in the history of Spain.

The following extract is part of the second of five letters Cortes sent to Charles V, describing the wonders he beheld.

THE CONQUEST OF MEXICO—1520

EXTRACT FROM THE SECOND LETTER TO EMPEROR CHARLES V

30th October, 1520

EIGHT leagues from the city of Cholula are two very lofty and remarkable mountains; in the latter part of August their summits are covered with snow; and from the highest, by night as well as by day, a volume of smoke arises, equal in bulk to a spacious house; it ascends above the mountain to the clouds as straight as an arrow, and with such force, that although a very strong wind is always blowing on the mountain, it does not turn the smoke from its course. As I have desired to render your Highness a very minute account of every thing in this part of the world, I wished to ascertain the cause of this phenomenon, as it appeared to me, and I despatched ten of my companions, such as I thought suitable for this purpose, with several natives of the country for guides, charging them to use every endeavor to ascend the mountain and find out the cause of that smoke, whence and how it was produced. They went, and struggled with all their might to

reach the summit, but were unable on account of the great quantity of
snow that lay on the mountain, and the whirlwinds of ashes that swept
over it, and also because they found the cold above insupportable; but they
reached very near the summit, and while they were there the smoke began
to issue forth with so much force and noise that it seemed as if the whole
Sierra was crumbling to the ground; so they descended, and brought with
them a considerable quantity of snow and icicles, that we might see them,
as it was something quite new in this region on account of its being in so
warm a latitude, according to the opinion of our pilots, who place it in
20°, which is the same parallel as the Island of Española, where the heat is
at all times extreme. While on their way to the mountain, the party discovered a road, and inquired of their Indian companions where it led, who
told them to Culua,[1] and that it was a good road, while the other, which
the Culuans wished us to take, was not a good one. The Spaniards followed this road until they began to ascend the mountain, between which
and the other elevation it passed; and from it they discovered the plains of
Culua, and the great city of Temixtitan, and the lakes in that province,
of which I shall hereafter give your Highness an account; they returned
overjoyed on having discovered so good a road, and God knows how much
joy I felt on the occasion.

Having obtained all the information I could from the Spaniards who
had returned from their visit to the mountain, as well as from the natives concerning the road they had discovered, I addressed myself to the
envoys of Muteczuma, who accompanied me as guides to their country,
and said to them, that I would take the new route instead of that which
they had recommended, as it was shorter. They answered that I was right,
that the new route was shorter and more level, and that the reason
they had not pointed it out to me was, that we should have to pass one
day through the territory of Guasucingo, whose inhabitants were their
enemies, and would not furnish supplies, as was done in the territory of
Muteczuma; but that since I preferred that route, they would cause provisions to be sent in that direction. And thus we set forth, not without
some apprehension that they would persist in their endeavors to entrap us;
but as we had already declared what route it was our intention to take, it
did not seem to me worth while to change our plan, or to return on our
steps, lest they should imagine that our courage failed us. On the day that
I left the city of Cholula, I advanced four leagues to some villages in the
state of Guasucingo, where we were well received by the natives, who
gave me a number of female slaves, some cotton cloth, and several small
pieces of gold, amounting altogether to very little, as the people are not
well supplied with it, on account of their belonging to the league and
party of the Tlascalans, and being so closely hemmed in on all sides by
the territory of Muteczuma, that they could have no trade with any other
province but their own; whence they lived very poorly. The next day I

[1]Mexico.

entered the pass between the two mountains already mentioned, and in descending it we discovered the province of Chalco, in the territory of Muteczuma, two leagues from us, and when we had reached the inhabited parts, we found a newly constructed building for our quarters, and so large that all my men and myself were comfortably lodged in it, although I had with me more than four thousand Indians, natives of the provinces of Tlascaltecal, Guasucingo, Churultecal, and Cempoal, for all of whom there was an abundant supply of provisions; and there were large fires in all the lodging-rooms, with a plenty of wood, as it was very cold on account of the proximity of the two mountains, which were covered with snow.

There came to me at this place several persons, apparently of some rank, among whom was one that I was told was a brother of Muteczuma. They brought me gold to the value of 3000 *pesos*, and said on behalf of that sovereign, that he had sent me this present, and at the same time requested that I would retrace my steps, and not think of visiting his city, as the country was ill supplied with provisions, and the road that led to it was bad; and that the city was all on the water, so that I could not enter it except in canoes, and with many other inconveniences that would obstruct my course. They added, that I might have all that I asked, which Muteczuma, their sovereign, had commanded them to give me; and that they would agree to pay me every year a certain sum *(certum quid)*, which they would carry to the sea, or wherever I wished. I received them kindly, and spoke to them of our Spain, of which they had heard much, addressing myself especially to the one who was said to be a brother of Muteczuma.

In answer to their official communication, I said,—that if it was in my power to return, I would do so to oblige Muteczuma; but that I had come into this country by the command of your Majesty, and that I was particularly charged to render an account of Muteczuma and his great city, of the fame of which your Highness had long since heard—that they might assure him from me, that I was extremely desirous he should take my visit to him in good part, since it would be productive of no injury, but rather of advantage to his person and country; that after I had seen him, if it was still his wish not to have my company, I would then return; and that we should be better able to agree in person, as to the homage he should render to your Highness, than through the agency of others, however trustworthy they might be. With this answer they returned. Judging from the appearance of our quarters, and the arrangements made respecting them, it struck me that the Indians intended to attack us that night; but on perceiving this, I took such precautions as, coming to their knowledge, changed their determination; and they drew off that night very secretly a large force, which they had placed in the mountains adjacent to our camp, as was observed by many of our scouts and sentinels.

As soon as it was day I set out for a town two leagues distant, called Amaqueruca, in the province of Chalco, which contains a population, including the villages within two leagues of it, of more than twenty thousand inhabitants. In this place they quartered us in the excellent houses of the governor. Many persons, apparently of a superior rank, here waited upon me, and announced that Muteczuma, their sovereign lord, had sent them to receive me at this place, with orders to provide every thing necessary to supply our wants. The governor of this province and town presented me with forty slaves and 3000 castellanos, and during the two days that I was there supplied us with an abundance of provisions. The next day—accompanied by the envoys of Muteczuma who received us here—I departed and reached for the night a small place four leagues distant, situated partly upon a great lake, and partly upon a rough, rocky mountain, where we were well lodged. Here likewise they would have tried our strength, but that they desired to do so without danger to themselves, as it seemed, by attacking us in the night, when they expected to take us by surprise. But as I was well informed of their intentions, they found that I had anticipated their designs.

That night I placed a strong guard, who took and killed fifteen or twenty spies that came in canoes on the lake, or descended the mountain to see whether I was prepared to resist an attack. Thus few of them returned to give the information they were sent to obtain; and finding us always upon our guard, they concluded to change their plans, and to suffer us to proceed in safety. The next morning when I was about leaving that place, there arrived ten or twelve of the most distinguished personages, as I afterwards learned, and among them a young man of about twenty-five years of age, to whom all showed particular marks of respect; and after he had alighted from a litter in which he came, the others began to remove stones out of his path, and to clear up the ground before him.

As soon as they arrived they announced that they had come on the part of Muteczuma, their liege lord, who had sent them to accompany me, and begged that I would pardon him for not coming himself to receive me, which he was unable to do on account of indisposition; but that the city was now near at hand, and as I was still determined to visit it, he would receive us there, when I should learn his willingness to do homage to your Highness. But nevertheless, he entreated that if it was possible, I would not go to the city, for I should meet with much trouble and want, and he would be ashamed not to be able to provide for me there in the manner he wished. The envoys also earnestly insisted on the same thing, and were extremely importunate; at the same time assuring me that they would protect us on the route if I persisted in proceeding. I made them a courteous reply, and calmed their anxiety by the mildest language in my power, giving them to understand that my visit would not be attended with injury, but advantage to Muteczuma. And thus they took their leave, after I had made them presents of some things that I had brought with me. I soon followed them, being accompanied by many persons who appeared to be of great consideration, as I afterwards learned was the case.

As I was pursuing the road that led along the shore of the great lake, at the distance of a league from the place of our departure, I discovered upon the surface of the water a small town, that might contain from one to two thousand inhabitants, well fortified and defended with towers, as it appeared on the outside, but without any entrance. A league farther on we came to a causeway of the width of a spear's length, running two thirds of a league into the lake, which led to a city that, although small, was the most beautiful we had yet seen, composed of well-constructed houses and towers, having the foundations laid with great regularity and wholly in the water. In this city, which contains about two thousand inhabitants, we were well received, and entertained with a handsome repast. The chief magistrate and other persons of rank came to see me, and requested that I would pass the night there. But some of Muteczuma's people who were with me advised me not to stop, but to go on to another city, three leagues distant, called Iztapalapa, belonging to a brother of Muteczuma, and I accordingly did so. The road from the city where we had our repast, the name of which does not now occur to me, was by another causeway, which is a full league in length to terra firma. Having arrived at the city of Iztapalapa, the cacique came to receive me at some distance from the town, together with another dignitary of a great city about three leagues off, called Calnaacan, accompanied by many other distinguished personages, who were expecting my arrival there, and presented me with 3 or 4000 castellanos, some slaves, and cotton cloth, giving me altogether a very agreeable reception.

The city of Iztapalapa contains twelve or fifteen thousand houses; it is situated on the shore of a large salt lake, one-half of it being built upon the water, and one-half on terra firma. The governor or chief of the city has several new houses, which, although they are not yet finished, are equal to the better class of houses in Spain—being large and well constructed, in the stone work, the carpentry, the floors, and the various appendages necessary to render a house complete, excepting the reliefs and other rich work usual in Spanish houses. There are also many upper and lower rooms—cool gardens, abounding in trees and odoriferous flowers; also pools of fresh water, well constructed, with stairs leading to the bottom. There is also a very extensive kitchen garden attached to the house, and over it a belvidere with beautiful corridors and halls; and within the garden a large square pond of fresh water, having its walls formed of handsome hewn stone; and adjacent to it there is a promenade, consisting of a tiled pavement so broad that four persons can walk on it abreast, and four hundred paces square, or sixteen hundred paces round; enclosed on one side towards the wall of the garden by canes, intermingled with *vergas*, and on the other side by shrubs and sweet-scented plants. The pond contains a great variety of fish and water-fowl, as wild ducks, teal, and others so numerous that they often cover the surface of the water.

The next day after my arrival at this city I departed on my route, and having proceeded half a league, I entered upon a causeway that extends two leagues through the centre of the salt lake, until it reaches the great city of Temixtitan, which is built in the middle of the lake. This causeway is as broad as two spears' length, and well constructed, so that eight horsemen can ride on it abreast; and within two leagues, on either side of this causeway, there are three cities, one of which, called Mesicalsingo, is built for the most part on the lake, and the two others, called Nyciaca and Huchilohuchico, are situated along its borders, with many houses on the water. The former of these cities contains about three thousand families, the second more than six thousand, and the third four or five thousand; in all of them are well built houses and towers, especially the residences of the governors and principal men, and the mosques or temples, in which they have their idols. In these cities there is a considerable trade in salt, which is manufactured from the water of the lake, and from a deposit on the grounds washed by the lake, which they boil in some way, and make into loaves, selling it to the natives and persons out of the district or province.

I pursued my course over the above-mentioned causeway, and having proceeded half a league before arriving at the body of the city of Temixtitan, I found at its intersection with another causeway, which extends from this point to terra firma, a very strong fortress with two towers, surrounded by a double wall, twelve feet in height, with an embattled parapet, which commands the two causeways, and has only two gates, one for entering, and the other for departure. There came to meet me at this place nearly a thousand of the principal inhabitants of the great city, all uniformly dressed according to their custom in very rich costumes; and as soon as they had come within speaking distance, each one, as he approached me, performed a salutation in much use among them, by placing his hand upon the ground and kissing it; and thus I was kept waiting about an hour, until all had performed the ceremony. Connected with the city is a wooden bridge ten paces wide, where the causeway is open to allow the water free ingress and egress, as it rises and falls; and also for the security of the city, as they can remove the long and wide beams of which the bridge is formed, and replace them whenever they wish; and there are many such bridges in different parts of the city, as your Highness will perceive hereafter from the particular account I shall give of it.

When we had passed the bridge, the Señor Muteczuma came out to receive us, attended by about two hundred nobles, all bare-footed and dressed in livery, or a peculiar garb of fine cotton, richer than is usually worn; they came in two processions in close proximity to the houses on each side of the street, which is very wide and beautiful, and so straight that you can see from one end of it to the other, although it is two thirds of a league in length, having on both sides large and elegant houses and temples. Muteczuma came through the centre of the street, attended by two lords, one upon his right, and the other upon his left hand, one of whom was the same nobleman who, as I have mentioned, came to meet me in a litter; and the other was the brother of Muteczuma, lord of the city of Iztapalapa, which I had left the same day; all three were dressed in the same manner, except that Muteczuma wore shoes, while the others were without them. He was supported on the arms of both, and as we approached, I alighted and advanced alone to salute him; but the two attendant lords stopped me to prevent my touching him, and they and he both performed the ceremony of kissing the ground; after which he directed his brother who accompanied him to remain with me; the latter accordingly took me by the arm, while Muteczuma, with his other attendant, walked a short distance in front of me, and after he had spoken to me, all the other nobles also came up to address me, and then went away in two processions with great regularity, one after the other, and in this manner returned to the city. At the time I advanced to speak to Muteczuma, I took off from myself a collar of pearls and glass diamonds, and put it around his neck.

After having proceeded along the street, one of his servants came bringing two collars formed of shell fish, enclosed in a roll of cloth, which were made from the shells of colored prawns or periwinkles, held by them in high estimation; and from each collar depended eight golden prawns, finished in a very perfect manner, about a foot and a half in length. When these were brought, Muteczuma turned towards me and put them round my neck; he then returned along the street in the order already described, until he reached a very large and splendid palace, in which we were to be quartered, which had been fully prepared for our reception. He there took me by the hand and led me into a spacious saloon, in front of which was a court, through which we entered. Having caused me to sit down on a piece of rich carpeting, which he had ordered to be made for his own use, he told me to wait his return there, and then went away. After a short space of time, when my people were all bestowed in their quarters, he returned with many and various jewels of gold and silver, feather-work, and five or six thousand pieces of cotton cloth, very rich and of varied texture and finish. After having presented these to me, he sat down on another piece of carpet they had placed for him near me, and being seated he discoursed as follows:

"It is now a long time since, by means of written records, we learned from our ancestors that neither myself nor any of those who inhabit this region were descended from its original inhabitants, but from strangers who emigrated hither from a very distant land; and we have also learned that a prince, whose vassals they all were, conducted our people into these parts, and then returned to his native land. He afterwards came again to this country, after the lapse of much time, and found that his people had intermarried with the native inhabitants, by whom they had many children, and had built towns in which they resided; and when he desired them to return with him, they were unwilling to go, nor were they disposed to acknowledge him as their sovereign; so he departed from the country, and we have always heard that his descendants would come to conquer this land, and reduce us to subjection as his vassals; and according to the direction from which you say you have come, namely, the quarter where the sun rises, and from what you say of the great lord or king who sent you hither, we believe and are assured that he is our natural sovereign, especially as you say that it is a long time since you first had knowledge of us.

Therefore be assured that we will obey you, and acknowledge you for our sovereign in place of the great lord whom you mention, and that there shall be no default or deception on our part. And you have the power in all this land, I mean wherever my power extends, to command what is your pleasure, and it shall be done in obedience thereto, and all that we have is at your disposal. And since you are in your own proper land and your own house, rest and refresh yourselves after the toils of your journey, and the conflicts in which you have been engaged, which have been brought upon you, as I well know, by all the people from Putunchán to this place; and I am aware that the Cempoallans and Tlascalans have told you much evil of me, but believe no more than you see with your own eyes, especially from those who are my enemies, some of whom were once my subjects, and having revelled upon your arrival, make these statements to ingratiate themselves in your favor. These people, I know, have informed you that I possessed houses with walls of gold, and that my carpets and other things in common use were of the texture of gold; and that I was a god, or made myself one, and many other such things. The houses you see are of stone and lime and earth." And then he opened his robes and showed his person to me saying, "You see that I am composed of flesh and bone like yourselves, and that I am mortal, and palpable to the touch," at the same time pinching his arm and body with his hands; "see," he continued, "how they have deceived you. It is true I have some things of gold, which my ancestors have left me; all that I have is at your service whenever you wish it. I am now going to my other houses where I reside; you will be here provided with every thing necessary for yourself and your people, and will suffer no embarrassment, as you are in your own house and country."

I answered him in respect to all that he had said, expressing my acknowledgments, and adding whatever the occasion seemed to demand, especially endeavoring to confirm him in the belief that your Majesty was the sovereign they had looked for; and after this he took his leave, and having gone, we were liberally supplied with fowls, bread, fruits, and other things required for the use of our quarters. In this way I was for six days amply provided with all that was necessary, and visited by many of the nobility.

I mentioned, most Catholic Sire, at the commencement of this letter, that at the time I departed from the city of Vera Cruz in quest of this Señor Muteczuma, I left there one hundred and fifty men to erect a fort, which had been already begun; and I also stated that I had left many towns and fortified places in the neighborhood of the city in subjection to the royal dominion of your Highness, and the inhabitants secure and decided in their allegiance to your Majesty. While I was in the city of Churultecal, I received letters from the commander, whom I had stationed in my place at Vera Cruz, informing me that Qualpopoca, lord of the city of Almeria, had sent messengers to announce that he desired to become a subject of your Highness, and if he had not appeared before, and still did not appear, to render that homage which it was his duty to yield, and to offer himself with all his territories as a vassal to your Majesty, the reason was, that he would be compelled to pass through the enemies' country, which he had not done in consequence of his apprehension of an attack from them; but that if I would despatch to him four Spaniards, they might accompany him, and the people through whose lands they would have to pass, knowing for what purpose they came, would not molest them; and thus he would be able to come to us at once.

The captain, believing that Qualpopoca was sincere in what he said, as many others had done the same thing, sent four Spaniards to him; but when he had got them into his power, he ordered them to be put to death, in such a way that it might not appear to have been done through his means; and thus two of them were killed, while the others effected their escape across the mountains, though wounded. Thereupon the captain marched against the city of Almeria with fifty Spaniards, two horsemen, and two pieces of fire-arms, and a force of from eight to ten thousand friendly Indians, with which he fought the inhabitants of that city and killed many of them, driving the rest away, and burning and destroying the city. The Indians who had accompanied him, being enemies to the Almerians, aided in the attack with great spirit and vigor. Qualpopoca himself, together with the other caciques, his allies, who had come to his assistance, escaped by flight, and some prisoners who were taken in the city gave information as to the people engaged in its defence, and the cause of their killing the Spaniards that had been sent to them. They said that Muteczuma had ordered Qualpopoca and the others who had come there as his vassals, (for such they were), that when I left the city of Vera Cruz, they should fall upon those who had rebelled and entered the service of your Highness; and that they should devise every means of destroying the Spaniards I had left there, so that they might not aid or favor us; and that accordingly, in consequence of these orders, they had done so.

Six days having passed, most powerful Prince, since I entered the great city of Temixtitan, and having seen some things in it, though but a few compared with what there was to be seen and noted, it seemed to me, judging from these things, and from what I had observed of the country, that it would subserve the interests of your Majesty and our own security if Mutezuma was in my power, and not wholly free from restraint; in order that he might not be diverted from the resolution and willing spirit which he showed in the service of your Majesty, especially as we Spaniards were somewhat troublesome and difficult to please; lest feeling annoyed on any occasion, he should do us some serious injury, and even might cause all memory of us to perish, in the exercise of his great power. It also appeared to me that if he was under my control, all the other countries that were subject to him would be more easily brought to the knowledge and service of your Majesty, as afterwards actually happened.

I resolved, therefore, to take him and place him in my quarters, which were of great strength; and revolving in my mind how this could be effected without occasioning any tumult or disturbance, I recollected what the officer whom I had left in command at Vera Cruz, had written me concerning the occurrences in the city of Almeria, which I have already related, and which, as he was informed, had all taken place in pursuance of orders from Muteczuma.

Having used the precaution to station guards at the corners of the streets, I went to the palace of Muteczuma, as I had before often done to visit him; and after conversing with him in a sportive manner on agreeable topics, and receiving at his hands some jewels of gold, and one of his own daughters, together with several daughters of his nobles for some of my company, I then said to him, "that I had been informed of what had taken place in the city of Nautecal or Almeria, and of the fate of the Spaniards, who had been killed there; that Qualpopoca alleged in defence of his conduct, that whatever he had done was in pursuance of orders from him, which, as his vassal, he could not disregard; that I did not believe it was so, but nevertheless, in order to clear himself from the imputation, it seemed to me proper that he should send for Qualpopoca and the other principal men of that city, who had been concerned in the slaughter of the Spaniards, that the truth of the matter might be known, and those men punished, by which means he would satisfy your Majesty of his loyal disposition beyond all dispute; lest instead of the rewards which your Majesty would order to be given him, the reports of these outrages might provoke your Majesty's anger against him, on account of his having commanded the injury to be done; since I was well satisfied that the truth was contrary to what those men had declared."

Immediately Muteczuma ordered certain of his followers to be called, to whom he gave a small stone resembling a seal, which he wore upon his arm, and ordered them to go to the city of Almeria, which is sixty or seventy leagues from Mextitán, and conduct Qualpopoca hither; and having ascertained what others were concerned in the murder of the Spaniards, to have them come likewise; that if they refused to come voluntarily, they should be brought as prisoners; and if they resisted, they should call upon the communities adjacent to that city, which he indicated to them, for an armed force to assist in taking the offenders; and that they should by no means return without them.

These persons departed at once, and when they had gone, I said to Muteczuma, that I was pleased with his diligence in this matter, since I should have to render an account to your Majesty of the Spaniards who had been killed. As for what remained of my duty in the premises, I must have him in my quarters until the truth was more clearly ascertained, and himself shown to be free from blame; and I begged him to suffer no uneasiness on this account, as he would not be treated as a prisoner, but left in the full possession of his liberty; that no obstacle should be interposed to his enjoying the service of his followers, who would continue to be at his command; that he might select an apartment, such as would please him, in the palace I occupied, where he would be at his ease; that he might rest assured that nothing should be allowed to give him pain or inconvenience; and that in addition to his own servants, my companions would cheerfully obey all his commands. Much conversation and discourse followed in regard to this arrangement, too long to be described at length, and even to be repeated to your Majesty, being not only prolix, but scarcely material to the case; and, therefore, I shall say no more than that, finally, he expressed his willingness to go with me.

He immediately gave orders to have the apartment he wished to occupy put in order for his use, which was well situated and handsomely fitted up; and this being done, many nobles came to him, stripped of their robes, which they carried hanging upon their arms, and bare-footed, bringing a litter, not in the best order, on which, with tears in their eyes, they placed him in deep silence; and in this manner we proceeded to the quarters which I occupied, without exciting any commotion in the city, although some signs of a disturbance began to appear. But as soon as Muteczuma heard of it, he sent orders forbidding any movement; and thus all remained quiet as before, and continued so during the whole time that Muteczuma was my prisoner, since he was entirely at his ease, with the same attendance that he had been accustomed to in his own palace, which was very large and splendid, as I shall hereafter relate; and I and my companions did every thing in our power to gratify his wishes.

Fifteen or twenty days after his imprisonment, the messengers arrived that Muteczuma had sent in quest of Qualpopoca and the others concerned in the murder of the Spaniards; and they brought with them that chief and his sons, together with fifteen persons who were said to be men of rank, and implicated in the affair. Qualpopoca was brought on a litter, much in the style of a governor, as in fact he was. They were delivered into my hands, and I caused them to be placed under a strong guard; and when they acknowledged that they had killed the Spaniards, I directed them to be asked if they were the vassals of Muteczuma? Qualpopoca replied—"If I have any other sovereign, who is it?" as much as to say that he had no other, and that they were his vassals. I also inquired if what had been done by them was by his command? They answered, no; although afterwards, when the sentence of death by burning was about to be executed upon them, they all with one voice declared that Muteczuma had sent to command it to be done, and that they had acted in pursuance of his orders.

So they were publicly burned in a square of the city, without creating any disturbance; and on the day of their execution, as they confessed that Muteczuma had directed them to kill the Spaniards, I caused him to be put in irons, which threw him into great consternation. On the same day, however, after having spoken to him, I caused his irons to be removed, and left him quite satisfied; and from that time I exerted myself to gratify his wishes, and render him contented by all means in my power. I publicly announced and declared to all the natives of the country, as well to the governors as to the people who came to me, that your Majesty's service would be promoted by Muteczuma's remaining at the head of his government, only acknowledging your Majesty's superiority, and that your

Majesty would be pleased by their obeying and respecting Muteczuma as their sovereign, as they had done before my arrival in the country.

Such was the kindness of my treatment towards him, and his own contentment with his situation, that when at different times I tempted him with the offer of his liberty, begging that he would return to his palace, he as often replied that he was well pleased with his present quarters, and did not wish to leave them, as he wanted nothing that he was accustomed to enjoy in his own palace; and that in case he went away, there would be reason to fear the importunities of the local governors, his vassals, might lead him to act against his own wishes, and in opposition to your Majesty, while he desired in every possible manner to promote your Majesty's service; that so far he had informed them what he desired to have done, and was well content to remain where he was; and should they wish to suggest anything to him, he could answer that he was not at liberty, and thus excuse himself from attending to them. Several times he asked permission to visit his pleasure-houses for the purpose of recreation, both within the city and without, and in no instance was his request denied. He often made an excursion, attended by five or six Spaniards, one or two leagues out of the city, and always returned in fine spirits to his quarters where I had placed him; and whenever he went out, he made many presents of jewels and cotton cloth, both to the Spaniards by whom he was accompanied, and to his own people, who followed him in such numbers that there were never less than three thousand men in his retinue, most of whom were nobles and persons of distinction; and he also gave many banquets and entertainments to those who accompanied him, which they considered worth relating.

When I discovered that Muteczuma was fully devoted to the service of your Highness, I requested him that, in order to enable me to render a complete account to your Majesty of the productions of the country, he would point out to me the mines from which gold was obtained; to which he consented with the greatest readiness, saying that it would give him pleasure to do so. He immediately sent for several of his public servants, and assigned them to four provinces, two to each province, in which he said the gold was obtained; and he asked me to allow some of the Spaniards to go with him, that they might observe the manner in which gold was procured; and I accordingly deputed two Spaniards for the same number of his own men.

One party of them went to a province called Cuzula, eighty leagues from the great city of Temixtitan, whose inhabitants are vassals of Muteczuma, where they were shown three rivers, from all of which they brought me specimens of gold, of a good quality, although procured with little trouble, and without any other instruments than those used by the Indians. On their route they passed through three provinces, that, according to the report of the Spaniards, contained very fine land, many villages and cities, with much scattered population, and buildings equal to any in Spain. They mentioned particularly a house and castle, the latter larger, of greater strength, and better built than the castle of Burgos; and the people of one of these provinces, called Tamazulapa, were better clothed than those of any other we had seen, as it justly appeared to them. Another party of our envoys went to a province called Malinaltebeque, [in Oaxaca], which is also seventy leagues from the great city, but more towards the seacoast. They brought me specimens of gold from a great river that passes through it.

The other party visited a region beyond this river, inhabited by a people speaking a different language from those of Culua, and called Tenis; whose chief ruler is named Coatelicamar. His territory is situated on a lofty and rough mountainous range, with a population inured to war, who fight with spears of twenty-five to thirty palms' length; he is independent of Muteczuma. The messengers with the Spaniards did not dare enter this province, as it was not subject to Muteczuma, without first notifying the governor, and asking his permission, announcing that they had come with certain Spaniards to see the gold mines that were in his country, for whom they requested a favorable reception in my name and that of Muteczuma, their lord. Coatelicamar answered, that he was very willing the Spaniards should enter his province and see the mines, with any thing else they pleased; but that the Culuans, who were subjects of Muteczuma, must not do so, as they were his enemies. The Spaniards were somewhat at a loss whether to go alone or not; their companions advised them not to go, as they would be put to death, alleging that it was for the purpose of being able to destroy them, that he would not consent to the Culuans accompanying them. At length, however, they resolved to go alone, and were well received by the governor and his people, who showed them seven or eight mines from which they said gold was procured; and in their presence some of the Indians got out a quantity of the precious metal, of which specimens were brought to me. Coatelicamar sent by these Spaniards several messengers, offering himself and his land to the service of your Majesty, and accompanying his professions with presents of gold and cotton cloth. The other party of envoys visited a province called Tuchitebeque, on the same route, towards the sea, twelve leagues from the province of Malinaltebeque, where I have already said gold was found, and there they were shown two other streams, from which also they obtained specimens of gold.

The Spaniards who went to the province of Malinaltebeque informed me that it contained every convenience for establishing farming stations, and procuring gold; on this account I requested Muteczuma to establish a plantation there for your Majesty. He accordingly set to work for this purpose with so much diligence, that within two months from the time I spoke to him on the subject, sixty fanegas of maize, and ten of beans were planted, together with two thousand cacao trees, which bear a fruit resembling the almond, that is sold after being ground, and is held in such estimation, that it is used as money throughout all the country, and employed in purchases in the markets and every where else. He had also erected four very good houses, in one of which beside the apartments there was a pool of water, in which they placed five hundred geese, there held in high esti-

mation, as they make a profitable use of their feathers, which they strip off
every year and weave into thin cloth. They also placed there fifteen hundred domestic fowls; and altogether the improvements were valued by
Spaniards who saw them at different times, exclusively of the soil, at
20,000 *pesos* of gold.

I likewise inquired of Muteczuma if there were on the coast of the sea
any river or bay into which ships could enter, and lie with safety. He
answered that he did not know, but that he would cause a chart of the
coast to be painted, showing the rivers and bays, and that I might send
Spaniards to examine them, for which purpose he would despatch suitable
persons with them as guides; and he did so. The next day they brought
me a chart of the whole coast, painted on cloth; on which appeared a river
that discharged into the sea, with a wider mouth, according to the chart,
than any others; this seemed to be between the mountains called Sanmyn,
which extend to a bay until then believed by the pilots to separate the land
at a province called Mazamalco. Muteczuma told me that I might select
whom I would wish to send, and that he would provide the means for their
examining and ascertaining every thing; I immediately designated ten men
and among them several pilots and persons acquainted with the sea.

Being furnished with the provision he made for them, they departed,
and proceeded along the coast from the port of Chalchilmeca, called San
Juan, where I first landed, for sixty leagues and upwards, without finding
any river or bay where ships could enter; although there were many large
ones on the coast, which they sounded in canoes; and in this manner they
arrived at the province of Quacalco above-mentioned, where was the river
represented on the chart. The governor of this province, named Tuchintecla, received them well, and furnished them with canoes to explore the
river. They found two fathoms and a half of water at its entrance, in the
shallowest part, and ascending twelve leagues, the least depth they found
was five or six fathoms; judging from their observations, it was thought
that the river continued for thirty leagues of the same depth. There were
numerous and large towns on its banks, and the whole province was level,
and well fortified, rich in all the productions of the earth, and containing
a numerous population, who are not vassals or subjects of Muteczuma, but
rather his enemies. The governor of the country, when the Spaniards arrived there, ordered that the Mexicans should not enter his territory, because they were his enemies; and when our people returned to me with
this account, he sent several persons in their company, by whom he trans-
mitted to me jewels of gold, skins of tigers, feathers, precious stones, and
cotton cloth; and they informed me from him, that Tuchintecla, their
sovereign, had heard of me a long time ago, for the people of Putunchán,
on the river of Grijalva, who were his friends, had told him of my passing
through their country, and making war upon them, because they opposed
my entrance into their town; and how afterwards we left them as friends
and vassals of your Majesty. He also offered himself and his whole province
to the service of your Majesty, and begged me to receive him as a friend,

on condition that the Mexicans should not enter his country, giving me
liberty to examine all it contained, and of choosing whatever I pleased for
your Majesty's use, of which he would yield an annual tribute.

When I was informed by the Spaniards that the province they had visited,
was in a situation to be colonized, and that they had discovered a harbor in
it, I was much gratified since from the time that I had first set foot in this
country, I had constantly sought to find some harbor upon its coast, where
I might found a settlement, but I had not been able to discover one, nor
is there any on all the coast, from the river San Antonio, which is next the
Grijalva, to that of Panuco, which is down the coast, where certain Spaniards
under Francisco de Garay, went for the purpose of establishing a colony,
as I shall hereafter relate to your Majesty. In order to satisfy myself in
relation to the province, the harbor, and the good will of the natives, I resolved to send thither certain of my company, who would be able to judge
of the country from their observation and experience. They went in company with the messengers that the Lord Tuchintecla had sent to me, carrying several things that I sent to him as presents. Having arrived there, they
were well received by him, and applied themselves to survey and sound the
port and river, and to examine the sites the place afforded for a town. They
afterwards brought me a full and correct report of their observations, and
declared that everything requisite for a settlement was to be found there.
The governor himself was gratified, and expressed a great desire to become
a vassal of your Majesty. As soon as they had returned, I despatched a
captain with one hundred and fifty men for the purpose of tracing, planning
and settling the town, and erecting a fortress, as the governor had consented to it, and offered whatever was necessary, or they might require for
the purpose; and he even built six houses on the spot selected for the town,
and said that he was very well pleased that we should go there to found a
colony, and dwell upon his land.

I have, in the preceding pages, most powerful Sire, stated that at the
time I entered the great city of Temixtitan, a great lord had met me on my
route who came on behalf of Muteczuma; and according to what I afterwards learned, he was a near relative of that monarch, possessing a province
next to that of Muteczuma, and called Haculuacán. The capital of it was
a very large city, adjacent to the salt lake; it is six leagues distant from the
city of Temixtitan, as the canoes go by the lake, and ten leagues by land.
The name of the city was Tezcuco, and it contained about thirty thousand
families. There are in it, Sire, splendid houses, mosques or temples, and
oratories of great magnitude, and well finished. The markets are also very
extensive; and besides this city, there are two others, one three leagues from
Tezcuco, called Acuruman, and the other six leagues, called Otumpa. Each
of these contains three or four thousand families. This province and seignory
of Haculuacán has numerous other villages and hamlets, and excellent lands,
well cultivated. It borders on one side upon that of Tascaltecal, of which
I have already spoken to your Majesty.

The governor, who is named Cacamazin, after the imprisonment of Muteczuma, rebelled, both against your Majesty, to whom he professed allegiance, and against Muteczuma. Although he was several times summoned to come and render obedience to your Majesty's commands, he never would. Beside the requisitions I made of him, Muteczuma also sent his commands to him, to which he answered, that if they wanted any thing of him they should go to his country, where they should see what he was, and what service he was obliged to perform. I was told that he had a large force of armed men in readiness at a moment's warning. As neither by demonstrations nor requisitions was I able to induce him to yield, I spoke to Muteczuma, and asked his advice what it was best for us to do, in order that we might not leave his rebellion unpunished. He answered, that should we resolve on war, it would be attended with much danger, as he was a great lord, and possessed much strength and many people; and he could not be attacked without the risk of great destruction of life. But that there were several of the principal persons of Cacamazin who resided in Mexico at his charge, and that he would speak to them on the subject, in order to induce some of Cacamazin's followers to come to Mexico, and thus being secured, they might favor our attempt, and their master be taken without risk.

And so it turned out; Muteczuma laid his plans in such a manner, that a number of his leading men persuaded Cacamazin to meet them in the city of Tezcuco, for the purpose of taking measures in relation to the affairs of the state, (in which their station entitled them to a voice), and who were grieved by the course he was pursuing, which would involve the ruin of the country. Accordingly they assembled in a splendid palace of Cacamazin, situated near the shore of the lake, which was built in such a manner that canoes could pass under it, and from thence issue forth upon the lake. At that place a number of boats were stationed, properly manned and equipped, in case Cacamazin should offer any resistance when taken. While he was consulting with his chiefs, they seized him, and before it was discovered by his attendants, they secured him in a boat, and launched out upon the lake, directing their course to the great city, which, as I have already stated, was six leagues distant. Having arrived there, they placed him on a litter, as his condition required, and they had been accustomed to do, and brought him to me; I immediately caused him to be put in irons, and to be carefully guarded. Having advised with Muteczuma, I conferred the government of the province on his son, called Cucuzcasin, in the name of your Majesty; and I directed all the communities and lords of the province to obey him as their ruler, until your Majesty should order otherwise. Accordingly, from that time he was recognized and obeyed as their sovereign, in the same manner as Cacamazin had been; and he also obeyed all the commands that I imposed on him in your Majesty's name.

A few days after the imprisonment of Cacamazin, Muteczuma called together all the governors of the neighboring cities and states, and when they were assembled, he sent an invitation to me to join them; on my arrival, he addressed them as follows: "My brethren and friends, you know that for a long period you, your fathers, and ancestors have been the subjects and vassals of my predecessors and myself, and that both by them and me you have been always well treated and honored. You have also done all that is due from good and loyal vassals to their liege lords; and I also believe that you have heard from your ancestors, that they were not natives of this land, but that they came to it from a great distance, under the conduct of a sovereign whose subjects they all were; he left them here, but after a considerable time he returned, and found that our ancestors had become numerous and well established in this country, having intermarried with the women of the land, by whom they had many children. On this account they were unwilling to go back with him, or to acknowledge him as their sovereign whereupon he went away, saying that he would return, or send so great a force as would compel them to submit to him. You knew well that we have always looked for him; and according to what this captain has told us of the king and lord, who has sent him here, and also considering the quarter from which he says he has come, I hold it certain, and you must be of the same opinion, that this is the sovereign that we have expected; especially as he informs us, that he had some knowledge of us there. And since our predecessors did not render their just service to their sovereign lord, let us perform our duty; and let us render thanks to our gods, that he, who was so long expected by them, has come in our day. I must, therefore, entreat, since all this is well known to you, that hereafter, instead of regarding me as your sovereign, you will recognize and obey that great king, as he is our natural ruler, and receive this his captain in place of him; and all the tributes and services which till now you have rendered to me, you will hereafter render and yield to him, as I likewise contribute and yield all that he requires of me; and thus besides performing your duty, you will gratify and oblige me."

All this he said weeping, with more tears and sighs than becomes a man to exhibit; and likewise all the princes who were present wept so much, that for a long time they were unable to answer. And I assure your sacred Majesty that there was not a Spaniard who heard the discourse, that did not feel great compassion. After their grief had abated, they answered, that they recognized him as their sovereign, and had engaged to do whatever he might command; and that on this account, as well as for the reasons he had assigned, they were willing to act as he required; and that, from henceforth forever, they declared themselves the vassals of your Majesty and all, and each for himself, would there promise, and did promise, to do and fulfil all that was commanded in the name of your Majesty as became good and loyal vassals; and to aid with tribute and services as they had heretofore done for Muteczuma, and as was their duty, together with whatever else might be required of them in the name of your Majesty. All this passed in the presence of a public notary, and was confirmed by a formal act; as well as by the testimony of many of our countrymen whom I had requested to be present.

After this solemn act and acknowledgment on the part of these lords towards your Majesty, I one day spoke to Muteczuma and said that your

Highness needed gold for certain works that he had ordered to be completed, and I wished him to send some of his people, and I would send some of mine, to the lands and abodes of those lords who had submitted themselves on that occasion, to ask them to supply your Majesty with some part of what they possessed; since besides the necessity your Majesty had for the gold, it would serve as a beginning of their fealty, and your Highness would form a better opinion of their disposition to render him service by such a demonstration; and I also requested that he himself would give me what gold he had, as well as other things, in order that I might transmit them to your Majesty. He immediately requested that I would designate the Spaniards whom I wished to send on this business, and he distributed them two by two, and five by five, among many provinces and cities, the names of which I do not recollect, the records having perished, as they were numerous and different, some eighty, some one hundred leagues from the great city of Temixtitan; and with them he sent some of his own people, and directed them to go to the governors of provinces and cities, and say that I commanded each one of them to give a certain proportion of gold, which he prescribed.

Accordingly all those caciques to whom he sent contributed freely what he demanded of them, as well jewels as plates and leaves of gold and silver, and whatever else they possessed; and melting down all that admitted it, we found that the fifth part belonging to your Majesty amounted to 32,400 *pesos* of gold and upwards, without reckoning the jewels of gold and silver, the feather-work, and precious stones, together with many other valuable articles that I set apart for your sacred Majesty, worth more than 100,000 ducats. These besides their monied value, were of so costly and curious workmanship, that considering their novelty and wonderful beauty, no price could be set on them; nor is it probable that any one of all the princes of the world to whose knowledge they might come, could produce any articles of equal splendor. It may seem to your Majesty like a fabulous story, but it is true, that all the natural objects, both on sea and land, of which Muteczuma has any knowledge, are imitated in gold and silver, as well as in precious stones and feathers, in such perfection that they appear almost the same. He gave me numerous specimens of many of these for your Highness, besides other things of which I had given him drawings, which he caused to be wrought in gold, such as images, crucifixes, medals, jewels, and necklaces, together with many other articles, of which he had imitations made. They assigned to your Majesty a fifth part of the silver, amounting to one hundred marks and upwards, which at my request the natives worked up into large and small dishes, porringers, cups, and spoons; and they made them as perfectly as they could understand their form from our description.

Besides these, Muteczuma gave me a large quantity of his cotton stuff, which, considering it was cotton without silk, could not be equalled in the whole world, either in texture, or in the variety and beauty of the colors, or in the workmanship. It comprised male and female apparel of remarkable elegance; ornamental hangings for bedchambers, superior beyond comparison to those made of silk; together with other fabrics of cotton, as tapestries, designed for halls and temples; counterpanes, composed of feathers interwoven with cotton, and extremely beautiful; and many other articles, so numerous and ingenious, that I am unable to describe them to your Majesty. He also presented me with a dozen serbatans, used by himself for shooting, made with such admirable skill that they also exceed my power of description. There were depicted on them a great variety of birds, animals, trees, flowers, and various other objects; the rims and extremities, of the width of a span, as well as the centre, were inlaid with gold, and curiously carved. To these he added a pouch of gold net-work, together with an infinite variety of other things.

CHAPTER V

John Hawkins—1532–1595

The three slave-trading voyages made by John Hawkins started a new era in the history of the English in America. These expeditions were equipped for the sole purpose of trading Negroes seized along the coast of Guinea, and sold profitably in San Domingo. Hawkins' first venture was so successful that he sailed almost immediately on a second voyage. Once more he captured and sold hapless Negroes for rich store of gold, silver, pearls, and other jewels, for which profitable undertaking he was knighted by Queen Elizabeth on his return to England. It is hard to realize that no onus attached to engaging in this wretched trade in human cargo. These slave-traders were as sincere in their enterprise as were the early navigators bent on exploration.

The third expedition of Hawkins came to a sorry end. There was such a demand for slaves to work the plantations of the early Spanish settlers that Hawkins persisted, despite the fact that the Spaniards had been warned not to trade with him. He was attacked by a powerful Spanish fleet, and escaped with the loss of all but two of his ships. For this treachery the English sought revenge for nearly two hundred years.

After a brief record of the first voyage by Richard Hakluyt, the accounts that follow are by John Sparke, who went on the second voyage, and by Hawkins himself, describing the ill-fated third voyage.

THREE VOYAGES—1562, 1564, 1567

First Voyage

The first voyage of the right worshipfull and valiant knight sir John Hawkins, sometimes treasurer of her Majesties navie Roial, made to the West Indies 1562.

MASTER JOHN HAUKINS having made divers voyages to the Iles of the Canaries, and there by his good and upright dealing being growen in love and favour with the people, informed himselfe amongst them by diligent inquisition, of the state of the West India, whereof hee had received some knowledge by the instructions of his father, but increased the same by the advertisements and reports of that people. And being amongst other particulars assured, that Negros were very good marchandise in Hispaniola, and that store of Negros might easily bee had upon the coast of Guinea, resolved with himselfe to make triall thereof, and communicated that devise with his worshipfull friendes of London: namely with Sir Lionell Ducket, sir Thomas Lodge, M. Gunson his father in law, sir William Winter, M. Bromfield, and others. All which persons liked so well of his intention, that they became liberall contributers and adventurers in the action. For which purpose there were three good ships immediatly provided: The one called the Salomon of the burthen of 120. tunnes, wherein M. Haukins himselfe went as Generall: The second the Swallow of 100. tunnes, wherein went for Captaine M. Thomas Hampton: and the third the Jonas a barke of 40. tunnes, wherein the Master supplied the Captaines roome: in which small fleete M. Hawkins tooke with him not above 100. men for feare of sicknesse and other inconveniences, whereunto men in long voyages are commonly subject.

With this companie he put off and departed from the coast of England in the moneth of October 1562. and in his course touched first at Teneriffe, where hee received friendly intertainement. From thence he passed to Sierra Leona, upon the coast of Guinea, which place by the people of the countrey is called Tagarin, where he stayed some good time, and got into his possession, partly by the sworde, and partly by other meanes, to the number of 300. Negros at the least, besides other merchandises which that countrey yeeldeth. With this praye hee sayled over the Ocean sea unto the Iland of Hispaniola, and arrived first at the port of Isabella: and there hee had reasonable utterance of his English commodities, as also of some part of his Negros, trusting the Spaniards no further, then that by his owne strength he was able still to master them. From the port of Isabella he went to Puerto de Plata, where he made like sales, standing alwaies upon his guard: from thence also hee sayled to Monte Christi another port on the North side of Hispaniola, and the last place of his touching, where he had peaceable traffique, and made vent of the whole number of his Negros: for which he received in those 3. places by way of exchange such quantitie of merchandise, that hee did not onely lade his owne 3. shippes with hides, ginger, sugars, and some quantitie of pearles, but he fraighted also two other hulkes with hides and other like commodities, which hee sent into Spaine. And thus leaving the Iland, he returned and disemboqued, passing out by the Ilands of the Caycos, without further entring into the bay of Mexico, in this his first voyage to the West India. And so with prosperous successe and much gaine to himselfe and the aforesayde adventurers, he came home, and arrived in the moneth of September 1563.

SECOND VOYAGE

The voyage made by M. John Hawkins Esquire, and afterward knight, Captaine of the Jesus of Lubek, one of her Majesties shippes, and Generall of the Salomon, and other two barkes going in his companie, to

the coast of Guinea, and the Indies of Nova Hispania, begun in An.
Dom. 1564.

MASTER JOHN HAWKINS with the Jesus of Lubek, a shippe of 700. and the
Salomon a shippe of 140. the Tiger a barke of 50. and the Swallow of 30.
tunnes, being all well furnished with men to the number of one hundreth
threescore and tenne, as also with ordinance and victuall requisite for such
a voyage, departed out of Plymmouth the 18. day of October, in the yeere
of our Lord 1564. with a prosperous winde. . . .

The fourth of November they had sight of the Iland of Madera, and the
sixt day of Teneriffe, which they thought to have beene the Canarie, in
that they supposed themselves to have beene to the Eastward of Teneriffe,
and were not. . . . To speake somewhat of these Ilands, being called in
olde time Insulæ fortunatæ, by the meanes of the flourishing thereof, the
fruitfulnesse of them doeth surely exceede farre all other that I have heard
of: for they make wine better than any in Spaine, they have grapes of such
bignesse, that they may bee compared to damsons, and in taste inferiour to
none: for sugar, suckets, raisins of the Sunne, and many other fruits,
abundance: for rosine & raw silke, there is great store, they want neither
corne, pullets, cattell, nor yet wilde foule: they have many Camels also,
which being young, are eaten of the people for victuals, and being olde,
they are used for caryage of necessaries: whose propertie is as hee is taught
to kneele at the taking of his loade, and unlading againe: his nature is to
ingender backward contrary to other beastes: of understanding very good,
but of shape very deformed, with a little bellie, long misshapen legges, and
feete very broad of flesh, without a hoofe, all whole, saving the great toe,
a backe bearing up like a molehill, a large and thin necke, with a little head,
with a bunch of hard flesh, which nature hath given him in his breast to
leane upon. This beast liveth hardly, and is contented with strawe and
stubble, but of force strong, being well able to carrie 500. weight. In one
of these Ilands called Fierro, there is by the reports of the inhabitants, a
certaine tree that raineth continually, by the dropping whereof the inhabitants and cattell are satisfied with water, for other water have they none
in all the Iland. And it raineth in such abundance, that it were incredible
unto a man to beleeve such a vertue to bee in a tree, but it is knowen to be
a divine matter, and a thing ordeined by God, at whose power therein wee
ought not to marvell, seeing he did by his providence as we read in the
Scriptures, when the children of Israel were going into the land of promise,
feede them with Manna from heaven, for the space of 40. yeeres. Of the trees
aforesaid wee saw in Guinie many, being of great height, dropping continually, but not so abundantly as the other, because the leaves are nar-
rower, and are like the leaves of a peare tree. About these Ilands are certaine
flitting Ilands, which have beene oftentimes seene, and when men approched
neere them, they vanished: as the like hath bene of these Ilands nowe
knowen by the report of the inhabitants, which were not found of long
time one after the other: and therefore it should seeme hee is not yet borne

to whom God hath appoynted the finding of them. In this Iland of Teneriffe there is a hill called The Pike, because it is piked, which is in heigth by their reports twentie leagues, having both winter and summer abundance of snowe in the top of it: this Pike may bee seene in a cleere day fiftie leagues off, but it sheweth as though it were a blacke cloude a great heigth in the element. I have heard of none to be compared with this in heigth, but in the Indias I have seene many, and in my judgement not inferiour to the Pike, and so the Spaniards write.

The 15. of November at night we departed from Teneriffe, and the 20. of the same wee had sight of ten Caravels, that were fishing at sea, with whome we would have spoken, but they fearing us, fled into a place of Barbarie, called Cape de las Barbas.

The twentieth, the ships pinnesse with two men in her, sayling by the ship, was overthrowen by the oversight of them that went in her, the winde being so great, that before they were espied, and the ship had cast about for them, she was driven half a league to leeward of the pinnesse, and had lost sight of her, so that there was small hope of recoverie, had not Gods helpe and the Captaines deligence bene, who having wel marked which way the pinnesse was by the Sunne, appointed 24 of the lustiest rowers in the great boate, to rowe to the wind-wardes, and so recovered, contrary to all mens expectations, both the pinnesse and the men sitting upon the keele of her.

The 25 he came to Cape Blanco, which is upon the coast of Africa, and a place where the Portugals do ride, that fish there in the moneth of November especially, and is a very good place of fishing, for Pargoes, Mullet, and Dogge fish. In this place the Portugals have no holde for their defence, but have rescue of the Barbarians, whom they entertaine as their souldiers, for the time of their being there and for their fishing upon that coast of Africa, doe pay a certaine tribute to the king of the Moores. The people of that part of Africa are tawnie, having long haire without any apparell, saving before their privie members. Their weapons in warres are bowes and arrowes.

The 26 we departed from S. Avis Baye, within Cape Blanco, where we refreshed our selves with fish, and other necessaries: and the 29 wee came to Cape Verde, which lieth in 14 degrees, and a halfe. These people are all blacke, and are called Negros, without any apparell, saving before their privities: of stature goodly men, and well liking by reason of their food, which passeth all other Guyneans for kine, goats, pullin, rise, fruits, and fish. Here wee tooke fishes with heads like conies, and teeth nothing varying, of a jolly thickenesse, but not past a foote long, and is not to be eaten without flaying or cutting off his head.

The 10 of December, we had a Northeast winde, with raine and storme, which weather continuing two dayes together, was the occasion that the Salomon, and Tygre loste our companie: for whereas the Jesus, and pinnesse ankered at one of the Islands called Sambula, the twelfth day, the Salomon and Tygre came not thither till the 14. In this Island we stayed certaine daies, going every day on shore to take the Inhabitants, with burning and spoiling their townes, who before were Sapies, and were conquered by the Samboses, Inhabitants beyond Sierra Leona. These Samboses had inhabited there three yeres before our comming thither, and in so short space have so planted the ground, that they had great plentie of Mil, Rise, Rootes, Pompions, Pullin, goates, of small frye dried, every house full of the Countrey fruite planted by Gods providence, as Palmito trees, fruites like dates, and sundry other in no place in all that Countrey so aboundantly, whereby they lived more deliciously then other. These inhabitants have diverse of the Sapies, which they tooke in the warres as their slaves, whome onely they kept to till the ground, in that they neither have the knowledge thereof, nor yet will worke themselves, of whome wee tooke many in that place, but of the Samboses none at all, for they fled into the maine. All the Samboses have white teeth as we have, farre unlike to the Sapies which doe inhabite about Rio grande, for their teeth are all filed, which they doe for a braverie, to set out themselves, and doe jagge their flesh, both legges, armes, and bodies, as workemanlike, as a Jerkinmaker with us pinketh a jerkin. These Sapies be more civill then the Samboses: for whereas the Samboses live most by the spoile of their enemies, both in taking their victuals, and eating them also. The Sapies doe not eate mans flesh, unlesse in the warre they be driven by necessitie thereunto, which they have not used but by the example of the Samboses, but live onely with fruites, and cattell, whereof they have great store. This plentie is the occasion that the Sapies desire not warre, except they be therunto provoked by the invasions of the Samboses, whereas the Samboses for want of foode are inforced thereunto, and therefore are not woont onely to take them that they kill, but also keepe those that they take, untill such time as they want meate, and then they kill them. There is also another occasion that provoketh the Samboses to warre against the Sapies which is for covetousnes of their riches. For whereas the Sapies have an order to burie their dead in certaine places appointed for that purpose, with their golde about them, the Samboses digge up the ground, to have the same treasure: for the Samboses have not the like store of golde, that the Sapies have. In this Island of Sambula we found about 50 boates called Almadyes, or Canoas, which are made of one peece of wood, digged out like a trough but of a good proportion, being about 8 yards long, and one in breadth, having a beakhead and a sterne very proportionably made, and on the out side artifically carved, and painted red and blewe: they are able to cary twenty or thirty men, but they are about the coast able to cary threescore and upward. In these canoas they rowe standing upright, with an oare somewhat longer then a man, the ende whereof is made about the breadth and length of a mans hand, of the largest sort. They row very swift, and in some of them foure rowers and one to steere make as much way, as a paire of oares in the Thames of London.

Their Townes are pretily divided with a maine streete at the entring in, that goeth thorough their Towne, and another overthwart street, which maketh their townes crosse wayes: their houses are built in a ranke very

orderly in the face of the street, and they are made round, like a dovecote,
with stakes set full of Palmito leaves, in stead of a wall: they are not much
more then a fathome large, and two of heigth, & thatched with Palmito
leaves very close, other some with reede, and over the roofe thereof, for
the better garnishing of the same, there is a round bundle of reede, pretily
contrived like a louer: in the inner part they make a loft of stickes, whereupon they lay all their provision of victuals: a place they reserve at their
enterance for the kitchin, and the place they lie in is devided with certaine
mattes artificially made with the rine of Palmito trees: their bedsteades are
of small staves layd along, and raysed a foote from the ground, upon which
is layde a matte, and another upon them when they list: for other covering they have none. In the middle of the towne there is a house larger and
higher then the other, but in forme alike, adjoyning unto the which there
is a place made of foure good stancions of woode, and a round roofe over
it, the grounde also raised round with claye a foote high, upon the which
floore were strawed many fine mats: this is the Consultation-house, the like
whereof is in all Townes, as the Portugals affirme: in which place, when
they sitte in Counsell the King or Captaine sitteth in the midst, and the
Elders upon the floore by him: (for they give reverence to their Elders)
and the common sorte sitte round about them. There they sitte to examine
matters of theft, which if a man be taken with, to steale but a Portugal cloth
from another, hee is sold to the Portugals for a slave. They consult also,
and take order what time they shall goe to warres: and as it is certainely
reported by the Portugals, they take order in gathering of the fruites in
the season of the yeere, and also of Palmito wine, which is gathered by a
hole cut in the top of a tree, and a gourde set for the receiving thereof,
which falleth in by droppes, and yeeldeth fresh wine againe within a moneth,
and this devided part and portion-like to every man, by the judgement of
the Captaine and Elders, every man holdeth himselfe contented: and this
surely I judge to be a very good order: for otherwise, whereas scarsitie of
Palmito is, every man would have the same, which might breed great strife:
but of such things, as every man doeth plant for himselfe, the sower thereof
reapeth it to his owne use, so that nothing is common, but that which is
unset by mans hands. In their houses there is more common passage of
Lizardes like Evats, and other greater, of blacke and blew colour, of neere
a foote long, besides their tailes, then there is with us of Mise in great
houses. The Sapies and Samboses also use in their warres bowes, and arrowes made of reedes, with heads of yron poysoned with the juyce of a
Cucumber, whereof I had many in my handes. In their battels they have
target-men, with broad wicker targets, and darts with heades at both endes,
of yron, the one in forme of a two edged sworde, a foote and an halfe
long, and at the other ende, the yron long of the same length made to
counterpease it, that in casting it might flie level, rather then for any other
purpose as I can judge. And when they espie the enemie, the Captaine to
cheere his men, cryeth Hungry, and they answere Heygre, and with that
every man placeth himselfe in order, for about every target man three

bowemen will cover themselves, and shoote as they see advantage: and when they give the onset, they make such terrible cryes, that they may bee heard two miles off. For their beliefe, I can heare of none that they have, but in such as they themselves imagine to see in their dreames, and so worshippe the pictures, whereof wee sawe some like unto devils.

In this Island aforesayde wee sojourned unto the one and twentieth of December, where having taken certaine Negros, and asmuch of their fruites, rise, and mill, as we could well cary away, (whereof there was such store, that wee might have laden one of our Barkes therewith) wee departed, and at our departure divers of our men being desirous to goe on shore, to fetch Pompions, which having prooved, they found to bee very good, certaine of the Tygres men went also, amongst the which there was a Carpenter, a yong man, who with his fellowes having fet many, and caryed them downe to their boates, as they were ready to depart, desired his fellow to tary while he might goe up to fetch a few which he had layed by for him selfe, who being more licorous then circumspect, went up without weapon, and as he went up alone, possibly being marked of the Negros that were upon the trees, espying him what hee did, perceaving him to be alone, and without weapon, dogged him, and finding him occupyed in binding his Pompions together, came behinde him, overthrowing him and straight cutte his throate, as hee afterwardes was found by his fellowes, who came to the place for him, and there found him naked.

The two and twentieth the Captaine went into the River, called Callowsa, with the two Barkes, and the Johns Pinnesse, and the Salomons boate, leaving at anker in the Rivers mouth the two shippes, the River being twenty leagues in, where the Portugals roade: hee came thither the five and twentieth, and dispatched his businesse, and so returned with two Caravels, loaden with Negros.

The 27. the Captaine was advertised by the Portugals of a towne of the Negros called Bymba, being in the way as they returned, where was not onely great quantitie of golde, but also that there were not above fortie men, and an hundred women and children in the Towne, so that if hee would give the adventure upon the same, hee might gette an hundreth slaves: with the which tydings hee being gladde, because the Portugals shoulde not thinke him to bee of so base a courage, but that hee durst give them that, and greater attempts: and being thereunto also the more provoked with the prosperous successe hee had in other Islands adjacent, where he had put them all to flight, and taken in one boate twentie together, determined to stay before the Towne three or foure houres, to see what hee could doe: and thereupon prepared his men in armour and weapon together, to the number of fortie men well appointed, having to their guides certaine Portugals, in a boat, who brought some of them to their death: wee landing boat after boat, and divers of our men scattering themselves, contrary to the Captaines will, by one or two in a company, for the hope that they had to finde golde in their houses, ransacking the same, in the meane time the Negros came upon them, and hurte many being thus scattered, whereas if five or sixe had bene together, they had bene able, as their companions did, to give the overthrow to 40 of them, and being driven downe to take their boates, were followed so hardly by a route of Negros, who by that tooke courage to pursue them to their boates, that not onely some of them, but others standing on shore, not looking for any such matter by meanes that the Negros did flee at the first, and our companie remained in the towne, were suddenly so set upon that some with great hurt recovered their boates; othersome not able to recover the same, tooke the water, and perished by meanes of the oaze. While this was doing, the Captaine who with a dosen men, went through the towne, returned, finding 200 Negros at the waters side, shooting at them in the boates, and cutting them in pieces which were drowned in the water, at whose comming, they ranne all away: so he entred his boates, and before he could put off from the shore, they returned againe, and shot very fiercely and hurt divers of them. Thus wee returned backe some what discomforted, although the Captaine in a singular wise maner caried himselfe, with countenance very cheerefull outwardly, as though hee did litle weigh the death of his men, nor yet the great hurt of the rest, although his heart inwardly was broken in pieces for it; done to this ende, that the Portugals being with him, should not presume to resist against him, nor take occasion to put him to further displeasure or hinderance for the death of our men: having gotten by our going ten Negros, and lost seven of our best men, whereof M. Field Captaine of the Salomon, was one, and we had 27 of our men hurt. In the same houre while this was doing, there happened at the same instant, a marveilous miracle to them in the shippes, who road ten leagues to sea-ward, by many sharkes or Tiburons, who came about the ships: among which, one was taken by the Jesus, and foure by the Salomon, and one very sore hurt escaped: and so it fell out of our men, whereof one of the Jesus men, and foure of the Salomons were killed, and the fift having twentie wounds was rescued, and scaped with much adoe.

The 28 they came to their ships, the Jesus, and the Salomon, and the 30 departed from thence to Taggarin.

The first of January the two barkes, and both the boates forsooke the ships, and went into a river called the Casserroes, and the 6 having dispatched their businesse, the two barkes returned, and came to Taggarin, where the two ships were at anker. Not two dayes after the comming of the two ships thither, they put their water caske a shore, and filled it with water, to season the same, thinking to have filled it with fresh water afterward: and while their men were some on shore, and some at their boates, the Negros set upon them in the boates, and hurt divers of them, and came to the caskes, and cut of the hoopes of twelve buts, which lost us 4 or 5 dayes time, besides great want we had of the same: sojourning at Taggarin, the Swallow went up the river about her trafficke, where they saw great townes of the Negros, and Canoas, that had threescore men in a piece: there they understood by the Portugals, of a great battell betweene them of Sierra Leona side, and them of Taggarin: they of Sierra Leona, had prepared three hun-

dred Canoas to invade the other. The time was appointed not past sixe
dayes after our departure from thence, which we would have seene, to the
intent we might have taken some of them, had it not bene for the death and
sickenesse of our men, which came by the contagiousnes of the place, which
made us to make hast away.

The 18 of Januarie at night, wee departed from Taggarin, being bound
for the West Indies, before which departure certaine of the Salomons men
went on shore to fill water in the night, and as they came on shore with
their boat being ready to leape on land, one of them espied an Negro in a
white coate, standing upon a rocke, being ready to have received them when
they came on shore, having in sight of his fellowes also eight or nine, some
in one place leaping out, and some in another, but they hid themselves
streight againe: whereupon our men doubting they had bene a great companie, and sought to have taken them at more advantage, as God would,
departed to their ships, not thinking there had bene such a mischiefe pretended toward them, as then was in deede. Which the next day we understood of a Portugal that came downe to us, who had trafficked with the
Negros, by whom hee understood, that the king of Sierra Leona had made
all the power hee could, to take some of us, partly for the desire he had to
see what kinde of people we were, that had spoiled his people at the Idols,
whereof he had newes before our comming, and as I judge also, upon other
occasions provoked by the Tangomangos, but sure we were that the armie
was come downe, by meanes that in the evening wee saw such a monstrous
fire, made by the watring place, that before was not seene, which fire is the
only marke for the Tangomangos to know where their armie is alwayes. If
these men had come downe in the evening, they had done us great displeasure, for that wee were on shore filling water: but God, who worketh
all things for the best, would not have it so, and by him we escaped without danger, his name be praysed for it.

The 29 of this same moneth we departed with all our shippes from Sierra
Leona, towardes the West Indies, and for the space of eighteene dayes, we
were becalmed, having nowe and then contrary windes, and some Ter-
nados, amongst the same calme, which happened to us very ill, beeing but
reasonably watered, for so great a companie of Negros, and our selves,
which pinched us all, and that which was worst, put us in such feare that
many never thought to have reached to the Indies, without great death of
Negros, and of themselves: but the Almightie God, who never suffereth his
elect to perish, sent us the sixteenth of Februarie, the ordinary Brise, which
is the Northwest winde, which never left us, till wee came to an Island of
the Canybals, called Dominica, where wee arrived the ninth of March, upon
a Saturday: and because it was the most desolate place in all the Island, we
could see no Canybals, but some of their houses where they dwelled, and as
it should seeme forsooke the place for want of fresh water, for wee could
finde none there but raine water, and such as fell from the hilles, and remained as a puddle in the dale, whereof wee filled for our Negros. The
Canybals of that Island, and also others adjacent are the most desperate

warriers that are in the Indies, by the Spaniardes report, who are never able to conquer them, and they are molested by them not a little, when they are driven to water there in any of those Islands: of very late, not two moneths past, in the said Island, a Caravel being driven to water, was in the night sette upon by the inhabitants, who cutte their cable in the halser, whereby they were driven a shore, and so taken by them, and eaten. The greene Dragon of Newhaven, whereof was Captaine one Bontemps, in March also, came to one of those Islands, called Granada, and being driven to water, could not doe the same for the Canybals, who fought with him very desperatly two dayes. For our part also, if we had not lighted upon the desertest place in all that Island, wee could not have missed, but should have bene greatly troubled by them, by all the Spaniards reports, who make them devils in respect of me.

The tenth day at night, we departed from thence, and the fifteenth had sight of nine Islands, called the Testigos: and the sixteenth of an Island, called Margarita, where wee were entertayned by the Alcalde, and had both Beeves and sheepe given us, for the refreshing of our men: but the Governour of the Island, would neither come to speake with our Captaine, neither yet give him any licence to trafficke: and to displease us the more, whereas wee had hired a Pilote to have gone with us, they would not onely not suffer him to goe with us, but also sent word by a Caravel out of hand, to Santo Domingo, to the Vice-roy, who doeth represent the kings person, of our arrivall in those partes, which had like to have turned us to great displeasure, by the meanes that the same Vice-roy did send word to Cape de la Vela, and to other places along the coast, commanding them that by the vertue of his authoritie, and by the obedience that they owe to their Prince, no man should trafficke with us, but should resist us with all the force they could. In this Island, notwithstanding that wee were not within foure leagues of the Towne, yet were they so afraid, that not onely the Governour himselfe, but also all the inhabitants forsooke their Towne, assembling all the Indians to them and fled into the mountaines, as wee were partly certified, and also sawe the experience our selves, by some of the Indians comming to see us who by three Spaniards a horsebacke passing hard by us, went unto the Indians, having every one of them their bowes, and arrowes, procuring them away, who before were conversant with us.

Here perceiving no trafficke to be had with them, nor yet water for the refreshing of our men, we were driven to depart the twentieth day, and the 2 and twentieth we came to a place in the maine called Cumana, whither the Captaine going in his Pinnisse, spake with certaine Spaniards, of whom he demanded trafficke, but they made him answere, they were but souldiers newely come thither, and were not able to by one Negro: whereupon hee asked for a watring place, and they pointed him a place two leagues off, called Santa Fè, where we found marveilous goodly watering, and commodious for the taking in thereof: for that the fresh water came into the Sea, and so our shippes had aboord the shore twentie fathome water. Neere about this place, inhabited certaine Indians, who the next day after we came thither, came down to us, presenting mill and cakes of breade, which they had made of a kinde of corne called Maiz, in bignesse of a pease, the eare whereof is much like to a teasell, but a spanne in length, having thereon a number of granes. Also they brought down to us Hennes, Potatoes and Pines, which we bought for beades, pewter whistles, glasses, knives, and other trifles. These Potatoes be the most delicate rootes that may be eaten, and doe farre exceed our passeneps or carets. Their pines be of the bignes of two fists, the outside whereof is of the making of a pine-apple, but it is soft like the rinde of a Cucomber, and the inside eateth like an apple, but it is more delicious then any sweet apple sugred. These Indians being of colour tawnie like an Olive, having every one of them both men and women, haire all blacke, and no other colour, the women wearing the same hanging downe to their shoulders, and the men rounded, and without beards, neither men nor women suffering any haire to growe in any part of their body, but dayly pull it off as it groweth. They goe all naked, the men covering no part of their body but their yard, upon the which they weare a gourd or piece of cane, made fast with a thrid about their loynes, leaving the other parts of their members uncovered, whereof they take no shame. The women also are uncovered, saving with a cloth which they weare a hand-breath, where-with they cover their privities both before and behind. These people be very small feeders, for travelling they cary but two small bottels of gourdes, wherein they put in one the juice of Sorrell whereof they have great store, and in the other flowre of their Maiz, which being moist, they eate, taking sometime of the other. These men cary every man his bowe and arrowes, whereof some arrowes are poisoned for warres, which they keepe in a Cane together, which Cane is of the bignesse of a mans arme, other some with broad heades of iron wherewith they stricke fish in the water: the experience whereof we saw not once nor twise, but dayly for the time we taried there, for they are so good archers that the Spaniards for feare thereof arme themselves and their horses with quilted canvas of two ynches thicke, and leave no place of their body open to their enemies, saving their eyes which they may not hide, and yet oftentimes are they hit in that so small a scantling: their poyson is of such a force, that a man being stricken there-with dyeth within foure and twentie howers, as the Spaniards do affirme, & in my judgement it is like there can be no stronger poyson as they make it, using thereunto apples which are very faire and red of colour, but are a strong poyson, with the which together with venemous Bats, Vipers, Adders and other serpents, they make a medley, and therewith anoint the same.

The Indian women delight not when they are yong in bearing of chil-dren, because it maketh them have hanging breastes which they account to bee great deforming in them, and upon that occasion while they bee yong, they destroy their seede, saying, that it is fittest for olde women. Moreover, when they are delivered of childe, they goe straight to washe themselves, without making any further ceremonie for it, not lying in bed as our women doe. The beds which they have are made of Gossopine cotton, and wrought artificially of divers colours, which they cary about

with them when they travell, and making the same fast to two trees, lie
therein they and their women. The people be surely gentle and tractable,
and such as desire to live peaceably, or els had it bene unpossible for the
Spaniards to have conquered them as they did, and the more to live now
peaceably, they being so many in number, and the Spaniards so few.

From hence we departed the eight and twentie, and the next day we
passed betweene the maine land, and the Island called Tortuga, a very lowe
Island, in the yeere of our Lorde God one thousande five hundred sixty
five aforesaide, and sayled along the coast untill the first of Aprill, at which
time the Captaine sayled along in the Jesus pinnesse to discerne the coast,
and saw many Caribes on shore, and some also in their Canoas, which made
tokens unto him of friendship, and shewed him golde, meaning thereby that
they would trafficke for wares. Whereupon he stayed to see the maners of
them, and so for two or three trifles they gave such things as they had
about them, and departed: but the Caribes were very importunate to have
them come on shore, which if it had not bene for want of wares to trafficke
with them, he would not have denyed them, because the Indians which we
saw before were very gentle people, and such as do no man hurt. But as
God would have it, hee wanted that thing, which if hee had had, would
have bene his confusion: for these were no such kinde of people as wee
tooke them to bee, but more devilish a thousand partes and are eaters and
devourers of any man they can catch, as it was afterwards declared unto
us at Burboroata, by a Caravel comming out of Spaine with certaine souldiers, and a Captaine generall sent by the king for those Eastward parts of
the Indians, who sayling along in his pinnesse, as our Captaine did to descry
the coast, was by the Caribes called a shoore with sundry tokens made to
him of friendshippe, and golde shewed as though they desired trafficke,
with the which the Spaniard being mooved, suspecting no deceite at all,
went ashore amongst them: who was no sooner ashore, but with foure or
five more was taken, the rest of his company being invaded by them, saved
themselves by flight, but they that were taken, paied their ransome with
their lives, and were presently eaten. And this is their practise to toll with
their golde the ignorant to their snares: they are bloodsuckers both of
Spaniards, Indians, and all that light in their laps, not sparing their owne
countreymen if they can conveniently come by them. Their policie in fight
with the Spaniards is marveilous: for they chuse for their refuge the mountaines and woodes where the Spaniards with their horses cannot follow
them, and if they fortune to be met in the plaine where one horseman may
overrunne 100. of them, they have a devise of late practised by them to
pitch stakes of wood in the ground, and also small iron pikes to mischiefe
their horses, wherein they shew themselves politique warriers. They have
more abundance of golde then all the Spaniards have, and live upon the
mountaines where the Mines are in such number, that the Spaniards have
much adoe to get any of them from them, and yet sometimes by assembling
a great number of them, which happeneth once in two yeeres, they get a
piece from them, which afterwards they keepe sure ynough.

Thus having escaped the danger of them, wee kept our course along the coast, and came the third of April to a Towne called Burboroata, where his ships came to an ancker, and hee himselfe went a shore to speake with the Spaniards, to whom hee declared himselfe to be an Englishman, and came thither to trade with them by the way of marchandize, and therefore required licence for the same. Unto whom they made answere, that they were forbidden by the king to traffique with any forren nation, upon penaltie to forfeit their goods, therfore they desired him not to molest them any further, but to depart as he came, for other comfort he might not looke for at their handes, because they were subjects and might not goe beyond the law. But hee replied that his necessitie was such, as he might not so do: for being in one of the Queens Armadas of England, and having many souldiers in them, hee had neede both of some refreshing for them, and of victuals, and of money also, without the which hee coulde not depart, and with much other talke perswaded them not to feare any dishonest part of his behalfe towards them, for neither would hee commit any such thing to the dishonour of his prince, nor yet for his honest reputation and estimation, unlesse hee were too rigorously dealt withall, which hee hoped not to finde at their handes, in that it should be well redound to their profite as his owne, and also hee thought they might doe it without danger, because their princes were in amitie one with another, and for our parts wee had free traffique in Spain and Flanders, which are in his dominions, and therefore he knew no reason why he should not have the like in all his dominions. To the which the Spaniards made answere, that it lay not in them to give any licence, for that they had a governour to whom the government of those parts was committed, but if they would stay tenne dayes, they would send to their governour who was threescore leagues off, and would returne answere within the space appointed, of his minde.

In the meane time they were contented hee should bring his ships into harbour, and there they would deliver him any victuals he would require. Whereupon the fourth day we went in, where being one day and receiving all things according to promise, the Captaine advised himselfe, that to remaine there tenne dayes idle, spending victuals and mens wages, and perhaps in the ende receive no good answere from the governour, it were meere follie, and therefore determined to make request to have licence for the sale of certaine leane and sicke Negros which hee had in his shippe like to die upon his hands if he kept them ten dayes, having little or no refreshing for them, whereas other men having them, they would bee recovered well ynough. And this request hee was forced to make, because he had not otherwise wherewith to pay for victuals & for necessaries which he should take: which request being put in writing and presented, the officers and townedwellers assembled together, and finding his request so reasonable, granted him licence for thirtie Negros, which afterwards they caused the officers to view, to the intent they should graunt to nothing but that were very reasonable, for feare of answering thereunto afterwards. This being past, our Captaine according to their licence, thought to have made sale, but the day past and none came to buy, who before made shewe that they had great neede of them, and therefore wist not what to surmise of them, whether they went about to prolong the time of the Governour his answere because they would keepe themselves blamelesse, or for any other pollicie hee knew not, and for that purpose sent them worde, marveiling what the matter was that none came to buy them. They answered, because they had granted licence onely to the poore to buy those Negros of small price, and their money was not so ready as other mens of more wealth. More then that, as soone as ever they sawe the shippes, they conveyed away their money by their wives that went into the mountaines for feare, & were not yet returned, & yet asked two dayes to seeke their wives and fetch their money. Notwithstanding, the next day divers of them came to cheapen, but could not agree of price, because they thought the price too high. Whereupon the Captaine perceiving they went about to bring downe the price, and meant to buy, and would not confesse if hee had licence, that he might sell at any reasonable rate, as they were worth in other places, did send for the principals of the Towne, and made a shewe hee would depart, declaring himselfe to be very sory that he had so much troubled them, and also that he had sent for the governour to come downe, seeing nowe his pretence was to depart, whereat they marveiled much, and asked him what cause mooved him thereunto, seeing by their working he was in possibilitie to have his licence.

To the which he replied, that it was not onely a licence that he sought, but profit, which he perceived was not there to bee had, and therefore would seeke further, and withall shewed him his writings what he payed for his Negros, declaring also the great charge he was at in his shipping, and mens wages, and therefore to countervaile his charges, hee must sell his Negros for a greater price then they offered. So they doubting his departure, put him in comfort to sell better there then in any other place. And if it fell out that he had no licence that he should not loose his labour in tarying, for they would buy without licence. Whereupon, the Captaine being put in comfort, promised them to stay, so that hee might make sale of his leane Negros, which they granted unto. And the next day did sell some of them, who having bought and payed for them, thinking to have had a discharge of the Customer, for the custome of the Negros, being the Kings duetie, they gave it away to the poore for Gods sake, and did refuse to give the discharge in writing, and the poore not trusting their wordes, for feare, least hereafter it might bee demaunded of them, did refraine from buying any more, so that nothing else was done untill the Governours comming downe, which was the fourteenth day, and then the Captaine made petition, declaring that hee was come thither in a shippe of the Queenes Majesties of England, being bound to Guinie, and thither driven by winde and weather, so that being come thither, hee had neede of sundry necessaries for the reparation of the said Navie, and also great need of money for the paiment of his Souldiours, unto whom hee had promised paiment, and therefore, although hee would, yet would not they depart without it, &

for that purpose he requested licence for the sale of certaine of his Negros, declaring that although they were forbidden to traffique with strangers, yet for that there was a great amitie betweene their princes, and that the thing perteined to our Queenes highnesse, he thought hee might doe their prince great service, and that it would bee well taken at his hands, to doe it in this cause. The which allegations with divers others put in request, were presented unto the Governour, who sitting in counsell for that matter, granted unto his request for licence. But yet there fell out another thing which was the abating of the Kings Custome, being upon every slave 30. duckets, which would not be granted unto.

Whereupon the Captaine perceiving that they would neither come neere his price hee looked for by a great deale, nor yet would abate the Kings Custome of that they offered, so that either hee must be a great looser by his wares, or els compell the officers to abate the same Kings Custome which was too unreasonable, for to a higher price hee coulde not bring the buyers; Therefore the sixteenth of April hee prepared one hundred men well armed with bowes, arrowes, harquebuzes and pikes, with the which hee marched to the townewards, and being perceived by the Governour, he straight with all expedition sent messengers to knowe his request, desiring him to march no further forward untill he had answere againe, which incontinent he should have. So our Captaine declaring how unreasonable a thing the Kings Custome was, requested to have the same abated, and to pay seven and a halfe per centum, which is the ordinarie Custome for wares through his dominions there, and unto this if they would not graunt, hee would displease them. And this word being caried to the Governour, answere was returned that all things should bee to his content, and thereupon hee determined to depart, but the souldiers and Mariners finding so little credite in their promises, demanded gages for the performance of the premisses, or els they would not depart. And thus they being constrained to send gages, wee departed, beginning our traffique, and ending the same without disturbance.

Thus having made traffique in the harborough untill the 28. our Captaine with his ships intended to goe out of the roade, and purposed to make shew of his departure, because nowe the common sort having imployed their money, the rich men were come to towne, who made no shew that they were come to buy, so that they went about to bring downe the price, and by this pollicie the Captaine knew they would be made the more eager, for feare least we departed, and they should goe without any at all.

The nine and twentie wee being at ancker without the road, a French ship called the Greene Dragon of Newhaven, whereof was Captaine one Bon Temps came in, who saluted us after the maner of the Sea, with certaine pieces of Ordinance, and we resaluted him with the like againe: with whom having communication, he declared that hee had bene at the Mine in Guinie, and was beaten off by the Portugals gallies, and inforced to come thither to make sale of such wares as he had: and further that the like was happened unto the Minion: besides the Captaine Davie Carlet and a Marchant, with a dozen Mariners betrayed by the Negros at their first arrivall

thither, and remayning prisoners with the Portugals; and besides other mis-
adventures of the losse of their men, happened through the great lacke of
fresh water, with great doubts of bringing home the ships: which was
most sorrowfull for us to understand.

Thus having ended our traffique here the 4. of May, we departed, leaving the Frenchman behinde us, the night before the which the Caribes,
whereof I have made mention before, being to the number of 200. came in
their Canoas to Burboroata, intending by night to have burned the towne,
and taken the Spaniards, who being more vigilant because of our being
there, then their custome was, perceiving them comming, raised the towne,
who in a moment being a horsebacke, by meanes their custome is for all
doubts to keepe their horses ready sadled, in the night set upon them, &
tooke one, but the rest making shift for themselves, escaped away. But
this one, because he was their guide, and was the occasion that divers times
they had made invasion upon them, had for his traveile a stake thrust through
his fundament, and so out at his necke.

The sixt of May aforesaide, wee came to an yland called Curaçao, where
wee had thought to have anckered, but could not find ground, and having
let fal an ancker with two cables, were faine to weigh it againe: and the
seventh sayling along the coast to seeke an harborow, and finding none,
wee came to an ancker where we rode open in the Sea. In this place we
had traffique for hides, and found great refreshing both of beefe, mutton
and lambes, whereof there was such plentie, that saving the skinnes, we had
the flesh given us for nothing, the plentie whereof was so abundant, that
the worst in the ship thought scorne not onely of mutton, but also of
sodden lambe, which they disdained to eate unrosted.

The increase of cattell in this yland is marveilous, which from a doozen
of each sort brought thither by the governour, in 25. yeres he had a hundreth thousand at the least, & of other cattel was able to kill without spoile
of the increase 1500. yeerely, which hee killeth for the skinnes, and of the
flesh saveth onely the tongues, the rest hee leaveth to the foule to de-
voure. And this I am able to affirme, not onely upon the Governours owne
report, who was the first that brought the increase thither, which so re-
maineth unto this day, but also by that I saw my selfe in one field, where
an hundred oxen lay one by another all whole, saving the skinne and
tongue taken away. And it is not so marveilous a thing why they doe
thus cast away the flesh in all the ylands of the West Indies, seeing the
land is great, and more then they are able to inhabite, the people fewe,
having delicate fruites and meates ynough besides to feede upon, which
they rather desire, and the increase which passeth mans reason to beleeve
when they come to a great number: for in S. Domingo an yland called by
the finders thereof Hispaniola, is so great quantitie of cattell, and such increase therof, that notwithstanding the daily killing of them for their hides,
it is not possible to asswage the number of them, but they are devoured by
wilde dogs, whose number is such by suffering them first to range the
woods and mountaines, that they eate and destroy 60000. a yeere, and yet

small lacke found of them. And no marveile, for the said yland is almost as bigge as all England, and being the first place that was founde of all the Indies, and of long time inhabited before the rest, it ought therefore of reason to be most populous: and to this houre the Viceroy and counsell royall abideth there as in the chiefest place of all the Indies, to prescribe orders to the rest for the kings behalfe, yet have they but one Citie and 13. villages in all the same yland, whereby the spoile of them in respect of the increase is nothing.

The 15. of the foresaid moneth wee departed from Curaçao, being not a little to the rejoycing of our Captaine and us, that wee had there ended our trafique: but notwithstanding our sweete meate, wee had sower sauce, for by reason of our riding so open at sea, what with blastes whereby our anckers being a ground, three at once came home, and also with contrary windes blowing, whereby for feare of the shore we were faine to hale off to have anker-hold, sometimes a whole day and a night we turned up and downe; and this happened not once, but halfe a dozen times in the space of our being there.

The 16. wee passed by an yland called Aruba, and the 17. at night anckered sixe houres at the West ende of Cabo de la Vela, and in the morning being the 18. weighed againe, keeping our course, in the which time the Captaine sailing by the shore in the pinnesse, came to the Rancheria, a place where the Spaniards use to fish for pearles, and there spoke with a Spaniard, who tolde him how far off he was from Rio de la Hacha, which because he would not overshoot, he ankered that night againe, & the 19. came thither; where having talke with the kings treasurer of the Indies resident there, he declared his quiet trafique in Burboroata, & shewed a certificate of the same, made by the governour thereof, & therefore he desired to have the like there also: but the treasurer made answere that they were forbidden by the Viceroy and councill of S. Domingo, who having intelligence of our being on the coast, did sende expresse commission to resist us, with all the force they could, insomuch that they durst not trafique with us in no case, alleaging that if they did, they should loose all that they did trafique for, besides their bodies at the magistrates commaundement. Our Captaine replied, that hee was in an Armada of the Queenes Majesties of England, and sent about other her affaires, but driven besides his pretended voyage, was inforced by contrary windes to come into those parts, where he hoped to finde such friendship as hee should doe in Spaine, to the contrary whereof hee knewe no reason, in that there was amitie betwixt their princes. But seeing they would contrary to all reason go about to withstand his trafique, he would it should not be said by him, that having the force he hath, to be driven from his trafique perforce, but he would rather put it in adventure to try whether he or they should have the better, and therefore willed them to determine either to give him licence to trade, or else to stand to their owne harmes: So upon this it was determined hee should have licence to trade, but they would give him such a price as was the one halfe lesse than he had sold for before, and thus they sent word they would do, and none otherwise, and if it liked him not, he might do what he would, for they were not determined to deale otherwise with him. Whereupon, the captaine waying their unconscionable request, wrote to them a letter, that they dealt too rigorously with him, to go about to cut his throte in the price of his commodities, which were so reasonably rated, as they could not by a great deale have the like at any other mans handes. But seeing they had sent him this to his supper, hee would in the morning bring them as good a breakfast. And therefore in the morning being the 21. of May, hee shot off a whole Culvering to summon the towne, and preparing one hundred men in armour, went a shore, having in his great boate two Faulcons of brasse, and in the other boates double bases in their noses, which being perceived by the Townesmen, they incontinent in battell aray with their drumme and ensigne displayed, marched from the Towne to the sands, of footemen to the number of an hundred and fiftie, making great bragges with their cries, and weaving us a shore, whereby they made a semblance to have fought with us in deed. But our Captaine perceiving them so bragge, commanded the two Faulcons to be discharged at them, which put them in no small feare to see (as they afterward declared) such great pieces in a boate. At every shot they fell flat to the ground, and as wee approched neere unto them, they broke their aray, and dispersed themselves so much for feare of the Ordinance, that at last they went all away with their ensigne. The horsemen also being about thirtie, made as brave a shew as might be, coursing up and downe with their horses, their brave white leather Targets in the one hand, and their javelings in the other, as though they would have received us at our landing. But when wee landed, they gave ground, and consulted what they should doe, for little they thought wee would have landed so boldly: and therefore as the Captaine was putting his men in aray, and marched forward to have encountred with them, they sent a messenger on horsebacke with a flagge of truce to the Captaine, who declared that the Treasurer marveiled what he meant to doe to come a shore in that order, in consideration that they had granted to every reasonable request that he did demaund: but the Captaine not well contented with this messenger, marched forwards. The messenger prayed him to stay his men, and saide, if hee would come apart from his men, the Treasurer would come and speake with him, whereunto hee did agree to commune together. The Captaine onely with his armour without weapon, and the Treasurer on horsebacke with his javeling, was afraide to come neere him for feare of his armour, which he said was worse then his weapon, and so keeping aloofe communing together, granted in fine to all his requests. Which being declared by the Captaine to the company, they desired to have pledges for the performance of all things, doubting that otherwise when they had made themselves stronger, they would have bene at defiance with us: and seeing that now they might have what they would request, they judged it to be more wisedome to be in assurance then to be forced to make any more labours about it. So upon this, gages were sent, and we made our trafique quietly with them.

In the mean time while we stayed here, wee watered a good breadth off from the shore, where by the strength of the fresh water running into the Sea, the salt water was made fresh. In this River we saw many Crocodils of sundry bignesses, but some as bigge as a boate, with 4. feete, a long broad mouth, and a long taile, whose skinne is so hard, that a sword wil not pierce it. His nature is to live out of the water as a frogge doth, but he is a great devourer, and spareth neither fish, which is his common food, nor beastes, nor men, if hee take them, as the proofe thereof was knowen by a Negro, who as hee was filling water in the River was by one of them caried cleane away, and never seene after. His nature is ever when hee would have his prey, to cry and sobbe like a Christian body, to provoke them to come to him, and then hee snatcheth at them, and thereupon came this proverbe that is applied unto women when they weepe, Lachrymæ Crocodili, the meaning whereof is, that as the Crocodile when hee crieth, goeth then about most to deceive, so doeth a woman most commonly when she weepeth. Of these the Master of the Jesus watched one, and by the banks side stroke him with a pike of a bill in the side, and after three or foure times turning in sight, hee sunke downe, and was not afterward seene. In the time of our being in the Rivers Guinie, wee sawe many of a monstrous bignesse, amongst the which the Captaine being in one of the Barks comming downe the same, shot a Faulcon at one, which very narowly hee missed, and with a feare hee plunged into the water, making a streame like the way of a boate.

The 31. of May wee departed, keeping our course to Hispaniola, and the fourth of June wee had sight of an yland, which wee made to be Jamaica, marveiling that by the vehement course of the Seas we should be driven so farre to leeward: for setting our course to the West end of Hispaniola we fel with the middle of Jamaica, notwithstanding that to al mens sight it shewed a headland, but they were all deceived by the clouds that lay upon the land two dayes together, in such sort that we thought it to be the head land of the said yland. And a Spaniard being in the ship, who was a Marchant, and inhabitant in Jamaica, having occasion to go to Guinie, and being by treason taken of the Negros, & afterwards bought by the Tangomangos, was by our Captaine brought from thence, and had his passage to go into his countrey, who perceiving the land, made as though he knew every place thereof, and pointed to certaine places which he named to be such a place, and such a mans ground, and that behinde such a point was the harborow, but in the ende he pointed so from one point to another, that we were a leeboord of all places, and found our selves at the West end of Jamaica before we were aware of it, and being once to leeward, there was no getting up againe, so that by trusting of the Spaniards knowledge, our Captaine sought not to speake with any of the inhabitants, which if he had not made himselfe sure of, he would have done as his custome was in other places: but this man was a plague not onely to our Captaine, who made him loose by overshooting the place 2000. pounds by hides, which hee might have gotten, but also to himselfe, who being three yeeres out of his Countrey, and in great misery in Guinie, both among the Negros and Tangomangos, and in hope to come to his wife and friendes, as he made sure accompt, in that at his going into the pinnesse, when he went to shore he put on his new clothes, and for joy flung away his old, could not afterwards finde any habitation, neither there nor in all Cuba, which we sailed all along, but it fell out ever by one occasion or other, that wee were put beside the same, so that he was faine to be brought into England, and it happened to him as it did to a duke of Samaria, when the Israelites were besieged, and were in great misery with hunger, & being tolde by the Prophet Elizæus, that a bushell of flower should be sold for a sickle, would not beleeve him, but thought it unpossible: and for that cause Elizæus prophesied hee should see the same done, but hee should not eate thereof: so this man being absent three yeeres, and not ever thinking to have seene his owne Countrey, did see the same, went upon it, and yet was it not his fortune to come to it, or to any habitation, whereby to remaine with his friends according to his desire. . . .

On the 20. of June, wee fell with the West end of Cuba, called Cape S. Anthony, where for the space of three dayes wee doubled along, till wee came beyond the shoales, which are 20. leagues beyond S. Anthony. And the ordinary Brise taking us, which is the Northeast winde, put us the 24. from the shoare, and therefore we went to the Northwest to fetch wind, and also to the coast of Florida to have the helpe of the current, which was judged to have set to the Eastward: so the 29. wee found our selves in 27. degrees, and in the soundings of Florida, where we kept our selves the space of foure dayes, sailing along the coast as neere as we could, in tenne or twelve fadome water, having all the while no sight of land.

The fift of July we had sight of certeine Islands of sand, called the Tortugas (which is lowe land) where the captaine went in with his pinnesse, and found such a number of birds, that in halfe an houre he laded her with them; and if they had beene ten boats more, they might have done the like. These Islands beare the name of Tortoises, because of the number of them, which there do breed, whose nature is to live both in the water and upon land also, but breed onely upon the shore, in making a great pit wherein they lay egges, to the number of three or foure hundred, and covering them with sand, they are hatched by the heat of the Sunne; and by this meanes commeth the great increase. Of these we tooke very great ones, which have both backe and belly all of bone, of the thicknes of an inch: the fish whereof we proved, eating much like veale; and finding a number of egges in them, tasted also of them, but they did eat very sweetly. Heere wee ankered six houres, and then a faire gale of winde springing, we weyed anker, and made saile toward Cuba, whither we came the sixt day. We made account (as it was indeed) that Havana was but eight leagues to wind-ward, but by the perswasion of a French man, who made the captaine beleeve he knew, we unawares overshot Havana; at which place wee thought to have watered: but not knowing that wee had overshot the same, sailed along the coast, seeking it, and the eleventh day in the morning, by certeine knowen marks, we understood that we had overshot it 20 leagues: in which coast ranging, we found no convenient watering place, whereby there was no remedy but to disemboque, and to water upon the coast of Florida.

In ranging this coast along, the captaine found it to be all an Island, and therefore it is all lowe land, and very scant of fresh water, but the countrey was marvellously sweet, with both marish and medow ground, and goodly woods among. There they found sorell to grow as abundantly as grasse, and where their houses were, great store of maiz and mill, and grapes of great bignesse, but of taste much like our English grapes. Also Deere great plentie, which came upon the sands before them. Their houses are not many together, for in one house an hundred of them do lodge; they being made much like a great barne, and in strength not inferiour to ours, for they have stanchions and rafters of whole trees, and are covered with palmito-leaves, having no place divided, but one small roome for their king and queene. In the middest of this house is a hearth, where they make great fires all night, and they sleepe upon certeine pieces of wood hewen in for the bowing of their backs, and another place made high for their heads, which they put one by another all along the walles on both sides. In their houses they remaine onely in the nights, and in the day they desire the fields, where they dresse their meat, and make provision for victuals, which they provide onely for a meale from hand to mouth. There is one thing to be marvelled at, for the making of their fire, and not onely they but also the Negros doe the same, which is made onely by two stickes, rubbing them one against another: and this they may doe in any place they come, where they finde sticks sufficient for the purpose. In their apparell the men onely use deere skinnes, wherewith some onely cover their privy members, othersome use the same as garments to cover them before and behind; which skinnes are painted, some yellow and red, some blacke & russet, and every man according to his owne fancy. They do not omit to paint their bodies also with curious knots, or antike worke, as every man in his owne fancy deviseth, which painting, to make it continue the better, they use with a thorne to pricke their flesh, and dent in the same, whereby the painting may have better hold. In their warres they use a sleighter colour of painting their faces, thereby to make themselves shew the more fierce; which after their warres ended, they wash away againe. In their warres they use bowes and arrowes, whereof their bowes are made of a kind of Yew, but blacker then ours, and for the most part passing the strength of the Negros or Indians, for it is not greatly inferior to ours: their arrowes are also of a great length, but yet of reeds like other Indians, but varying in two points, both in length and also for nocks and feathers, which the other lacke, whereby they shoot very stedy: the heads of the same are vipers teeth, bones of fishes, flint stones, piked points of knives, which they have gotten of the French men, broke the same, & put the points of them in their arrowes head: some of them have their heads of silver, othersome that have want of these, put in a kinde of hard wood, notched, which pierceth as farre as any of the rest. In their fight, being in the woods, they use a marvellous pollicie for their owne safegard, which is by clasping a tree in their armes, and yet shooting notwithstanding: this policy they used with the French men in their fight, whereby it appeareth that they are people of some policy: and although they are called by the Spanyards Gente triste, that is to say, Bad people, meaning thereby, that they are not men of capacity: yet have the French men found them so witty in their answeres, that by the captaines owne report, a counseller with us could not give a more profound reason.

The women also for their apparell use painted skinnes, but most of them gownes of mosse, somewhat longer then our mosse, which they sowe together artificially, and make the same surplesse wise, wearing their haire downe to their shoulders, like the Indians. . . .

The ground yeeldeth naturally grapes in great store. . . . Also it yeeldeth roots passing good, Deere marvellous store, with divers other beasts, and fowle, serviceable to the use of man. These be things wherewith a man may live, having corne or maiz wherewith to make bread: for maiz maketh good savory bread, and cakes as fine as flowre. Also it maketh good meale, beaten and sodden with water, and eateth like pap wherewith we feed children. It maketh also good beverage, sodden in water, and nourishable; which the Frenchmen did use to drinke of in the morning, and it assuageth their thirst, so that they had no need to drinke all the day after. And this maiz was the greatest lacke they had, because they had no labourers to sowe the same, and therfore to them that should inhabit the land it were requisit to have labourers to till and sowe the ground: for they having victuals of their owne, whereby they neither rob nor spoile the inhabitants, may live not onely quietly with them, who naturally are more desirous of peace then of warres, but also shall have abundance of victuals profered them for nothing: for it is with them as it is with one of us, when we see another man ever taking away from us, although we have enough besides, yet then we thinke all too little for our selves: for surely we have heard the Frenchmen report, and I know it by the Indians, that a very little contenteth them: for the Indians with the head of maiz rosted, will travell a whole day, and when they are at the Spanyards finding, they give them nothing but sodden herbs & maiz: and in this order I saw threescore of them feed who were laden with wares, and came fifty leagues off. The Floridians when they travell, have a kinde of herbe dried, who with a cane and an earthen cup in the end, with fire, and the dried herbs put together, doe sucke thorow the cane the smoke thereof, which smoke satisfieth their hunger, and therwith they live foure or five dayes without meat or drinke, and this all the Frenchmen used for this purpose: yet do they holde opinion withall, that it causeth water & fleame to void from their stomacks. The commodities of this land are more then are yet knowen to any man: for besides the land it selfe, whereof there is more then any king Christian is able to inhabit, it flourisheth with medow, pasture ground, with woods of

Cedar and Cypres, and other sorts, as better can not be in the world. They have for apothecary herbs, trees, roots and gummes great store, as Storax liquida, Turpintine, Gumme, Myrrhe, and Frankinsence, with many others, whereof I know not the names. Colours both red, blacke, yellow, & russet, very perfect, wherewith they so paint their bodies, and Deere skinnes which they weare about them, that with water it neither fadeth away, nor altereth colour. Golde and silver they want not: for at the Frenchmens first comming thither they had the same offered them for little or nothing, for they received for a hatchet two pound weight of golde, because they knew not the estimation thereof: but the souldiers being greedy of the same, did take it from them, giving them nothing for it: the which they perceiving, that both the Frenchmen did greatly esteeme it, and also did rigorously deale with them, by taking the same away from them, at last would not be knowen they had any more, neither durst they weare the same for feare of being taken away: so that saving at their first comming, they could get none of them: and how they came by this golde and silver the French men know not as yet, but by gesse, who having travelled to the Southwest of the cape, having found the same dangerous, by meanes of sundry banks, as we also have found the same: and there finding masts which were wracks of Spanyards comming from Mexico, judged that they had gotten treasure by them. For it is most true that divers wracks have beene made of Spanyards, having much treasure: for the Frenchmen having travelled to the cape-ward an hundred and fiftie miles, did finde two Spanyards with the Floridians, which they brought afterward to their fort, whereof one was in a caravel comming from the Indies, which was cast away fourteene yeeres ago, & the other twelve yeeres; of whose fellowes some escaped, othersome were slain by the inhabitants. It seemeth they had estimation of their golde & silver, for it is wrought flat and graven, which they weare about their neckes; othersome made round like a pancake, with a hole in the midst, to boulster up their breasts withall, because they thinke it a deformity to have great breasts. As for mines either of gold or silver, the Frenchmen can heare of none they have upon the Island, but of copper, whereof as yet also they have not made the proofe, because they were but few men: but it is not unlike, but that in the maine where are high hilles, may be golde and silver as well as in Mexico, because it is all one maine. The Frenchmen obteined pearles of them of great bignesse, but they were blacke, by meanes of rosting of them, for they do not fish for them as the Spanyards doe, but for their meat: for the Spanyards use to keepe dayly afishing some two or three hundred Indians, some of them that be of choise a thousand: and their order is to go in canoas, or rather great pinnesses, with thirty men in a piece, whereof the one halfe, or most part be divers, the rest doe open the same for the pearles: for it is not suffered that they should use dragging, for that would bring them out of estimation, and marre the beds of them. The oisters which have the smallest sort of pearles are found in seven or eight fadome water, but the greatest in eleven or twelve fadome.

The Floridians have pieces of unicornes hornes which they weare about their necks, whereof the Frenchmen obteined many pieces. Of those unicornes they have many; for that they doe affirme it to be a beast with one horne, which comming to the river to drinke, putteth the same into the water before he drinketh. Of this unicornes horne there are of our company, that having gotten the same of the Frenchmen, brought home thereof to shew. It is therfore to be presupposed that there are more commodities aswell as that, which for want of time, and people sufficient to inhabit the same, can not yet come to light: but I trust God will reveale the same before it be long, to the great profit of them that shal take it in hand. Of beasts in this countrey besides deere, foxes, hares, polcats, conies, owraces, & leopards, I am not able certeinly to say: but it is thought that there are lions and tygres as well as unicornes; lions especially; if it be true that is sayd, of the enmity betweene them and the unicornes: for there is no beast but hath his enemy, as the cony the polcat, a sheepe the woolfe, the elephant the rinoceros; and so of other beasts the like: insomuch, that whereas the one is, the other can not be missing. And seeing I have made mention of the beasts of this countrey, it shall not be from my purpose to speake also of the venimous beasts, as crocodiles, whereof there is great abundance, adders of great bignesse, whereof our men killed some of a yard and a halfe long. Also I heard a miracle of one of these adders, upon the which a faulcon seizing, the sayd adder did claspe her tail about her; which the French captaine seeing, came to the rescue of the faulcon, and tooke her slaying the adder; and this faulcon being wilde, he did reclaim her, and kept her for the space of two moneths, at which time for very want of meat he was faine to cast her off. On these adders the Frenchmen did feed, to no little admiration of us, and affirmed the same to be a delicate meat. And the captaine of the Frenchmen saw also a serpent with three heads and foure feet, of the bignesse of a great spaniell, which for want of a harquebuz he durst not attempt to slay. Of fish also they have in the river, pike, roch, salmon, trout, and divers other small fishes, and of great fish, some of the length of a man and longer, being of bignesse accordingly, having a snout much like a sword of a yard long. There be also of sea fishes, which we saw comming along the coast flying, which are of the bignesse of a smelt, the biggest sort whereof have foure wings, but the other have but two: of these wee sawe comming out of Guinea a hundred in a company, which being chased by the gilt-heads, otherwise called the bonitos, do to avoid them the better, take their flight out of the water, but yet are they not able to flie farre, because of the drying of their wings, which serve them not to flie but when they are moist, and therefore when they can flie no further they fall into the water, and having wet their wings, take a new flight againe. These bonitos be of bignesse like a carpe, and in colour like a makarell, but it is the swiftest fish in swimming that is, and followeth her prey very fiercely, not onely in the water, but also out of the water: for as the flying fish taketh her flight, so doeth this bonitio leape after them, and taketh them sometimes above the water. There were some of those bonitos, which being galled by a fisgig, did follow our shippe comming out of Guinea

500. leagues. There is a sea-fowle also that chaseth this flying fish aswell as the bonito: for as the flying fish taketh her flight, so doth this fowle pursue to take her, which to beholde is a greater pleasure then hawking, for both the flights are as pleasant, and also more often then an hundred times: for the fowle can flie no way, but one or other lighteth in her pawes, the number of them are so abundant. There is an innumerable yoong frie of these flying fishes, which commonly keepe about the ship, and are not so big as butter-flies, and yet by flying do avoid the unsatiablenesse of the bonito. Of the bigger sort of these fishes wee tooke many, which both night and day flew into the sailes of our ship, and there was not one of them which was not woorth a bonito: for being put upon a hooke drabling in the water, the bonito would leap thereat, and so was taken. Also, we tooke many with a white cloth made fast to a hooke, which being tied so short in the water, that it might leape out and in, the greedie bonito thinking it to be a flying fish leapeth thereat, and so is deceived. We tooke also dolphins which are of very goodly colour and proportion to behold, and no lesse delicate in taste. Fowles also there be many, both upon land and upon sea: but concerning them on the land I am not able to name them, because my abode was there so short. But for the fowle of the fresh rivers, these two I noted to be the chiefe, whereof the Flemengo is one, having all red feathers, and long red legs like a herne, a necke according to the bill, red, whereof the upper neb hangeth an inch over the nether; and an egript, which is all white as the swanne, with legs like to an hearnshaw, and of bignesse accordingly, but it hath in her taile feathers of so fine a plume, that it passeth the estridge his feather. Of the sea-fowle above all other not common in England, I noted the pellicane, which is fained to be the lovingst bird that is; which rather than her yong should want, wil spare her heart bloud out of her belly: but for all this lovingnesse she is very deformed to beholde; for she is of colour russet: notwithstanding in Guinea I have seene of them as white as a swan, having legs like the same, and a body like a hearne, with a long necke, and a thick long beake, from the nether jaw whereof downe to the breast passeth a skinne of such a bignesse, as is able to receive a fish as big as ones thigh, and this her big throat and long bill doeth make her seem so ougly.

Here I have declared the estate of Florida, and the commodities therein to this day knowen, which although it may seeme unto some, by the meanes that the plenty of golde and silver, is not so abundant as in other places, that the cost bestowed upon the same will not be able to quit the charges: yet am I of the opinion, that by that which I have seene in other Islands of the Indians, where such increase of cattell hath bene, that of twelve head of beasts in five & twenty yeeres, did in the hides of them raise a thousand pound profit yerely, that the increase of cattell onely would raise profit sufficient for the same: for wee may consider, if so small a portion did raise so much gaines in such short time, what would a greater do in many yeres? and surely I may this affirme, that the ground of the Indians for the breed of cattell, is not in any point to be compared to this of Florida, which all the yeere long is so greene, as any time in the Summer with us: which surely is not to be marvelled at, seeing the countrey standeth in so watery a climate: for once a day without faile they have a shower of raine; which by meanes of the countrey it selfe, which is drie, and more fervent hot then ours, doeth make all things to flourish therein. And because there is not the thing we all seeke for, being rather desirous of present gaines, I doe therefore affirme the attempt thereof to be more requisit for a prince, who is of power able to go thorow with the same, rather then for any subject.

From thence wee departed the 28 of July, upon our voyage homewards, having there all things as might be most convenient for our purpose: and tooke leave of the Frenchmen that there still remained, who with diligence determined to make as great speede after, as they could. Thus by meanes of contrary windes oftentimes, wee prolonged our voyage in such manner that victuals scanted with us, so that we were divers times (or rather the most part) in despaire of ever comming home, had not God of his goodnesse better provided for us, then our deserving. In which state of great miserie, wee were provoked to call upon him by fervent prayer, which mooved him to heare us, so that we had a prosperous winde, which did set us so farre shot, as to be upon the banke of Newfound land, on Saint Bartholomews eve, and we sounded therupon, finding ground at an hundred and thirty fadoms, being that day somewhat becalmed, and tooke a great number of fresh codde-fish, which greatly relieved us: and being very glad thereof, the next day we departed, and had lingring little gales for the space of foure or five dayes, at the ende of which we sawe a couple of French shippes, and had of them so much fish as would serve us plentifully for all the rest of the way, the Captaine paying for the same both golde and silver, to the just value thereof, unto the chiefe owners of the saide shippes, but they not looking for any thing at all, were glad in themselves to meete with such good intertainement at sea, as they had at our hands. After which departure from them, with a good large winde the twentieth of September we came to Padstow in Cornewall, God be thanked, in safetie, with the losse of twentie persons in all the voyage, and with great profit to the venturers of the said voyage, as also to the whole realme, in bringing home both golde, silver, Pearles and other jewels great store. His name therefore be praised for evermore. Amen.

The names of certaine Gentlemen that were in this voyage.

M. John Hawkins.
M. John Chester, { sir William Chesters sonne.
M. Anthony Parkhurst.
M. Fitzwilliam.
M. Thomas Woorley.
M. Edward Lacie, { with divers others.

{ The Register and true accounts of all herein expressed hath beene approved by me John Sparke the younger, who went upon the same voyage, and wrote the same.

THIRD VOYAGE

The third troublesome voyage made with the Jesus of Lubeck, the Minion, and foure other ships, to the parts of Guinea, and the West Indies, in the yeeres 1567 and 1568 by M. John Hawkins.

THE ships departed from Plimmouth, the second day of October, Anno 1567 and had reasonable weather untill the seventh day, at which time fortie leagues North from Cape Finister, there arose an extreme storme, which continued foure dayes, in such sort, that the fleete was dispersed, and all our great boats lost, and the Jesus our chiefe shippe, in such case, as not thought able to serve the voyage: whereupon in the same storme we set our course homeward, determining to give over the voyage: but the eleventh day of the same moneth, the winde changed with faire weather, whereby we were animated to followe our enterprise, and so did, directing our course with the Ilands of the Canaries, where according to an order before prescribed, all our shippes before dispersed, met at one of those Ilands, called Gomera, where we tooke water, and departed from thence the fourth day of November, towards the coast of Guinea, and arrived at Cape Verde, the eighteenth of November: where we landed 150 men, hoping to obtaine some Negros, where we got but fewe, and those with great hurt and damage to our men, which chiefly proceeded of their envenomed arrowes: and although in the beginning they seemed to be but small hurts, yet there hardly escaped any that had blood drawen of them, but died in strange sort, with their mouthes shut some tenne dayes before they died, and after their wounds were whole; where I my selfe had one of the greatest woundes, yet thankes be to God, escaped. From thence we past the time upon the coast of Guinea, searching with all diligence the rivers from Rio Grande, unto Sierra Leona, till the twelfth of Januarie, in which time we had not gotten together a hundreth and fiftie Negros: yet notwithstanding the sicknesse of our men, and the late time of the yeere commanded us away: and thus having nothing wherewith to seeke the coast of the West Indias, I was with the rest of our company in consultation to goe to the coast of the Mine, hoping there to have obtained some golde for our wares, and thereby to have defraied our charge. But even in that present instant, there came to us a Negro, sent from a king, oppressed by other Kings his neighbours, desiring our aide, with promise that as many Negros as by these warres might be obtained, aswell of his part as of ours, should be at our pleasure: whereupon we concluded to give aide, and sent 120 of our men, which the 15 of Januarie, assaulted a towne of the Negros of our Allies adversaries, which had in it 8000 Inhabitants, being very strongly impaled and fenced after their manner, but it was so well defended, that our men prevailed not, but lost sixe men and fortie hurt: so that our men sent forthwith to me for more helpe: whereupon considering that the good successe of this enterprise might highly further the commoditie of our voyage, I went my selfe, and with the helpe of the king of our side, assaulted the towne, both by land and sea, and very hardly with fire (their houses being covered with dry Palme leaves) obtained the towne, put the Inhabitants to flight, where we tooke 250 persons, men, women, & children, and by our friend the king of our side, there were taken 600 prisoners, whereof we hoped to have had our choise: but the Negro (in which nation is seldome or never found truth) meant nothing lesse: for that night he remooved his campe and prisoners, so that we were faine to content us with those few which we had gotten our selves.

Now had we obtained between foure and five hundred Negros, wherwith we thought it somewhat reasonable to seeke the coast of the West Indies, and there, for our Negros, and other our merchandize, we hoped to obtaine, whereof to countervaile our charges with some gaines, wherunto we proceeded with all diligence, furnished our watering, tooke fuell, and departed the coast of Guinea the third of Februarie, continuing at the sea with a passage more hard, then before hath bene accustomed till the 27 day of March, which day we had sight of an Iland, called Dominica, upon the coast of the West Indies, in fourteene degrees: from thence we coasted from place to place, making our traffike with the Spaniards as we might, somewhat hardly, because the king had straightly commanded all his Governors in those parts, by no meanes to suffer any trade to be made with us: notwithstanding we had reasonable trade, and courteous entertainement, from the Ile of Margarita unto Cartagena, without any thing greatly worth the noting, saving at Capo de la Vela, in a towne called Rio de la Hacha (from whence come all the pearles) the treasurer who had the charge there, would by no meanes agree to any trade, or suffer us to take water, he had fortified his towne with divers bulwarkes in all places where it might be entered, and furnished himselfe with an hundred Hargabuziers, so that he thought by famine to have inforced us to have put a land our Negros: of which purpose he had not greatly failed, unlesse we had by force entred the towne: which (after we could by no meanes obtaine his favour) we were enforced to doe, and so with two hundred men brake in upon their bulwarkes, and entred the towne with the losse onely of two men of our partes, and no hurt done to the Spaniards because after their voley of shot discharged, they all fled.

Thus having the town with some circumstance, as partly by the Spaniards desire of Negros, and partly by friendship of the Treasurer, we obtained a secret trade: whereupon the Spaniards resorted to us by night, and bought of us to the number of 200 Negros: in all other places where we traded the Spaniards inhabitants were glad of us and traded willingly.

At Cartagena the last towne we thought to have seene on the coast, we could by no meanes obtaine to deale with any Spaniard, the governour was so straight, and because our trade was so neere finished we thought not good either to adventure any landing, or to detract further time, but in peace departed from thence the 24 of July, hoping to have escaped the time of their stormes which then soone after began to reigne, the which they call Furicanos, but passing by the West end of Cuba, towards the coast of Florida there happened to us the 12 day of August an extreme storme which continued by the space of foure dayes, which so beat the Jesus, that we cut downe all her higher buildings, her rudder also was sore shaken, and withall was in so extreme a leake that we were rather upon the point to leave her then to keepe her any longer, yet hoping to bring all to good passe, we sought the coast of Florida, where we found no place nor Haven for our ships, because of the shalownesse of the coast: thus being in greater dispaire, and taken with a newe storme which continued other 3 days, we were inforced to take for our succour the Port which serveth the citie of Mexico called Saint John de Ullua, which standeth in 19 degrees: in seeking of which Port we tooke in our way 3 ships which carried passengers to the number of an hundred, which passengers we hoped should be a meane to us the better to obtaine victuals for our money, & a quiet place for the repairing of our fleete. Shortly after this the 16 of September we entered the Port of Saint John de Ullua and in our entrie the Spaniardes thinking us to be the fleete of Spaine, the chiefe officers of the Countrey came aboord us, which being deceived of their expectation were greatly dismayed: but immediately when they sawe our demand was nothing but victuals, were recomforted. I found also in the same Port twelve ships which had in them by report two hundred thousand pound in gold & silver, all which (being in my possession, with the kings Iland as also the passengers before in my way thitherward stayed) I set at libertie, without the taking from them the waight of a groat: onely because I would not be delayed of my dispatch, I stayed two men of estimation and sent post immediately to Mexico, which was two hundred miles from us, to the Presidentes and Councell there, shewing them of our arrivall there by the force of weather, and the necessitie of the repaire of our shippes and victuals, which wantes we required as friends to king Philip to be furnished of for our money: and that the Presidents and Councell there should with all convenient speede take order, that at the arrivall of the Spanish fleete, which was dayly looked for, there might no cause of quarrell rise beweene us and them, but for the better maintenance of amitie, their commandement might be had in that behalfe. This message being sent away the sixteenth day of September at night, being the very day of our arrivall, in the next morning which was the seventeenth day of the same moneth, we sawe open of the Haven thirteene great shippes, and understanding them to bee the fleete of Spaine, I sent immediatly to advertise the Generall of the fleete of my being there, doing him to understand, that before I would suffer them to enter the Port, there should some order of condiions passe betweene us for our safe being there, and maintenance of peace. Now it is to be understood that this Port is made by a little Iland of stones not three foote above the water in the highest place, and but a bowshoot of length any way, this Iland standeth from the maine land two bow shootes or more, also it is to be understood that there is not in all this coast any other place for ships to arrive in safety, because the North winde hath there such violence, that unlesse the shippes be very safely mored with their ankers fastened upon this Iland, there is no remedie for these North windes but death: also the place of the Haven was so little, that of necessitie the shippes must ride one aboord the other, so that we could not give place to them, nor they to us: and here I beganne to bewaile that which after followed, for now, said I, I am in two dangers, and forced to receive the one of them. That was, either I must have kept out the fleete from entring the Port, the which with Gods helpe I was very able to doe, or else suffer them to enter in with their accustomed treason, which they never faile to execute, where they may have opportunitie, to compasse it by any meanes: if I had kept them out, then had there bene present shipwracke of all the fleete which amounted in value to sixe Millions, which was in value of our money 1800000. li. which I considered I was not able to answere, fearing the Queenes Majesties indignation in so waightie a matter. Thus with my selfe revolving the doubts, I thought rather better to abide the Jutt of the uncertainty, then the certaintie. The uncertaine doubt I account was their treason which by good policie I hoped might be prevented, and therefore as chusing the least mischiefe I proceeded to conditions. Now was our first messenger come and returned from the fleete with report of the arrivall of a Viceroy, so that hee had authoritie, both in all this Province of Mexico (otherwise called Nueva Espanna) and in the sea, who sent us word that we should send our conditions, which of his part should (for the better maintenance of amitie between the Princes) be both favourably granted, and faithfully performed, with many faire wordes how passing the coast of the Indies he had understood of our honest behaviour towardes the inhabitants where we had to doe, aswell elsewhere as in the same Port, the which I let passe: thus following our demand, we required victuals for our money, and licence to sell as much ware as might furnish our wants, and that there might be of either part twelve gentlemen as hostages for the maintenance of peace: and that the Iland for our better safetie might be in our owne possession, during our abode there, and such ordinance as was planted in the same Iland which were eleven peeces of brasse: and that no Spaniard might land in the Iland with any kind of weapon: these conditions at the first he somewhat misliked, chiefly the guard of the Iland to be in our owne keeping, which if they had had, we had soone knowen our fare: for with the first North winde they had cut our cables and our ships had gone ashore: but in the ende he concluded to our request, bringing the twelve hostages to ten, which with all speede of either part were received, with a writing from the Viceroy signed with his hande and sealed with his seale of all the conditions concluded, & forthwith a trumpet blowen with commandement that none of either part should be meane to violate the peace upon paine of death: and further it was concluded that the two Generals of the fleetes should meete, and give faith ech to other for the performance of the premisses which was so done. Thus at the end of 3 dayes all was concluded & the fleete entered the Port, saluting one an-other as the maner of the sea doth require. Thus as I said before, thursday we entred the Port, Friday we saw the fleete, and on munday at night they entered the Port: then we laboured 2. daies placing the English ships by themselves & the Spanish ships by themselves, the captaines of ech part & inferiour men of their parts promising great amity of al sides: which even as with all fidelitie it was ment on our part, so the Spaniards ment nothing lesse on their parts, but from the maine land had furnished themselves with a supply of men to the number of 1000, and ment the next thursday being the 23 of September at dinner time to set upon us on all sides. The same Thursday in the morning the treason being at hand, some appearance shewed, as shifting of weapon from ship to ship, planting and bending of ordinance from the ships to the Iland where our men warded, passing too and fro of companies of men more then required for their necessary busines, & many other ill likelihoods, which caused us to have a vehement suspition, and therewithall sent to the Viceroy to enquire what was ment by it, which sent immediatly straight commandement to unplant all things suspicious, and also sent word that he in the faith of a Viceroy would be our defence from all villanies. Yet we being not satisfied with this answere, because we suspected a great number of men to be hid in a great ship of 900 tunnes, which was mored next unto the Minion, sent againe to the Viceroy the master of the Jesus which had the Spanish tongue, and required to be satisfied if any such thing were or not. The Viceroy now seeing that the treason must be discovered, foorthwith stayed our master, blew the Trumpet, and of all sides set upon us: our men which warded a shore being stricken with sudden feare, gave place, fled, and sought to recover succour of the ships; the Spaniardes being before provided for the purpose landed in all places in multitudes from their ships which they might easily doe without boates, and slewe all our men a shore without mercie, a fewe of them escaped aboord the Jesus. The great ship which had by the estimation three hundred men placed in her secretly, immediatly fell aboord the Minion, but by Gods appointment, in the time of the suspicion we had, which was onely one halfe houre, the Minion was made readie to avoide, and so leesing her hedfasts, and hayling away by the sternefastes she was gotten out: thus with Gods helpe she defended the violence of the first brunt of these three hundred men. The Minion being past out, they came aboord the Jesus, which also with very much a doe and the losse of manie of our men were defended and kept out. Then there were also two other ships that assaulted the Jesus at the same instant, so that she had hard getting loose, but yet with some time we had cut our head-fastes and gotten out by the sterne-fastes. Nowe when the Jesus and the Minion were gotten about two shippes length from the Spanish fleete, the fight beganne so hotte on all sides that within one houre the Admirall of the Spaniards was supposed to be sunke, their Viceadmirall burned and one other of their principall ships supposed to be sunke, so that the shippes were little able to annoy us.

Then it is to be understood, that all the Ordinance upon the Ilande was in the Spaniardes handes, which did us so great annoyance, that it cut all the mastes and yardes of the Jesus, in such sort that there was no hope to carrie her away: also it sunke our small shippes, wereupon we determined to place the Jesus on that side of the Minion, that she might abide all the batterie from the land, and so be a defence for the Minion till night, and then to take such reliefe of victuall and other necessaries from the Jesus, as the time would suffer us, and to leave her. As we were thus determining, and had placed the Minion from the shot of the land, suddenly the Spaniards had fired two great shippes which were comming directly with us, and having no meanes to avoide the fire, it bredde among our men a marvellous feare, so that some sayd, let us depart with the Minion, other said, let us see whither the winde will carrie the fire from us. But to be short, the Minions men which had alwayes their sayles in a readinesse, thought to make sure worke, and so without either consent of the Captaine or Master cut their saile, so that very hardly I was received into the Minion.

The most part of the men that were left alive in the Jesus, made shift and followed the Minion in a small boat, the rest which the little boate was not able to receive, were inforced to abide the mercie of the Spaniards (which I doubt was very little) so with the Minion only and the Judith (a small barke of 50 tunne) we escaped, which barke the same night forsooke us in our great miserie: we were now remooved with the Minion from the Spanish ships two bow-shootes, and there rode all that night: the next morning we recovered an Iland a mile from the Spaniardes, where there tooke us a North winde, and being left onely with two ankers and two cables (for in this conflict we lost three cables and two ankers) we thought alwayes upon death which ever was present, but God preserved us to a longer time.

The weather waxed reasonable, and the Saturday we set saile, and having a great number of men and little victuals our hope of life waxed lesse and lesse: some desired to yeeld to the Spaniards, some rather desired to obtaine a place where they might give themselves to the Infidels, and some had rather abide with a little pittance the mercie of God at Sea: so thus with many sorowful hearts we wandred in an unknowen Sea by the space of 14 days, till hunger inforced us to seek the land, for hides were thought very good meat, rats, cats, mice and dogs, none escaped that might be gotten, parrats and monkeyes that were had in great price, were thought there very profitable if they served the turne one dinner: thus in the end the 8 day of October we came to the land in the botome of the same bay of Mexico in 23 degrees and a halfe, where we hoped to have found inhabitants of the Spaniards, reliefe of victuals, and place for the repaire of our ship, which was so sore beaten with shot from our enemies and brused with shooting off our owne ordinance, that our wearie and weake armes were scarce able to defende and keepe out water. But all things happened to the contrary, for we found neither people, victuall, nor haven of reliefe, but a place where having faire weather with some perill we might land a boat: our people being forced with hunger desired to be set on land, whereunto I consented.

And such as were willing to land I put them apart, and such as were desirous to goe homewardes, I put apart, so that they were indifferently parted a hundred of one side and a hundred of the other side: these hundred men we set a land with all diligence in this little place beforesaid, which being landed, we determined there to take in fresh water, and so with our little remaine of victuals to take the sea.

The next day having a land with me fiftie of our hundreth men that remained for the speedier preparing of our water aboord, there arose an extreame storme, so that in three days we could by no meanes repaire aboord our ship: the ship also was in such perill that every houre we looked for shipwracke.

But yet God againe had mercie on us, and sent faire weather, we had aboord our water, and departed the sixteenth day of October, after which day we had faire and prosperous weather till the sixteenth day of November, which day God be praysed we were cleere from the coast of the Indies, and out of the chanell and gulfe of Bahama, which is betweene the Cape of Florida, and the Ilandes of Lucayo. After this growing neere to the colde countrey, our men being oppressed with famine, died continually, and they that were left, grew into such weakenesse that we were scantly able to manage our shippe, and the winde being alwayes ill for us to recover England, we determined to goe with Galicia in Spaine, with intent there to relieve our companie and other extreame wantes. And being arrived the last day of December in a place neere unto Vigo called Ponte Vedra, our men with excesse of fresh meate grew into miserable disseases, and died a great part of them. This matter was borne out as long as it might be, but in the end although there were none of our men suffered to goe a land, yet by accesse of the Spaniards, our feeblenesse was knowen to them. Whereupon they ceased not to seeke by all meanes to betray us, but with all speede possible we departed to Vigo, where we had some helpe of certaine English ships and twelve fresh men, wherewith we repaired our wants as we might, and departing the 20 day of January 1568 arrived in Mounts bay in Cornewall the 25 of the same moneth, praised be God therefore.

If all the miseries and troublesome affaires of this sorowfull voyage should be perfectly and thoroughly written, there should neede a painefull man with his pen, and as great a time as he had that wrote the lives and deathes of the Martyrs.

JOHN HAWKINS.

CHAPTER VI

Martin Frobisher—1535?—1594

Captain Martin Frobisher was born in Yorkshire, England. Like Hawkins, he had engaged in the traffic of slaves, though not so profitably, before he was fired with the ambition to discover a Northwest passage from Europe to Asia. For years he tried to secure the means of carrying out this project. Finally, in 1576, under the patronage of the Earl of Warwick, he set sail for the New World. Among other things, he hoped to establish English colonies along the Pacific coast of America. He thought he had succeeded in his search for the mysterious Northwest Passage and hurried back to England with the news, hoping to return the following year better equipped for a longer expedition. But from this first voyage he brought back with him a curious black stone which, upon investigation, was found to contain gold. Consequently, his second and third voyages evolved into a search for gold, and the original enterprise was virtually abandoned. The inadvertent possession of this small stone proved disastrous to Frobisher's dream, but nevertheless he is recognized as one of the great English navigators. The following record of his three voyages is written by George Best, a member of the expedition.

THREE VOYAGES—1576, 1577, & 1578

First Voyage

A true discourse of the three Voyages of discoverie, for the finding of a passage to Cathaya, by the Northwest, under the conduct of Martin Frobisher, Generall. Penned by Master George Best, a Gentleman employed in the same voyages. . . .

GENERALL captaine Frobisher . . . is thorowly furnished of the knowledge of the sphere and all other skilles appertaining to the arte of navigation, as also for the confirmation he hath of the same by many yeres experience both by sea and land, and being persuaded of a new and nerer passage to Cataya then by Capo de buona Sperança, which the Portugals yerely use: he began first with himselfe to devise, and then with his friends to conferre, and layed a plaine plat unto them that that voyage was not onely possible by the Northwest, but also he could prove easie to be performed. And further, he determined and resolved with himselfe to go make full proofe thereof, and to accomplish or bring true certificate of the truth, or els never to re- turne againe, knowing this to be the only thing of the world that was left yet undone, whereby a notable minde might be made famous and fortunate. But although his will were great to performe this notable voyage, whereof he had conceived in his minde a great hope by sundry sure reasons and secret intelligence, which here for sundry causes I leave untouched, yet he wanted altogether meanes and ability to set forward, and performe the same. Long time he conferred with his private friends of these secrets, and made also many offers for the performing of the same in effect unto sundry merchants of our countrey above 15 yeres before he attempted the same, as by good witnesse shall well appeare (albeit some evill willers which challenge to themselves the fruits of other mens labours have greatly in- jured him in the reports of the same, saying that they have bene the first authours of that action, and that they have learned him the way, which themselves as yet have never gone) but perceiving that hardly he was hearkened unto of the merchants, which never regard vertue without sure, certaine, and present gaines, he repaired to the Court (from whence, as from the fountaine of our Common wealth, all good causes have their chiefe in- crease and maintenance) and there layed open to many great estates and learned men the plot and summe of his device. And amongst many honour- able minds which favoured his honest and commendable enterprise, he was specially bound and beholding to the right honourable Ambrose Dudley earle of Warwicke, whose favourable minde and good disposition hath al- wayes bene ready to countenance and advance all honest actions with the authours and executers of the same: and so by meanes of my lord his hon- ourable countenance he received some comfort of his cause, and by litle and litle, with no small expense and paine brought his cause to some per- fection, and had drawen together so many adventurers and such summes of money as might well defray a reasonable charge to furnish himselfe to sea withall.

He prepared two small barks of twenty and five and twenty tunne a piece, wherein he intended to accomplish his pretended voyage. Wherefore, being furnished with the foresayd two barks, and one small pinnesse of ten tun burthen, having therein victuals and other necessaries for twelve moneths provision, he departed upon the sayd voyage from Blacke-wall the 15 of June anno Domini 1576.

One of the barks wherein he went was named The Gabriel, and the other The Michael; and sailing Northwest from England upon the 11 of July he had sight of an high and ragged land, which he judged to be Fris- land (whereof some authors have made mention) but durst not approch the same by reason of the great store of ice that lay alongst the coast, and the great mists that troubled them not a litle. Not farre from thence he lost company of his small pinnesse, which by meanes of the great storme he supposed to be swallowed up of the Sea, wherein he lost onely foure men.

Also the other barke named The Michael mistrusting the matter, conveyed themselves privily away from him, and returned home, with great report that he was cast away.

The worthy captaine notwithstanding these discomforts, although his mast was sprung, and his toppe mast blowen overboord with extreame foule weather, continued his course towards the Northwest, knowing that the sea at length must needs have an ending, & that some land should have a beginning that way; and determined therefore at the least to bring true proofe what land and sea the same might be so farre to the Northwestwards, beyond any man that hath heretofore discovered. And the twentieth of July he had sight of an high land, which he called Queene Elizabeths Forland, after her Majesties name. And sailing more Northerly alongst that coast, he descried another forland with a great gut, bay, or passage, divided as it were two maine lands or continents asunder. There he met with store of exceeding great ice all this coast along, and coveting still to continue his course to the Northwards, was alwayes by contrary winde deteined overthwart these straights, and could not get beyond. Within few dayes after he perceived the ice to be well consumed and gone, either there ingulfed in by some swift currents or indrafts, carried more to the Southwards of the same straights, or els conveyed some other way: wherefore he determined to make proofe of this place, to see how farre that gut had continuance, and whether he might carry himselfe thorow the same into some open sea on the backe side, whereof he conceived no small hope, and so entred the same the one and twentieth of July, and passed above fifty leagues therein, as he reported, having upon either hand a great maine or continent. And that land upon his right hand as he sailed Westward he judged to be the continent of Asia, and there to be divided from the firme of America, which lieth upon the left hand over against the same.

This place he named after his name, Frobishers streights, like as Magellanus at ye Southwest end of the world, having discovered the passage to the South sea (where America is divided from the continent of that land, which lieth under the South pole) and called the same straights, Magellanes straits.

After he had passed 60 leagues into this foresayd straight, he went ashore, and found signes where fire had bene made.

He saw mighty deere that seemed to be mankinde, which ranne at him, and hardly he escaped with his life in a narrow way, where he was faine to use defence and policy to save his life.

In this place he saw and perceived sundry tokens of the peoples resorting thither. And being ashore upon the top of a hill, he perceived a number of small things fleeting in the sea afarre off, which he supposed to be porposes or seales, or some kinde of strange fish; but comming neerer, he discovered them to be men in small boats made of leather. And before he could descend downe from the hill, certaine of those people had almost cut off his boat from him, having stollen secretly behinde the rocks for that purpose, where he speedily hasted to his boat, and bent himselfe to his halberd, and narrowly escaped the danger, and saved his boat. Afterwards he had sundry conferences with them, and they came aboord his ship, and brought him salmon and raw flesh and fish, and greedily devoured the same before our mens faces. And to shew their agility, they tried many masteries upon the ropes of the ship after our mariners fashion, and appeared to be very strong of their armes, and nimble of their bodies. They exchanged coats of seales, and beares skinnes, and such like, with our men; and received belles, looking glasses, and other toyes, in recompense thereof againe. After great curtesie, and many meetings, our mariners, contrary to their captaines direction, began more easily to trust them; and five of our men going ashore were by them intercepted with their boat, and were never since heard of to this day againe: so that the captaine being destitute of boat, barke, and all company, had scarsely sufficient number to conduct backe his barke againe. He could now neither convey himselfe ashore to rescue his men (if he had bene able) for want of a boat; and againe the subtile traitours were so wary, as they would after that never come within our mens danger. The captaine notwithstanding desirous to bring some token from thence of his being there, was greatly discontented that he had not before apprehended some of them: and therefore to deceive the deceivers he wrought a pretty policy; for knowing wel how they greatly delighted in our toyes, and specially in belles, he rang a pretty lowbell, making signes that he would give him the same that would come and fetch it. And because they would not come within his danger for feare, he flung one bell unto them, which of purpose he threw short, that it might fall into the sea and be lost. And to make them more greedy of the matter he rang a louder bell, so that in the end one of them came nere the ship side to receive the bell; which when he thought to take at the captaines hand, he was thereby taken himselfe: for the captaine being readily provided let the bell fall, and caught the man fast, and plucked him with maine force boat and all into his barke out of the sea. Whereupon when he found himselfe in captivity, for very choler and disdaine he bit his tongue in twaine within his mouth: notwithstanding, he died not thereof, but lived untill he came in England, and then he died of cold which he had taken at sea.

Now with this new pray (which was a sufficient witnesse of the captaines farre and tedious travell towards the unknowen parts of the world, as did well appeare by this strange infidell, whose like was never seene, read, nor heard of before, and whose language was neither knowen nor understood of any) the sayd captaine Frobisher returned homeward, and arrived in England in Harwich the 2 of October following, and thence came to London 1576, where he was highly commended of all men for his great and notable attempt, but specially famous for the great hope he brought of the passage to Cataya.

And it is especially to be remembred that at their first arrivall in those parts there lay so great store of ice all the coast along so thicke together, that hardly his boat could passe unto the shore. At length, after divers attempts he commanded his company, if by any possible meanes they could get ashore, to bring him whatsoever thing they could first finde, whether it were living or dead, stocke or stone, in token of Christian possession, which thereby he tooke in behalfe of the Queenes most excellent Majesty, thinking that thereby he might justify the having and injoying of the same things that grew in these unknowen parts.

Some of his company brought floures, some greene grasse; and one brought a piece of blacke stone much like to a sea cole in colour, which by the waight seemed to be some kinde of metall or minerall. This was a thing of no account in the judgement of the captaine at the first sight; and yet for novelty it was kept in respect of the place from whence it came.

After his arrivall in London, being demanded of sundry his friends what thing he had brought them home out of that countrey, he had nothing left to present them withall but a piece of this blacke stone. And it fortuned a gentlewoman one of the adventurers wives to have a piece therof, which by chance she threw and burned in the fire, so long, that at the length being taken forth, and quenched in a litle vinegar, it glistered with a bright marquesset of golde. Whereupon the matter being called in some question, it was brought to certaine Goldfiners in London to make assay thereof, who gave out that it held golde, and that very richly for the quantity. Afterwards, the same Goldfiners promised great matters thereof if there were any store to be found, and offered themselves to adventure for the searching of those parts from whence the same was brought. Some that had great hope of the matter sought secretly to have a lease at her Majesties hands of those places, whereby to injoy the masse of so great a publike profit unto their owne private gaines.

In conclusion, the hope of more of the same golde ore to be found kindled a greater opinion in the hearts of many to advance the voyage againe. Whereupon preparation was made for a new voyage against the yere following, and the captaine more specially directed by commission for the searching more of this golde ore then for the searching any further discovery of the passage. And being well accompanied with divers resolute and forward gentlemen, her Majesty then lying at the right honourable the lord of Warwicks house in Essex, he came to take his leave, and kissing her hignesse hands, with gracious countenance & comfortable words departed toward his charge.

SECOND VOYAGE

A true report of such things as happened in the second voyage of captaine Frobisher, pretended for the discovery of a new passage to Cataya, China and the East India, by the Northwest. Ann. Dom. 1577.

BEING furnished with one tall ship of her Majesties, named The Ayde, of two hundred tunne, and two other small barks, the one named The Gabriel, the other The Michael, about thirty tun a piece, being fitly appointed with men, munition, victuals, and all things necessary for the voyage, the sayd captaine Frobisher, with the rest of his company came aboord his ships riding at Blackwall, intending (with Gods helpe) to take the first winde and tide serving him, the 25 day of May, in the yere of our Lord God 1577.

On Whitsunday being the 26 of May, Anno 1577, early in the morning, we weighed anker at Blackwall, and fell that tyde downe to Gravesend, where we remained untill Monday at night.

On munday morning the 27 of May, aboord the Ayde we received all the Communion by the Minister of Gravesend, and prepared us as good Christians towards God, and resolute men for all fortunes: and towards night we departed to Tilbery Hope.

Tuesday the eight and twenty of May, about nine of the clocke at night, we arrived at Harwitch in Essex and there stayed for the taking in of certaine victuals, untill Friday being the thirtieth of May, during which time came letters from the Lordes of the Councell, straightly commanding our Generall, not to exceede his complement and number appointed him, which was, one hundred and twentie persons: whereupon he discharged many proper men which with unwilling mindes departed.

He also dismissed all his condemned men, which he thought for some purposes very needefull for the voyage, and towards night upon Friday the one and thirtieth of May we set saile, and put to the Seas againe. And sayling Northward alongst the East coasts of England and Scotland, the seventh day of June we arrived in Saint Magnus sound in Orkney Ilands, called in latine Orcades.

After we had provided us here of matter sufficient for our voyage the eight of June wee set sayle againe, and passing through Saint Magnus sound having a merrie winde by night, came cleare and lost sight of all the land, and keeping our course West Northwest by the space of two dayes, the winde shifted upon us so that we lay in traverse on the Seas, with contrary windes, making good (as neere as we could) our course to the westward, and sometime to the Northward, as the winde shifted. And hereabout we met with 3 saile of English fishermen from Iseland, bound homeward, by whom we wrote our letters unto our friends in England. We traversed these Seas by the space of 26 dayes without sight of any land, and met with much drift wood, & whole bodies of trees. We sawe many monsterous fishes and strange foules, which seemed to live onely by the Sea, being there so farre distant from any land. At length God favoured us with more prosperous windes, and after wee had sayled foure dayes with good winde in the Poop, the fourth of July the Michaell being formost a head shot off a peece of Ordinance, and stroke all her sayles, supposing that they descryed land which by reason of the thicke mistes they could not make perfit: howbeit, as well our account as also the great alteration of the water, which became more blacke and smooth, did plainely declare we were not farre off the coast. Our Generall sent his Master aboord the Michaell (who had beene with him the yeere before) to beare in with the place to make proofe thereof, who descryed not the land perfect, but sawe sundry huge Ilands of yce, which we deemed to be not past twelve leagues from the shore, for about tenne of the clocke at night being the fourth of July, the weather being more cleare, we made the land perfect and knew it to be Frislande.

Our Generall prooved landing here twice, but having spent foure dayes and nightes sayling alongst this land, finding the coast subject to such bitter colde and continuall mistes, he determined to spend no more time therein, but to beare out his course towardes the streightes called Frobishers streights after the Generals name, who being the first that ever passed beyond 58 degrees to the Northwardes, for any thing that hath beene yet knowen of certaintie of New found land, otherwise called the continent or firme lande land of America, discovered the saide straights this last yere 1576.

Betweene Frisland and the straights we had one great storme, wherein the Michaell was somewhat in danger, having her Stirrage broken, and her toppe Mastes blowen over boord, & being not past 50 leagues short of the straights by our account, we stroke sayle & lay a hull, fearing the continuance of the storme, the winde being at the Northeast, and having lost companie of the Barkes in that flaw of winde, we happily met again the seventeenth day of July, having the evening before seene divers Ilands of fleeting yce, which gave an argument that we were not farre from land. Our Generall in the morning from the maine top (the weather being reasonable cleare) descried land, but to be better assured he sent the two Barkes two contrarie courses, whereby they might discry either the South or North foreland, the Ayde lying off and on at Sea, with a small sayle by an Iland of yce, which was the marke for us to meete togither againe. And about noone, the weather being more cleare, we made the North forland perfite, which otherwise is called Halles Iland, and also the small Iland bearing the name of the sayde Hall whence the Ore was taken up which was brought into England this last yeere 1576 the said Hall being present at the finding & taking up thereof, who was then Maister in the Gabriell with Captaine Frobisher. At our arrivall here all the Seas about this coast were so covered over with huge quantitie of great yce, that we thought these places might onely deserve the name of Mare Glaciale, and be called the Isie Sea.

God having blessed us with so happie a land-fall, we bare into the straights which runne in next hand, and somewhat further up to the Northwarde, and came as neere the shore as wee might for the yce, and upon the eighteenth day of July our Generall taking the Goldfiners with him, attempted to goe on shore with a small rowing Pinnesse, upon the small Ilande where the Ore was taken up, to proove whether there were any store thereof to be found, but he could not get in all that Iland a peece so bigge as a Walnut, where the first was found. But our men which sought the other Ilands thereabouts found them all to have good store of the Ore, whereupon our Generall with these good tidings returned aboord about tenne of the clocke at night, and was joyfully welcommed of the company with a volie of shot. He brought egges, foules, and a young Seale aboord, which the companie had killed ashore, and having found upon those Ilands ginnes set to catch fowle, and stickes newe cut, with other things, he well perceived that not long before some of the countrey people had resorted thither.

Having therefore found those tokens of the peoples accesse in those parts, and being in his first voyage well acquainted with their subtill and cruell disposition, hee provided well for his better safetie, and on Friday the ninteenth of July in the morning early, with his best companie of Gentlemen and souldiers, to the number of fortie persons, went on shore, aswell to discover the Iland and habitation of the people, as also to finde out some fit harborowe for our shippes. And passing towardes the shoare with no small difficultie by reason of the abundance of yce which lay alongst the coast so thicke togither that hardly any passage through them might be discovered, we arrived at length upon the maine of Halles greater Iland, and found there also aswell as in the other small Ilands good store of the Ore. And leaving his boates here with sufficient guarde we passed up into the countrey about two English miles, and recovered the toppe of a high hill, on the top whereof our men made a Columne or Crosse of stones heaped up of a good heigth togither in good sort, and solemnely sounded a Trumpet, and saide certaine prayers kneeling about the Ensigne, and honoured the place by the name of Mount Warwicke, in remembrance of the Right Honorable the Lord Ambrose Dudley Earle of Warwick, whose noble mind and good countenance in this, as in all other good actions, gave great encouragement and good furtherance. This done, we retyred our companies not seeing any thing here worth further discoverie, the countrey seeming barren and full of ragged mountaines and in most parts covered with snow.

And thus marching towards our botes, we espied certaine of the countrey people on the top of Mount Warwick with a flag wafting us backe againe and making great noise, with cries like the mowing of Buls seeming greatly desirous of conference with us: whereupon the Generall being therewith better acquainted, answered them againe with the like cries, whereat and with the noise of our trumpets they seemed greatly to rejoyce, skipping, laughing and dancing for joy. And hereupon we made signes unto them, holding up two fingers, commanding two of our men to go apart from our companies, whereby they might do the like. So that forthwith two of our men & two of theirs met togither a good space from company, neither partie having their weapons about them. Our men gave them pins and points and such trifles as they had. And they likewise bestowed on our men two bow cases and such things as they had. They earnestly desired our men to goe up into their countrey, and our men offered them like kindnesse aboord our ships, but neither part (as it seemed) admitted or trusted the others curtesie. Their maner of traffique is thus, they doe use to lay downe of their marchandise upon the ground, so much as they meane to part withal, and so looking that the other partie with whom they make trade should doe the like, they themselves doe depart, and then if they doe like of their Mart they come againe, and take in exchange the others marchandise, otherwise if they like not, they take their owne and depart.

The day being thus well neere spent, in haste wee retired our companies into our boates againe, minding foorthwith to search alongst the coast for some harborow fit for our shippes, for the present necessitie thereof was much, considering that all this while they lay off and on betweene the two landes, being continually subject aswell to great danger of fleeting yce, which environed them, as to the sodaine flawes which the coast seemeth much subject unto. But when the people perceived our departure, with great tokens of affection they earnestly called us backe againe, following us almost to our boates: whereupon our Generall taking his Master with him, who was best acquainted with their maners, went apart unto two of them, meaning, if they could lay sure hold upon them, forcibly to bring them aboord, with intent to bestow certaine toyes and apparell upon the one, and so to dismisse him with all arguments of curtesie, and retaine the other for an Interpreter. The Generall and his Maister being met with their two companions togither, after they had exchanged certaine things the one with the other, one of the Salvages for lacke of better marchandise, cut off the tayle of his coat (which is a chiefe ornament among them) and gave it unto our Generall for a present. But he presently upon a watchword given with his Maister sodainely laid hold upon the two Salvages. But the ground underfoot being slipperie with the snow on the side of the hill, their handfast fayled and their prey escaping ranne away and lightly recovered their bow and arrowes, which they had hid not farre from them behind the rockes. And being onely two Salvages in sight, they so fiercely, desperately, and with such fury assaulted and pursued our Generall and his Master, being altogether unarmed, and not mistrusting their subtiltie that they chased them to their boates, and hurt the Generall in the buttocke with an arrow, who the rather speedily fled backe, because they suspected a greater number behind the rockes. Our souldiers (which were commanded before to keepe their boates) perceiving the danger, and hearing our men calling for shot came speedily to rescue, thinking there had bene a greater number. But when the Salvages heard the shot of one of our calivers (and yet having first bestowed their arrowes) they ranne away, our men speedily following them. But a servant of my Lorde of Warwick, called Nicholas Conger a good footman, and uncombred with any furniture having only a dagger at his backe overtooke one of them, and being a Cornishman and a good wrastler, shewed his companion such a Cornish tricke, that he made his sides ake against the ground for a moneth after. And so being stayed, he was taken alive and brought away, but the other escaped.

Thus with their strange and new prey our men repaired to their boates, and passed from the maine to a small Iland of a mile compasse, where they resolved to tarrie all night; for even now a sodaine storme was growen so great at sea, that by no meanes they could recover their ships. And here every man refreshed himselfe with a small portion of victuals which was laide into the boates for their dinners, having neither eate nor drunke all the day before. But because they knewe not how long the storme might last, nor how farre off the shippes might be put to sea, nor whether they should ever recover them againe or not, they made great spare of their victuals, as it greatly behoved them: For they knew full well that the best cheare the countrey could yeeld them, was rockes and stones, a hard food to live withall, and the people more readie to eate them then to give them wherewithall to eate. And thus keeping verie good watch and warde, they lay there all night upon hard cliffes of snow and yce both wet, cold, and comfortlesse.

These things thus hapning with the company on land, the danger of the ships at Sea was no lesse perilous. For within one houre after the Generals departing in the morning by negligence of the Cooke in over-heating, and the workman in making the chimney, the Ayde was set on fire, and had bene the confusion of the whole if by chance a boy espying it, it had not bene speedily with great labour and Gods helpe well extinguished.

This day also were diverse stormes and flawes, and by nine of the clocke at night the storme was growen so great, & continued such untill the morning, that it put our ships at sea in no small perill: for having mountaines of fleeting yce on every side, we went roomer for one, and loofed for another, some scraped us, and some happily escaped us, that the least of a M. were as dangerous to strike as any rocke, and able to have split asunder the strongest ship of the world. We had a scope of cleare without yce, (as God would) wherein we turned, being otherwise compassed on every side about: but so much was the winde and so litle was our sea roome, that being able to beare onely our forecourse we cast so oft about, that we made fourteene bordes in eight glasses running, being but foure houres: but God being our best Steresman, & by the industry of Charles Jackman and Andrew Dyer the masters mates, both very expert Mariners, & Richard Cox ye maister Gunner, with other very carefull sailers, then within bord, and also by the helpe of the cleare nights which are without darkenesse, we did happily avoide those present dangers, whereat since wee have more marvelled then in the present danger feared, for that every man within borde, both better and worse had ynough to doe with his hands to hale ropes, and with his eyes to looke out for danger. But the next morning being the 20 of July, as God would, the storme ceased, and the Generall espying the ships with his new Captive and whole company, came happily abord, and reported what had passed a shoare, whereupon altogither upon our knees we gave God humble and hartie thankes, for that it had pleased him, from so speedy peril to send us such speedy deliverance, and so from this Northerne shore we stroke over towards the Southerland.

The one and twentieth of July, we discovered a bay which ranne into the land, that seemed a likely harborow for our ships, wherefore our Generall rowed thither with his boats, to make proofe thereof, and with his goldfiners to search for Ore, having never assayed any thing on the South shore as yet, and the first small Iland which we landed upon. Here all the sands and clifts did so glister and had so bright a marquesite, that it seemed all to be gold, but upon tryall made, it proved no better than black-lead, and verified the proverbe. All is not gold that glistereth.

Upon a small Iland, within this sound called Smithes Iland (because he first set up his forge there) was found a Mine of silver, but was not wonne out of the rockes without great labour. Here our goldfiners made say of such Ore as they found upon the Northerland, and found foure sortes thereof to holde gold in good quantitie. Upon another small Iland here was also found a great dead fish, which as it should seeme, had bene embayed with yce, and was in proportion round like to a Porpose, being about twelve foote long, and in bignesse answerable, having a horne of two yardes long growing out of the snoute or nostrels. This horne is wreathed and straite, like in fashion to a Taper made of waxe, and may truely be thought to be the sea Unicorne. This horne is to be seene and reserved as a Jewell by the Queenes Majesties commandement, in her Wardrope of Robes.

Tuesday the three and twentieth of July, our Generall with his best company of gentlemen, souldiers and saylers, to the number of seventie persons in all, marched with ensigne displayde, upon the continent of the Southerland (the supposed continent of America) where, commanding a Trumpet to sound a call for every man to repaire to the ensigne, he declared to the whole company how much the cause imported for the service of her Majestie, our countrey, our credits, and the safetie of our owne lives, and therefore required every man to be conformable to order, and to be directed by those he should assigne. And he appointed for leaders, Captaine Fenton, Captaine Yorke, and his Lieutenant George Beste: which done, we cast our selves into a ring, and altogither upon our knees, gave God humble thanks for that it had pleased him of his great goodnesse to preserve us from such imminent dangers, beseeching likewise the assistance of his holy spirite, so to deliver us in safetie into our Countrey, whereby the light and truth of these secrets being knowen, it might redound to the more honour of his holy name, and consequently to the advancement of our common wealth. And so, in as good sort as the place suffered, we marched towards the tops of the mountaines, which were no lesse painfull in climbing then dangerous in descending, by reason of their steepnesse & yce. And having passed about five miles, by such unwieldie wayes, we returned unto our ships without sight of any people, or likelihood of habitation. Here diverse of the Gentlemen desired our Generall to suffer them to the number of twentie or thirtie persons to march up thirtie or fortie leagues in the countrey, to the end they might discover the Inland, and doe some acceptable service for their countrey. But he not contented with the matter he sought for, and well considering the short time he had in hand, and the greedie desire our countrey hath to a present savour and returne of gaine, bent his whole indevour only to find a Mine to fraight his ships, and to leave the rest (by Gods helpe) hereafter to be well accomplished.

The next flood toward the morning we weyed ancker, and went further up the straights . . . In one of the small Ilands here we found a Tombe, wherein the bones of a dead man lay together, and our savage Captive being with us, & being demanded by signes whether his countreymen had not slaine this man and eat his flesh so from the bones, he made signes to the contrary, and that he was slaine with Wolves and wild beasts. Here also was found hid under stones good store of fish, and sundry other things of the inhabitants; as sleddes, bridles, kettels of fish-skinnes, knives of bone, and such other like. And our Savage declared unto us the use of all those things. And taking in his hand one of those countrey bridles, he caught one of our dogges and hampred him handsomely therein, as we doe our horses, and with a whip in his hand, he taught the dogge to drawe in a sled as we doe horses in a coach, setting himselfe thereupon like a guide: so that we might see they use dogges for that purpose that we do our horses. And we found since by experience, that the lesser sort of dogges they feede fatte, and keepe them as domesticall cattell in their tents for their eating, and the greater sort serve for the use of drawing their sleds.

The twentie ninth of July, about five leagues from Beares sound, we discovered a Bay which being fenced on ech side with smal Ilands lying off the maine, which breake the force of the tides, and make the place free from any indrafts of yce, did proove a very fit harborow for our ships, where we came to ancker under a small Ilande, which now together with the sound is called by the name of that right Honourable and vertuous Ladie, Anne Countesse of Warwicke. And this is the furthest place that this yeere we have entred up within the streites, and is reckoned from the Cape of the Queenes foreland, which is the entrance of the streites not above 30 leagues. Upon this Iland was found good store of the Ore, which in the washing helde gold to our thinking plainly to be seene: where-upon it was thought best rather to load here, where there was store and indifferent good, then to seeke further for better, and spend time with jeoperdie. And therefore our Generall setting the Myners to worke, and shewing first a good president of a painefull labourer and a good Captaine in himselfe, gave good examples for others to follow him: whereupon every man both better and worse, with their best endevours willingly layde to their helping hands. And the next day, being the thirtieth of July, the Michaell was sent over to Jackmans sound, for the Ayde and the whole companie to come thither. Upon the maine land over against the Countesses Iland we discovered and behelde to our great marvell the poore caves and houses of those countrey people, which serve them (as it should seeme) for their winter dwellings, and are made two fadome under grounde, in compasse round, like to an Oven, being joyned fast one by another, hav-ing holes like to a Foxe or Conny berry, to keepe and come togither. They undertrenched these places with gutters so, that the water falling from the hilles above them, may slide away without their annoyance: and are seated commonly in the foote of a hill, to shield them better from the cold windes, having their doore and entrance ever open towards the South. From the ground upward they builde with whales bones, for lacke of timber, which bending one over another, are handsomely compacted in the top together, and are covered over with Sealesskinnes, which in stead of tiles, fence them from the raine. In which house they have only one roome, having the one halfe of the floure raised with broad stones a foot higher than ye other, whereon strawing Mosse, they make their nests to sleep in. They defile these dennes most filthily with their beastly feeding, & dwell so long in a place (as we thinke) untill their sluttishnes lothing them, they are forced to seeke a sweeter ayre, and a new seate, and are (no doubt) a dispersed and wandring nation, as the Tartarians, and live in hords and troupes, without any certaine abode, as may appeare by sundry circumstances of our experience.

Here our captive being ashore with us, to declare the use of such things as we saw, stayd himselfe alone behind the company, and did set up five small stickes round in a circle one by another, with one smal bone placed just in the middest of all: which thing when one of our men perceived, he called us backe to behold the matter, thinking that hee had meant some charme or witchcraft therein. But the best conjecture we could make thereof was, that hee would thereby his countreymen should understand, that for our five men which they betrayed the last yeere (whom he signified by the five stickes) he was taken and kept prisoner, which he signified by the bone in the midst. For afterwards when we shewed him the picture of his countreman, which the last yeere was brought into England (whose counterfeit we had drawen, with boate and other furniture, both as he was in his own, & also in English apparel) he was upon the sudden much amazed thereat, and beholding advisedly the same with silence a good while, as though he would streine courtesie whether should begin the speech (for he thought him no doubt a lively creature) at length began to question with him, as with his companion, and finding him dumb and mute, seemed to suspect him, as one disdeinfull, and would with a little helpe have growen into choller at the matter, untill at last by feeling and handling, hee found him but a deceiving picture. And then with great noise and cryes, ceased not wondring, thinking that we could make men live or die at our pleasure. . . .

The morning following being the first of August, Captaine Yorke with the Michael came into Jackmans sound, and declared unto the company there, that the last night past he came to anker in a certaine baye (which sithens was named Yorkes sound) about foure leagues distant from Jackmans sound, being put to leeward of that place for lacke of winde, where he discovered certaine tents of the countrey people, where going with his company ashore, he entred into them, but found the people departed, as it should seeme, for feare of their comming. But amongst sundry strange things which in these tents they found, there was rawe and new killed flesh of unknowen sorts, with dead carcasses and bones of dogs, and I know not what. They also beheld (to their greatest marveile) a dublet of Canvas made after the English fashion, a shirt, a girdle, three shoes for contrary feete, and of unequall bignesse, which they well conjectured to be the apparell of our five poore countreymen, which were intercepted the last yeere by these Countrey people, about fiftie leagues from this place, further within the Straights. Whereupon our men being in good hope, that some of them might be here, and yet living: the Captaine devising for the best left his mind behind him in writing, with pen, yncke, and paper also, whereby our poore captive countrymen, if it might come to their hands, might know their friends minds, and of their arrivall, and likewise returne their answere. And so without taking any thing away in their tents, leaving there also looking glasses, points, and other of our toyes (the better to allure them by such friendly meanes) departed aboord his Barke, with intent to make haste to the Aide, to give notice unto the company of all such things as he had there discovered: and so meant to returne to these tents againe, hoping that he might by force or policie intrappe or intice the people to some friendly conference. Which things when he had delivered to the whole company there, they determined forthwith to go in hand with the matter. Hereupon Captaine Yorke with the master of the Aide and his mate (who the night before had bene at the tents, and came over from the other side in the Michael with him) being accompanied with the Gentlemen and souldiers to the number of thirty or forty persons in two small rowing Pinnasses made towards the place, where the night before they discovered the tents of those people, and setting Charles Jackman, being the masters Mate, ashore with a convenient number, for that he could best guide them to the place, they marched over land, meaning to compasse them on the one side, whilest the Captaine with his boates might entrap them on the other side. But landing at last at the place where the night before they left them, they found them with their tents removed. Notwithstanding, our men which marched up into the countrey, passing over two or three mountaines, by chance espied certaine tents in a valley underneath them neere unto a creeke by the Sea side, which because it was not the place where the guide had bene the night before, they judged them to be another company, and besetting them about, determined to take them if they could. But they having quickly discried our companie, lanched one great & another smal boat, being about 16 or 18 persons, and very narrowly escaping, put themselves to sea. Wherupon our souldiers discharged their Calivers, and followed them, thinking the noise therof being heard to our boats at sea, our men there would make what speede they might to that place. And thereupon indeede our men which were in the boates (crossing upon them in the mouth of the sound whereby their passage was let from getting sea roome, wherein it had bene impossible for us to overtake them by rowing) forced them to put themselves ashore upon a point of land within the sayd sound (which upon the occasion of the slaughter there, was since named The bloody point) whereunto our men so speedily followed, that they had little leisure left them to make any escape. But so soone as they landed, ech of them brake his Oare, thinking by that meanes to prevent us, in carying away their boates for want of Oares. And desperately returning upon our men, resisted them manfully in their landing, so long as their arrowes and dartes lasted, and after gathering up those arrowes which our men shot at them, yea, and plucking our arrowes out of their bodies incountred afresh againe, and maintained their cause untill both weapons and life fayled them. And when they found they were mortally wounded, being ignorant what mercy meaneth, with deadly fury they cast themselves headlong from off the rockes into the sea, least perhaps their enemies should receive glory or prey of their dead carcaises, for they supposed us belike to be Canibals or eaters of mans flesh. In this conflict one of our men was dangerously hurt in the belly with one of their arrowes, and of them were slaine five or sixe, the rest by flight escaping among the rockes, saving two women, whereof the one being old and ugly, our men thought shee had bene a devill or some witch, and therefore let her goe: the other being yong, and cumbred with a sucking childe at her backe, hiding her selfe behind the rockes, was espied by one of our men, who supposing she had bene a man, shot through the haire of her head, and pierced through the childs arme, whereupon she cried out, and our Surgeon meaning to heale her childes arme, applyed salves thereunto. But she not acquainted with such kind of surgery, plucked those salves away, and by continuall licking with her owne tongue, not much unlike our dogs, healed up the childes arme. And because the day was welneere spent our men made haste unto the rest of our company which on the other side of the water remained at the tents, where they found by the apparell, letter, and other English furniture, that they were the same company which Captaine Yorke discovered the night before, having removed themselves from the place where he left them.

And now considering their sudden flying from our men, and their desperate maner of fighting, we began to suspect that we had heard the last newes of our men which the last yere were betrayed of these people. And considering also their ravenous and bloody disposition in eating any kind of raw flesh or carrion howsoever stinking, it is to bee thought that they had slaine and devoured our men: For the dublet which was found in their tents had many holes therein being made with their arrowes and darts.

But now the night being at hand, our men with their captives and such poore stuffe as they found in their tents, returned towards their ships, when being at sea, there arose a sudden flaw of winde, which was not a little dangerous for their small boates: but as God would they came all safely aboord. And with these good newes they returned (as before mentioned) into the Countesse of Warwicks sound unto us. And betweene Jackmans sound, from whence they came, and the Countesse of Warwicks sound betweene land and land, being thought the narrowest place of the Straights were judged nine leagues over at the least: and Jackmans sound being upon the Southerland, lyeth directly almost over against the Countesses sound, as is reckoned scarce thirty leagues within the Straights from the Queenes Cape, which is the entrance of the Streits of the Southerland. This Cape being named Queene Elizabeths Cape, standeth in the latitude of 62 degrees and a halfe to the Northwards of New found land, and upon the same continent, for any thing that is yet knowen to the contrary.

Having now got a woman captive for the comfort of our man, we brought them both together, and every man with silence desired to behold the maner of their meeting and entertainment, the which was more worth the beholding than can be well expressed by writing. At their first encountring they beheld each the other very wistly a good space, without speech or word uttered, with great change of colour and countenance, as though it seemed the griefe and disdeine of their captivity had taken away the use of their tongues and utterance: the woman at the first very suddenly, as though she disdeined or regarded not the man, turned away, and began to sing as though she minded another matter: but being againe brought together, the man brake up the silence first, and with sterne and stayed countenance, began to tell a long solemne tale to the woman, whereunto she gave good hearing, and interrupted him nothing, till he had finished, and afterwards, being growen into more familiar acquaintance by speech, they were turned together, so that (I thinke) the one would hardly have lived without the comfort of the other. And for so much as we could perceive, albeit they lived continually together, yet they did never use as man & wife, though the woman spared not to doe all necessary things that appertained to a good houswife indifferently for them both, as in making cleane their Cabin, and every other thing that appertained to his ease: for when he was seasicke, she would make him cleane, she would kill and flea the dogs for their eating, and dresse his meate. Only I thinke it worth the noting, the continencie of them both: for the man would never shift himselfe, except he had first caused the woman to depart out of his cabin, and they both were most shamefast, least any of their privie parts should be discovered, either of themselves, or any other body.

On Munday the sixth of August, the Lieutenant with all the Souldiers, for the better garde of the Myners and the other things a shore, pitched their tents in the Countesses Island, and fortifyed the place for their better defence as well as they could, and were to the number of forty persons, when being all at labour, they might perceive upon the top of a hill over against them a number of the countrey people wafting with a flag, and making great outcries unto them, and were of the same companie, which had encountred lately our men upon the other shore, being come to complaine their late losses, and to entreate (as it seemed) for restitution of the woman and child, which our men in the late conflict had taken and brought away; whereupon the Generall taking the savage captive with him, and setting the woman where they might best perceive her in the highest place of the Island, went over to talke with them. This captive at his first encounter of his friends fell so out into teares that he could not speake a word in a great space, but after a while, overcomming his kindnesse, he talked at full with his companions, and bestowed friendly upon them such toyes and trifles as we had given him, whereby we noted, that they are very kind one to another, and greatly sorrowfull for the losse of their friends. Our Generall by signes required his five men which they tooke captive the last yere, and promised them, not only to release those which he had taken, but also to reward them with great gifts and friendship. Our Savage made signes in answere from them that our men should be delivered us, and were yet living, and made signes likewise unto us that we should write our letters unto them, for they knew very well the use we have of writing, and received knowledge thereof, either of our poore captive countreymen which they betrayed, or else by this our new captive who hath seene us dayly write, and repeate againe such words of his language as we desired to learne: but they for this night, because it was late, departed without any letter, although they called earnestly in hast for the same. And the next morning early being the seventh of August, they called againe for the letter, which being delivered unto them, they speedily departed, making signes with three fingers, and pointing to the Sunne, that they meant to returne within 3 dayes, untill which time we heard no more of them, & about the time appointed they returned, in such sort as you shal afterwards heare.

This night because the people were very neere unto us, the Lieutenant caused the Trumpet to sound a call, and every man in the Island repayring to the Ensigne, he put them in minde of the place so farre from their countrey wherein they lived, and the danger of a great multitude which they were subject unto, if good watch and warde were not kept, for at every low water the enimie might come almost dryfoot from the mayne unto us, wherefore he willed every man to prepare him in good readinesse upon all sudden occasions, and so giving the watch their charge, the company departed to rest.

I thought the Captaines letter well worth the remembring, not for the circumstance of curious enditing, but for the substance and good meaning therein contained, and therefore have repeated here the same, as by himselfe it was hastily written.

The forme of M. Martin Frobishers letter to the English captives.

In the name of God, in whom we all beleeve, who (I trust) hath preserved your bodies and soules amongst these infidels, I commend me unto you. I will be glad to seeke by al means you can devise for your deliverance, either with force, or with any commodities within my ships, which I will not spare for your sakes, or any thing else I can doe for you. I have aboord, of theirs, a man, a woman, and a child, which I am contented to deliver for you, but the man which I caried away from hence the last yeere is dead in England. Moreover you may declare unto them, that if they deliver you not, I will not leave a man alive in their countrey. And thus, if one of you can come to speake with mee, they shall have either the man, woman, or childe in pawne for you. And thus unto God whom I trust you doe serve, in hast I leave you, and to him wee will dayly pray for you. This Tuesday morning the seventh of August. Anno 1557.

Yours to the uttermost of my power,
MARTIN FROBISHER.

I have sent you by these bearers, penne, ynke, and paper, to write backe unto me againe, if personally you cannot come to certifie me of your estate.

Now had the Generall altered his determination for going any further into the Streites at this time for any further discovery of the passage, having taken a man and a woman of that countrey, which he thought sufficient for the use of language: & having also met with these people here, which intercepted his men the last yere, (as the apparell and English furniture which was found in their tents, very well declared) he knew it was but a labour lost to seeke them further off, when he had found them there at hand. And considering also the short time he had in hand, he thought it best to bend his whole endevour for the getting of Myne, and to leave the passage further to be discovered hereafter. For his commission directed him in this voyage, onely for the searching of the Ore, and to deferre the further discovery of the passage untill another time.

THIRD VOYAGE

The third voyage of Captaine Frobisher, pretended for the discoverie of Cataia, by Meta Incognita, Anno Do. 1578.

THE Generall being returned from the second voyage, immediately after his arrivall in England, repaired with all hast to the Court being then at Windsore, to advertise her Majestie of his prosperous proceeding, and good successe in this last voyage, & of the plenty of gold Ore, with other matters of importance which he had in these Septentrionall parts discovered. He was courteously enterteyned, and hartily welcommed of many noble men, but especially for his great adventure, commended of her Majestie, at whose hands he received great thankes, and most gracious countenance, according to his deserts. Her Highnesse also greatly commended the rest of the Gentlemen in this service, for their great forwardnes in this so dangerous an attempt: but especially she rejoyced very much, that among them there was so good order of governement, so good agreement, every man so ready in his calling, to do whatsoever the General should command, which due commendation gratiously of her Majestie remembred, gave so great encouragement to all the Captaines and Gentlemen, that they, to continue her Highnesse so good and honourable opinion of them, have since neither spared labour, limme, nor life, to bring this matter (so well begun) to a happie and prosperous ende.

And finding that the matter of the golde Ore had appearance & made shew of great riches & profit, & the hope of the passage to Cataya, by this last voyage greatly increased, her Majestie appointed speciall Commissioners chosen for this purpose, gentlemen of great judgement, art, and skill, to looke thorowly, into the cause, for the true triall and due examination thereof, and for the full handling of all matters thereunto appertaining. And because that place and countrey hath never heretofore beene discovered, and therefore had no speciall name, by which it might be called and knowen, her Majestie named it very properly Meta Incognita, as a marke and bound utterly hitherto unknowen.

The commissioners after sufficient triall and proofe made of the Ore, and having understood by sundrie reasons, and substantiall grounds, the possibilitie and likelyhood of the passage, advertised her highnesse, that the cause was of importance, and the voyage greatly worthy to be advanced againe. Whereupon preparation was made of ships and all other things necessary, with such expedition, as the time of the yeere then required. And because it was assuredly made accompt of, that the commoditie of Mines, there already discovered, would at the least countervaile in all respects the adventurers charge, and give further hope & likelyhood of greater matters to follow. It was thought needfull, both for the better guard of those parts already found, and for further discovery of the Inland and secrets of those countreys, & also for further search of the passage to Cataya (whereof the hope continually more & more increaseth) that certaine numbers of chosen souldiers and discreet men for those purposes should be assigned to inhabite there. Whereupon there was a strong fort or house of timber, artificially framed, & cunningly devised by a notable learned man here at home, in ships to be caried thither, wherby those men that were appointed to winter & stay there the whole yere, might aswell bee defended from the danger of the snow and colde ayre, as also fortified from the force or offence of those countrey people, which perhaps otherwise with too great multitudes might oppresse them. And to this great adventure and notable exploit many well minded and forward yong Gentlemen of our countrey willingly have offered themselves.

First Captaine Fenton, Lieutenant generall for Captaine Frobisher, and in charge of the company with him there, Captaine Best, and Captaine Filpot, unto whose good discretions the government of that service was chiefly commended, who, as men not regarding peril in respect of the profit and common wealth of their countrey, were willing to abide the first brunt & adventure of those dangers among a savage and brutish kinde of people, in a place hitherto ever thought for extreme cold not habitable. The whole number of men which had offered, and were appointed to inhabite Meta Incognita all the yeere, were one hundreth persons, wherof 40 should be mariners for the use of ships, 30 Miners for gathering the gold Ore together for the next yere, and 30 souldiers for the better guard of the rest, within which last number are included the Gentlemen, Goldfiners, Bakers, Carpenters, & all necessary persons.

To each of the Captaines was assigned one ship, aswel for the further searching of the coast & countrey there, as for to returne & bring backe their companies againe, if the necessity of the place so urged, or by miscarying of the fleet the next yere, they might be disappointed of their further provision. Being therfore thus furnished with al necessaries, there were ready to depart upon the said voyage 15 saile of good ships, wherof the whole number was to returne again with their loding of gold Ore in the end of the sommer, except those 3 ships, which should be left for the use of those Captains which should inhabit there the whole yere. And be-

ing in so good readinesse, the Generall with all the Captaines came
Court, then lying at Greenwich, to take their leave of her Majesti
whose hands they all received great incouragement, and gracious coun
nance. Her highnesse besides other good gifts, and greater promises, bestowed on the Generall a faire chaine of golde, and the rest of the Captaines kissed her hand, tooke their leave, and departed every man towards
their charge.

Articles and orders to be observed for the Fleete, set downe by Captaine
  Frobisher Generall, and delivered in writing to every Captaine, as well
  for keeping company, as for the course, the 31 of May.

1 Inprimis, to banish swearing, dice, and card-playing, and filthy communication, and to serve God twice a day, with the ordinary service usuall
in Churches of England, and to cleare the glasse, according to the old
order of England.

2 The Admiral shall carie the light, & after his light be once put out,
no man to goe a head of him, but every man to fit his sailes to follow as
neere as they may, without endangering one another.

3 That no man shall by day or by night depart further from the Admirall then the distance of one English mile, and as neere as they may,
without danger one of another.

4 If it chance to grow thicke, and the wind contrary, either by day or
by night, that the Admirall be forced to cast about, before her casting
about shee shall give warning, by shooting off a peece, and to her shall
answere the Viceadmirall and the Rereadmirall each of them with a piece,
if it bee by night, or in a fogge; and that the Viceadmirall shall answere
first, and the Rereadmirall last.

5 That no man in the Fleete descrying any sayle or sayles, give upon
any occasion any chace before he have spoken with the Admirall.

6 That every evening all the Fleete come up and speake with the Admirall, at seven of the Clocke, or betweene that and eight, and if the
weather will not serve them all to speake with the Admirall, then some
shall come to the Viceadmirall, and receive the order of their course of
Master Hall chiefe Pilot of the Fleete, as he shall direct them.

7 If to any man in the Fleete there happen any mischance, they shall
presently shoote off two peeces by day, and if it be by night, two peeces,
and shew two lights.

8 If any man in the Fleete come up in the night, & hale his fellow
knowing him not, he shall give him this watch-word, Before the world
was God. The other shall answere him (if he be one of our Fleete), After
God came Christ his Sonne. So that if any be found amongst us, not of
our owne company, he that first descrieth any such sayle or sayles, shall
give warning to the Admirall by himselfe or any other that he can speake
to, that sailes better then he, being neerest unto him.

9 That every ship in the fleete in the time of fogs, which continually

winds, and most part calmes, shall keepe a reasonable
...t, drumme, or otherwise, to keepe themselves cleere one

...out so thicke or mistie that we lay it to hull, the Admirall
...arning with a piece, and putting out three lights one over an-
...he end that every man may take in his sailes, and at his setting
...s againe doe the like, if it be not cleere.

11 If any man discover land by night, that he give the like warning, that
he doth for mischances, two lights, and two pieces, if it be by day one piece,
and put out his flagge, and strike all his sailes he hath aboord.

12 If any ship shall happen to lose company by force of weather, then any
such ship or ships shall get her into the latitude of   , and so keepe that
latitude untill they get Frisland. And after they be past the West parts of
Frisland, they shall get them into the latitude of   , and   , and not to the
Northward of   ; and being once entred within the Streites, al such ships
shal every watch shoote off a good piece, and looke out well for smoke and
fire which those that get in first shall make every night, untill all the fleete
be come together.

13 That upon the sight of an Ensigne in the mast of the Admirall (a piece
being shot off) the whole fleete shall repaire to the Admirall, to understand
such conference as the Generall is to have with them.

14 If we chance to meete with any enemies, that foure ships shall attend
upon the Admirall, viz. the Francis of Foy, the Moone, the Barke Dennis,
and the Gabriel: and foure upon my Lieutenant generall in the Judith, viz.
the Hopewel, the Armenal, the Beare, and the Salomon: and the other foure
upon the Vizadmirall, the Anne Francis, the Thomas of Ipswich, the Em-
manuel, and the Michael.

15 If there happen any disordred person in the Fleete, that he be taken
and kept in safe custodie untill he may conveniently be brought aboord the
Admirall, and there to receive such punishment as his or their offences shall
deserve.

By me Martin Frobisher.

Our Departure from England

HAVING received these articles of direction we departed from Harwich the
one and thirtieth of May. And sayling along the South part of England
Westward, we at length came by the coast of Ireland at Cape Cleare the
sixth of June, and gave chase there to a small barke which was supposed to
be a Pyrat, or Rover on the Seas, but it fell out indeede that they were poore
men of Bristow, who had met with such company of Frenchmen as had
spoiled and slaine many of them, and left the rest so sore wounded that
they were like to perish in the sea, having neither hand nor foote hole to
helpe themselves with, nor victuals to sustaine their hungry bodies. Our
Generall, who well understood the office of a Souldier and an Englishman,
and knew well what the necessitie of the sea meaneth, pitying much the

miserie of the poore men, relieved them with Surgerie and salves to heale their hurtes, and with meate and drinke to comfort their pining hearts; some of them having neither eaten nor drunke more than olives and stinking water in many dayes before, as they reported. And after this good deede done, having a large wind, we kept our course upon our sayd voyage without staying for the taking in of fresh water, or any other provision, whereof many of the fleete were not throughly furnished: and sayling towards the Northwest parts from Ireland, we mette with a great current from out of the Southwest, which caried us (by our reckoning) one point to the Northeastwards of our sayd course, which current seemed to us to continue it selfe towards Norway, and other the Northeast parts of the world, whereby we may be induced to beleeve, that this is the same which the Portugals meete at Capo de buona Speranza, where striking over from thence to the Streites of Magellan, and finding no passage there for the narrownesse of the sayde Streites, runneth along into the great Bay of Mexico, where also having a let of land, it is forced to strike backe againe towards the Northeast, as we not onely here, but in another place, also, further to the Northwards, by good experience this yeere have found, as shalbe hereafter in his place more at large declared.

Now had we sayled about foureteene dayes, without sight of any land, or any other living thing, except certaine foules, as Wilmots, Nodies, Gulles, &c. which there seeme onely to live by sea.

We were forced many times to stemme and strike great rockes of yce, and so as it were make way through mighty mountaines. By which meanes some of the fleete, where they found the yce to open, entred in, and passed so farre within the danger thereof, with continuall desire to recover their port, that it was the greatest wonder of the world that they ever escaped safe, or were ever heard of againe. For even at this present we missed two of the fleete, that is, the Judith, wherein was the Lieutenant generall Captaine Fenton; and the Michael, whom both we supposed had bene utterly lost, having not heard any tidings of them in moe than 20 dayes before.

And one of our fleete named the Barke Dennis, being of an hundreth tunne burden, seeking way in amongst these yce, received such a blow with a rocke of yce that she sunke downe therewith in the sight of the whole fleete. Howbeit having signified her danger by shooting off a peece of great Ordinance, new succour of other ships came so readily unto them, that the men were all saved with boats.

Within this ship that was drowned there was parcell of our house which was to bee erected for them that should stay all the winter in Meta Incognita.

This was a more fearefull spectacle for the Fleete to beholde, for that the outragious storme which presently followed, threatned them the like fortune and danger. For the Fleete being thus encompassed (as aforesayd) on every side with yce, having left much behind them, thorow which they passed, and finding more before them, thorow which it was not possible to passe, there arose a sudden terrible tempest at the Southeast, which blowing from

the maine sea, directly upon the place of the Streites, brought together all
the yce a sea-boorde of us upon our backes, and thereby debard us of turning backe to recover sea-roome againe: so that being thus compassed with
danger on every side, sundry men with sundry devises sought the best way
to save themselves. Some of the ships, where they could find a place more
cleare of yce, and get a little birth of sea roome, did take in their sayles, and
there lay a drift. Other some fastened & mored Anker upon a great Island
of yce, and roade under the Lee therof, supposing to be better guarded
thereby from the outragious winds, and the danger of the lesser fleeting yce.
And againe some where so fast shut up, and compassed in amongst an infinite number of great countreys and Islands of yce, that they were faine to
submit themselves and their ships to the mercy of the unmercifull yce, and
strengthened the sides of their ships with junckes of cables, beds, Mastes,
plankes and such like, which being hanged over boord on the sides of their
ships, might the better defend them from the outragious sway and strokes
of the said yce. But as in greatest distresse, men of best valour are best to
bee discerned, so it is greatly worthy commendation and noting with what
invincible minde every Captaine encouraged his company, and with what
incredible labour the painefull Mariners and poore Miners (unacquainted
with such extremities) to the everlasting renowne of our nation, did over-
come the brunt of these so great and extreme dangers: for some, even without boord upon the yce, and some within boord upon the sides of their
ships, having poles, pikes, pieces of timber, and Ores in their handes, stoode
almost day and night without any rest, bearing off the force, and breaking
the sway of the yce with such incredible paine and perill, that it was wonderful to beholde. . . .

The seventh of July as men nothing yet dismayed, we cast about towards
the inward, and had sight of land, which rose in forme like the Northerland
of the straights, which some of the Fleete, and those not the worst Mariners,
judged to be the North Foreland, howbeit other some were of contrary
opinion. But the matter was not well to be discerned by reason of the thicke
fogge which a long time hung upon the coast, & the new falling snow which
yeerely altereth the shape of the land, and taketh away oftentimes the
Mariners markes. And by reason of the darke mists which continued by the
space of twentie dayes togither, this doubt grewe the greater and the longer
perilous.

But whilest the Fleete lay thus doubtfull amongst great store of yce in a
place they knew not without sight of Sunne, whereby to take the height,
and so to know the true elevation of the pole, and without any cleere of
light to make perfite the coast, the Generall with the Captaines and Masters
of his ships, began doubtfully to question of the matter. But Christopher Hall
chiefe Pilot of the voyage delivered a plaine and publique opinion in the
hearing of the whole Fleete, that hee had never seene the foresayd coast
before, and that he could not make it for any place of Frobishers Streits, as
some of the Fleete supposed, and yet the landes doe lie and trend so like,
that the best Mariners therein may bee deceived. . . .

The Generall albeit with the first perchance he found out the error, and that this was not the olde straights, yet he perswaded the Fleete alwayes that they were in their right course, and knowen straights. Howbeit I suppose he rather dissembled his opinion therein then otherwise, meaning by that policie (being himselfe led with an honourable desire of further discoverie) to induce the Fleete to follow him, to see a further proofe of that place. And as some of the companie reported, he hath since confessed that if it had not bene for the charge and care he had of the Fleete and fraughted ships, he both would and could have gone through to the South Sea, called Mar del Sur, and dissolved the long doubt of the passage which we seeke to find to the rich countrey of Cataya.

Our men that sayled furthest in the same mistaken straights (having the maine land upon their starboord side) affirme that they met with the outlet or passage of water which commeth thorow Frobishers straights, and followeth as all one into this passage.

Some of our companie also affirme that they had sight of a continent upon their larboord-side being 60 leagues within the supposed straights: howbeit except certaine Ilands in the entrance hereof we could make no part perfect thereof. All the foresaid tract of land seemeth to be more fruitfull and better stored of Grasse, Deere, Wild foule, as Partridges, Larkes, Seamewes, Guls, Wilmots, Falcons and Tassel gentils, Ravens, Beares, Hares, Foxes, and other things, than any other part we have yet discovered, and is more populous. And here Luke Ward, a Gentleman of the companie, traded marchandise, and did exchange knives, bels, looking glasses, &c. with those countrey people, who brought him foule, fish, beares skinnes, and such like, as their countrey yeeldeth for the same. Here also they saw of those greater boats of the countrey, with twentie persons in a peece.

Now after the Generall had bestowed these many dayes here, not without many dangers, he returned backe againe. And by the way sayling alongst this coast (being the backeside of the supposed continent of America) and the Queenes Foreland, he perceived a great sound to goe thorow into Frobishers straights. Whereupon he sent the Gabriel the one and twentieth of July, to proove whether they might goe thorow and meete againe with him in the straights, which they did: and as wee imagined before, so the Queenes foreland prooved an Iland, as I thinke most of these supposed continents will. And so he departed towardes the straights, thinking it were high time now to recover his Port, and to provide the Fleete of their lading, whereof he was not a little carefull, as shall by the processe and his resolute attempts appeare.

. . . . Long time now the Anne Francis had layne beating off and on all alone before the Queenes foreland, not being able to recover their Port for yce, albeit many times they dangerously attempted it, for yet the yce choaked up the passage, and would not suffer them to enter. And having never seene any of the fleete since twenty dayes past, when by reason of the thicke mistes they were severed in the mistaken straights, they did now this present 23 of July overthwart a place in the straights called Hattons Hedland, where they met with seven ships of ye Fleete againe, which good hap did not onely rejoyce them for themselves, in respect of the comfort which they received by such good companie, but especially that by this meanes they were put out of doubt of their deare friends, whose safeties long time they did not a little suspect and feare.

At their meeting they haled the Admirall after the maner of the Sea, and with great joy welcommed one another with a thundring volly of shot. And now every man declared at large the fortunes and dangers which they had passed.

The foure and twentieth of July we met with the Francis of Foy, who with much adoe sought way backe againe, through the yce from out of the mistaken straights, where (to their great perill) they prooved to recover their Port. They brought the first newes of the Vizadmirall Captaine Yorke, who many dayes with themselves, and the Busse of Bridgewater was missing. They reported that they left the Vizeadmirall reasonably cleare of the yce, but the other ship they greatly feared, whom they could not come to helpe, being themselves so hardly distressed as never men more. Also they told us of the Gabriel, who having got thorow from the backside, and Western point of the Queenes foreland, into Frobishers straights, fell into their company about the cape of Good hope.

And upon the seven and twentieth of July, the ship of Bridgewater got out of the yce and met with the Fleete which lay off and on under Hattons Hedland. They reported of their marvellous accidents and dangers, declaring their ship to be so leake that they must of necessitie seeke harborow, having their stem so beaten within their huddings, that they had much adoe to keepe themselves above water. . . .

*　　　　*　　　　*

The report of these dangers by these ships thus published amongst the fleete, with the remembrance of the perils past, and those present before their face, brought no small feare and terror into the hearts of many considerate men. So that some beganne privily to murmure against the Generall for this wilfull maner of proceeding. Some desired to discover some harborow thereabouts to refresh themselves and reforme their broken vessels for a while, untill the North and Northwest windes might disperse the yce, and make the place more free to passe. Other some forgetting themselves, spake more undutifully in this behalfe, saying: that they had as leeve be hanged when they came home, as without hope of safetie to seeke to passe, and so to perish amongst the yce.

The Generall not opening his eares to the peevish passion of any private person, but chiefly respecting the accomplishment of the cause he had undertaken (wherein the chiefe reputation and fame of a Generall and Captaine consisteth) and calling to his remembrance the short time he had in hand to provide so great number of ships their loading, determined with this resolution to passe and recover his Port, or else there to burie himselfe with his attempt.

Where he saw the yce never so little open, he gate in at one gappe and out at another, and so himselfe valiantly led the way thorow before to induce the Fleete to follow after, and with incredible paine and perill at length gat through the yce, and upon the one and thirtieth of July recovered his long wished Port after many attempts and sundry times being put backe, and came to anker in the Countesse of Warwicks sound. At their arrivall here they perceived two ships at anker within the harborough, whereat they began much to marvell and greatly to rejoyce, for those they knew to be the Michael, wherein was the Lieutenant generall Captaine Fenton, and the small Barke called the Gabriel, who so long time were missing, and never heard of before, whom every man made the last reckoning, never to heare of againe.

Here every man greatly rejoyced of their happie meeting, and welcommed one another after the Sea manner with their great Ordinance, and when each partie had ripped up their sundry fortunes and perils past, they highly praysed God, and altogither upon their knees gave him due, humble and hearty thankes, and Maister Wolfall a learned man, appointed by her Majesties Councell to be their Minister and Preacher made unto them a godly sermon, exhorting them especially to be thankfull to God for their strange and miraculous deliverance in those so dangerous places, and putting them in mind of the uncertainetie of mans life, willed them to make themselves alwayes readie as resolute men to enjoy and accept thankefully whatsoever adventure his divine Providence should appoint. This maister Wolfall being well seated and setled at home in his owne Countrey, with a good and large living, having a good honest woman to wife and very towardly children, being of good reputation among the best, refused not to take in hand this painefull voyage, for the onely care he had to save soules, and to reforme those Infidels if it were possible to Christianitie: and also partly for the great desire he had that this notable voyage so well begunne, might be brought to perfection: and therefore he was contented to stay there the whole yeare if occasion had served, being in every necessary action as forward as the resolutest men of all. Wherefore in this behalfe he may rightly be called a true Pastor and minister of Gods word, which for the profite of his flocke spared not to venture his owne life. . . .

*   *   *

The Generall after his arrivall in the Countesses sound, spent no time in vaine, but immediatly at his first landing called the chiefe Captaines of his Councell together, and consulted with them for the speedier execution of such things as then they had in hand. At first, for searching and finding out good Minerall for the Miners to be occupied on. Then to give good Orders to bee observed of the whole company on shore. And lastly, to consider for the erecting up of the Fort and House for the use of them which were to abide there the whole yeere. . . .

The Muster of the men being taken, and the victuals with all other things viewed and considered, every man was set to his charge, as his place and office required. The Myners were appointed where to worke, and the Mariners discharged their shippes.

In the meane time, whilest the Mariners plyed their worke, the Captaines sought out new Mynes, the Goldfiners made tryall of the Ore, the Mariners discharged their shippes, the Gentlemen for example sake laboured heartily, and honestly encouraged the inferiour sort to worke. So that the small tyme of that little leisure that was left to tarrie, was spent in vaine.

The second of August the Gabriel arrived, who came from the Vize-admirall, and beeing distressed sore with Yce, put into Harborough neere unto Mount Oxford. And now was the whole Fleete arrived safely at their Port, excepting foure, besides the Shippe that was lost: that is, the Thomas Allen, the Anne Francis, the Thomas of Ipswich, and the Moone, whose absence was some lette unto the workes and other proceedings, aswell for that these Shippes were furnished with the better sorte of Myners, as with other provision for the habitation. . . .

The Fleet now being in some good readinesse for their lading, the Generall calling together the Gentlemen and Captaines to consult, told them that he was very desirous that some further discovery should be attempted, and that he would not onely by Gods helpe bring home his Ships laden with Ore, but also meant to bring some certificate of a further discovery of the Countrey, which thing to bring to passe (having sometime therein consulted) they found very hard, and almost invincible. And considering that already they had spent sometime in searching out the trending and fashion of the mistaken straites, therefore it could not be sayd, but that by this voyage they have notice of a further discovery, and that the hope of the passage thereby is much furthered and encreased, as appeared before in the discourse thereof. Yet notwithstanding if any meanes might be further devised, the Captaines were contented and willing, as the Generall shoulde appoynt and commaund, to take any enterprise in hand. Which after long debating was found a thing very impossible, and that rather consultation was to be had of returning homeward, especially for these causes following. First the darke foggy mists, the continuall falling snowe and stormy weather which they commonly were vexed with, and now daily ever more and more increased, have no small argument of the Winters drawing neere. And also the frost every night was so hard congealed within the sound, that if by evill hap they should bee long kept in with contrary winds, it was greatly to be feared, that they should be shut up there fast the whole yeere, which being utterly unprovided, would be their utter destruction. Againe, drinke was so scant throughout all the Fleet by meanes of the great leakage, that not onely the provision which was layd in for the habitation was wanting and wasted, but also each shippes severall provision spent and lost, which many of our company to their great griefe found in their returne since, for all the way homewards they dranke nothing but water.

Thanks be to God, all the Fleete arrived safely in England about the first of October, some in one place and some in another.

CHAPTER VII

Sir Francis Drake—1540?–1596

Sir Francis Drake had been in command of the Judith *during Hawkins' third voyage, when they were furiously attacked and routed by the Spaniards. It was his resolve to avenge the alleged wrong against the English, as well as an unconquerable desire to break the sea power of Spain, that led Drake to undertake this new venture. He set sail in 1577 with the unofficial blessing of Queen Elizabeth, and fought and plundered his way up and down the Spanish main. Having acquired a rich booty, he determined not to risk returning by way of the Straits of Magellan, where the Spaniards were obviously lying in wait for him.*

He struck a course northward across the Pacific, and discovered the coast of Oregon and that part of California which now belongs to the United States. He returned triumphantly to England three years later, and was knighted by the Queen. Drake helped to create the sea power which gave England, rather than Spain, control of the seas for nearly four hundred years. The narrative of the journey is by a seaman who made the voyage.

DRAKE'S FAMOUS VOYAGE—1577–1580

[NARRATIVE BY FRANCIS PRETTY, ONE OF DRAKE'S GENTLEMEN AT ARMS]

The famous voyage of Sir Francis Drake into the South sea, and therehence about the whole Globe of the earth, begun in the yeere of our Lord, 1577.

THE 15. day of November, in the yeere of our Lord 1577. M. Francis Drake, with a fleete of five ships and barkes, and to the number of 164. men, gentlemen and sailers, departed from Plimmouth, giving out his pretended voyage for Alexandria: but the wind falling contrary, hee was forced the next morning to put into Falmouth haven in Cornewall, where such and so terible a tempest tooke us, as few men have seene the like, and was in deed o vehement, that all our ships were like to have gone to wracke: but it pleased God to preserve us from that extremitie, and to afflict us onely for hat present with these two particulars: The mast of our Admirall which vas the Pellican, was cut over boord for the safegard of the ship, and the

Marigold was driven ashore, and somewhat bruised: for the repairing of which damages wee returned againe to Plimmouth, and having recovered those harmes, and brought the ships againe to good state, we set forth the second time from Plimmouth, and set saile the 13. day of December following.

The 25. day of the same moneth we fell with the Cape Cantin, upon the coast of Barbarie, and coasting along, the 27. day we found an Island called Mogador, lying one mile distant from the maine, betweene which Island and the maine, we found a very good and safe harbour for our ships to ride in, as also very good entrance, and voyde of any danger.

On this Island our Generall erected a pinnesse, whereof he brought out of England with him foure already framed. While these things were in doing, there came to the waters side some of the inhabitants of the countrey, shewing foorth their flags of truce, which being seene of our Generall, hee sent his ships boate to the shore, to know what they would: they being willing to come aboord, our men left there one man of our company for a pledge, and brought two of theirs aboord our ship, which by signes shewed our Generall, that the next day they would bring some provision, as sheepe, capons and hennes, and such like: whereupon our Generall bestowed amongst them some linnen cloth and shooes, and a javeling, which they very joyfully received, and departed for that time.

The next morning they failed not to come againe to the waters side, and our Generall againe setting out our boate, one of our men leaping over rashly ashore, and offering friendly to imbrace them, they set violent hands on him, offering a dagger to his throte if hee had made any resistance, and so laying him on a horse, caried him away: so that a man cannot be too circumspect and warie of himselfe among such miscreants.

Our pinnesse being finished, wee departed from this place the 30. and last day of December, and coasting along the shore, wee did descrie, not contrary to our expectation, certaine Canters which were Spanish fishermen, to whom we gave chase and tooke three of them, and proceeding further we met with 3. Caravels and tooke them also.

The 17. day of January we arrived at Cape Blanco, where we found a ship riding at anchor, within the Cape, and but two simple Mariners in her, which ship we tooke and caried her further into the harbour, where we remained 4. dayes, and in that space our Generall mustered, and trayned his men on land in warlike maner, to make them fit for all occasions.

In this place we tooke of the Fishermen such necessaries as wee wanted, and they could yeeld us, and leaving heere one of our litle barkes called the Benedict, wee tooke with us one of theirs which they called Canters, being of the burden of 40. tunnes or thereabouts.

All of these things being finished, wee departed this harbour the 22. of Januarie, carying along with us one of the Portugall Caravels which was bound to the Islands of Cape Verde for salt, whereof good store is made in one of those Islands.

The master or Pilot of that Caravel did advertise our Generall that upon one of those Islands called Mayo, there was great store of dryed Cabritos, which a few inhabitants there dwelling did yeerely make ready for such of the kings Ships as did there touch, beeing bound for his countrey of Brasile or elsewhere. Wee fell with this Island the 27. of January, but the Inhabitants would in no case traffique with us, being thereof forbidden by the kings Edict: yet the next day our Generall sent to view the Island, and the likelihoodes that might be there of provision of victuals, about threescore and two men under the conduct and government of Master Winter and Master Doughtie, and marching towards the chiefe place of habitation in this Island (as by the Portugall wee were informed) having travailed to the mountaines the space of three miles, and arriving there somewhat before the day breake, we arrested our selves to see day before us, which appearing, we found the inhabitants to be fled: but the place, by reason that it was manured, wee found to be more fruitfull than the other part, especially the valleys among the hils.

Here we gave our selves a litle refreshing, as by very ripe and sweete grapes, which the fruitfulnesse of the earth at that season of the yeere yeelded us: and that season being with us the depth of Winter, it may seeme strange that those fruites were then there growing: but the reason thereof is this, because they being betweene the Tropike and the Equinoctiall, the Sunne passeth twise in the yeere through their Zenith over their heads, by meanes whereof they have two Summers, & being so neere the heate of the line, they never lose the heate of the Sunne so much, but the fruites have their increase and continuance in the midst of Winter. The Island is wonderfully stored with goates and wilde hennes, and it hath salt also without labour, save onely that the people gather it into heapes, which continually in great quantitie is increased upon the sands by the flowing of the sea, and the receiving heate of the Sunne kerning the same, so that of the increase thereof they keepe a continuall traffique with their neighbours.

Amongst other things we found here a kind of fruit called Cocos, which because it is not commonly knowen with us in England, I thought good to make some description of it.

The tree beareth no leaves nor branches, but at the very top the fruit groweth in clusters, hard at the top of the stemme of the tree, as big every severall fruite as a man's head: but having taken off the uttermost barke, which you shall find to bee very full of strings or sinowes, as I may terme them, you shall come to a hard shell which may holde a quantitie in liquor a pint commonly, or some a quart, and some lesse: within that shell of the thicknesse of halfe an inch good, you shall have a kinde of hard substance and very white, no lesse good and sweete than almonds: within that againe a certaine cleare liquor, which being drunke, you shall not onely finde it very delicate and sweete, but most comfortable and cordiall.

After wee had satisfied our selves with some of these fruites, wee marched further into the Island, and saw great store of Cabritos alive, which were so chased by the inhabitants, that wee could doe no good towards our provision, but they had layde out as it were to stoppe our mouthes withall, certaine olde dryed Cabritos, which being but ill, and small and few, wee made no account of.

Being returned to our ships, our Generall departed hence the 31. of this moneth, and sayled by the Island of S. Iago, but farre enough from the danger of the inhabitants, who shot and discharged at us three peeces, but they all fell short of us, and did us no harme. The Island is fayre and large, and as it seemeth, rich and fruitfull, and inhabited by the Portugals, but the mountaines and high places of the Island are sayd to be possessed by the Moores, who having bin slaves to the Portugals, to ease themselves, made escape to the desert places of the Island, where they abide with great strength.

Being before this Island, we espied two ships under sayle, to the one of which wee gave chase, and in the end boorded her with a ship-boat without resistance, which we found to be a good prize, and she yeelded unto us good store of wine: which prize our Generall committed to the custodie of Master Doughtie, and reteining the Pilot, sent the rest away with his Pinnesse, giving them a Butte of wine and some victuals, and their wearing clothes, and so they departed.

The same night wee came with the Island called by the Portugals, Ilha del fogo, that is, the burning Island: in the Northside whereof is a consuming fire, the matter is sayde to be of Sulphure, but notwithstanding it is like to bee a commodious Island, because the Portugals have built, and doe inhabite there.

Upon the South side thereof lyeth a most pleasant and sweete Island, the trees whereof are alwayes greene and faire to looke upon, in respect whereof they call it Ilha Brava, that is, the brave Island. From the bankes thereof into the sea doe run in many places reasonable streames of fresh waters easie to be come by, but there was no convenient roade for our ships: for such was the depth, that no ground could bee had for anchoring, and it is reported, that ground was never found in that place, so that the tops of Fogo burne not so high in the ayre, but the rootes of Brava are quenched as low in the sea.

Being departed from these Islands, we drew towards the line, where wee were becalmed the space of 3. weekes, but yet subject to divers great stormes, terrible lightnings and much thunder: but with this miserie we had the commoditie of great store of fish, as Dolphins, Bonitos, and flying fishes, whereof some fell into our shippes, wherehence they could not rise againe for want of moisture, for when their wings are drie, they cannot flie.

From the first day of our departure from the Islands of Cape Verde, wee sayled 54. dayes without sight of land, and the first land that we fell with was the coast of Brasil, which we saw the fift of April in ye height of 33. degrees towards the pole Antarctike, and being discovered at sea by the inhabitants of the countrey, they made upon the coast great fires for a sacrifice (as we learned) to the devils, about which they use conjurations making heapes of sande and other ceremonies, that when any ship shall goe about to stay upon their coast, not onely sands may be gathered together in shoalds in every place, but also that stormes and tempests may arise, to the casting away of ships and men, whereof (as it is reported) there have bene divers experiments.

The seventh day in a mightie great storme both of lightning, rayne and thunder, wee lost the Canter which we called the Christopher: but the eleventh day after, by our Generals great care in dispersing his ships, we found her againe, and the place where we met, our Generall called the Cape of Joy, where every ship tooke in some water. Heere we found a good temperature and sweete ayre, a very faire and pleasant countrey with an exceeding fruitfull soyle, where were great store of large and mightie Deere, but we came not to the sight of any people: but traveiling further into the countrey, we perceived the footing of people in the clay-ground, shewing that they were men of great stature. Being returned to our ships, we wayed anchor, and ranne somewhat further, and harboured our selves betweene a roeke and the maine, where by meanes of the rocke that brake the force of the sea, we rid very safe, and upon this rocke we killed for our provision certaine sea-wolves, commonly called with us Seales.

From hence we went our course to 36. degrees, and entred the great river of Plate, and ranne into 54. and 55. fadomes and a halfe of fresh water, where wee filled our water by the ships side: but our Generall finding here no good harborough, as he thought he should, bare out againe to sea the 27. of April, and in bearing out we lost sight of our Flieboate wherein master Doughtie was, but we sayling along, found a fayre and reasonable good Bay wherein were many, and the same profitable Islands, one whereof had so many Seales, as would at the least have laden all our Shippes, and the rest of the Islands are as it were laden with foules which is wonderfull to see, and they of divers sortes. It is a place very plentifull of victuals, and hath in it no want of fresh water.

Our Generall after certaine dayes of his abode in this place, being on shore in an Island, the people of the countrey shewed themselves unto him, leaping and dauncing, and entred into traffique with him, but they would not receive any thing at any mans hands, but the same must bee cast upon the ground. They are of cleane, comely, and strong bodies, swift on foote, and seeme to be very active.

The eighteenth day of May our Generall thought it needfull to have a care of such Ships as were absent, and therefore indevouring to seeke the Flieboate wherein master Doughtie was, we espied her againe the next day: and whereas certaine of our ships were sent to discover the coast and to search an harbour, the Marygold and the Canter being imployed in that businesse, came unto us and gave us understanding of a safe harbour that they had found, wherewith all our ships bare, and entred it, where we watered and made new provision of victuals, as by Seales, whereof we slew to the number of 200. or 300. in the space of an houre.

Here our Generall in the Admirall rid close aboord the Flie-boate, and tooke out of her all the provision of victuals and what els was in her, and halling her to the Lande, set fire to her, and so burnt her to save the iron worke: which being a doing, there came downe of the countrey certaine of the people naked, saving only about their waste the skinne of some beast with the furre or haire on, and something also wreathed on their heads: their faces were painted with divers colours, and some of them had on their heads the similitude of hornes, every man his bow which was an ell in length, and a couple of arrowes. They were very agill people and quicke to deliver, and seemed not to be ignorant in the feates of warres, as by their order of ranging a few men, might appeare. These people would not of a long time receive any thing at our handes; yet at length our Generall being ashore, and they dauncing after their accustomed maner about him, and hee once turning his backe towards them, one leapt suddenly to him, and tooke his cap with his golde band off his head, and ran a litle distance from him and shared it with his fellow, the cap to the one, and the band to the other.

Having dispatched all our businesse in this place, wee departed and set sayle, and immediatly upon our setting foorth we lost our Canter which was absent three or foure dayes: but when our General had her againe, he tooke out the necessaries, and so gave her over neere to the Cape of Good hope.

The next day after being the twentieth of June, wee harboured our selves againe in a very good harborough, called by Magellan Port S. Julian, where we found a gibbet standing upon the maine, which we supposed to be the place where Magellan did execution upon some of his disobedient and rebellious company.

The two and twentieth day our Generall went ashore to the maine, and in his companie, John Thomas, and Robert Winterhie, Oliver the Master gunner, John Brewer, Thomas Hood, and Thomas Drake, and entring on land, they presently met with two or three of the countrey people, and Robert Winterhie having in his hands a bowe and arrowes, went about to make a shoote of pleasure, and in his draught his bowstring brake, which the rude Savages taking as a token of warre, began to bend the force of their bowes against our company, and drove them to their shifts very narrowly.

In this Port our Generall began to enquire diligently of the actions of M. Thomas Doughtie, and found them not to be such as he looked for, but tending rather to contention or mutinie, or some other disorder, whereby (without redresse) the successe of the voyage might greatly have bene hazarded: whereupon the company was called together and made acquainted with the particulars of the cause, which were found partly by master Doughties owne confession, and partly by the evidence of the fact, to be true: which when our Generall saw, although his private affection to M. Doughtie (as hee then in the presence of us all sacredly protested) was great, yet the care he had of the state of the voyage, of the expectation of her Majestie, and of the honour of his countrey did more touch him (as indeede it ought) then the private respect of one man: so that the cause being throughly heard, and all things done in good order as neere as might be to the course of our lawes in England, it was concluded that M. Doughtie should receive punishment according to the qualitie of the offence: and he

SIR FRANCIS DRAKE—1540?–1596 159

seeing no remedie but patience for himselfe, desired before his death to receive the Communion, which he did at the hands of M. Fletcher our Minister, and our Generall himselfe accompanied him in that holy action: which being done, and the place of execution made ready, hee having embraced our Generall and taken his leave of all the companie, with prayer for the Queenes majestie and our realme, in quiet sort laid his head to the blocke, where he ended his life. This being done, our Generall made divers speaches to the whole company, perswading us to unitie obedience, love, and regard of our voyage; and for the better confirmation thereof, willed every man the next Sunday following to prepare himselfe to receive the Communion, as Christian brethren and friends ought to doe, which was done in very reverent sort, and so with good contentment every man went about his businesse.

The 17. day of August we departed the port of S. Julian, & the 20. day we fell with the streight or freat of Magellan going into the South sea, at the Cape or headland whereof we found the bodie of a dead man, whose flesh was cleane consumed.

The 21. day we entred the streight, which we found to have many turnings, and as it were shuttings up, as if there were no passage at all, by meanes whereof we had the wind often against us, so that some of the fleete recovering a Cape or point of land, others should be forced to turne backe againe, and to come to an anchor where they could.

In this streight there be many faire harbors, with store of fresh water, but yet they lacke their best commoditie: for the water is there of such depth, that no man shal find ground to anchor in, except it bee in some narow river or corner, or betweene some rocks, so that if any extreme blasts or contrary winds do come (whereunto the place is much subject) it carieth with it no small danger.

The land on both sides is very huge & mountainous, the lower mountains whereof, although they be monstrous and wonderfull to looke upon for their height, yet there are others which in height exceede them in a strange maner, reaching themselves above their fellowes so high, that betweene them did appeare three regions of cloudes.

These mountaines are covered with snow: at both the Southerly and Easterly partes of the streight there are Islands, among which the sea hath his indraught into the streights, even as it hath in the maine entrance of the freat.

This streight is extreme cold, with frost and snow continually; the trees seeme to stoope with the burden of the weather, and yet are greene continually, and many good and sweete herbes doe very plentifully grow and increase under them.

The bredth of the streight is in some place a league, in some other places 2. leagues, and three leagues, and in some other 4. leagues, but the narrowest place hath a league over.

The 24. of August we arrived at an Island in the streights, where we found great store of foule which could not flie, of the bignesse of geese,

whereof we killed in lesse then one day 3000. and victualled our selves
throughly therewith.

*   *   *

The 8. of Februarie following, wee fell with the fruitfull Island of Barateve, having in the meane time suffered many dangers by windes and shoalds.
The people of this Island are comely in body and stature, and of a civill
behaviour, just in dealing, and courteous to strangers, whereof we had the
experience sundry wayes, they being most glad of our presence, and very
ready to releeve our wants in those things which their Countrey did yeelde.
The men goe naked, saving their heads and privities, every man having
something or other hanging at their eares. Their women are covered from
the middle downe to the foote, wearing a great number of bracelets upon
their armes, for some had 8. upon each arme, being made some of bone,
some of horne, and some of brasse, the lightest whereof by our estimation
waied two ounces apeece.

With this people linnen-cloth is good marchandize, and of good request,
whereof they make rols for their heads, and girdles to weare about them.
Their Island is both rich and fruitfull: rich in golde, silver, copper, and
sulphur, wherein they seeme skilfull and expert, not onely to trie the same,
but in working it also artificially into any forme and fashion that pleaseth
them.

Their fruits be divers and plentifull, as nutmegs, ginger, long pepper, lem-
mons, cucumbers, cocos, figu, sagu, with divers other sorts: and among all
the rest, wee had one fruite, in bignesse, forme, and huske, like a Bay berry,
hard of substance, and pleasant of taste, which being sodden, becommeth
soft, and is a most good and wholesome victuall, whereof we tooke reasonable store, as we did also of the other fruits and spices: so that to confesse
a trueth, since the time that we first set out of our owne Countrey of England, we happened upon no place (Ternate onely excepted) wherein we
found more comforts and better meanes of refreshing.

At our departure from Barateve, we set our course for Java major, where
arriving, we found great courtesie, and honourable entertainment. This
Island is governed by 5. Kings, whom they call Rajah: as Rajah Donaw,
and Rajah Mang Bange, and Rajah Cabuccapollo, which live as having one
spirite, and one minde.

Of these five we had foure a shipboord at once, and two or three often.
They are wonderfully delighted in coloured clothes, as red and greene:
their upper parts of their bodies are naked, save their heads, whereupon
they weare a Turkish roll, as do the Maluccians: from the middle down-
ward they weare a pintado of silke, trailing upon the ground, in colour as
they best like.

The Maluccians hate that their women should bee seene of strangers: but
these offer them of high courtesie, yea the kings themselves.

The people are of goodly stature, and warlike, well provided of swords
and targets, with daggers, all being of their owne worke, and most artifi-

cially done, both in tempering their mettall, as also in the forme, whereof we bought reasonable store.

They have an house in every village for their common assembly: every day they meete twise, men, women, and children, bringing with them such victuals as they thinke good, some fruites, some rice boiled, some hennes roasted, some sagu, having a table made 3. foote from the ground, whereon they set their meate, that every person sitting at the table may eate, one rejoycing in the company of another.

They boile their rice in an earthen pot, made in forme of a sugar loafe, being ful of holes, as our pots which we water our gardens withall, and it is open at the great ende, wherein they put their rice drie, without any moisture. In the meane time they have ready another great earthen pot, set fast in a fornace, boiling full of water, whereinto they put their pot with rice, by such measure, that they swelling become soft at the first, and by their swelling stopping the holes of the pot, admit no more water to enter, but the more they are boiled, the harder and more firme substance they become, so that in the end they are a firme & good bread, of the which with oyle, butter, sugar, and other spices, they make divers sorts of meates very pleasant of taste, and nourishing to nature.

The French pocks is here very common to all, and they helpe themselves, sitting naked from ten to two in the Sunne, whereby the venemous humour is drawen out. Not long before our departure, they tolde us, that not farre off there were such great Ships as ours, wishing us to beware: upon this our Captaine would stay no longer.

From Java Major we sailed for the cape of Good Hope, which was the first land we fell withall: neither did we touch with it, or any other land, untill we came to Sierra Leona, upon the coast of Guinea: notwithstanding we ranne hard aboord the Cape, finding the report of the Portugals to be most false, who affirme, that it is the most dangerous Cape of the world, never without intolerable stormes and present danger to travailers, which come neere the same.

This Cape is a most stately thing, and the fairest Cape we saw in the whole circumference of the earth, and we passed by it the 18. of June.

From thence we continued our course to Sierra Leona, on the coast of Guinea, where we arrived the 22. of July, and found necessarie provisions, great store of Elephants, Oisters upon trees of one kind, spawning and increasing infinitely, the Oister suffering no budde to grow. We departed thence the 24. day.

We arrived in England the third of November 1580. being the third yeere of our departure.

VOYAGE TO THE CALIFORNIA COAST

The course which Sir Francis Drake held from the haven of Guatulco in the South sea on the backe side of Nueva Espanna, to the North-west of California as far as fourtie three degrees: and his returne back along the said Coast to thirtie eight degrees: where finding a faire and goodly haven, he landed, and staying there many weekes, and discovering many excellent things in the countrey and great shewe of rich minerall matter, and being offered the dominion of the countrey by the Lord of the same, hee tooke possession thereof in the behalfe of her Majestie, and named it Nova Albion.

WEE kept our course from the Isle of Cano (which lyeth in eight degrees of Northerly latitude, and within two leagues of the maine of Nicaragua, where wee calked and trimmed our ship) along the coast of Nueva Espanna, untill we came to the Haven and Towne of Guatulco, which (as we were informed) had but seventeene Spaniards dwelling in it, and we found it to stand in fifteene degrees and fiftie minutes.

Assoone as we were entred this Haven we landed, and went presently to the towne, and to the Towne house, where we found a Judge sitting in judgement, he being associate with three other officers, upon three Negroes that had conspired the burning of the Towne: both which Judges, and prisoners we tooke, and brought them a shippeboord, and caused the chiefe Judge to write his letter to the Towne, to command all the Townesmen to avoid, that we might safely water there. Which being done, and they departed, wee ransaked the Towne, and in one house we found a pot of the quantitie of a bushell full of royals of plate, which we brought to our ship.

And here one Thomas Moone one of our companie, took a Spanish gentleman as he was flying out of the Towne, and searching him, he found a chaine of Gold about him, and other jewels, which we tooke and so let him goe.

At this place our Generall among other Spaniards, set a shore his Portugall Pilote, which he tooke at the Island of Cape Verde, out of a ship of Saint Marie port of Portugall, and having set them a shoare, we departed thence.

Our General at this place and time thinking himselfe both in respect of his private injuries received from the Spaniards, as also of their contempts and indignities offered to our Countrey and Prince in generall, sufficiently satisfied, and revenged: and supposing that her Majestie at his returne would rest contented with his service, purposed to continue no longer upon the Spanish coastes, but began to consider and to consult of the best way for his Countrey.

He thought it not good to returne by the Streights, for two speciall causes: the one, least the Spaniards should there waite, and attend for him in great number and strength, whose handes he being left but one ship, could not possibly escape. The other cause was the dangerous situation of the mouth of the Streights of the South side, with continuall stormes raining and blustring, as he found by experience, besides the shoals and sands upon the coast, wherefore he thought it not a good course to adventure that way: he resolved therefore to avoide these hazards, to goe forward to the Islands of the Malucos, and therehence to saile the course of the Portugales by the Cape of Bona Sperança.

Upon this resolution, he began to thinke of his best way for the Malucos, and finding himselfe, where hee now was, becalmed, hee sawe that of necessitie hee must bee enforced to take a Spanish course, namely to saile somewhat Northerly to get a winde. Wee therefore set saile, and sayled 800 leagues at the least for a good winde, and thus much we sayled from the 16 of Aprill after our olde stile till the third of June.

The fift day of June being in fortie three degrees towardes the pole Arcticke, being speedily come out of the extreame heate, wee found the ayre so colde, that our men being pinched with the same, complayned of the extremitie thereof, and the further we went, the more the colde increased upon us, whereupon we thought it best for that time to seeke land, and did so, finding it not mountainous, but low plaine land, & we drew backe againe without landing, til we came within thirtie eight degrees towardes the line. In which height it pleased God to send us into a faire and good Bay, with a good winde to enter the same.

In this Bay wee ankered the sevententh of June, and the people of the Countrey, having their houses close by the water side, shewed themselves unto us, and sent a present to our Generall.

When they came unto us, they greatly wondred at the things which we brought, but our Generall (according to his naturall and accustomed humanitie) curteously intreated them, and liberally bestowed on them necessarie things to cover their nakednesse, whereupon they supposed us to be gods, and would not be perswaded to the contrary: the presentes which they sent unto our Generall were feathers, and cals of net worke.

Their houses are digged round about with earth, and have from the uttermost brimmes of the circle clifts of wood set upon them, joyning close together at the toppe like a spire steeple, which by reason of that closenesse are very warme.

Their bed is the ground with rushes strawed on it, and lying about the house, they have the fire in the middest. The men goe naked, the women take bulrushes and kembe them after the maner of hempe, and thereof make their loose garments, which being knit about their middles, hang downe about their hippes, having also about their shoulders a skinne of Deere, with the haire upon it. These women are very obedient and serviceable to their husbands.

After they were departed from us, they came and visited us the second time, and brought with them feathers and bags of Tabacco for presents: And when they came to the toppe of the hil (at the bottome whereof wee had pitched our tents) they stayed themselves, where one appointed for speaker, wearied himselfe with making a long oration, which done, they left their bowes upon the hill and came downe with their presents.

In the meane time the women remaining on the hill, tormented themselves lamentably, tearing their flesh from their cheekes, whereby we perceived that they were about a sacrifice. In the meane time our Generall, with his companie, went to prayer, and to reading of the Scriptures, at which exercise they were attentive and seemed greatly to be affected with it: but when they were come unto us they restored againe unto us those things which before we had bestowed upon them.

The newes of our being there being spread through the countrey, the people that inhabited round about came downe, and amongst them the king himself, a man of a goodly stature, and comely personage, with many other tall and warlike men: before whose comming were sent two Ambassadours to our Generall, to signifie that their king was comming, in doing of which message, their speech was continued about halfe an howre. This ended, they by signes requested our Generall to send something by their hand to their king, as a token that his comming might bee in peace: wherein our Generall having satisfied them, they returned with glad tidings to their king, who marched to us with a princely Majestie, the people crying continually after their maner, and as they drewe neere unto us, so did they strive to behave themselves in their actions with comelinesse.

In the fore front was a man of a goodly personage, who bare the scepter, or mace before the king, whereupon hanged two crownes, a lesse and a bigger, with three chaines of a merveilous length: the crownes were made of knit work wrought artificially with feathers of divers colours; the chaines were made of a bony substance and few be the persons among them that are admitted to weare them: and of that number also the persons are stinted, as some ten, some twelve, &c. Next unto him which bare the scepter, was the king himselfe, with his Guarde about his person, clad with Conie skinnes, and other skinnes: after them followed the naked common sort of people, every one having his face painted, some with white, some with blacke, and other colours, and having in their hands one thing or other for a present, not so much as their children, but they also brought their presents.

In the meane time, our Generall gathered his men together, and marched within his fenced place, making against their approching, a very warlike shewe. They being trooped together in their order, and a general salutation being made, there was presently a generall silence. Then he that bare the scepter before the king, being informed by another, whome they assigned to that office, with a manly and loftie voice, proclaimed that which the other spake to him in secret, continuing halfe an houre: which ended, and a generall Amen as it were given, the king with the whole number of men, and women (the children excepted) came downe without any weapon, who descending to the foote of the hill, set themselves in order.

In comming towards our bulwarks and tents, the scepter bearer began a song, observing his measures in a dance, and that with a stately countenance, whom the king with his Garde, and every degree of persons following, did in like maner sing and dance, saving onely the women which daunced and kept silence. The General permitted them to enter within our bulwark, where they continued their song and daunce a reasonable time.

When they had satisfied themselves, they made signes to our Generall to sit downe, to whom the king, and divers others made several orations, or rather supplication, that he would take their province and kingdom into his hand, and become their king, making signes that they would resigne unto him their right and title of the whole land, and become his subjects. In which to perswade us the better, the king and the rest, with one consent and with great reverence, joyfully singing a song, did set the crowne upon his head, inriched his necke with all their chaines, and offered unto him many other things, honouring him by the name of Hioh, adding thereunto as it seemed a signe of triumph: which thing our Generall thought not meete to reject, because hee knewe not what honour and profite it might bee to our countrey. Wherefore in the name, and to the use of her Majestie, he tooke the scepter, crowne and dignitie of the said Countrey in his hands, wishing that the riches & treasure thereof might so conveniently be transported to the inriching of her kingdome at home, as it aboundeth in the same.

The common sort of the people leaving the king and his Guarde with our Generall, scattered themselves together with their sacrifices among our people, taking a diligent viewe of every person; and such as pleased their fancie, (which were the yongest) they inclosing them about offred their sacrifices unto them with lamentable weeping, scratching, and tearing the flesh from their faces with their nayles, whereof issued abundance of blood. But wee used signes to them of disliking this, and stayed their hands from force, and directed them upwardes to the living God, whome onely they ought to worshippe. They shewed unto us their wounds, and craved helpe of them at our handes, whereupon wee gave them lotions, plaisters and ointments agreeing to the state of their griefes, beseeching God to cure their deseases. Every thirde day they brought their sacrifices unto us, untill they understoode our meaning, that we had no pleasure in them: yet they could not be long absent from us, but daily frequented our company to the houre of our departure, which departure seemed so grievous unto them, that their joy was turned into sorrow. They intreated us, that being absent wee would remember them, and by stelth provided a sacrifice, which we misliked.

Our necessarie businesse being ended, our Generall with his companie traveiled up into the Countrey to their villages, where we found heardes of Deere by a thousand in a companie, being most large and fat of body.

We found the whole countrey to bee a warren of a strange kinde of Conies, their bodyes in bignes as be the Barbary Conies, their heads as the heades of ours, the feet of a Want, and the taile of a Rat being of great length: under her chinne on either side a bagge, into the which shee gathereth her meate when she hath filled her belly abroad. The people eate their bodies, and make great account of their skinnes, for their Kings coate was made of them.

Our Generall called this countrey, Nova Albion, and that for two causes: the one in respect of the white bankes and cliffes, which ly towards the sea:

and the other, because it might have some affinitie with our Countrey in name, which sometime was so called.

There is no part of earth here to bee taken up, wherein there is not some speciall likelihood of gold or silver.

At our departure hence our Generall set up a monument of our being there; as also of her Majesties right and title to the same, namely a plate nailed upon a faire great poste, whereupon was ingraven her Majesties name, the day and yeere of our arrivall there, with the free giving up of the Province and people into her Majesties hands, together with her highnes picture and armes, in a peice of six pence of current English money under the plate, where under was also written the name of our Generall.

It seemeth that the Spaniards hitherto had never bene in this part of the countrey, neither did ever discover the land by many degrees to the Southwards of this place.

CHAPTER VIII

Sir Walter Raleigh—1552–1618

Although Sir Walter Raleigh is best known to history as a pioneer in the movement to colonize America, his efforts in this direction met with dismal failure. Nevertheless, it was his indomitable spirit of enterprise which led England to become one of the most powerful nations on earth.

Raleigh was a great favorite of Queen Elizabeth, from whom he obtained a charter empowering him to establish English colonies along the American coast. A knighthood was bestowed upon him for the discovery of Virginia, although he himself never went on any of the Virginia expeditions.

Raleigh fell out of favor with the Queen after his marriage, and his fortunes definitely waned with her death. Shortly after the accession of King James he was unjustly accused of treason and thrown into the Tower of London for thirteen years' imprisonment. He was finally released by promising King James untold riches if he would grant a commission to sail to Guiana.

Raleigh's plans for this voyage were thwarted from the start by the Spanish ambassador. On his return in 1618 he was once more unjustly arrested for treason and this time, as a sop to the king of Spain, he was beheaded.

The accounts of the Virginia expeditions which follow were addressed to Raleigh by those who made the voyages. The fateful Guiana expedition, made by Raleigh himself, is here beautifully and eloquently recounted in his own words.

THE DISCOVERY OF VIRGINIA

The Voyages and Navigations of the English nation to Virginia, and the severall discoveries therof chiefly at the charges of the honourable Sir Walter Ralegh knight, from 33 to 40 degrees of latitude: together with the successe of the English colonies there planted: as likewise a description of the Countrey, with the Inhabitants, and the manifold commodities. The first voyage made to the coasts of America, with two barks, where in were Captaines M. Philip Amadas, and M. Arthur Barlowe, who discovered part of the Countrey now called Virginia, Anno 1584. Written by one of the said Captaines, and sent to sir Walter Ralegh knight, at whose charge and direction, the said voyage was set forth.

THE 27 day of Aprill, in the yeere of our redemption, 1584 we departed the West of England, with two barkes well furnished with men and victuals, having received our last and perfect directions by your letters, confirming the former instructions, and commandements delivered by your selfe at our leaving the river of Thames. And I thinke it a matter both unnecessary, for the manifest discoverie of the Countrey, as also for tediousnesse sake, to remember unto you the diurnall of our course, sayling thither and returning: onely I have presumed to present unto you this briefe discourse, by which you may judge how profitable this land is likely to succeede, as well to your selfe, (by whose direction and charge, and by whose servantes this our discoverie hath bene performed) as also to her Highnesse, and the Common wealth, in which we hope your wisedome wilbe satisfied, considering that as much by us hath bene brought to light, as by those smal meanes, and number of men we had, could any way have bene expected, or hoped for.

The tenth of May we arrived at the Canaries, and the tenth of June in this present yeere, we were fallen with the Islands of the West Indies, keeping a more Southeasterly course then was needefull, because wee doubted that the current of the Bay of Mexico, disbogging betweene the Cape of Florida and Havana, had bene of greater force then afterwardes we found it to bee. At which Islands we found the ayre very unwholsome, and our men grew for the most part ill disposed: so that having refreshed our selves with sweet water, & fresh victuall, we departed the twelfth day of our arrivall there. These Islands, with the rest adjoyning, are so well knowen to your selfe, and to many others, as I will not trouble you with the remembrance of them.

The second of July, we found shole water, wher we smelt so sweet, and so strong a smel, as if we had bene in the midst of some delicate garden abounding with all kinde of odoriferous flowers, by which we were assured, that the land could not be farre distant: and keeping good watch, and bearing but slacke saile, the fourth of the same moneth we arrived upon the coast, which we supposed to be a continent and firme lande, and we sayled along the same a hundred and twentie English miles before we could finde any entrance, or river issuing into the Sea. The first that appeared unto us, we entred, though not without some difficultie, & cast anker about three harquebuz-shot within the havens mouth, on the left hand of the same: and after thankes given to God for our safe arrivall thither, we manned our boats, and went to view the land next adjoyning, and to take possession of the same, in the right of the Queenes most excellent Majestie, as rightfull Queene, and Princesse of the same, and after delivered the same over to your use, according to her Majesties grant, and letters patents, under her Highnesse great Seale. Which being performed, according to the ceremonies used in such enterprises, we viewed the land about us, being, whereas we first landed, very sandie and low towards the waters side, but so full of grapes, as the very beating and surge of the Sea overflowed them, of which we found such plentie, as well there as in all places else, both on the sand and on the greene soile on the hils, as in the plaines, as well on every little shrubbe, as also climing towardes the tops of high

Cedars, that I thinke in all the world the like abundance is not to be found: and my selfe having seene those parts of Europe that most abound, find such difference as were incredible to be written.

We passed from the Sea side towardes the toppes of those hilles next adjoyning, being but of meane higth, and from thence wee behelde the Sea on both sides to the North, and to the South, finding no ende any of both wayes. This lande lay stretching it selfe to the West, which after wee found to bee but an Island of twentie miles long, and not above sixe miles broade. Under the banke or hill whereon we stoode, we behelde the vallyes replenished with goodly Cedar trees, and having discharged our harquebuz-shot, such a flocke of Cranes (the most part white) arose under us, with such a cry redoubled by many ecchoes, as if an armie of men had showted all together.

This Island had many goodly woodes full of Deere, Conies, Hares, and Fowle, even in the middest of Summer in incredible abundance. The woodes are not such as you finde in Bohemia, Moscovia, or Hercynia, barren and fruitles, but the highest and reddest Cedars of the world, farre bettering the Cedars of the Açores, of the Indies, or Lybanus, Pynes, Cypres, Sassa-phras, the Lentisk, or the tree that beareth the Masticke, the tree that beareth the rine of blacke Sinamon, of which Master Winter brought from the streights of Magellan, and many other of excellent smell and qualitie. We remained by the side of this Island two whole dayes before we saw any people of the Countrey: the third day we espied one small boate row-ing towardes us having in it three persons: this boat came to the Island side, foure harquebuz-shot from our shippes, and there two of the people remaining, the third came along the shoreside towards us, and wee being then all within boord, he walked up and downe upon the point of the land next to us: then the Master and the Pilot of the Admirall, Simon Ferdi-nando, and the Captaine Philip Amadas, my selfe, and others rowed to the land, whose comming this fellow attended, never making any shewe of feare or doubt. And after he had spoken of many things not understood by us, we brought him with his owne good liking, aboord the ships, and gave him a shirt, a hat & some other things, and made him taste of our wine, and our meat, which he liked very wel: and after having viewed both barks, he departed, and went to his owne boat againe, which hee had left in a little Cove or Creeke adjoyning: assoone as hee was two bow shoot into the water, he fell to fishing, and in lesse then halfe an houre, he had laden his boate as deepe, as it could swimme, with which hee came againe to the point of the lande, and there he devided his fish into two parts, pointing one part to the ship, and the other to the pinnesse: which, after he had (as much as he might) requited the former benefites received, de-parted out of our sight.

The next day there came unto us divers boates, and in one of them the Kings brother, accompanied with fortie or fiftie men, very handsome and goodly people, and in their behaviour as mannerly and civill as any of Europe. His name was Granganimo, and the king is called Wingina, the countrey Wingandacoa, and now by her Majestie Virginia. The maner of his comming was in this sort: hee left his boates altogether as the first man did a little from the shippes by the shore, and came along to the place over against the ships, followed with fortie men. When he came to the place, his servants spread a long matte upon the ground, on which he sate downe, and at the other ende of the matte foure others of his companie did the like, the rest of his men stood round about him, somewhat a farre off: when we came to the shore to him with our weapons, hee never mooved from his place, nor any of the other foure, nor never mistrusted any harme to be offred from us, but sitting still he beckoned us to come and sit by him, which we performed: and being set hee made all signes of joy and welcome, striking on his head and his breast and afterwardes on ours, to shewe wee were all one, smiling and making shewe the best he could of all love, and familiaritie. After hee had made a long speech unto us, wee presented him with divers things, which hee received very joyfully, and thankefully. None of the company durst speake one worde all the time: onely the foure which were at the other ende, spake one in the others eare very softly.

The King is greatly obeyed, and his brothers and children reverenced: the King himselfe in person was at our being there, sore wounded in a fight which hee had with the King of the next countrey, called Wingina, and was shot in two places through the body, and once cleane through the thigh, but yet he recovered: by reason whereof and for that hee lay at the chiefe towne of the countrey, being six dayes journey off, we saw him not at all.

After we had presented this his brother with such things as we thought he liked, wee likewise gave somewhat to the other that sat with him on the matte: but presently he arose and tooke all from them and put it into his owne basket, making signes and tokens, that all things ought to bee delivered unto him, and the rest were but his servant, and followers. A day or two after this, we fell to trading with them, exchanging some things that we had, for Chamoys, Buffe, and Deere skinnes: when we shewed him all our packet of merchandize, of all things that he sawe, a bright tinne dish most pleased him, which hee presently tooke up and clapt it before his breast, and after made a hole in the brimme thereof and hung it about his necke, making signes that it would defende him against his enemies arrowes: for those people maintaine a deadly and terrible warre, with the people and King adjoyning. We exchanged our tinne dish for twentie skinnes, woorth twentie Crownes, or twentie Nobles: and a copper kettle for fiftie skins woorth fifty Crownes. They offered us good exchange for our hatchets, and axes, and for knives, and would have given any thing for swordes: but wee would not depart with any. After two or three dayes the Kings brother came aboord the shippes, and dranke wine, and eat of our meat and of our bread, and liked exceedingly thereof: and after a few dayes overpassed, he brought his wife with him to the ships, his daughter and two or three children: his wife was very well favoured, of meane stature, and very bashfull: shee had on her backe a long cloake of leather, with the furre side next to her body, and before her a piece of the same: about her forehead shee had a bande of white Corall, and so had her hus-band many times: in her eares shee had bracelets of pearles hanging downe to her middle, (whereof wee delivered your worship a little bracelet) and those were of the bignes of good pease. The rest of her women of the better sort had pendants of copper hanging in either eare, and some of the children of the kings brother and other noble men, have five or sixe in either eare: he himselfe had upon his head a broad plate of golde, or copper, for being unpolished we knew not what mettal it should be, neither would he by any meanes suffer us to take it off his head, but feeling it, it would bow very easily. His apparell was as his wives, onely the women weare their haire long on both sides, and the men but on one. They are of colour yellowish, and their haire black for the most part, and yet we saw children that had very fine aburne, and chestnut coloured haire.

After that these women had bene there, there came downe from all parts great store of people, bringing with them leather, corall, divers kindes of dies very excellent, and exchanged with us: but when Granganimo the kings brother was present, none durst trade but himselfe: except such as weare red pieces of copper on their heads like himselfe: for that is the difference betweene the noble men, and the governours of countreys, and the meaner sort. And we both noted there, and you have understood since by these men, which we brought home, that no people in the worlde cary more respect to their King, Nobilitie, and Governours, then these doe. The Kings brothers wife, when she came to us (as she did many times) was followed with forty or fifty women always: and when she came into the shippe, she left them all on land, saving her two daughters, her nurse and one or two more. The Kings brother alwayes kept this order, as many boates as he would come withall to the shippes, so many fires would hee make on the shore a farre off, to the end we might understand with what strength and company he approched. Their boates are made of one tree, either of Pine or of Pitch trees: a wood not commonly knowen to our people, nor found growing in England. They have no edge-tooles to make them withall: if they have any they are very fewe, and those it seemes they had twentie yeres since, which, as those two men declared, was out of a wrake which happened upon their coast of some Christian ship, being beaten that way by some storme and outragious weather, whereof none of the people were saved, but only the ship, or some part of her be-ing cast upon the sand, out of whose sides they drew the nayles and the spikes, and with those they made their best instruments. The manner of making their boates is thus: they burne downe some great tree, or take such as are winde fallen, and putting gumme and rosen upon one side thereof, they set fire into it, and when it hath burnt it hollow, they cut out the coale with their shels, and ever where they would burne it deeper or wider they lay on gummes, which burne away the timber, and by this meanes they fashion very fine boates, and such as will transport twentie men. Their oares are like scoopes, and many times they set with long pooles, as the depth serveth.

The Kings brother had great liking of our armour, a sword, and divers other things which we had: and offered to lay a great boxe of pearle in gage for them: but we refused it for this time, because we would not make them knowe, that we esteemed thereof, untill we had understoode in what places of the countrey the pearle grew: which now your Worshippe doeth very well understand.

He was very just of his promise: for many times we delivered him merchandize upon his word, but ever he came within the day and performed his promise. He sent us every day a brase or two of fat Bucks, Conies, Hares, Fish the best of the world. He sent us divers kindes of fruites, Melons, Walnuts, Cucumbers, Gourdes, Pease, and divers rootes, and fruites very excellent good, and of their Countrey corne, which is very white, faire and well tasted, and groweth three times in five moneths: in May they sow, in July they reape, in June they sow, in August they reape: in July they sow, in September they reape: onely they cast the corne into the ground, breaking a little of the soft turfe with a wodden mattock, or picke axe: our selves prooved the soile, and put some of our Pease in the ground, and in tenne dayes they were of fourteene ynches high: they have also Beanes very faire of divers colours and wonderfull plentie: some growing naturally, and some in their gardens, and so have they both wheat and oates.

The soile is the most plentifull, sweete, fruitfull and wholsome of all the worlde: there are above fourteene severall sweete smelling timber trees, and the most part of their underwoods are Bayes and such like: they have those Okes that we have, but farre greater and better. After they had bene divers times aboord our shippes, my selfe, with seven more went twentie mile into the River, that runneth towarde the Citie of Skicoak, which River they call Occam: and the evening following, wee came to an Island, which they call Roanoak, distant from the harbour by which we entred, seven leagues: and at the North end thereof was a village of nine houses, built of Cedar, and fortified round about with sharpe trees, to keepe out their enemies, and the entrance into it made like a turne pike very artificially; when wee came towardes it, standing neere unto the waters side, the wife of Granganimo the kings brother came running out to meete us very cheerefully and friendly, her husband was not then in the village; some of her people shee commanded to drawe our boate on shore for the beating of the billoe: others she appointed to cary us on their backes to the dry ground, and others to bring our oares into the house for feare of stealing. When we were come into the utter roome, having five roomes in her house, she caused us to sit downe by a great fire, and after tooke off our clothes and washed them, and dryed them againe: some of the women plucked off our stockings and washed them, some washed our feete in warme water, and shee her selfe tooke great paines to see all things ordered in the best maner shee could, making great haste to dresse some meate for us to eate.

After we had thus dryed our selves, she brought us into the inner roome, where shee set on the boord standing along the house, some wheate like furmentie, sodden Venison, and roasted, fish sodden, boyled, and roasted, Melons rawe, and sodden, rootes of divers kindes, and divers fruites: their drinke is commonly water, but while the grape lasteth they drinke wine, and for want of caskes to keepe it, all the yere after they drink water, but it is sodden with Ginger in it, and blacke Sinamon, and sometimes Sassaphras, and divers other wholesome, and medicinable hearbes and trees. We were entertained with all love and kindnesse, and with as much bountie (after their maner) as they could possibly devise. We found the people most gentle, loving, and faithfull, voide of all guile and treason, and such as live after the maner of the golden age. The people onely care howe to defend themselves from the cold in their short winter, and to feed themselves with such meat as the soile affoordeth: there meate is very well sodden and they make broth very sweet and savorie: their vessels are earthen pots, very large, white and sweete, their dishes are wodden platters of sweet timber: within the place where they feede was their lodging, and within that their Idoll, which they worship, of whome they speake incredible things. While we were at meate, there came in at the gates two or three men with their bowes and arrowes from hunting, whom when wee espied, we beganne to looke one towardes another, and offered to reach our weapons: but assoone as shee espied our mistrust, shee was very much mooved, and caused some of her men to runne out, and take away their bowes and arrowes and breake them, and withall beate the poore fellowes out of the gate againe. When we departed in the evening and would not tary all night, she was very sory, and gave us into our boate our supper halfe dressed, pottes and all, and brought us to our boate side, in which wee lay all night, remooving the same a prettie distance from the shoare: shee perceiving our jelousie, was much grieved, and sent divers men and thirtie women, to sit all night on the banke side by us, and sent us into our boates five mattes to cover us from the raine, using very many wordes to intreate us to rest in their houses: but because wee were fewe men, and if wee had miscaried, the voyage had bene in very great danger, wee durst not adventure any thing, though there was no cause of doubt: for a more kinde and loving people there can not be found in the worlde, as farre as we have hitherto had triall.

Beyond this Island there is the maine lande, and over against this Island falleth into this spacious water, the great river called Occam by the inhabitants on which standeth a towne called Pomeiock, & sixe dayes journey from the same is situate their greatest citie, called Skicoak, which this people affirme to be very great: but the Savages were never at it, only they speake of it by the report of their fathers and other men, whom they have heard affirme it to bee above one houres journey about.

Into this river falleth another great river, called Cipo, in which there is found great store of Muskles in which there are pearles: likewise there descendeth into this Occam, another river, called Nomopana, on the one side whereof standeth a great towne called Chawanook, and the Lord of that towne and countrey is called Pooneno: this Pooneno is not subject to the king of Wingandacoa, but is a free Lord: beyond this country is there another king, whom they cal Menatonon, and these three kings are in league with each other. Towards the Southwest, foure dayes journey is situate a towne called Sequotan, which is the Southermost towne of Wingandacoa, neere unto which, sixe and twentie yeres past there was a ship cast away, whereof some of the people were saved, and those were white people, whom the countrey people preserved.

And after ten dayes remaining in an out Island unhabited, called Woco-kon, they with the help of some of the dwellers of Sequotan, fastened two boates of the countrey together & made mastes unto them, and sailes of their shirtes, and having taken into them such victuals as the countrey yeelded, they departed after they had remained in this out Island 3 weekes: but shortly after it seemed they were cast away, for the boates were found upon the coast, cast a land in another Island adjoyning: other then these, there was never any people apparelled, or white of colour, either seene or heard of amongst these people, and these aforesaid were seene onely of the inhabitantes of Secotan, which appeared to be very true, for they wondred marvelously when we were amongst them at the whitenes of our skins, ever coveting to touch our breasts, and to view the same. Besides they had our ships in marvelous admiration, & all things els were so strange unto them, as it appeared that none of them had ever seene the like. When we discharged any piece, were it but an harqubuz, they would tremble thereat for very feare, and for the strangenesse of the same: for the weapons which themselves use are bowes and arrowes: the arrowes are but of small canes, headed with a sharpe shell or tooth of a fish sufficient ynough to kill a naked man. Their swordes be of wood hardened: likewise they use wooden breastplates for their defence. They have besides a kinde of club, in the end whereof they fasten the sharpe hornes of a stagge, or other beast. When they goe to warres they cary about with them their idol, of whom they aske counsel, as the Romans were woont of the Oracle of Apollo. They sing songs as they march towardes the battell in stead of drummes and trumpets: their warres are very cruell and bloody, by reason whereof, and of their civill dissentions which have happened of late yeeres amongst them, the people are marvelously wasted, and in some places the countrey left desolate.

Adjoyning to this countrey aforesaid called Secotan beginneth a countrey called Pomovik, belonging to another king whom they call Piemacum, and this king is in league with the next king adjoyning towards the setting of the Sunne, and the countrey Newsiok, situate upon a goodly river called Neus: these kings have mortall warre with Wingina king of Wing-andacoa: but about two yeeres past there was a peace made betweene the King Piemacum, and the Lord of Secotan, as these men which we have brought with us to England, have given us to understand: but there re-maineth a mortall malice in the Secotanes, for many injuries & slaughters done upon them by this Piemacum. They invited divers men, and thirtie women of the best of his countrey to their towne to a feast: and when they were altogether merry, & praying before their Idol, (which is nothing els but a meer illusion of the devil) the captaine or Lord of the town came suddenly upon them, and slewe them every one, reserving the women and children: and these two have oftentimes since perswaded us to surprize Piemacum his towne, having promised and assured us, that there will be found in it great store of commodities. But whether their perswasion be to the ende they may be revenged of their enemies, or for the love they beare to us, we leave that to the tryall hereafter.

Beyond this Island called Roanoak, are maine Islands very plentifull of fruits and other naturall increases, together with many townes, and villages, along the side of the continent, some bounding upon the Islands, and some stretching up further into the land.

When we first had sight of this countrey, some thought the first land we saw to bee the continent: but after we entred into the Haven, we saw before us another mighty long Sea: for there lyeth along the coast a tracte of Islands, two hundreth miles in length, adjoyning to the Ocean sea, and betweene the Islands, two or three entrances: when you are entred betweene them (these Islands being very narrow for the most part, as in most places sixe miles broad, in some places lesse, in fewe more) then there appeareth another great Sea, containing in bredth in some places, forty, and in some fifty, in some twenty miles over, before you come unto the continent: and in this inclosed Sea there are above an hundreth Islands of divers bignesses, whereof one is sixteene miles long, at which we were, finding it a most pleasant and fertile ground, replenished with goodly Cedars, and divers other sweete woods, full of Corrants, of flaxe, and many other notable commodities, which we at that time had no leasure to view. Besides this Island there are many, as I have sayd, some of two, of three, of foure, of five miles, some more, some lesse, most beautifull and pleasant to behold, replenished with Deere, Conies, Hares and divers beasts, and about them the goodliest and best fish in the world, and in greatest abundance.

Thus Sir, we have acquainted you with the particulars of our discovery, made this present voyage, as farre foorth as the shortnesse of the time we there continued would affoord us take viewe of: and so contenting our selves with this service at this time, which wee hope hereafter to inlarge, as occasion and assistance shalbe given, we resolved to leave the countrey, and to apply our selves to returne for England which we did accordingly, and arrived safely in the West of England about the middest of September.

·   ·   ·   ·   ·

A briefe and true report of the new found land of Virginia: of the commodities there found, and to be raised, aswell merchantable as others: Written by Thomas Heriot, servant to Sir Walter Ralegh, a member of the Colony, and there imployed in discovering a full twelvemoneth.

To the Adventurers, Favourers, and Welwillers of the enterprise for
the inhabiting and planting in Virginia.

SINCE the first undertaking by Sir Walter Ralegh to deale in the action of
discovering of that countrey which is now called and knowen by the name
of Virginia, many voyages having beene thither made at sundry times to
his great charge; as first in the yere 1584, and afterwards in the yeres 1585,
1586, and now of late this last yeere 1587: there have bene divers and variable reports, with some slanderous and shamefull speeches bruted abroad
by many that returned from thence: especially of that discovery which
was made by the Colony transported by Sir Richard Grinvile in the yere
1585, being of all others the most principall, and as yet of most effect, the
time of their abode in the countrey being a whole yere, when as in the
other voyage before they stayed but six weeks, and the others after were
onely for supply and transportation, nothing more being discovered then
had bene before. Which reports have not done a little wrong to many that
otherwise would have also favoured and adventured in the action, to the
honour and benefit of our nation, besides the particular profit and credit
which would redound to themselves the dealers therein, as I hope by the
sequel of events, to the shame of those that have avouched the contrary,
shall be manifest, if you the adventurers, favourers and welwillers doe but
either increase in number, or in opinion continue, or having beene doubtfull, renew your good liking and furtherance to deale therein according
to the woorthinesse thereof already found, and as you shall understand
hereafter to be requisit. Touching which woorthinesse through cause of
the diversity of relations and reports, many of your opinions could not be
firme, nor the minds of some that are well disposed be setled in any certaintie.

I have therefore thought it good, being one that have beene in the discoverie, and in dealing with the naturall inhabitants specially imployed:
and having therefore seene and knowen more then the ordinary, to im-
part so much unto you of the fruits of our labours, as that you may know
how injuriously the enterprise is slandered. . . .

Of our company that returned, some for their misdemeanour and ill
dealing in the countrey have bene there worthily punished, who by reason of their bad natures, have maliciously not onely spoken ill of their
Governours, but for their sakes slandered the countrey it selfe. The like
also have those done which were of their consort.

Some being ignorant of the state thereof, notwithstanding since their
returne amongst their friends & acquaintance, and also others, especially
if they were in company where they might not be gainsayd, would seeme
to know so much as no men more, and make no men so great travellers as
themselves. They stood so much, as it may seeme, upon their credit and
reputation, that having bene a twelvemoneth in the countrey, it would have
bene a great disgrace unto them, as they thought, if they could not have
sayd much, whether it were true or false. Of which some have spoken of

more then ever they saw, or otherwise knew to be there. Other some have not bene ashamed to make absolute deniall of that, which although not by them, yet by others is most certainly and there plentifully knowen, & other some make difficulties of those things they have no skill of.

The cause of their ignorance was, in that they were of that many that were never out of the Island where we were seated, or not farre, or at the least wise in few places els, during the time of our abode in the country: or of that many, that after gold & silver was not so soone found, as it was by them looked for, had litle or no care of any other thing but to pamper their bellies: or of that many which had litle understanding, lesse discretion, and more tongue then was needfull or requisite.

Some also were of a nice bringing up, only in cities or townes, or such as never (as I may say) had seene the world before. Because there were not to be found any English cities, nor such faire houses, nor at their owne wish any of their old accustomed dainty food, nor any soft beds of downe or feathers, the countrey was to them miserable, and their reports thereof according.

Because my purpose was but in briefe to open the cause of the variety of such speeches, the particularities of them, and of many envious, malicious, and slanderous reports and devices els, by our owne countreymen besides, as trifles that are not worthy of wise men to be thought upon, I meane not to trouble you withall, but will passe to the commodities, the substance of that which I have to make relation of unto you.

The Treatise whereof, for your more ready view and easier understanding, I will divide into three speciall parts. . . .

The first part of Merchantable commodities.

SILKE of grasse, or Grasse silke. There is a kind of grasse in the country, upon the blades whereof there groweth very good silke in forme of a thin glittering skin to be stript off. It groweth two foot & an halfe high or better: the blades are about two foot in length, and halfe an inch broad. The like groweth in Persia, which is in the selfe same climate as Virginia, of which very many of the Silke works that come from thence into Europe are made. Hereof if it be planted and ordered as in Persia, it cannot in reason be otherwise, but that there will rise in short time great profit to the dealers therein, seeing there is so great use and vent thereof aswel in our countrey as elsewhere. And by the meanes of sowing and planting it in good ground, it will be farre greater, better, and more plentifull then it is. Although notwithstanding there is great store thereof in many places of the countrey growing naturally and wild, which also by proofe here in England, in making a piece of Silke grogran, we found to be excellent good.

Worme silke. In many of our journeys we found Silke-wormes faire and great, as bigge as our ordinary Walnuts. Although it hath not bene our hap to have found such plenty, as elswhere to be in the countrey we have heard of, yet seeing that the countrey doth naturally breed and nourish them, there is no doubt but if arte be added in planting of Mulberie trees, and others, fit for them in commodious places, for their feeding & nourishing, and some of them carefully gathered & husbanded in that sort, as by men of skil is knowen to be necessary: there wil rise as great profit in time to the Virginians, as thereof doth now to the Persians, Turks, Italians and Spanyards.

Flaxe and Hempe. The trueth is, that of Hempe and Flaxe there is no great store in any one place together, by reason it is not planted but as the soile doth yeeld of it selfe: and howsoever the leafe and stemme or stalke do differ from ours, the stuffe by judgement of men of skill is altogether as good as ours.

Allum. There is a veine of earth along the sea coast for the space of forty or fifty miles, whereof by the judgement of some that have made triall here in England, is made good Allum, of that kind which is called Roch allum. The richnesse of such a commodity is so well knowen, that I need not to say any thing thereof. The same earth doth also yeeld White coprasse, Nitrum, and Alumen plumeum, but nothing so plentifully as the common Allum, which be also of price, and profitable.

Wapeih. A kind of earth so called by the naturall inhabitants, very like to Terra sigillata, and having bene refined, it hath bene found by some of our Physicians and Chyrurgians, to be of the same kind of vertue, and more effectuall. The inhabitants use it very much for the cure of sores and wounds: there is in divers places great plenty, and in some places of a blew sort.

Pitch, Tarre, Rozen and Turpentine. There are those kinds of trees which yeeld them abundantly and great store. In the very same Island where we were seated, being fifteene miles of length, and five or sixe miles in breadth, there are few trees els but of the same kinde, the whole Island being full.

Sassafras, called by the inhabitants Winauk, a kind of wood of most pleasant and sweet smell, and of most rare vertues in physicke for the cure of many diseases. It is found by experience to be far better and of more uses then the wood which is called Guaiacum, or Lignum vitæ.

Cedar. A very sweet wood, and fine timber, whereof if nests of chests be there made, or timber thereof fitted for sweet and fine bedsteds, tables, desks, lutes, virginals, and many things els, (of which there hath bene proofe made already) to make up fraight with other principall commodities, will yeeld profit.

Wine. There are two kindes of grapes that the soile doth yeeld naturally, the one is small and sowre, of the ordinary bignesse as ours in England, the other farre greater and of himselfe lushious sweet. When they are planted and husbanded as they ought, a principall commodity of wines by them may be raised.

Oile. There are two sorts of Walnuts, both holding oile; but the one farre more plentifull then the other. When there are mils and other devices for the purpose, a commodity of them may be raised, because there are infinite store. There are also three severall kindes of berries in the forme of Oke-akornes, which also by the experience and use of the inhabitants, we find to yeeld very good and sweet oile. Furthermore, the beares of the countrey are commonly very fat, and in some places there are many. Their fatnesse, because it is so liquid, may well be termed oile, and hath many speciall uses.

Furres. All along the Sea coast there are great store of Otters, which being taken by weares and other engines made for the purpose, wil yeeld good profit. We hope also of Marterne furres, and make no doubt by the relation of the people, but that in some places of the countrey there are store, although there were but two skinnes that came to our hands. Luzernes also we have understanding of, although for the time we saw none.

Deers skinnes dressed after the maner of Chamoes, or undressed, are to be had of the naturall inhabitants thousands yerely by way of traffike for trifles, and no more waste or spoile of Deere then is and hath bene ordinarily in time before.

Civet-cats. In our travels there was found one to have bin killed by a Savage or inhabitant, & in another place the smel where one or more had lately bene before, whereby we gather, besides then by the relation of the people, that there are some in the country: good profit will rise by them.

Iron. In two places of the countrey specially, one about fourescore, & the other six score miles from the fort or place where we dwelt, we found nere the water side the ground to be rocky, which by the triall of a Minerall man was found to holde iron richly. It is found in many places of the country els: I know nothing to the contrary, but that it may be allowed for a good merchantable commodity, considering there the small charge for the labour & feeding of men, the infinite store of wood, the want of wood & deerenesse thereof in England, and the necessity of ballasting of ships.

Copper. An hundred and fifty miles into the maine in two townes we found with the inhabitants divers small plates of Copper, that had bene made as we understood by the inhabitants that dwell further into the country, where as they say are mountaines and rivers that yeeld also white graines of mettall, which is to be deemed Silver. For confirmation whereof, at the time of our first arrivall in the countrey, I saw, with some others with me, two small pieces of Silver grosly beaten, about the weight of a testron, hanging in the eares of a Wiroans or chiefe lord that dwelt about fourescore miles from us: of whom through inquiry, by the number of dayes and the way, I learned that it had come to his hands from the same place or neere, where I after understood the Copper was made, and the white graines of metall found. The aforesayd Copper we also found by triall to holde Silver.

Pearle. Sometimes in feeding on Muscles we found some Pearle: but it was our happe to meet with ragges, or of a pide colour: not having yet discovered those places where we heard of better and more plenty. . . .

Sweet gummes of divers kinds, and many other Apothecary drugges, of which we will make speciall mention, when we shall receive it from such men of skill in that kinde, that in taking reasonable paines shal discover them more particularly then we have done, and then now I can make relation of, for want of the examples I had provided and gathered, and are now lost, with other things by casualty before mentioned.

Dies of divers kinds: There is Shoemake well knowen, and used in England for blacke: the seed of an herbe called Wasebur, little small roots called Chappacor, and the barke of the tree called by the inhabitants Tango-mockonomindge: which dies are for divers sorts of red: their goodnesse for our English clothes remaine yet to be prooved. The inhabitants use them only for the dying of haire, and colouring of their faces, and mantles made of Deere skinnes: and also for the dying of rushes to make artificiall works withall in their mats and baskets.

Woad: a thing of so great vent and uses amongst English Diers, which can not be yeelded sufficiently in our owne countrey for spare of ground, may be planted in Virginia, there being ground enough. The growth thereof need not to be doubted, when as in the Islands of the Açores it groweth plentifully, which are in the same climate. So likewise of Madder.

We caried thither Sugar-canes to plant, which being not so well preserved as was requisite, and besides the time of the yeere being past for their setting when we arrived, we could not make that proofe of them as we desired. Notwithstanding, seeing that they grow in the same climate, in the South part of Spaine, and in Barbary, our hope in reason may yet continue. So likewise for Orenges and Limmons. There may be planted also Quinses. Whereby may grow in reasonable time, if the action be diligently prosecuted, no small commodities in Sugars, Suckets, and Marmelades.

The second part of such commodities as Virginia is knowen to yeeld for victuall and sustenance of mans life, usually fed upon by the naturall inhabitants; as also by us, during the time of our abode: and first of such as are sowed and husbanded.

Pagatowr, a kinde of graine so called by the inhabitants: the same in the West Indies is called Mayz: English men call it Guiny-wheat or Turkey-wheat, according to the names of the countreys from whence the like hath beene brought. The graine is about the bignesse of our ordinary English peaze, and not much different in forme and shape: but of divers colours: some white, some red, some yellow, and some blew. All of them yeeld a very white and sweet flowre: being used according to his kinde, it maketh a very good bread. We made of the same in the countrey some Mault, whereof was brewed as good Ale as was to be desired. So likewise by the helpe of Hops, therof may be made as good Beere. . . .

Okindgier, called by us Beanes, because in greatnesse and partly in shape they are like to the beanes in England, saving that they are flatter, of more divers colours, and some pide. The leafe also of the stemme is much different. In taste they are altogether as good as our English peaze.

Wickonzowr, called by us Peaze, in respect of the Beanes, for distinction sake, because they are much lesse, although in forme they little differ: but in goodnesse of taste much like, and are far better then our English Peaze. Both the beanes and peaze are ripe in ten weeks after they are set. . . .

There is an herbe which is sowed apart by it selfe, and is called by the inhabitants Uppowoc: in the West Indies it hath divers names, according to the severall places and countreys where it groweth and is used: the Spanyards generally call it Tabacco. The leaves thereof being dried and brought into pouder, they use to take the fume or smoake thereof, by sucking it thorow pipes made of clay, into their stomacke and head; from whence it purgeth superfluous fleame and other grosse humours, and openeth all the pores and passages of the body: by which meanes the use thereof not onely preserveth the body from obstructions, but also (if any be, so that they have not bene of too long continuance) in short time breaketh them: whereby their bodies are notably preserved in health, and know not many grievous diseases, wherewithall we in England are often times afflicted.

This Uppowoc is of so precious estimation amongst them, that they thinke their gods are marvellously delighted therewith: whereupon sometime they make hallowed fires, and cast some of the pouder therin for a sacrifice: being in a storme upon the waters, to pacifie their gods, they cast some up into the aire and into the water: so a weare for fish being newly set up, they cast some therein and into the aire: also after an escape of danger, they cast some into the aire likewise: but all done with strange gestures, stamping, sometime dancing, clapping of hands, holding up of hands, staring up into the heavens, uttering therewithall, and chattering strange words and noises.

We our selves, during the time we were there, used to sucke it after their maner, as also since our returne, and have found many rare and woonderfull experiments of the vertues thereof: of which the relation would require a volume by it selfe: the use of it by so many of late men and women of great calling, as els, and some learned Physicians also, is sufficient witnesse.

And these are all the commodities for sustenance of life, that I know and can remember, they use to husband: all els that follow, are found growing naturally or wilde.

Of Beasts

Deere, in some places there are great store: neere unto the Sea coast they are of the ordinary bignesse of ours in England, and some lesse: but further up into the countrey, where there is better food, they are greater: they differ from ours onely in this, their tailes are longer, and the snags of their hornes looke backward.

Conies. Those that we have seene, and all that we can heare of are of a gray colour like unto Hares: in some places there are such plenty that all the people of some townes make them mantles of the furre or flue of the skinnes of those which they usually take.

Saquenuckot and Maquowoc, two kinds of small beasts greater then Conies, which are very good meat. We never tooke any of them our selves but sometime eat of such as the inhabitants had taken and brought unto us.

Squirels, which are of a grey colour, we have taken and eaten.

Beares, which are of blacke colour. The beares of this countrey are good meat. The inhabitants in time of Winter do use to take & eat many: so also sometime did we. They are taken commonly in this sort: In some Islands or places where they are, being hunted for, assoone as they have spiall of a man, they presently run away, and then being chased, they clime and get up the next tree they can: from whence with arrowes they are shot downe starke dead, or with those wounds that they may after easily be killed. We sometime shot them downe with our calievers.

I have the names of eight and twenty severall sorts of beasts, which I have heard of to be here and there dispersed in the countrey, especially in the maine: of which there are only twelve kinds that we have yet discovered; and of those that be good meat we know only them before mentioned. The inhabitants sometime kill the Lion, and eat him: and we sometime as they came to our hands of their Woolves or Woolvish dogs, which I have not yet set downe for good meat, least that some would understand my judgement therein to be more simple then needeth, although I could alleage the difference in taste of those kinds from ours, which by some of our company have bene experimented in both.

Of Fowle

Turkie cocks and Turkie hennes, Stockdoves, Partridges, Cranes, Hernes, and in Winter great store of Swannes and Geese. . . .

There are also Parrots, Faulcons, and Marlin hauks, which although with us they be not used for meat, yet for other causes I thought good to mention.

Of Fish

For foure moneths of the yeere, February, March, Aprill and May, there are plenty of Sturgeons. And also in the same moneths of Herrings, some of the ordinary bignesse of ours in England, but the most part farre greater, of eighteene, twenty inches, and some two foot in length and better: both these kinds of fish in those moneths are most plentifull, and in best season, which we found to be most delicate and pleasant meat.

There are also Trouts, Porpoises, Rayes, Oldwives, Mullets, Plaice, and very many other sorts of excellent good fish, which we have taken and eaten, whose names I know not but in the countrey language: we have the pictures of twelve sorts more, as they were drawn in the countrey, with their names.

The inhabitants use to take them two maner of wayes; the one is by a kinde of weare made of reeds, which in that country are very strong: the other way, which is more strange, is with poles made sharpe at one end, by shooting them into the fish after the maner as Irish men cast darts, either as they are rowing in their boats, or els as they are wading in the shallowes for the purpose.

There are also in many places plenty of these kinds which follow:
Sea-crabs, such as we have in England.

Oisters, some very great, and some small, some round, and some of a long shape: they are found both in salt water and brackish, and those that we had out of salt water are farre better then the other, as in our countrey.

Also Muscles, Scalops, Periwinkles, and Crevises.

Seekanauk, a kinde of crusty shel-fish, which is good meat, about a foot in bredth, having a crusty taile many legges like a crab, and her eyes in her backe. They are found in shallowes of waters, and sometime on the shore.

There are many Tortoises both of land and sea kinde, their backs and bellies are shelled very thicke; their head, feet, and taile, which are in appearance, seeme ougly, as though they were members of a serpent or venimous beasts; but notwithstanding they are very good meat, as also their eggs. Some have bene found of a yard in bredth and better.

And thus have I made relation of all sorts of victuall that we fed upon for the time we were in Virginia, as also the inhabitants themselves, as farre forth as I know and can remember, or that are specially woorthy to be remembered.

Of the Nature and Maners of the People

It resteth I speake a word or two of the naturall inhabitants, their natures and maners, leaving large discourse thereof until time more convenient hereafter: nowe onely so farre foorth, as that you may know, how that they in respect of troubling our inhabiting and planting, are not to be feared, but that they shall have cause both to feare and love us, that shall inhabite with them.

They are a people clothed with loose mantles made of deere skinnes, and aprons of the same round about their middles, all els naked, of such a difference of statures onely as wee in England, having no edge tooles or weapons of yron or steele to offend us withall, neither knowe they how to make any: those weapons that they have, are onely bowes made of Witch-hazle, and arrowes of reedes, flat edged truncheons also of wood about a yard long, neither have they any thing to defend themselves but targets made of barkes, and some armours made of sticks wickered together with thread.

Their townes are but small, and neere the Sea coast but fewe, some contayning but tenne or twelve houses; some 20. the greatest that we have seene hath bene but of 30. houses: if they bee walled, it is onely done with barkes of trees made fast to stakes, or els with poles onely fixed upright, and close one by another.

Their houses are made of small poles, made fast at the tops in round forme after the maner as is used in many arbories in our gardens of England, in most townes covered with barkes, and in some with artificiall mats made of long rushes, from the tops of the houses downe to the ground. The length of them is commonly double to the breadth, in some places they are but 12. and 16. yards long, and in other some we have seene of foure and twentie.

In some places of the Countrey, one onely towne belongeth to the government of a Wiroans or chiefe Lord, in other some two or three, in some sixe, eight, and more: the greatest Wiroans that yet wee had dealing with, had but eighteene townes in his government, and able to make not above seven or eight hundreth fighting men at the most. The language of every government is different from any other, and the further they are distant, the greater is the difference.

Their maner of warres amongst themselves is either by sudden surprising one an other most commonly about the dawning of the day, or moone-light, or els by ambushes, or some subtile devises. Set battels are very rare, except it fall out where there are many trees, where either part may have some hope of defence, after the delivery of every arrow, in leaping behind some or other.

If there fall out any warres betweene us and them, what their fight is likely to bee, wee having advantages against them so many maner of wayes, as by our discipline, our strange weapons and devises else, especially Ordinance great and small, it may easily bee imagined: by the experience wee have had in some places, the turning up of their heeles against us in running away was their best defence.

In respect of us they are a people poore, and for want of skill and judgement in the knowledge and use of our things, doe esteeme our trifles before things of greater value: Notwithstanding, in their proper maner (considering the want of such meanes as we have), they seeme very ingenious. For although they have no such tooles, nor any such crafts, Sciences and Artes, as wee, yet in those things they doe, they shew excellencie of wit. And by how much they upon due consideration shall finde our maner of knowledges and crafts to exceede theirs in perfection, and speede for doing or execution, by so much the more is it probable that they should desire our friendship and love, and have the greater respect for pleasing and obeying us. Whereby may bee hoped, if meanes of good government be used, that they may in short time bee brought to civilitie, and the imbracing of true Religion.

Some religion they have already, which although it be farre from the trueth, yet being as it is, there is hope it may be the easier and sooner reformed.

They beleeve that there are many gods, which they call Mantoac, but of different sorts & degrees, one onely chiefe and great God, which hath bene from all eternitie. Who, as they affirme, when hee purposed to make the world, made first other gods of a principall order, to be as meanes and instruments to be used in the creation and government to follow, and after the Sunne, moone, and starres as pettie gods, and the instruments of the other order more principal. First (they say) were made waters, out of which by the gods was made all diversitie of creatures that are visible or invisible.

For mankinde they say a woman was made first, which by the working of one of the gods, conceived and brought foorth children: And in such sort they say they had their beginning. But how many yeeres or ages have passed since, they say they can make no relation, having no letters nor other such meanes as we to keepe Records of the particularities of times past, but onely tradition from father to sonne.

They thinke that all the gods are of humane shape, and therefore they represent them by images in the formes of men, which they call Kewasowok, one alone is called Kewas: them they place in houses appropriate or temples, which they call Machicomuck, where they worship, pray, sing, and make many times offring unto them. In some Machicomuck we have seene but one Kewas, in some two, and in other some three. The common sort thinke them to be also gods.

They beleeve also the immortalitie of the soule, that after this life as soone as the soule is departed from the body, according to the workes it hath done, it is either caried to heaven the habitacle of gods, there to enjoy perpetuall blisse and happinesse, or els to a great pitte or hole, which they thinke to be in the furthest parts of their part of the world toward the Sunne set there to burne continually: the place they call Popogusso.

For the confirmation of this opinion, they tolde me two stories of two men that had bene lately dead and revived againe, the one happened but few yeeres before our comming into the Countrey of a wicked man, which having bene dead and buried, the next day the earth of the grave being seene to move, was taken up againe, who made declaration where his soule had bene, that is to say, very neere entring into Popogusso, had not one of the gods saved him, and gave him leave to returne againe, and teach his friends what they should do to avoyd that terrible place of torment. The other happened in the same yeere we were there, but in a towne that was 60. miles from us, and it was told me for strange newes, that one being dead, buried, and taken up againe as the first, shewed that although his body had lien dead in the grave, yet his soule was alive, & had travailed farre in a long broad way, on both sides whereof grew most delicate and pleasant trees, bearing more rare and excellent fruits, then ever hee had seene before, or was able to expresse, and at length came to most brave and faire houses, neere which he met his father that had bene dead before, who gave him great charge to goe backe againe, and shew his friendes what good they were to doe to enjoy the pleasures of that place, which when he had done he should after come againe.

What subtiltie soever be in the Wiroances and priestes, this opinion worketh so much in many of the common and simple sort of people, that it maketh them have great respect to their Governours, and also great care what they doe, to avoyd torment after death, and to enjoy blisse, although notwithstanding there is punishment ordeined for malefactours, as stealers, whoremongers, and other sorts of wicked doers, some punished with death, some with forfeitures, some with beating, according to the greatnesse of the facts.

And this is the summe of their Religion, which I learned by having speciall familiaritie with some of their priests. Wherein they were not so sure grounded, nor gave such credite to their traditions and stories, but through conversing with us they were brought into great doubts of their owne, and no small admiration of ours, with earnest desire in many, to learne more then wee had meanes for want of perfect utterance in their language to expresse.

Most things they sawe with us, as Mathematicall instruments, sea Compasses, the vertue of the load-stone in drawing yron, a perspective glasse whereby was shewed many strange sights, burning glasses, wilde firewoorkes, gunnes, hookes, writing and reading, spring-clockes that seeme to goe of themselves and many other things that wee had were so strange unto them, and so farre exceeded their capacities to comprehend the reason and meanes how they should be made and done, that they thought they were rather the workes of gods then of men, or at the leastwise they had bene given and taught us of the gods. Which made many of them to have such opinion of us, as that if they knew not the trueth of God and Religion already, it was rather to bee had from us whom God so specially loved, then from a people that were so simple, as they found themselves to be in comparison of us. Whereupon greater credite was given unto that wee spake of, concerning such matters.

Many times and in every towne where I came, according as I was able, I made declaration of the contents of the Bible, that therein was set foorth the true and onely God, and his mightie workes, that therein was conteined the true doctrine of salvation through Christ, with many particularities of Miracles and chiefe points of Religion, as I was able then to utter, and thought fit for the time. And although I told them the booke materially and of it selfe was not of any such vertue, as I thought they did conceive, but onely the doctrine therein conteined: yet would many be glad to touch it, to embrace it, to kisse it, to holde it to their breastes and heads, and stroke over all their body with it, to shew their hungry desire of that knowledge which was spoken of.

The Wiroans with whom we dwelt called Wingina, and many of his people would bee glad many times to be with us at our Prayers, and many times call upon us both in his owne towne, as also in others whither hee sometimes accompanied us, to pray and sing Psalmes, hoping thereby to be partaker of the same effects which we by that meanes also expected.

Twise this Wiroans was so grievously sicke that he was like to die, and as he lay languishing, doubting of any helpe by his owne priestes, and thinking hee was in such danger for offending us and thereby our God, sent for some of us to pray and bee a meanes to our God that it would please him either that he might live, or after death dwell with him in blisse, so likewise were the requests of many others in the like case.

On a time also when their corne began to wither by reason of a drought which happened extraordinarily, fearing that it had come to passe by reason that in some thing they had displeased us, many would come to us and desire us to pray to our God of England, that he would preserve their Corne, promising that when it was ripe we also should be partakers of the fruit.

There could at no time happen any strange sicknesse, losses, hurts, or any other crosse unto them, but that they would impute to us the cause or meanes thereof, for offending or not pleasing us. One other rare and strange accident, leaving others, wil I mention before I end, which moved the whole Countrey that either knew or heard of us, to have us in wonderfull admiration.

There was no towne where wee had any subtile devise practised against us, wee leaving it unpunished or not revenged (because we sought by all meanes possible to win them by gentlenesse) but that within a few dayes after our departure from every such Towne, the people began to die very fast, and many in short space, in some Townes about twentie, in some fourtie, and in one sixe score, which in trueth was very many in respect of their numbers. This happened in no place that we could learne, but where we had bin, where they used some practise against us, & after such time. The disease also was so strange, that they neither knewe what it was, nor how to cure it, the like by report of the oldest men in the Countrey never happened before, time out of minde. A thing specially observed by us, as also by the naturall inhabitants themselves. Insomuch that when some of the inhabitants which were our friends, and especially the Wiroans Wingina, had observed such effects in foure or five Townes to followe their wicked practises, they were perswaded that it was the worke of our God through our meanes, and that we by him might kill and slay whom we would without weapons, and not come neere them. And thereupon when it had happened that they had understanding that any of their enemies had abused us in our journeys, hearing that we had wrought no revenge with our weapons, and fearing upon some cause the matter should so rest: did come and intreate us that we would be a meanes to our God that they as others that had dealt ill with us might in like sort die, alleadging how much it would bee for our credite and profite, as also theirs, and hoping furthermore that we would doe so much at their requests in respect of the friendship we professed them.

Whose entreaties although wee shewed that they were ungodly, affirming that our God would not subject himselfe to any such prayers and requests of men: that indeede all things have bene and were to be done according to his good pleasure as he had ordeined: and that we to shewe our selves his true servants ought rather to make petition for the contrary, that they with them might live together with us, be made partakers of his trueth, and serve him in righteousnesse, but notwithstanding in such sort, that wee referre that, as all other things, to bee done according to his divine will and pleasure, and as by his wisedome he had ordeined to be best.

Yet because the effect fell out so suddenly and shortly after according to their desires, they thought neverthelesse it came to passe by our meanes, & that we in using such speeches unto them, did but dissemble the matter, and therefore came unto us to give us thankes in their maner, that although we satisfied them not in promise, yet in deedes and effect we had fulfilled their desires.

This marveilous accident in all the Countrey wrought so strange opinions of us, that some people could not tell whether to thinke us gods or men, and the rather because that all the space of their sicknes, there was no man of ours knowen to die, or that was specially sicke: they noted also that we had no women amongst us, neither that we did care for any of theirs.

Some therefore were of opinion that we were not borne of women, and therefore not mortall, but that we were men of an old generation many yeeres past, then risen againe to immortalitie.

Some would likewise seeme to prophecie that there were more of our generation yet to come to kill theirs and take their places, as some thought the purpose was, by that which was already done. Those that were immediatly to come after us they imagined to be in the aire, yet invisible and without bodies, and that they by our intreatie and for the love of us, did make the people to die in that sort as they did, by shooting invisible bullets into them.

To confirme this opinion, their Phisitions (to excuse their ignorance in curing the disease) would not be ashamed to say, but earnestly make the simple people beleeve, that the strings of blood that they sucked out of the sicke bodies, were the strings wherewithall the invisible bullets were tied and cast. Some also thought that wee shot them our selves out of our pieces, from the place where wee dwelt, and killed the people in any Towne that had offended us, as wee listed, howe farre distant from us soever it were. And other some said, that it was the speciall worke of God for our sakes, as we our selves have cause in some sort to thinke no lesse, whatsoever some doe, or may imagine to the contrary, specially some Astrologers, knowing of the Eclipse of the Sunne which we saw the same yeere before in our voyage thitherward, which unto them appeared very terrible. And also of a Comet which began to appeare but a fewe dayes before the beginning of the saide sicknesse. But to exclude them from being the speciall causes of so speciall an accident, there are further reasons then I thinke fit at this present to be alleadged. These their opinions I have set downe the more at large, that it may appeare unto you that there is good hope they may be brought through discreete dealing and government to the imbracing of the trueth, and consequently to honour, obey, feare and love us.

And although some of our company towards the end of the yeere, shewed themselves too fierce in slaying some of the people in some Townes, upon causes that on our part might easily ynough have bene borne withall: yet notwithstanding, because it was on their part justly deserved, the alteration of their opinions generally and for the most part concerning us is the lesse to be doubted. And whatsoever els they may be, by carefulnesse of our selves neede nothing at all to be feared.

The Conclusion

Now I have (as I hope) made relation not of so few and small things, but that the Countrey (of men that are indifferent and well disposed) may bee sufficiently liked: If there were no more knowen then I have mentioned, which doubtlesse and in great reason is nothing to that which remaineth to be discovered, neither the soyle, nor commodities. As we have reason so to gather by the difference we found in our travailes, for although al which I have before spoken of, have bene discovered and experimented not farre from the Sea coast, where was our abode and most of our travailing: yet sometimes as we made our journeys further into the maine and Countrey; we found the soile to be fatter, the trees greater and to grow thinner, the ground more firme and deeper mould, more and larger champions, finer grasse, and as good as ever we saw any in England; in some places rockie and farre more high and hilly ground, more plentie of their fruites, more abundance of beastes, the more inhabited with people, and of greater pollicie and larger dominions, with greater townes and houses.

Why may wee not then looke for in good hope from the inner parts of more and greater plentie, as well of other things, as of those which wee have already discovered? Unto the Spaniards happened the like in discovering the maine of the West Indies. The maine also of this Countrey of Virginia, extending some wayes so many hundreds of leagues, as otherwise then by the relation of the inhabitants wee have most certaine knowledge of, where yet no Christian prince hath any possession or dealing, cannot but yeelde many kinds of excellent commodities, which we in our discovery have not yet seene.

What hope there is els to bee gathered of the nature of the Climate, being answerable to the Iland of Japan, the land of China, Persia, Jury, the Ilands of Cyprus and Candy, the South parts of Greece, Italy and Spaine, and of many other notable and famous Countreys, because I meane not to be tedious, I leave to your owne consideration.

Whereby also the excellent temperature of the aire there at all seasons, much warmer then in England, and never so vehemently hot, as sometimes is under and betweene the Tropikes, or neere them, cannot be knowen unto you without further relation.

For the holsomnesse thereof I neede to say but thus much: that for all the want of provision, as first of English victuall, excepting for twentie dayes, we lived onely by drinking water, and by the victuall of the Countrey, of which some sorts were very strange unto us, and might have bene thought to have altered our temperatures in such sort, as to have brought us into some grievous and dangerous diseases: Secondly the want of English meanes, for the taking of beastes, fish and foule, which by the helpe onely of the inhabitants and their meanes could not bee so suddenly and easily provided for us, nor in so great number and quantities, nor of that choise as otherwise might have bene to our better satisfaction and contentment. Some want also we had of clothes. Furthermore in al our travailes, which were most specially and often in the time of Winter, our lodging was in the open aire upon the ground. And as I say for all this, there were but foure of our whole company (being one hundreth and eight) that died all the yeere, and that but at the latter ende thereof, and upon none of the aforesaide causes. For all foure, especially three, were feeble, weake, and sickly persons before ever they came thither, and those that knew them, much marveled that they lived so long being in that case, or had adventured to travaile.

Seeing therefore the aire there is so temperate and holsome, the soyle so fertile, and yeelding such commodities, as I have before mentioned, the voyage also thither to and fro being sufficiently experimented to be perfourmed twise a yeere with ease, and at any season thereof: And the dealing of Sir Walter Ralegh so liberall in large giving and granting lande there, as is already knowen, with many helpes and furtherances else: (The least that he hath granted hath bene five hundreth acres to a man onely for the adventure of his person) I hope there remaines no cause whereby the action should be misliked.

If that those which shall thither travaile to inhabite and plant bee but reasonably provided for the first yeere, as those are which were transported the last, and being there, doe use but that diligence and care, that is requisit, and as they may with ease: There is no doubt, but for the time following, they may have victuals that are excellent good and plentie ynough, some more English sorts of cattel also hereafter, as some have bene before, and are there yet remayning, may, and shall be (God willing) thither transported. So likewise, our kinde of fruites, rootes, and hearbes, may be there planted and sowed, as some have bene already, and prove well: And in short time also they may raise so much of those sorts of commodities which I have spoken of, as shall both enrich themselves, as also others that shall deale with them.

And this is all the fruit of our labours, that I have thought necessary to advertise you of at this present.

Thus referring my relation to your favourable constructions, expecting good successe of the action, from him which is to be acknowledged the authour and governour, not onely of this, but of all things els, I take my leave of you, this moneth of February 1587.

THE DISCOVERY OF GUIANA

The discoverie of the large, rich, and beautifull Empire of Guiana, with a relation of the great and golden citie of Manoa (which the Spaniards call El Dorado) and the provinces of Emeria, Aromaia, Amapaia, and other countries, with their rivers adjoyning. Performed in the yeere 1595 by Sir Walter Ralegh Knight, Captaine of Her Majesties Guard, Lorde Warden of the Stanneries, and Her Highnesse Lieutenant Generall of the Countie of Corne-wall.

To the right Honourable my singular good Lord and kinsman Charles Howard, Knight of the Garter, Baron and Counceller, and of the Admirals of England the most renowned: and to the right Honourable Sir Robert Cecyll knight, Counceller in her Highnesse Privie Councels.

FOR your Honours many Honourable and friendly partes, I have hitherto onely returned promises, and now for answere of both your adventures, I

have sent you a bundle of papers, which I have devided betwene your Lordship, and Sir Robert Cecyll in these two respects chiefly: First for that it is
reason, that wastful factors, when they have consumed such stockes as they
had in trust, doe yeeld some colour for the same in their account; secondly
for that I am assured, that whatsoever shall bee done, or written by me, shall
neede a double protection and defence.

The triall that I had of both your loves, when I was left of all, but of
malice and revenge, makes me still presume, that you wil be pleased (knowing what litle power I had to performe ought, and the great advantage of
forewarned enemies) to answer that out of knowledge, which others shal
but object out of malice. In my more happy times as I did especially Hon.
you both, so I found that your loves sought mee out in the darkest shadow
of adversitie, and the same affection which accompanied my better fortune,
sored not away from me in my many miseries: al which though I can not
requite, yet I shal ever acknowledge: & the great debt which I have no
power to pay, I can do no more for a time but confesse to be due.

It is true that as my errors were great, so they have yeelded very grievous
effects, & if ought might have bene deserved in former times to have coun-
terpoysed any part of offences, the fruit thereof (as it seemeth) was long
before fallen from the tree, & the dead stocke onely remained. I did therefore even in the winter of my life, undertake these travels, fitter for bodies
lesse blasted with mis-fortunes, for men of greater abilitie, and for mindes of
better incouragement, that thereby, if it were possible, I might recover but
the moderation of excesse, & the least tast of the greatest plenty formerly
possessed. If I had knowen other way to win, if I had imagined how greater
adventures might have regained, if I could conceive what farther meanes I
might yet use, but even to appease so powreful displeasure, I would not
doubt but for one yeere more to hold fast my soule in my teeth, till it were
performed. Of that litle remaine I had, I have wasted in effect all herein.
I have undergone many constructions. I have bene accompanyed with many
sorrowes, with labour, hunger, heat, sickenes, & perill: It appeareth notwithstanding that I made no other bravado of going to the sea, then was ment,
and that I was never hidden in Cornewall, or els where, as was supposed.
They have grosly belied me, that forejudged, that I would rather become a
servant to the Spanish king, then returne, and the rest were much mistaken,
who would have perswaded, that I was too easefull and sensuall to undertake
a journey of so great travell. But, if what I have done, receive the gracious
construction of a painefull pilgrimage, and purchase the least remission, I
shall thinke all too litle, & there were wanting to the rest many miseries.
But if both the times past, the present, and what may be in the future, doe
all by one graine of gall continue in eternall distast; I doe not then know
whether I should bewaile my selfe, either for my too much travell and
expence, or condemne my selfe for doing lesse then that, which can deserve
nothing.

From my selfe I have deserved no thankes, for I am returned a beggar, and
withered, but that I might have bettred my poore estate, it shall appeare by

the following discourse, if I had not onely respected her Majesties future Honour, and riches. It became not the former fortune in which I once lived, to goe journeys of picory, it had sorted ill with the offices of Honour, which by her Majesties grace I hold this day in England, to run from Cape to Cape, and from place to place, for the pillage of ordinaries prizes.

Many yeeres since, I had knowledge by relation, of that mighty, rich and beautiful Empire of Guiana, and of that great and golden Citie, which the Spaniards call El Dorado, and the naturals Manoa, which Citie was conquered, reedified, and inlarged by a yonger sonne of Guainacapa Emperour of Peru, at such time as Francisco Pizarro and others conquered the said Empire, from his two elder brethren, Guascar, and Atabalipa, both then contending for the same, the one being favoured by the Orejones of Cuzco, the other by the people of Caxamalca.

I sent my servant Jacob Whiddon the yere before, to get knowledge of the passages, and I had some light from Captaine Parker, sometime my servant, and nowe attending on your Lordship, that such a place there was to the Southward of the great Bay of Charuas, or Guanipa: but I found that it was 600 miles farther off then they supposed, and many other impediments to them unknowen and unheard.

After I had displanted Don Antonio de Berreo, who was upon the same enterprize, leaving my ships at Trinidad, at the Port called Curiapan, I wandred 400 miles into the said countrey by lande and river: the particulars I will leave to the following discourse. The countrey hath more quantity of gold by manifolde, then the best partes of the Indies, or Peru: All the most of the kings of the borders are already become her Majesties vassals: and seeme to desire nothing more then her Majesties protection and the returne of the English nation. It hath another ground and assurance of riches and glory, then the voyages of the West Indies, an easier way to invade the best parts thereof, then by the common course.

The king of Spaine is not so impoverished, by taking three or foure Port townes in America, as wee suppose, neither are the riches of Peru, or Nueva Espanna so left by the sea side, as it can bee easily washt away with a great flood, or springtide, or left dry upon the sandes on a lowe ebbe. The Port townes are fewe and poore in respect of the rest within the lande, and are of litle defence, and are onely rich, when the Fleets are to receive the treasure for Spaine: and we might thinke the Spaniards very simple, having so many horses and slaves, if they could not upon two dayes warning cary all the golde they have into the land, and farre enough from the reach of our foote-men, especially the Indies being (as they are for the most part) so mountanous, so full of woodes, rivers, and marishes. In the Port townes of the Province of Venezuela, as Cumana, Coro and S. Iago (whereof Coro and S. Iago were taken by Captaine Preston, and Cumana and S. Josepho by us) we found not the value of one riall of plate in either: but the Cities of Barquasimeta, Valencia, S. Sebastian, Cororo, S. Lucia, Laguna, Maracaiba, and Truxillo, are not so easely invaded: neither doeth the burning of those on the coast impoverish the king of Spaine, any one ducat: and if we sacke the river of Hacha, S. Marta, and Cartagena, which are the Portes of Nuevo reyno, and Popayan; there are besides within the land, which are indeed riche and populous, the townes and Cities of Merida, Lagrita, S. Christophoro, the great Cities of Pamplon S. Fe de Bogota, Tunxa and Mozo where the Esmeralds are found, the townes and Cities of Marequita, Velez, la Villa de Leva, Palma, Unda, Angustura, the great citie of Timana, Tocaima, S. Aguila, Pasto, Juago, the great Citie of Popaian it selfe, Los Remedios, and the rest. If we take the Ports and villages within the Bay of Uraba, in the kingdom or rivers of Dariene, and Caribana, the Cities and townes of S. Juan de Roydas, of Cassaris, of Antiocha, Caramanta, Cali, and Anserma have gold enough to pay the kings part, and are not easily invaded by the way of the Ocean: or if Nombre de Dios and Panama be taken in the Province of Castilla del oro, and the villages upon the rivers of Cenu & Chagre; Peru hath besides those & besides the magnificent cities of Quito & Lima so many ylands, ports, cities, and mines, as if I should name them with the rest, it would seem incredible to the reader: of all which, because I have written a particular treatise of the West Indies, I wil omit the repetition at this time, seeing that in the said treatise I have anatomized the rest of the sea-townes aswel of Nicaragua, Iucatan, Nueva Espanna, & the ylands, as those of the Inland, & by what meanes they may be best invaded, as far as any meane judgement can comprehend.

But I hope it shal appeare that there is a way found to answer every mans longing, a better Indies for her Majestie then the King of Spaine hath any: which if it shal please her highnes to undertake, I shal most willingly end the rest of my daies in folowing the same: if it be left to the spoile & sackage of common persons, if the love & service of so many nations be despised, so great riches, & so mighty an empire refused, I hope her majesty wil yet take my humble desire and my labor therin in gracious part, which, if it had not bin in respect of her highnes future honor & riches, could have laid hands on & ransomed many of the kings & Casiqui of the country, & have had a reasonable proportion of gold for their redemption: but I have chosen rather to beare the burden of poverty, then reproch, & rather to endure a second travel and the chances therof, then to have defaced an enterprise of so great assurance, untill I knew whether it pleased God to put a disposition in her princely & royal heart either to folow or foreslow the same: I wil therefore leave it to his ordinance that hath only power in all things, & do humbly pray that your honors wil excuse such errors, as without the defence of art, overrun in every part of the folowing discourse, in which I have neither studied phrase, forme nor fashion, that you will be pleased to esteeme mee as your owne (though over dearly bought) and I shall ever remaine ready to do you all honour and service.

W. R.

To the Reader.

BECAUSE there have bin divers opinions conceived of the gold oare broght from Guiana, and for that an Alderman of London & an officer of her

Majesties Mint, hath given out that the same is of no price, I have thought good by the addition of these lines to give answer aswel to the said malicious slander, as to other objections. It is true that while we abode at the yland of Trinidad, I was informed, by an Indian, that not far from the Port, where we ancored, there were found certaine mineral stones which they esteemed to be gold, & were thereunto perswaded the rather for that they had seene both English and Frenchmen gather, & imbark some quantities therof: upon this likelyhood I sent 40. men & gave order that each one should bring a stone of that mine to make trial of its goodnes: which being performed, I assured them at their returne that the same was Marcasite, & of no riches or value: notwithstanding divers, trusting more to their owne sence, then to my opinion, kept of the said Marcasite, and have tried therof since my returne in divers places. In Guiana it selfe I never saw Marcasite, but al the rocks, mountains, al stones in ye plaines, woods, & by the rivers side are in effect throughshining, and seem marvelous rich, which being tried to be no Marcasite, are the true signes of rich minerals, but are no other then El madre del oro (as the Spaniards terme them) which is the mother of gold, or as it is said by others the scum of gold: of divers sorts of these many of my company brought also into England, every one taking ye fairest for the best, which is not general. For mine own part I did not countermand any mans desire, or opinion, & I could have aforded them litle if I should have denied them the pleasing of their owne fancies therein: but I was resolved that gold must be found either in graines separate from the stone (as it is in most of the rivers in Guiana) or els in a kind of hard stone, which we call The white spar, of which I saw divers hils, & in sundry places, but had neither time nor men, nor instruments fit for labour. Neere unto one of the rivers I found of the said White sparre or flint a very great ledge or banke, which I endevoured to breake by al the meanes I could, because there appeared on the outside some smal graines of gold, but finding no meane to worke the same upon the upper part, seeking the sides and circuit of the said rocke, I found a clift in the same from whence with daggers, and with the head of an axe, we got out some smal quantitie therof, of which kind of white stone (wherin gold ingendred) we saw divers hils and rocks in every part of Guiana, wherein we traveiled. Of this there have bin many trials, and in London it was first assaid by M. Westwood a refiner dwelling in Wood-street, and it held after the rate of 12000. or 13000. pounds a tunne. Another sort was afterward tried by M. Bulmar & M. Dimock Assay-master, & it held after the rate of 23000. li. a tunne. There was some of it againe tried by M. Palmer comptroller of the Mint, and M. Dimock in goldsmiths hal, & it held after 26900. li. a tun. There was also at the same time, & by the same persons a trial made of the dust of the said mine which held 8 li. 6. ounces weight of gold in the 100: there was likewise at the same time a triall of an image of copper made in Guiana, which held a third part of gold, besides divers trials made in the countrey, & by others in London. But because there came ill with the good, & belike the said Alderman was not presented with the best, it hath pleased him therefore to scandall all the rest, and to deface the enterprize as much as in him lieth. It hath also bene concluded by divers, that if there had bin any such oare in Guiana, and the same discovered, that I would have brought home a greater quantitie thereof: first I was not bound to satisfie any man of the quantitie, but such onely as adventured, if any store had bin returned thereof: but it is very true that had al their mountaines bene of massie gold, it was impossible for us to have made any longer stay to have wrought the same: and whosoever hath seene with what strength of stone the best gold oare is invironed, hee will not thinke it easie to be had out in heapes, and especially by us, who had neither men, instruments, nor time (as it is said before) to performe the same. There were on this discovery no lesse then 100. persons, who can all witnesse, that when we past any branch of the river to view the land within, and staied from our boats but 6. houres, wee were driven to wade to the eyes, at our returne: and if wee attempted the same, the day following it was impossible either to ford it, or to swim it, both by reason of the swiftnesse, and also for that the borders were so pestred with fast woods, as neither boat nor man could find place, either to land or to imbarke: for in June, July, August and September, it is impossible to navigate any of those rivers: for such is the fury of the current, and there are so many trees and woods overflowne, as if any boat but touch upon any tree or stake, it is impossible to save any one person therein: and yer we departed the land it ranne with such swiftnes, as wee drave downe most commonly against the wind, little lesse than 100. miles a day: Besides our vessels were no other then whirries, one little barge, a small cockboat, and a bad Galiota, which we framed in hast for that purpose at Trinidad, and those little boats had 9. or 10. men a piece, with all their victuals, and armes. It is further true, that we were about 400. miles from our ships, and had bene a moneth from them, which also we left weakly manned in an open road, and had promised our returne in 15. dayes. Others have devised that the same oare was had from Barbary, and that we caried it with us into Guiana: surely the singularitie of that device I doe not well comprehend: for mine owne part, I am not so much in love with these long voyages, as to devise, therby to cozen my selfe, to lie hard, to fare worse, to be subjected to perils, to diseases, to ill savors, to be parched & withered, and withall to sustaine the care & labour of such an enterprize, except the same had more comfort, then the fetching of Marcasite in Guiana, or buying of gold oare in Barbary. But I hope the better sort wil judge me by themselves, & that the way of deceit is not the way of honor or good opinion: I have herein consumed much time, & many crownes, & I had no other respect or desire then to serve her Majestie and my country thereby. If the Spanish nation had bene of like beliefe to these detracters, we should litle have feared or doubted their attempts, wherewith we now are daily threatned. But if we now consider of the actions both of Charles the 5. who had the maidenhead of Peru, and the abundant treasures of Atabalipa, together with the affaires of the Spanish king now living, what territories he hath purchased, what he hath added to the acts of his predecessors, how many kingdoms he hath indangered, how many armies, garisons, & navies he hath and doth mainteine, the great losses which he hath repaired, as in 88. above 100. saile of great ships with their artillery, & that no yere is lesse unfortunate but that many vessels, treasures, and people are devoured, and yet notwithstanding he beginneth againe like a storme to threaten shipwrack to us all: we shall find that these abilities rise not from the trades of sacks, and Sivil oringes, nor from ought els that either Spaine, Portugal, or any of his other provinces produce: it is his Indian gold that indangereth and disturbeth all the nations of Europe, it purchaseth intelligence, creepeth into counsels, and setteth bound loyaltie at libertie, in the greatest Monarchies of Europe. If the Spanish king can keepe us from forren enterprizes, & from the impeachment of his trades, either by offer of invasion, or by besieging us in Britaine, Ireland, or elsewhere, hee hath then brought the worke of our peril in great forwardnes. Those princes which abound in treasure have great advantages over the rest, if they once constraine them to a defensive war, where they are driven once a yere or oftener to cast lots for their own garments, and from such shal all trades, & entercourse be taken away, to the general losse and impoverishment of the kingdom and common weale so reduced: besides when our men are constrained to fight, it hath not the like hope, as when they are prest & incouraged by the desire of spoile & riches. Farther, it is to be douted how those that in time of victory seeme to affect their neighbor nations, wil remaine after the first view of misfortunes, or il successe; to trust also to the doubtfulnes of a battel, is but a fearefull & uncertaine adventure, seeing therein fortune is as likely to prevaile, as vertue. It shall not be necessary to alleage all that might bee said, and therefore I will thus conclude, that whatsoever kingdome shalbe inforced to defend it selfe may be compared to a body dangerously diseased, which for a season may be preserved with vulgar medicines, but in a short time, and by litle and litle, the same must needs fall to the ground, & be dissolved. I have therefore laboured all my life, both according to my smal power, & perswasion, to advance al those attempts, that might either promise return of profit to our selves, or at least be a let and impeachment to the quiet course and plentifull trades of the Spanish nation, who in my weake judgement by such a warre were as easily indangered & brought from his powerfulnes, as any prince of Europe, if it be considered from how many kingdomes and nations his revenues are gathered, & those so weake in their owne beings, and so far severed from mutual succour. But because such a preparation and resolution is not to be hoped for in hast, & that the time which our enemies embrace, cannot be had againe to advantage, I wil hope that these provinces, and that Empire now by me discovered shal suffice to inable her Majestie & the whole kingdome, with no lesse quantities of treasure, then the king of Spaine hath in all the Indies East and West, which he possesseth, which if the same be considered and followed, ere the Spaniards enforce the same, and if her Majestie wil undertake it, I wil be contented to lose her highnesse favour & good opinion for ever, and my life withall, if the same be not found rather to exceed, then to equal whatsoever is in this discourse promised or declared.

I wil now referre the Reader to the following discourse, with the hope that the perillous and chargeable labours and indevors of such as thereby seeke the profit and honour of her Majestie, and the English nation, shall by men of qualitie and vertue receive such construction, and good acceptance, as themselves would looke to be rewarded withall in the like.

W. R.

The Discoverie of Guiana

On Thursday the 6. of February in the yere 1595. we departed England, and the Sunday following had sight of the North cape of Spaine, the winde for the most part continuing prosperous: we passed in sight of the Burlings, & the Rocke, and so onwards for the Canaries. . . .

Meeting with the ships at Puerta de los Espannoles, we found at the landing place a company of Spaniards who kept a guard at the descent, and they offering a signe of peace, I sent Captaine Whiddon to speake with them, whom afterward to my great griefe I left buried in the said yland after my returne from Guiana, being a man most honest and valiant. The Spaniards seemed to be desirous to trade with us, and to enter into termes of peace, more for doubt of their owne strength then for ought else, and in the ende upon pledge, some of them came abord: the same evening there stale also abord us in a small Canoa two Indians, the one of them being a Casique or Lord of the people called Cantyman, who had the yeere before bene with Captaine Whiddon, and was of his acquaintance. By this Cantyman wee understood what strength the Spaniards had, howe farre it was to their Citie, and of Don Antonio de Berreo the governour, who was said to be slaine in his second attempt of Guiana, but was not.

While we remained at Puerto de los Espannoles some Spaniards came abord us to buy linnen of the company, and such other things as they wanted, and also to view our ships and company, all which I entertained kindly and feasted after our maner: by meanes whereof I learned of one and another as much of the estate of Guiana as I could, or as they knew, for those poore souldiers having bene many yeeres without wine, a few draughts made them merrie, in which mood they vaunted of Guiana and of the riches thereof, and all what they knewe of the wayes and passages, my selfe seeming to purpose nothing lesse then the enterance or discoverie thereof, but bred in them an opinion that I was bound onely for the reliefe of those English which I had planted in Virginia, whereof the bruite was come among them; which I had performed in my returne, if extremitie of weather had not forst me from the said coast.

I found occasions of staying in this place for two causes: the one was to be revenged of Berreo, who the yere before 1594. had betraied eight of Captaine Whiddons men, and tooke them while he departed from them to seeke the Edward Bonaventure, which arrived at Trinidad the day before from the East Indies: in whose absence Berreo sent a Canoa abord the pinnesse onely with Indians and dogs inviting the company to goe with them into the woods to kill a deare, who like wise men in the absence of their Captaine followed the Indians, but were no sooner one harquebuze shot from the shore, but Berreos souldiers lying in ambush had them al, notwithstanding that he had given his word to Captaine Whiddon that they should take water and wood safely: the other cause of my stay was, for that by discourse with the Spaniards I dayly learned more and more of Guiana, of the rivers and passages, and of the enterprise of Berreo, by what meanes or fault he failed, and how he meant to prosecute the same.

While wee thus spent the time I was assured by another Casique of the North side of the yland, that Berreo had sent to Margarita and Cumana for souldiers, meaning to have given mee a cassado at parting, if it had bene possible. For although he had given order through all the yland that no Indian should come abord to trade with me upon paine of hanging & quartering, (having executed two of them for the same, which I afterwards founde) yet every night there came some with most lamentable complaints of his crueltie, how he had divided the yland and given to every souldier a part, that hee made the ancient Casiques which were Lords of the countrey to be their slaves, that he kept them in chaines, and dropped their naked bodies with burning bacon, and such other torments, which I found afterwards to be true: for in the city after I entred the same there were 5. of ye lords or litle kings (which they cal Casiques in the West Indies) in one chaine almost dead of famine, and wasted with torments.

So as both to be revenged of the former wrong, as also considering that to enter Guiana by small boats, to depart 400. or 500. miles from my ships, and to leave a garison in my backe interrested in the same enterprize, who also dayly expected supplies out of Spaine, I should have savoured very much of the asse: and therefore taking a time of most advantage I set upon the Corps du guard in the evening, and having put them to the sword, sent Captaine Calfield onwards with 60. souldiers, and my selfe followed with 40. more and so tooke their new City which they called S. Joseph by breake of day: they abode not any fight after a fewe shot, and all being dismissed but onely Berreo and his companion, I brought them with me abord, and at the instance of the Indians, I set their new citie of S. Joseph on fire.

The same day arrived Captaine George Gifford with your Lordships ship, and Captaine Keymis whom I lost on the coast of Spaine, with the Galego, and in them divers gentlemen and others, which to our little armie was a great comfort and supply.

We then hasted away towards our purposed discovery, and first I called all the Captaines of the yland together that were enemies to the Spaniards and by my Indian interpreter, which I caried out of England, I made them understand that I was the servant of a Queene, who was the great Casique of the North, and a virgine, and had more Casiqui under her then there were trees in that yland: that shee was an enemie to the Castellani in respect of their tyrannie and oppression, and that she delivered all such nations about her, as were by them oppressed, and having freed all the coast of the Northren world from their servitude, had sent mee to free them also, and withall to defend the countrey of Guiana from their invasion and conquest. I shewed them her Majesties picture which they so admired and honoured, as it had bene easie to have brought them idolatrous thereof.

The like and a more large discourse I made to the rest of the nations both in my passing to Guiana, and to those of the borders, so as in that part of the world her Majestie is very famous and admirable, whom they now call Ezrabeta Cassipuna Aquerewana, which is as much as Elizabeth, the great princesse or greatest commander. This done we left Puerto de los Espannoles, and returned to Curiapan, and having Berreo my prisoner I gathered from him as much of Guiana as hee knew.

This Berreo is a gentleman wel descended, and had long served the Spanish king in Millain, Naples, the Low countreis and elsewhere, very valiant and liberall, and a gentleman of great assurednes, and of a great heart: I used him according to his estate and worth in all things I could, according to the small meanes I had. . . .

Berreo for executing of Morequito, and other cruelties, spoiles, and slaughters done in Aromaia, hath lost the love of the Orenoqueponi, and of all the borderers, and dare not send any of his souldiers any further into the land then to Carapana, which he called the port of Guiana: but from thence by the helpe of Carapana he had trade further into the countrey, and alwayes appointed ten Spaniards to reside in Carapanas towne, by whose favour, and by being conducted by his people, those ten searched the countrey thereabouts, aswell for mines, as for other trades and commodities.

They also have gotten a nephew of Morequito, whom they have Christened, and named Don Juan, of whom they have great hope, endevouring by all meanes to establish him in the sayd province. Among many other trades, those Spaniards used canoas to passe to the rivers of Barema, Pawroma, & Dissequebe, which are on the south side of the mouth of Orenoque, and there buy women and children from the Canibals, which are of that barbarous nature, as they will for three or foure hatchets sell the sonnes and daughters of their owne brethren and sisters, and for somewhat more, even their owne daughters. Hereof the Spaniards make great profit: for buying a maid of twelve or thirteene yeres for three or foure hatchets, they sell them againe at Margarita in the West Indies for fifty and an hundred pezos, which is so many crownes.

The master of my shippe, John Dowglas, tooke one of the canoas which came laden from thence with people to be solde, and the most of them escaped; yet of those he brought, there was one as well favoured, and as well shaped as ever I saw any in England, and afterward I saw many of them, which but for their tawnie colour may be compared to any of Europe. They also trade in those rivers for bread of Cassavi, of which they buy an hundred pound weight for a knife, and sell it at Margarita for ten pezos. They also recover great store of Cotton, Brasill wood, and those beds which they call Hamacas or Brasill beds, wherein in hot countreyes all the Spaniards use to lie commonly, and in no other, neither did we our selves while we were there. By meanes of which trades, for ransome of divers of the Guianians, and for exchange of hatchets and knives, Berreo recovered some store of golde plates, eagles of golde, and images of men and divers birdes, and dispatched his campe-master for Spaine, with all that hee had gathered, therewith to levie souldiers, and by the shew thereof to draw others to the love of the enterprise. And having sent divers images aswell of men as beasts, birds & fishes, so curiously wrought in gold, he doubted not but to perswade the king to yeeld to him some further helpe.

After I had thus learned of his proceedings past and purposed, I told him that I had resolved to see Guiana, and that it was the end of my journey, and the cause of my comming to Trinidad, as it was indeed, (and for that purpose I sent Jacob Whiddon the yeere before to get intelligence with whom Berreo himselfe had speech at that time, and remembred how inquisitive Jacob Whiddon was of his proceedings, and of the countrey of Guiana) Berreo was stricken into a great melancholy and sadnesse, and used all the arguments he could to disswade me, and also assured the gentlemen of my company that it would be labour lost, and that they should suffer many miseries if they proceeded. And first he delivered that I could not enter any of the rivers with any barke or pinnesse, or hardly with any ships boat, it was so low, sandy, and full of flats, and that his companies were dayly grounded in their canoas, which drew but twelve inches water. Hee further sayde, that none of the countrey would come to speake with us, but would all flie; and if we followed them to their dwellings, they would burne their owne townes: and besides that, the way was long, the Winter at hand, and that the rivers beginning once to swell, it was impossible to stem the current, and that we could not in those small boats by any means cary victuall for halfe the time, and that (which indeed most discouraged my company) the kings and lords of all the borders of Guiana had decreed that none of them should trade with any Christians for golde, because the same would be their owne overthrow, and that for the love of gold the Christians meant to conquer and dispossesse them of all together.

Many and the most of these I found to be true. . . .

The Empire of Guiana is directly East from Peru towards the Sea, and lieth under the Equinoctial line, and it hath more abundance of golde then any part of Peru, and as many or more great Cities than ever Peru had when it flourished most: it is governed by the same lawes, and the Emperour and people observe the same religion, and the same forme and policies in government as were used in Peru, not differing in any part: and I have bene assured by such of the Spaniards as have seene Manoa the Imperial Citie of Guiana, which the Spaniards call El Dorado, that for the greatnesse, for the riches, and for the excellent seat, it farre exceedeth any of the world, at least of so much of the world as is knowen to the Spanish nation: it is founded upon a lake of salt water of 200. leagues long like unto Mare Caspium. And if we compare it to that of Peru, & but read the report of Francisco Lopez and others, it will seeme more then credible: and because we may judge of the one by the other, I thought good to insert part of the 120. Chapter of Lopez in his generall historie of the Indies, wherein he describeth the Court and magnificence of Guaynacapa, ancestour to the

Emperour of Guiana. All the vessels of his house, table and kitchin were of gold and silver, and the meanest of silver and copper for strength and hardnesse of metall. He had in his wardrobe hollow statues of gold which seemed giants, and the figures in proportion and bignesse of all the beasts, birds, trees, and hearbes, that the earth bringeth foorth: and of all the fishes that the sea or waters of his kingdome breedeth. He had also ropes, budgets, chestes and troughs of golde and silver, heapes of billets of gold, that seemed wood marked out to burne. Finally, there was nothing in his countrey, whereof he had not the counterfait in gold: Yea and they say, The Ingas had a garden of pleasure in an yland neere Puna, where they went to recreat themselves, when they would take the aire of the Sea, which had all kinde of garden-hearbs, flowers and trees of golde and silver, an invention, and magnificence till then never seene. Besides all this, he had an infinite quantitie of silver and golde unwrought in Cuzco which was lost by the death of Guascar, for the Indians hid it, seeing that the Spaniards tooke it, and sent it into Spaine. . . .

The great river of Orenoque or Baraquan hath nine branches which fall out on the North side of his owne maine mouth: on the South side it hath seven other fallings into the sea, so it disemboqueth by sixteene armes in all, betweene Ilands and broken ground, but the Ilands are very great, many of them as bigge as the Isle of Wight, and bigger, and many lesse. From the first branch on the North to the last of the South, it is at least 100 leagues, so as the rivers mouth is 300 miles wide at his entrance into the sea, which I take to be farre bigger then that of Amazones. All those that inhabit in the mouth of this river upon the severall North branches, are these Tivitivas, of which there are two chiefe lords which have continuall warres one with the other. The Ilands which lie on the right hand, are called Pallamos, and the land on the left, Horotomaka, and the river by which John Dowglas returned within the land from Amana to Capuri, they call Macuri.

These Tivitivas are a very goodly people and very valiant, and have the most manly speech and most deliberate that ever I heard, of what nation soever. In the Summer they have houses on the ground, as in other places: in the Winter they dwell upon the trees, where they build very artificiall townes and villages, as it is written in the Spanish story of the West Indies, that those people do in the low lands nere the gulfe of Uraba: for betweene May & September the river of Orenoque riseth thirty foot upright, and then are those ilands overflowen twenty foot high above the levell of the ground, saving some few raised grounds in the middle of them: and for this cause they are inforced to live in this maner. They never eat of any thing that is set or sowen: and as at home they use neither planting nor other manurance, so when they come abroad, they refuse to feed of ought, but of that which nature without labour bringeth forth. They use the tops of Palmitos for bread, and kill deere, fish, and porks, for the rest of their sustenance. They have also many sorts of fruits that grow in the woods, and great variety of birds and fowle.

And if to speake of them were not tedious, and vulgar, surely we saw in those passages of very rare colours and formes, not elsewhere to be found, for as much as I have either seene or read. Of these people those that dwell upon the branches of Orenoque, called Capuri and Macureo, are for the most part carpenters of canoas, for they make the most and fairest canoas, and sel them into Guiana for golde, and into Trinidad for tabacco, in the excessive taking whereof, they exceed all nations; and notwithstanding the moistnesse of the aire in which they live, the hardnesse of their diet, and the great labours they suffer to hunt, fish and fowle for their living; in all my life, either in the Indies or in Europe, did I never behold a more goodly or better favoured people or a more manly. They were woont to make warre upon all nations, and especially on the Canibals, so as none durst without a good strength trade by those rivers: but of late they are at peace with their neighbours, all holding the Spaniards for a common enemy. When their commanders die, they use great lamentation, and when they thinke the flesh of their bodies is putrified, and fallen from the bones, then they take up the carcase againe, and hang it in the caciques house that died, and decke his scull with feathers of all colours, and hang all his golde plates, about the bones of his armes, thighs, and legs. Those nations which are called Arwacas, which dwell on the South of Orenoque, (of which place and nation our Indian pilot was) are dispersed in many other places, and doe use to beat the bones of their lords into powder, and their wives and friends drinke it all in their severall sorts of drinks.

After we departed from the port of these Ciawani, wee passed up the river with the flood, and ankered the ebbe, and in this sort we went onward. The third day that we entred the river, our galley came on ground, and stucke so fast, as we thought that even there our discovery had ended, and that we must have left fourescore and ten of our men to have inhabited like rooks upon trees with those nations: but the next morning, after we had cast out all her ballast, with tugging and halling to and fro, we got her aflote, and went on. At foure dayes end wee fell into as goodly a river as ever I beheld, which was called The great Amana, which ranne more directly without windings and turnings then the other: but soone after the flood of the sea left us; and being inforced either by maine strength to row against a violent current, or to returne as wise as we went out, we had then no shift but to perswade the companies that it was but two or three dayes worke, and therefore desired them to take paines, every gentleman & others taking their turnes to row, and to spell one the other at the houres end. Every day we passed by goodly branches of rivers, some falling from the West, others from the East into Amana, but those I leave to the description in the Cart of discovery, where every one shalbe named with his rising and descent. When three dayes more were overgone, our companies began to despaire, the weather being extreame hote, the river bordered with very high trees, that kept away the aire, and the current against us every day stronger then other: but we evermore commanded our pilots to promise an ende the next day, and used it so long, as we were driven to assure them from foure reaches of the river to three, and so to two, and so to the next reach: but so long we laboured, that many dayes were spent, and wee driven to drawe our selves to harder allowance, our bread even at the last, and no drinke at all; and our men and our selves so wearied and scorched, and doubtfull withall, whether wee should ever performe it or no, the heat increasing as we drew towards the line; for wee were now in five degrees.

The further we went on (our victuall decreasing and the aire breeding great faintnesse) wee grew weaker and weaker, when wee had most need of strength and abilitie; for hourely the river ranne more violently then other against us, and the barge, wheries, and shippes boat of captaine Gifford and captaine Calfield, had spent all their provisions; so as we were brought into despaire and discomfort, had wee not perswaded all the company that it was but onely one dayes worke more to atteine the land where wee should be relieved of all wee wanted, and if we returned, that wee were sure to starve by the way, and that the world would also laugh us to scorne. On the banks of these rivers were divers sorts of fruits good to eat, flowers and trees of such variety, as were sufficient to make tenne volumes of herbals: we relieved our selves many times with the fruits of the countrey, and some-times with fowle and fish. Wee saw birds of all colours, some carnation, some crimson, orenge-tawny, purple, watchet, and of all other sorts both simple and mixt, and it was unto us a great good passing of the time to be-holde them, besides the reliefe we found by killing some store of them with our fowling pieces; without which, having little or no bread, and lesse drinke, but onely the thicke and troubled water of the river, we had beene in a very hard case.

Our olde pilot of the Ciawani tolde us, that if we would enter a branch of a river on the right hand with our barge and wheries, and leave the galley at anker the while in the great river, he would bring us to a towne of the Arwacas, where we should finde store of bread, hennes, fish, and of the countrey wine; and perswaded us, that departing from the galley at noone, we might returne yer night. I was very glad to heare this speech, and pres-ently tooke my barke, with eight musketiers, captaine Giffords whery, with himselfe and foure musketiers, and Captaine Calfield with his whery, and as many; and so we entred the mouth of this river: and because we were perswaded that it was so nere, we tooke no victuall with us at all. When we had rowed three houres, we marvelled we saw no signe of any dwelling, and asked the pilot where the towne was: he tolde us a little further. After three houres more, the Sun being almost set, we began to suspect that he led us that way to betray us: for hee confessed that those Spanyards which fled from Trinidad, and also those that remained with Carapana in Emeria, were joyned together in some village upon that river. But when it grew towards night; and wee demanded where the place was; hee tolde us but foure reaches more. When we had rowed foure and foure; we saw no signe; and our poore water-men, even heartbroken, and tired, were ready to give up the ghost: for wee had now come from the galley neere forty miles.

At the last we determined to hang the pilot; and if wee had well knowen the way backe againe by night, hee had surely gone; but our owne necessities pleaded sufficiently for his safety: for it was as darke as pitch, and the river began so to narrow it selfe, and the trees to hang over from side to side, as wee were driven with arming swords to cut a passage thorow those branches that covered the water. Wee were very desirous to finde this towne, hoping of a feast, because wee made but a short breakefast aboord the galley in the morning and it was now eight a clocke at night, and our stomacks began to gnawe apace: but whether it was best to returne or goe on, we beganne to doubt, suspecting treason in the pilot more and more: but the poore olde Indian ever assured us that it was but a little further, but this one turning and that turning: and at the last about one a clocke after midnight wee saw a light; and rowing towards it, wee heard the dogges of the village. When we landed wee found few people; for the lord of that place was gone with divers canoas above foure hundred miles off, upon a journey towardes the head of Orenoque to trade for golde, and to buy women of the Canibals, who afterward unfortunately passed by us as wee rode at an anker in the port of Morequito in the darke of the night, and yet came so neere us, as his canoas grated against our barges: he left one of his company at the port of Morequito, by whom wee understood that hee had brought thirty yoong women, divers plates of golde, and had great store of fine pieces of cotton cloth, and cotton beds. In his house we had good store of bread, fish, hennes, and Indian drinke, and so rested that night, and in the morning after we had traded with such of his people as came downe, we returned towards our gally, and brought with us some quantity of bread, fish, and hennes.

On both sides of this river, we passed the most beautifull countrey that ever mine eyes beheld: and whereas all that we had seene before was nothing but woods, prickles, bushes, and thornes, here we beheld plaines of twenty miles in length, the grasse short and greene, and in divers parts groves of trees by themselves, as if they had beene by all the arte and labour in the world so made of purpose: and still as we rowed, the deere came downe feeding by the waters side, as if they had beene used to a keepers call. Upon this river there were great store of fowle, and of many sorts: we saw in it divers sorts of strange fishes, and of marvellous bignes: but for lagartos it exceeded, for there were thousands of those ugly serpents; and the people call it for the abundance of them, The river of Lagartos, in their language. I had a Negro a very proper yoong fellow, who leaping out of the galley to swim in the mouth of this river, was in all our sights taken and devoured with one of those lagartos. In the meane while our companies in the gally thought we had bene all lost (for wee promised to returne before night) and sent the Lions whelps shippes boat with captaine Whiddon to follow us up the river; but the next day, after we had rowed up and downe some fourescore miles, we returned, and went on our way, up the great river; and when we were even at the last cast for want of victuals, captaine Gifford being before the galley and the rest of the boats, seeking out some place to land upon the banks to make fire, espied foure canoas comming downe the river; & with no small joy caused his men to trie the uttermost of their strengths, and after a while two of the foure gave over, and ranne themselves ashore, every man betaking himselfe to the fastnesse of the woods, the two other lesser got away, while he landed to lay holde on these; and so turned into some by-creeke, we knew not whither. Those canoas that were taken, were loaden with bread, and were bound for Margarita in the West Indies, which those Indians (called Arwacas) purposed to cary thither for exchange: but in the lesser there were three Spanyards, who having heard of the defeat of their governour in Trinidad, and that we purposed to enter Guiana, came away in those canoas: one of them was a cavallero, as the captaine of the Arwacas after tolde us, another a souldier, and the third a refiner.

In the meane time, nothing on the earth could have bene more welcome to us, next unto gold, then the great store of very excellent bread which we found in these canoas; for now our men cried, Let us goe on, we care not how farre. After that captaine Gifford had brought the two canoas to the galley, I tooke my barge, and went to the banks side with a dozen shot, where the canoas first ranne themselves ashore, and landed there, sending out captaine Gifford, and captaine Thyn on one hand, and captaine Calfield on the other, to follow those that were fled into the woods: and as I was creeping thorow the bushes, I sawe an Indian basket hidden, which was the refiners basket; for I found in it his quick-silver, salt-peter, and divers things for the triall of metals, and also the dust of such ore as he had refined, but in those canoas which escaped there was a good quantity of ore and gold. I then landed more men, and offered five hundred pound to what souldier soever could take one of those three Spanyards that we thought were landed. But our labours were in vaine in that behalfe; for they put themselves into one of the small canoas: and so while the greater canoas were in taking they escaped. But seeking after the Spanyards, we found the Arwacas hidden in the woods, which were pilots for the Spanyards, and rowed their canoas; of which I kept the chiefest for a pilot, and caried him with me to Guiana, by whom I understood where and in what countreyes the Spanyards had laboured for golde, though I made not the same knowen to all: for when the springs began to breake, and the rivers to raise themselves so suddenly, as by no meanes wee could abide the digging of any mine, especially for that the richest are defended with rocks of hard stones, which wee call the White spar, and that it required both time, men, and instruments fit for such a worke, I thought it best not to hover thereabouts, least if the same had beene perceived by the company, there would have beene by this time many barks and shippes set out, and perchance other nations would also have gotten of ours for pilots; so as both our selves might have beene prevented, and all our care taken for good usage of the people bene utterly lost, by those that onely respect present profit, and such violence or insolence offered, as the nations which are borderers would have changed their desire of our love and defence into hatred and violence. And for any longer stay to have brought a more quantity (which I heare hath beene often objected) whosoever had seene or proved the fury of that river after it

beganne to arise, and had bene a moneth and odde dayes, as we were, from
hearing ought from our shippes, leaving them meanly manned 400 miles
off, would perchance have turned somewhat sooner then we did, if all the
mountaines had bene golde, or rich stones. And to say the trueth, all the
branches and small rivers which fell into Orenoque were raised with such
speed, as if we waded them over the shooes in the morning outward, we
were covered to the shoulders homeward the very same day: and to stay
to digge out gold with our nailes, had bene Opus laboris but not Ingenii:
such a quantitie as would have served our turnes we could not have had,
but a discovery of the Mines to our infinite disadvantage wee had made, and
that could have bene the best profite of farther search or stay: for those
Mines are not easily broken, nor opened in hast, and I could have returned
a good quantitie of gold ready cast, if I had not shot at another marke, then
present profit.

This Arwacan Pilot with the rest, feared that wee would have eaten
them, or otherwise have put them to some cruel death (for the Spaniards,
to the end that none of the people in the passage towards Guiana or in
Guiana it selfe might come to speach with us, perswaded all the nations,
that we were men-eaters, and Canibals) but when the poore men and
women had seen us, and that wee gave them meate, and to every one something or other, which was rare and strange to them, they beganne to conceive the deceit and purpose of the Spaniards, who indeed (as they confessed) tooke from them both their wives and daughters dayly, and used
them for the satisfying of their owne lusts, especially such as they tooke in
this maner by strength. But I protest before the Majestie of the living God,
that I neither know nor beleeve, that any of our company one or other, by
violence or otherwise, ever knew any of their women, and yet we saw
many hundreds, and had many in our power, and of those very yong, and
excellently favoured, which came among us without deceit, starke naked.

Nothing got us more love amongst them then this usage: for I suffered
not any man to take from any of the nations so much as a Pina, or a Potato
roote, without giving them contentment, nor any man so much as to offer
to touch any of their wives or daughters: which course so contrary to the
Spaniards (who tyrannize over them in all things) drewe them to admire
her Majestie, whose commaundement I tolde them it was, and also wonderfully to honour our nation.

But I confesse it was a very impatient worke to keepe the meaner sort
from spoyle and stealing, when wee came to their houses: which because
in all I coulde not prevent, I caused my Indian interpreter at every place
when wee departed, to knowe of the losse or wrong done, and if ought
were stolen or taken by violence, either the same was restored, and the
partie punished in their sight, or else was payed for to their uttermost
demand.

They also much wondered at us, after they heard that we had slaine the
Spaniards at Trinidad, for they were before resolved, that no nation of
Christians durst abide their presence, and they wondered more when I had

made them know of the great overthrow that her Majesties armie and Fleete had given them of late yeeres in their owne Countreys.

After we had taken in this supply of bread, with divers baskets of rootes which were excellent meate, I gave one of the Canoas to the Arwacas, which belonged to the Spaniards that were escaped, and when I had dismissed all but the Captaine (who by the Spaniards was christened Martin) I sent backe in the same Canoa the olde Ciawan, and Ferdinando my first Pilot, and gave them both such things as they desired, with sufficient victuall to cary them backe, and by them wrote a letter to the ships, which they promised to deliver, and performed it, and then I went on, with my newe hired Pilot Martin the Arwacan: but the next or second day after, wee came aground againe with our Galley, and were like to cast her away, with all our victuall and provision, and so lay on the sand one whole night and were farre more in despaire at this time to free her then before, because wee had no tide of flood to helpe us, and therefore feared that all our hopes would have ended in mishaps: but we fastened an ancker upon the lande, and with maine strength drewe her off: and so the fifteenth day wee discovered afarre off the mountaines of Guiana to our great joy, and towards the evening had a slent of a Northerly winde that blewe very strong, which brought us in sight of the great river Orenoque; out of which this River discended wherein wee were: wee descried afarre off three other Canoas as farre as wee could descerne them, after whom wee hastened with our barge and wherries, but two of them passed out of sight, and the thirde entered up the great River, on the right hande to the Westward, and there stayed out of sight, thinking that wee meant to take the way Eastward towards the province of Carapana, for that way the Spaniards keepe, not daring to goe upwards to Guiana, the people in those parts being all their enemies, and those in the Canoas thought us to have bene those Spaniards that were fled from Trinidad, and had escaped killing: and when wee came so farre downe as the opening of that branch into which they slipped, being neere them with our barge and wherries, wee made after them, and ere they coulde land, came within call, and by our interpreter tolde them what wee were, wherewith they came backe willingly abord us: and of such fish and Tortugas egges as they had gathered, they gave us, and promised in the morning to bring the Lord of that part with them, and to do us all other services they could.

That night we came to an ancker at the parting of the three goodly Rivers (the one was the River of Amana by which we came from the North, and ranne athwart towards the South, the other two were of Orenoque which crossed from the West and ranne to the Sea towardes the East) and landed upon a faire sand, where wee found thousands of Tortugas egges, which are very wholesome meate, and greatly restoring, so as our men were nowe well filled and highly contented both with the fare, and neerenesse of the land of Guiana which appeared in sight.

In the morning there came downe according to promise the Lord of that border called Toparimaca, with some thirtie or fourtie followers, and brought us divers sorts of fruites, and of his wine, bread, fish, and flesh, whom wee also feasted as wee could, at least wee dranke good Spanish wine (whereof wee had a small quantitie in bottles) which above all things they love. I conferred with this Toparimaca of the next way to Guiana, who conducted our galley and boates to his owne port, and caried us from thence some mile and a halfe to his Towne, where some of our Captaines karoused of his wine till they were reasonable pleasant, for it is very strong with pepper, and the juice of divers hearbes, and fruites digested and purged, they keepe it in great earthen pots of tenne or twelve galons very cleane and sweete, and are themselves at their meetings and feastes the greatest karousers and drunkards of the world: when wee came to his towne wee found two Casiques, whereof one was a stranger that had bene up the River in trade, and his boates, people, and wife incamped at the port where wee anckered, and the other was of that countrey a follower of Toparimaca: they lay each of them in a cotten Hamaca, which wee call Brasill beds, and two women attending them with six cuppes and a little ladle to fill them, out of an earthen pitcher of wine, and so they dranke each of them three of those cups at a time one to the other, and in this sort they drinke drunke at their feastes and meetings.

That Casique that was a stranger had his wife staying at the port where wee anckered, and in all my life I have seldome seene a better favoured woman: Shee was of good stature, with blacke eyes, fat of body, of an excellent countenance, her haire almost as long as her selfe, tied up againe in pretie knots, and it seemed shee stood not in that awe of her husband, as the rest, for shee spake and discoursed, and dranke among the gentlemen and Captaines, and was very pleasant, knowing her owne comelinesse, and taking great pride therein. I have seene a Lady in England so like to her, as but for the difference of colour, I would have sworne might have bene the same.

The seat of this Towne of Toparimaca was very pleasant, standing on a little hill, in an excellent prospect, with goodly gardens a mile compasse round aboute it, and two very faire and large ponds of excellent fish adjoyning. This towne is called Arowocai: the people are of the nation called Nepoios, and are followers of Carapana. In that place I sawe very aged people, that wee might perceive all their sinewes and veines without any flesh, and but even as a case covered onely with skinne. The Lord of this place gave me an old man for Pilot, who was of great experience and traveile, and knew the River most perfectly both by day and night: and it shall bee requisite for any man that passeth it, to have such a Pilot, for it is foure, five, and six miles over in many places, and twentie miles in other places, with wonderfull eddies, and strong currents, many great ylands, and divers sholds, and many dangerous rockes, and besides upon any increase of winde so great a bilowe, as wee were sometimes in great perill of drowning in the galley, for the small boates durst not come from the shoare, but when it was very faire.

The next day we hasted thence, and having an Easterly winde to helpe us, we spared our armes from rowing: for after wee entred Orenoque, the

River lieth for the most part East and West, even from the Sea unto Quito in Peru. This River is navigable with barkes, litle lesse then a thousand miles, & from the place where we entred, it may be sailed up in small pinnesses to many of the best parts of Nuevo reyno de Granada, and of Popayan: and from no place may the cities of these parts of the Indies be so easily taken and invaded as from hence. All that day wee sailed up a branch of that River, having on the left hand a great yland which they call Assapana which may conteine some five and twentie miles in length, and sixe miles in breadth, the great body of the River running on the other side of this yland. Beyond that middle branch there is also another yland in the River called Iwana, which is twise as bigge as the yle of Wight, and beyond it, and betweene it and the maine of Guiana, runneth a thirde branch of Orenoque called Arraroopana: all three are goodly branches, and all navigable for great ships. I judge the river in this place to be at least thirty miles brode, reckoning the ylands which devide the branches in it, for afterwards I sought also both the other branches.

After wee reached to the head of the yland, called Assapana, a little to the Westward on the right hand there opened a river which came from the North, called Europa, and fel into the great River, and beyond it on the same side, wee anckered for that night, by another yland sixe miles long, and two miles broade, which they call Ocaywita: From hence in the morning wee landed two Guianians, which wee found in the Towne of Topari-maca, that came with us, who went to give notice of our comming to the Lord of that countrey called Putyma, a follower of Topiawari, chiefe Lord of Aromaia, who succeeded Morequito, whom (as you have heard before) Berreo put to death: but his towne being farre within the land, he came not unto us that day, so as we ankered againe that night neere the bankes of another yland, of bignesse much like the other, which they call Putapayma, over against which yland, on the maine lande, was a very high mountaine called Oecope: we coveted to ancker rather by these ylands in the River, then by the maine, because of the Tortugas egges, which our people found on them in great abundance, and also because the ground served better for us to cast our nets for fish, the maine bankes being for the most part stonie and high, and the rocks of a blew metalline colour, like unto the best steele-ore, which I assuredly take it to be: of the same blew stone are also divers great mountaines, which border this river in many places.

The next morning towards nine of the clocke, wee weighed ancker, and the brize increasing, we sailed alwayes West up the river, and after a while opening the land on the right side, the countrey appeared to bee champaine, and the bankes shewed very perfect red. I therefore sent two of the little barges with Captaine Gifford, and with him Captaine Thyn, Captaine Cal-field, my cosen Greenvile, my nephew John Gilbert, Captaine Eynus, Master Edward Porter, and my cosen Butshead Gorges, with some fewe souldiers, to march over the bankes of that red land, and to discover what maner of countrey it was on the other side, who at their returne found it all a plaine level, as farre as they went or could discerne, from the highest tree they could get upon: And my old Pilot, a man of great travell, brother to the Casique Toparimica tolde mee, that those were called the plaines of the Sayma, and that the same levell reached to Cumaná, and Caracas in the West Indies, which are a hundreth and twentie leagues to the North, and that there inhabited foure principall nations. The first were the Sayma, the next Assawai, the thirde and greatest the Wikiri, by whom Pedro Hernandez de Serpa before mentioned was overthrowen, as hee passed with three hundred horse from Cumaná towards Orenoque, in his enterprize of Guiana: the fourth are called Aroras, and are as blacke as Negros, but have smooth haire, and these are very valiant, or rather desperate people, and nations have the most strong poyson on their arrowes, and most dangerous of all nations.

There was nothing whereof I was more curious, then to finde out the true remedies of these poysoned arrowes: for besides the mortalitie of the wound they make, the partie shotte indureth the most insufferable torment in the world, and abideth a most ugly and lamentable death. . . . And it is more strange to know, that in all this time there was never Spaniard either by gift or torment that could atteine to the true knowledge of the cure, although they have martyred and put to invented torture I know not how many of them. But every one of these Indians know it not, no not one among thousands, but their soothsayers and priestes, who doe conceale it, and onely teach it but from the father to the sonne. . . .

Those medicines which are vulgar, and serve for the ordinarie poyson, are made of the juice of a roote called Tupara: the same also quencheth marveilously the heate of burning feavers, and healeth inward wounds, and broken veines, that bleed within the body. But I was more beholding to the Guianians then any other: for Anthonio de Berreo tolde mee that hee could never attaine to the knowledge thereof, and yet they taught mee the best way of healing as well thereof, as of all other poysons. Some of the Spaniards have bene cured in ordinary wounds, of the common poysoned arrowes with the juice of garlike: but this is a generall rule for all men that shall hereafter travel the Indies where poisoned arrowes are used, that they must abstaine from drinke, for if they take any licour into their body, as they shall bee marveilously provoked thereunto by drought, I say, if they drinke before the wound bee dressed, or soone upon it, there is no way with them but present death.

And so I will returne againe to our journey which for this thirde day we finished, and cast ancker againe neere the continent or the left hand betweene two mountaines, the one called Aroami, and the other Aio: I made no stay here but till midnight, for I feared hourely least any raine should fall, and then it had bene impossible to have gone any further up, notwithstanding that there is every day a very strong brize, and Easterly winde. I deferred the search of the countrey on Guiana-side, till my returne downe the river.

The next day we sailed by a great yland in the middle of the river called Manoripano, and as wee walked a while on the yland, while the Galley got a head of us, there came for us from the maine a small Canoa with seven or eight Guianians, to invite us to ancker at their port, but I deferred till my returne. It was that Casique to whom those Nepoios went, which came with us from the towne of Toparimaca: and so the fift day we reached as high up as the province of Aromaia the countrey of Morequito whom Berreo executed, and ankered to the West of an yland called Murrecotima, tenne miles long and five broad: and that night the Casique Aramiary (to whose towne we made our long and hungry voyage out of the river of Amana) passed by us.

The next day wee arrived at the port of Morequito, and anckered there, sending away one of our Pilots to seeke the king of Aromaia, uncle to Morequito slaine by Berreo as aforesaid. The next day following before noone hee came to us on foote from his house, which was foureteene English miles (himselfe being a hundreth and tenne yeeres olde) and returned on foote the same day, and with him many of the borderers, with many women and children, that came to wonder at our nation, and to bring us downe victuall, which they did in great plentie, as venison, porke, hennes, chickens, foule, fish, with divers sorts of excellent fruites and rootes, and great abundance of Pinas, the princes of fruites, that grow under the Sunne, especially those of Guiana. They brought us also store of bread, and of their wine, and a sort of Paraquitos, no bigger then wrennes, and of all other sorts both small and great; one of them gave mee a beast called by the Spaniards Armadilla, which they call Cassacam, which seemeth to be all barred over with smal plates somewhat like to a Rinoceros, with a white horne growing in his hinder parts, as bigge as a great hunting horne, which they use to winde in stead of a trumpet. Monardus writeth that a little of the powder of that horne put into the eare, cureth deafenesse.

After this olde King had rested a while in a little tent, that I caused to bee set up, I beganne by my interpreter to discourse with him of the death of Morequito his predecessour, and afterward of the Spaniards, and ere I went any farther I made him knowe the cause of my comming thither, whose servant I was, and that the Queenes pleasure was, I should undertake the voyage for their defence, and to deliver them from the tyrannie of the Spaniards, dilating at large (as I had done before to those of Trinidad) her Majesties greatnesse, her justice, her charitie to all oppressed nations, with as many of the rest of her beauties and vertues, as either I could expresse, or they conceive: all which being with great admiration attentively heard, and marveilously admired, I beganne to sound the olde man as touching Guiana, and the state thereof, what sort of common wealth it was, how governed, of what strength and policie, howe farre it extended, and what nations were friendes or enemies adjoyning, and finally of the distance and way to enter the same: hee tolde mee that himselfe and his people with all those downe the River towards the Sea, as farre as Emeria, the province of Carapana, were of Guiana, but that they called themselves Orenoqueponi, and that all the nations betweene the river and those mountaines in sight called Wacarima, were of the same cast and appellation: and that on the other side of those mountaines of Wacarima there was a large plaine (which after I discovered in my returne) called the valley of Amariocapana, in all that valley the people were also of the ancient Guianians.

I asked what nations those were which inhabited on the farther side of those mountaines, beyond the valley of Amariocapana: hee answered with a great sigh (as a man which had inward feeling of the losse of his Countrey and libertie, especially for that his eldest sonne was slaine in a battell on that side of the mountaines, whom hee most entirely loved) that hee remembred in his fathers life time when hee was very olde, and himselfe a yong man, that there came downe into that large valley of Guiana, a nation from so farre off as the Sunne slept, (for such were his owne words) with so great a multitude as they coulde not bee numbred nor resisted, and that they wore large coates, and hattes of crimson colour, which colour hee expressed, by shewing a piece of red wood, wherewith my tent was supported, and that they were called Orejones, and Epuremei, those that had slaine and rooted out so many of the ancient people, as there were leaves in the wood upon all the trees, and had nowe made themselves Lords of all, even to that mountaine foote called Curaa, saving onely of two nations, the one called Iwarawaqueri, and the other Cassipagotos, and that in the last battell fought betweene the Epuremei, and the Iwarawaqueri, his eldest sonne was chosen to carry to the aide of the Iwarawaqueri, a great troupe of the Orenoqueponi, and was there slaine with all his people and friendes, and that hee had now remayning but one sonne: and farther tolde mee that those Epuremei had built a great Towne called Macureguarai at the said mountaine foote, at the beginning of the great plaines of Guiana, which have no ende: and that their houses have many roomes, one over the other, and that therein the great King of the Orejones and Epuremei kept three thousande men to defend the borders against them, and withall dayly to invade and slay them: but that of late yeeres since the Christians offered to invade his territories, and those frontiers, they were all at peace, and traded one with another, saving onely the Iwarawaqueri, and those other nations upon the head of the river of Caroli, called Cassipagotos, which we afterwards discovered, each one holding the Spaniard for a common enemie.

After hee had answered thus farre, he desired leave to depart, saying that hee had farre to goe, that hee was olde, and weake, and was every day called for by death, which was also his owne phrase: I desired him to rest with us that night, but I could not intreate him, but hee tolde mee that at my returne from the countrey above, hee would againe come to us, and in the meane time provide for us the best he could, of all that his countrey yeelded; the same night hee returned to Orocotona his owne towne, so as hee went that day eight and twentie miles, the weather being very hot, the countrey being situate betweene foure and five degrees of the Equinoctial.

This Topiawari is helde for the prowdest, and wisest of all the Orenoqueponi, and so hee behaved himselfe towardes mee in all his answers at my returne, as I marveiled to finde a man of that gravitie and judgement, and of so good discourse, that had no helpe of learning nor breede.

The next morning we also left the port, and sailed Westward up to the

River, to view the famous River called Caroli, as well because it was marveilous of it selfe, as also for that I understoode it ledde to the strongest nations of all the frontiers, that were enemies to the Epuremei, which are subjects to Inga, Emperour of Guiana, and Manoa, and that night we anckered at another yland called Caiama, of some five or sixe miles in length, and the next day arrived at the mouth of Caroli. When we were short of it as lowe or further downe as the port of Morequito wee heard the great rore and fall of the River, but when wee came to enter with our barge and whirries thinking to have gone up some fourtie miles to the nations of the Cassipagotos, wee were not able with a barge of eight oares to row one stones cast in an houre, and yet the River is as broad as the Thames at Wolwich, and wee tried both sides, and the middle, and every part of the River, so as we incamped upon the bankes adjoyning, and sent off our Orenoquepone (which came with us from Morequito) to give knowledge to the nations upon the River of our being there, and that wee desired to see the Lordes of Canuria, which dwelt within the province upon that River, making them know that we were enemies to the Spaniards, (for it was on this River side that Morequito slewe the Frier, and those nine Spaniards which came from Manoa, the Citie of Inga, and tooke from them fourtie thousande pezos of golde) so as the next day there came downe a Lord or Casique called Wanuretona with many people with him, and brought all store of provisions to entertaine us, as the rest had done. And as I had before made my comming knowen to Topiawari, so did I acquaint this Casique therewith, and howe I was sent by her Majestie for the purpose aforesaide, and gathered also what I could of him touching the estate of Guiana, and I founde that those also of Caroli were not onely enemies to the Spaniards, but most of all to the Epuremei, which abound in golde, and by this Wanuretona, I had knowledge that on the head of this River were three mighty nations, which were seated on a great lake, from whence this River descended, & were called Cassipagotos, Eparagotos, and Arawagotos, and that all those either against the Spaniards, or the Epuremei would joyne with us, and that if wee entred the land over the mountaines of Curaa, we should satisfie our selves with gold and all other good things: he told us farther of a nation called Iwarawaqueri before spoken off, that held dayly warre with the Epuremei that inhabited Macureguarai the first civill towne of Guiana, of the subjects of Inga the Emperour.

Upon this river one Captaine George, that I tooke with Berreo tolde mee there was a great silver Mine, and that it was neere the banckes of the saide river. But by this time as well Orenoque, Caroli, as all the rest of the rivers were risen foure or five foote in height, so as it was not possible by the strength of any men, or with any boat whatsoever to rowe into the River against the streame. I therefore sent Captaine Thyn, Captaine Greenvile, my nephew John Gilbert, my cosen Butshead Gorges, Captaine Clarke, and some thirtie shotte more to coast the River by land, and to goe to a towne some twentie miles over the valley called Amnatapoi, and they found guides there, to goe farther towards the mountaine foote to another great towne

called Capurepana, belonging to a Casique called Haharacoa (that was a
nephew to olde Topiawari King of Arromaia our chiefest friend) because
this towne and province of Capurepana adjoyned to Macureguarai, which
was a frontier towne of the Empire: and the meane while my selfe with
Captaine Gifford, Captaine Calfield, Edward Hancocke, and some halfe a
dosen shotte marched over land to viewe the strange overfals of the river
of Caroli which rored so farre off, and also to see the plaines adjoyning,
and the rest of the province of Canuri: I sent also Captaine Whiddon, William Connocke, and some eight shotte with them, to see if they coulde finde
any Minerall stone alongst the river side. When we were come to the tops
of the first hilles of the plaines adjoyning to the river, we behelde that
wonderfull breach of waters, which ranne downe Caroli: and might from
that mountaine see the river howe it ranne in three parts, above twentie
miles off, and there appeared some tenne or twelve overfals in sight, every
one as high over the other as a Church-tower, which fell with that fury,
that the rebound of water made it seeme, as if it had bene all covered over
with a great shower of raine: and in some places wee tooke it at the first
for a smoke that had risen over some great towne. For mine owne part I
was well perswaded from thence to have returned, being a very ill foote-
man, but the rest were all so desirous to goe neere the saide strange thunder
of waters, as they drew me on by little and little, till wee came into the next
valley where we might better discerne the same.

I never saw a more beautifull countrey, nor more lively prospects, hils
so raised here and there over the valleys, the river winding into divers
branches, the plaines adjoyning without bush or stubble, all faire greene
grasse, the ground of hard sand easie to march on, either for horse or foote,
the deere crossing in every path, the birdes towards the evening singing on
every tree with a thousand severall tunes, cranes and herons of white, crimson, and carnation pearching in the rivers side, the aire fresh with a gentle
Easterly winde, and every stone that we stouped to take up, promised either
golde or silver by his complexion. Your Lordship shall see of many sorts,
and I hope some of them cannot bee bettered under the Sunne, and yet
we had no meanes but with our daggers and fingers to teare them out here
and there, the rockes being most hard of that minerall Sparre aforesaide,
which is like a flint, and is altogether as hard or harder, and besides the
veines lye a fathome or two deepe in the rockes. But we wanted all things
requisite save onely our desires and good will to have performed more if
it had pleased God. To be short, when both our companies returned, each
of them brought also severall sorts of stones that appeared very faire, but
were such as they found loose on the ground, and were for the most part
but coloured, and had not any golde fixed in them, yet such as had no
judgement or experience kept al that glistered, and would not be perswaded
but it was rich because of the lustre, and brought of those, and of Marquesite
with all, from Trinidad, and have delivered of those stones to be tried in
many places, and have thereby bred an opinion that all the rest is of the same:
yet some of these stones I shewed afterward to a Spaniard of the Caracas,

who tolde mee that it was El Madre del oro, that is the mother of gold, and that the Mine was farther in the ground.

But it shall be found a weake policie in me, either to betray my selfe, or my countrey with imaginations, neither am I so farre in love with that lodging, watching, care, perill, diseases, ill savours, bad fare, and many other mischiefes that accompany these voyages, as to woo my selfe againe into any of them, were I not assured that the Sunne covereth not so much riches in any part of the earth. Captaine Whiddon, and our Chirurgion Nicholas Millechap brought mee a kinde of stones like Saphires, what they may prove I know not. I shewed them to some of the Orenoqueponi, and they promised to bring mee to a mountaine, that had of them very large pieces growing Diamond wise: whether it be Christall of the mountaine, Bristol-Diamond, or Saphire I doe not yet know, but I hope the best, sure I am that the place is as likely as those from whence all the rich stones are brought, and in the same height or very neere.

On the left hand of this river Caroli are seated those nations which are called Iwarawakeri before remembred, which are enemies to the Epuremei: and on the head of it adjoyning to the great lake Cassipa, are situate those other nations which also resist Inga, and the Epuremei, called Cassepagotos, Eparegotos, and Arrawagotos. I farther understood that this lake of Cassipa is so large, as it is above one dayes journey for one of their Canoas to crosse, which may bee some fourtie miles, and that thereinto fall divers rivers, and that great stores of graines of gold are found in the Summer time when the lake falleth by the banckes, in those branches.

There is also another goodly river beyond Caroli which is called Arui, which also runneth thorow the lake Cassipa, and falleth into Orenoque farther West, making all that land betweene Caroli and Arui an yland, which is likewise a most beautifull countrey. Next unto Arui there are two rivers Atoica and Caora, and on that branch which is called Caora, are a nation of people, whose heads appeare not above their shoulders; which though it may be thought a meere fable, yet for mine owne part I am resolved it is true, because every childe in the provinces of Arromaia and Canuri affirme the same: they are called Ewaipanoma: they are reported to have their eyes in their shoulders, and their mouthes in the middle of their breasts, and that a long traine of haire groweth backward betweene their shoulders. The sonne of Topiawari, which I brought with me into England, told me that they are the most mighty men of all the land, and use bowes, arrowes, and clubbes thrice as big as any of Guiana, or of the Orenoqueponi, and that one of the Iwarawakeri tooke a prisoner of them the yeere before our arrivall there, and brought him into the borders of Aromaia his fathers countrey. And farther when I seemed to doubt of it, hee told me that it was no wonder among them, but that they were as great a nation, and as common as any other in all the provinces, and had of late yeeres slaine many hundreds of his fathers people, and of other nations their neighbours, but it was not my chance to heare of them till I was come away, and if I had but spoken one worde of it while I was there, I might have brought one of them with mee to put the matter out of doubt. Such a nation was written of by Mandevile, whose reports were holden for fables many yeeres, and yet since the East Indies were discovered, we find his relations true of such things as heretofore were held incredible: whether it be true or no, the matter is not great, neither can there bee any profit in the imagination; for mine owne part I saw them not, but I am resolved that so many people did not all combine, or forethinke to make the report.

When I came to Cumana in the West Indies afterwards by chance I spake with a Spaniard dwelling not farre from thence, a man of great travell, and after hee knew that I had bene in Guiana, and so farre directly West as Caroli, the first question hee asked me was, whether I had seene any of the Ewaipanoma, which are those without heads: who being esteemed a most honest man of his word, and in all things else, tolde mee that hee had seene many of them: I may not name him, because it may be for his disadvantage, but hee is well knowen to Monsieur Mucherons sonne of London, and to Peter Mucheron merchant of the Flemish shippe that was there in trade, who also heard what he avowed to be true of those people.

The fourth river to the West of Caroli is Casnero which falleth into Orenoque on this side of Amapaia, and that river is greater then Danubius, or any of Europe: it riseth on the South of Guiana from the mountaines which devide Guiana from Amazones, and I thinke it to bee navigable many hundreth miles: but wee had no time, meanes, nor season of the yeere, to search those rivers for the causes aforesayd, the Winter being come upon us, although the Winter and Summer as touching colde and heate differ not, neither doe the trees ever sensibly lose their leaves, but have alwayes fruit either ripe or greene, and most of them both blossome, leaves, ripe fruite, and greene at one time: but their Winter onely consisteth of terrible raines, and overflowing of the rivers, with many great stormes and gustes, thunder and lightnings, of which we had our fill, ere we returned.

On the North side, the first river that falleth into Orenoque is Cari, beyond it on the same side is the river of Limo, betweene these two is a great nation of Canibals, and their chiefe towne beareth the name of the river, and is called Acamacari: at this towne is a continuall market of women for three or foure hatchets a piece, they are bought by the Arwacas, and by them sold into the West Indies.

Betweene Dawney and Beta lyeth a famous Island in Orenoque now called Baraquan (for above Meta it is not knowen by the name of Orenoque) which is called Athule, beyond which, ships of burden cannot passe by reason of a most forcible overfall, and current of waters: but in the eddy al smaller vessels may be drawen even to Peru it selfe: But to speake of more of these rivers without the description were but tedious, and therefore I will leave the rest to the description. This river of Orenoque is navigable for ships little lesse then 1000 miles, and for lesser vessels neere 2000. By it (as aforesayd) Peru, Nuevo reyno, and Popaian, may be invaded: it also leadeth to the great empire of Inga, & to the provinces of Amapaia, and Anebas which abound in gold.

We left the mouth of Caroli, and arrived againe at the port of Morequito where we were before: for passing downe the streame we went without labour, and against the winde, little lesse then a hundreth miles a day. Assoone as I came to ankor, I sent away one for olde Topiawari, with whom I much desired to have further conference, and also to deale with him for some one of his countrey, to bring with us into England, as well to learne the language, as to conferre withall by the way, the time being nowe spent of any longer stay there. Within three houres after my messenger came to him, he arrived also, and with him such a rabble of all sorts of people, and every one loden with somewhat, as if it had beene a great market or faire in England: and our hungry companies clustered thicke and threefold among their baskets, every one laying hand on what he liked. After he had rested a while in my tent, I shut out all but our selves, and my interpreter, and told him that I knew that both the Epuremei and the Spaniards were enemies to him, his countrey and nations: that the one had conquered Guiana already, and the other sought to regaine the same from them both: and therefore I desired him to instruct me what he could, both of the passage into the golden parts of Guiana, and to the civill townes and apparelled people of Inga. Hee gave mee an answere to this effect: first that hee could not perceive that I meant to goe onward towards the citie of Manoa, for neither the time of the yeere served, neither could hee perceive any sufficient numbers for such an enterprize: and if I did, I was sure with all my company to bee buried there, for the Emperour was of that strength, as that many times so many men more were too fewe: besides hee gave mee this good counsell and advised mee to holde it in minde (as for himselfe hee knewe, hee could not live till my returne) that I should not offer by any meanes hereafter to invade the strong parts of Guiana without the helpe of all those nations which were also their enemies: for that it was impossible without those, either to bee conducted, to be victualled, or to have ought carried with us, our people not being able to indure the march in so great heate, and travell, unlesse the borderers gave them helpe, to carie with them both their meate and furniture: For hee remembred that in the plaines of Macureguarai three hundreth Spaniards were overthrowen, who were tired out, and had none of the borderers to their friendes: but meeting their enemies as they passed the frontier, were environed on all sides, and the people setting the long drie grasse on fire, smoothered them, so as they had no breath to fight, nor could discerne their enemies for the great smoke. He told me farther that 4 daies journey from his towne was Macureguarai, and that those were the next and neerest of the subjects of Inga, and of the Epuremei, and the first towne of apparelled and rich people, and that all those plates of gold which were scattered among the borderers and caried to other nations farre and neere, came from the sayd Macureguarai and were there made, but that those of the land within were farre finer, and were fashioned after the images of men, beastes, birds, and fishes. I asked him whether hee thought that those companies that I had there with me, were sufficient to take that towne or no? He told me that he thought they were. I then asked him, whether he would assist me with guides, and some companies of his people to joyne with us? He answered that he would go himselfe with al the borderers, if the rivers did remaine foordable, upon this condition that I would leave with him til my return againe fifty souldiers, which hee undertooke to victuall: I answered that I had not above fiftie good men in all there, the rest were labourers and rowers, & that I had no provision to leave with them of powder, shot, apparell, or ought else, and that without those things necessary for their defence, they should bee in danger of the Spaniards in my absence, who I knewe would use the same measure towards mine, that I offered them at Trinidad: And although upon the motion Captaine Calfield, Captaine Greenvile, my nephew John Gilbert and divers others were desirous to stay, yet I was resolved that they must needes have perished, for Berreo expected daylie a supply out of Spaine, and looked also hourely for his sonne to come downe from Nuevo reyno de Granada, with many horse and foote, and had also in Valencia in the Caracas, two hundreth horse ready to march, and I could not have spared above fortie, and had not any store at all of powder, leade, or match to have left with them, nor any other provision, either spade, pickeaxe, or ought else to have fortified withall.

When I had given him reason that I could not at this time leave him such a companie, he then desired mee to forbeare him and his countrey for that time, for he assured mee that I should bee no sooner three dayes from the coast, but those Epuremei would invade him, and destroy all the remaine of his people and friendes, if hee should any way either guide us or assist us against them.

He further alleaged, that the Spaniards sought his death, and as they had already murthered his Nephew Morequito lord of that province, so they had him seventeene dayes in a chaine before hee was king of the countrey, and ledde him like a dog from place to place, until hee had payde an hundreth plates of golde, and divers chaines of Spleen-stones for his ransome: and nowe since he became owner of that province, that they had many times layd waite to take him, and that they would bee nowe more vehement, when they should understand of his conference with the English, and because, sayd hee, they would the better displant me, if they cannot lay handes on mee, they have gotten a Nephew of mine called Eparacano, whom they have Christened Don Juan, and his sonne Don Pedro, whom they have also apparelled and armed, by whom they seeke to make a partie against me in mine owne coun-trey: hee also had taken to wife one Loviana of a strong familie, which are borderers and neighbours, and my selfe now being olde and in the handes of death am not able to travell nor to shifte, as when I was of yoonger yeeres: hee therefore prayed us to deferre it till the next yeere, when he would under-take to draw in all the borderers to serve us, and then also it would bee more seasonable to travell, for at this time of the yeere, wee should not bee able to passe any river, the waters were and would bee so growen ere our returne

He farther told me, that I could not desire so much to invade Macureguarai and the rest of Guiana, but that the borderers would be more vehement then I, for he yeelded for a chiefe cause that in the warres with the Epuremei they were spoyled of their women, and that their wives and daughters wer taken from them, so as for their owne parts they desired nothing of the golde or treasure, for their labours, but onely to recover women from the Epuremei: for hee farther complayned very sadly (as it had beene a matter of great consequence) that whereas they were wont to have tenne or twelve wives, they were now inforced to content themselves with three or foure, and that the lords of the Epuremei had fifty or a hundreth: And in truth they war more for women then either for gold or dominion: For the lords of countreys desire many children of their owne bodies, to increase their races and kinreds, for in those consist their greatest trust and strength. Divers of his followers afterwards desired mee to make haste againe, that they might sacke the Epuremei, and I asked them of what? They answered, of their women for us, and their gold for you: for the hope of those many of women they more desire the war, then either for gold, or for the recovery of their ancient territories. For what betweene the subjects of Inga, and the Spaniards, those frontiers are growen thinne of people, and also great numbers are fled to other nations farther off for feare of the Spaniards.

After I received this answere of the old man, we fell into consideration, whether it had bene of better advice to have entred Macureguarai, and to have begun a warre upon Inga at this time, yea or no, if the time of the yeere, and all things else had sorted. For mine owne part (as we were not able to march it for the rivers, neither had any such strength as was requisite, and durst not abide the comming of the Winter, or to tarie any longer from our ships) I thought it were evill counsell to have attempted it at that time, although the desire of gold will answere many objections: but it would have bin in mine opinion an utter overthrow to the enterprize, if the same should be hereafter by her Majesty attempted: for then (whereas now they have heard we were enemies to the Spaniards & were sent by her Majesty to relieve them) they would as good cheap have joyned with the Spaniards at our returne, as to have yeelded unto us, when they had proved that we came both for one errant, and that both sought but to sacke & spoile them, but as yet our desire of gold, or our purpose of invasion is not knowen to them of the empire: and it is likely that if her Majestie undertake the enterprize, they will rather submit themselves to her obedience then to the Spaniards, of whose cruelty both themselves and the borderers have already tasted: and therefore till I had knowen her Majesties pleasure, I would rather have lost the sacke of one or two townes (although they might have beene very profitable) then to have defaced or indangered the future hope of so many millions, & the great good, & rich trade which England may be possessed of thereby. I am assured nowe that they will all die even to the last man against the Spaniards in hope of our succour and returne: whereas otherwise if I had either layd handes on the borderers, or ransomed the lords, as Berreo did, or invaded the subjects of Inga, I know all had beene lost for hereafter.

After that I had resolved Topiawari lord of Aromaia, that I could not at this time leave with him the companies he desired, and that I was contented to forbeare the enterprize against the Epuremei till the next yeare, he freely gave me his onely sonne to take with me into England, and hoped, that though hee himselfe had but a short time to live, yet that by our meanes his sonne should be established after his death: and I left with him one Francis Sparrow, a servant of Captaine Gifford, (who was desirous to tarie, and could describe a countrey with his pen) and a boy of mine called Hugh Goodwin, to learne the language. I after asked the maner how the Epuremei wrought those plates of golde, and howe they could melt it out of the stone; hee tolde mee that the most of the golde which they made in plates and images, was not severed from the stone, but that on the lake of Manoa, and in a multitude of other rivers they gathered it in graines of perfect gold and in peeces as bigge as small stones, and that they put it to a part of copper, otherwise they could not worke it, and that they used a great earthern pot with holes round about it, and when they had mingled the gold and copper together, they fastened canes to the holes, and so with the breath of men they increased the fire till the metall ran, & then they cast it into moulds of stone and clay, and so make those plates and images. I have sent your Honors of two sortes such as I could by chance recover, more to shewe the maner of them, then for the value: For I did not in any sort make my desire of gold knowen, because I had neither time, nor power to have a greater quantity. I gave among them manie more peeces of gold, then I received, of the new money of 20 shillings with her Majesties picture to weare, with promise that they would become her servants thencefoorth.

I have also sent your Honours of the ore, whereof I know some is as rich as the earth yeeldeth any, of which I know there is sufficient, if nothing else were to bee hoped for. But besides that we were not able to tarrie and search the hils, so we had neither pioners, barres, ledges, nor wedges of yron to breake the ground, without which there is no working in mines: but wee saw all the hilles with stones of the colour of gold and silver, and we tried them to be no Marquesite, and therefore such as the Spaniards call El madre del oro, or, The mother of gold, which is an undoubted assurance of the generall abundance: and my selfe saw the outside of many mines of the Sparre, which I know to be the same that all covet in this world, and of those, more then I will speake of.

From the river of Mana, we crost another river in the said beautifull valley called Oiana, & rested our selves by a cleere lake, which lay in the middle of the said Oiana, and one of our guides kindling us fire with two stickes, wee stayed a while to drie our shirts, which with the heate hong very wette and heavie on our sholders. Afterwards wee sought the ford to passe over towards the mountaine called Iconuri, where Putijma foretold us of the mine. In this lake we saw one of the great fishes, as big as a wine pipe, which they call Manati, being most excellent and holsome meate. But after I perceived, that to passe the said river would require halfe a dayes march more, I was not able my selfe to endure it, and therefore I sent Captaine Keymis with six shot to goe on, and gave him order not to returne to the port of Putijma, which is called Chiparepare, but to take leisure, and to march downe the sayd valley, as farre as a river called Cumaca, where I promised to meete him againe, Putijma himselfe promising also to bee his guide: and as they marched, they left the townes of Emparepana, and Capurepana, on the right hand, and marched from Putijmas house downe the sayd valley of Amariocapana, and wee returning the same day to the rivers side, saw by the way many rockes, like unto gold ore, and on the left hand, a round mountaine which consisted of minerall stone.

From hence we rowed downe the streame, coasting the province of Parino: As for the branches of rivers which I overpasse in this discourse, those shall be better expressed in the description with the mountaines of Ajo, Ara, and the rest, which are situate in the provinces of Parino and Carricurrina. When we were come as farre downe as the land called Ariacoa, (where Orenoque devideth it selfe into three great branches, each of them being most goodly rivers) I sent away captaine Henrie Thin, and captaine Greenevile with the galley, the neerest way, and tooke with mee captaine Gifford, captaine Calfield, Edward Porter, and captaine Eynos with mine owne barge, and the two wherries, and went downe that branch of Orenoque, which is called Cararoopana, which leadeth towards Emeria the province of Carapana, and towards the East sea, as well to finde out captaine Keymis, whome I had sent over land, as also to acquaint my selfe with Carapana, who is one of the greatest of all the lords of the Orenoqueponi: and when I came to the river of Cumaca (to which Putijma promised to conduct captaine Keymis) I left captaine Eynos and master Porter in the sayd river to expect his comming, & the rest of us rowed downe the streame towards Emeria.

In this branch called Cararoopana were also many goodly Islands, some of sixe miles long, some of ten, and some of twenty. When it grew towards sunneset, we entred a branch of a river that fell into Orenoque called Winicapora: where I was enformed of the mountaine of Christall, to which in trueth for the length of the way, and the evill season of the yeere, I was not able to march, nor abide any longer upon the journey: wee saw it afarre off and it appeared like a white Church-tower of an exceeding height. There falleth over it a mighty river which toucheth no part of the side of the mountaine, but rusheth over the toppe of it, and falleth to the ground with so terrible a noyse and clamor, as if a thousand great bels were knockt one against another. I thinke there is not in the world so strange an over-fall, nor so wonderfull to behold: Berreo told mee that there were Diamonds and other precious stones on it, and that they shined very farre off: but what it hath I know not, neither durst he or any of his men ascend to the top of the sayd mountaine, those people adjoyning being his enemies (as they were) and the way to it so impassable.

Upon this river of Winicapora wee rested a while, and from thence marched into the countrey to a town called after the name of the river, whereof the captaine was one Timitwara, who also offered to conduct mee to the top of the sayd mountaine called Wacarima: But when wee came in first to the house of the sayd Timitwara, being upon one of their sayd feast dayes, we found them all as drunke as beggers, and the pots walking from one to another without rest: we that were weary, and hote with marching, were glad of the plenty though a small quantitie satisfied us, their drinke being very strong and headie, and so rested our selves a while; after wee had fedde, we drew our selves backe to our boats, upon the river and there came to us all the lordes of the countrey, with all such kinde of victuall as the place yeelded, and with their delicate wine of Pinas, and with abundance of hens, and other provisions, and of those stones which wee call Spleene-stones.

Wee understood by the chiefetaines of Winicapora, that their lord Carapana was departed from Emeria which was now in sight, & that he was fled to Cairamo, adjoyning to the mountains of Guiana, over the valley called Amariocapana, being perswaded by those tenne Spaniards which lay at his house, that we would destroy him, and his countrey.

But after these Cassiques of Winicapora & Saporatona his followers perceived our purpose, and saw that we came as enemies to the Spaniards onely, and had not so much as harmed any of those nations, no though we found them to be of the Spaniards owne servants, they assured us that Carapana would be as ready to serve us, as any of the lords of the provinces, which we had passed; and that he durst doe no other till this day but entertaine the Spaniards, his countrey lying so directly in their way, and next of all other to any entrance that should be made in Guiana on that side.

And they farther assured us, that it was not for feare of our comming that he was remooved, but to be acquited of the Spaniards or any other that should come hereafter. For the province of Cairoma is situate at the mountaine foote, which devideth the plaines of Guiana from the countreys of the Orenoqueponi: by meanes whereof if any should come in our absence into his townes, hee would slip over the mountaines into the plaines of Guiana among the Epuremei, where the Spaniards durst not follow him without great force.

But in mine opinion, or rather I assure my selfe, that Carapana (being a notable wise and subtil fellow, a man of one hundred yeeres of age, and therefore of great experience) is remooved, to looke on, and if he finde that we returne strong he will be ours, if not, hee will excuse his departure to the Spaniards, and say it was for feare of our comming.

On the Island of Assapano we feasted our selves with that beast which is called Armadilla presented unto us before at Winicapora, and the day following we recovered the galley at ankor at the port of Toparimaca, & the same evening departed with very foule weather and terrible thunder, and showers, for the Winter was come on very farre: the best was, we went no lesse then 100 miles a day, downe the river; but by the way we entred, it was impossible to returne, for that the river of Amana, being in the bottome of the bay of Guanipa, cannot be sayled backe by any meanes, both the brize and current of the sea were so forcible: and therefore wee followed a branch of Orenoque called Capuri, which entred into the sea Eastward of our ships, to the end we might beare with them before the wind, and it was not without neede, for we had by that way as much to crosse of the maine sea after we came to the rivers mouth, as between Gravelyn and Dover, in such boats as your Hon. hath heard.

To speake of what past homeward were tedious, either to describe or name any of the rivers, Islands, or villages of the Tivitivas which dwell on trees: we will leave all those to the generall mappe.

Now that it hath pleased God to sende us safe to our shippes, it is time to leave Guiana to the Sunne, whom they worshippe, and steare away towardes the North: I will therefore in a fewe wordes finish the discovery thereof.

On the hithermost part of Orenoque, as at Toparimaca, and Winicapora, those are of a nation called Nepoios, and are of the followers of Carapana, Lord of Emeria. Betweene Winicapora and the port of Morequito which standeth in Aromaia, and all those in the valley of Amariocapana are called Orenoqueponi, and did obey Morequito, and are now followers of Topiawari. Upon the river of Caroli, are the Canuri, which are governed by a woman (who is inheritrix of that Province) who came farre off to see our Nation, and asked me diverse questions of her Majestie, being much delighted with the discourse of her Majesties greatness, and wondering at such reports as we truely made of her Highnesse many vertues: And upon the head of Caroli, and on the lake of Cassipa, are the three strong Nations of the Cassipagotos. Right South into the land are the Capurepani, and Emparepani, and beyond those adjoyning to Macureguarai (the first citie of Inga) are the Iwarawakeri: all these are professed enemies to the Spaniards, and to the rich Epuremei also. To the West of Caroli are diverse nations of Canibals, and of those Ewaipanoma without heads. Directly West are the Amapaias and Anebas, which are also marveilous rich in gold. The rest towards Peru we will omit. On the North of Orenoque, betweene it and the West Indies are the Wikiri, Saymi, and the rest before spoken of, all mortall enemies to the Spaniardes. On the South side of the maine mouth of Orenoque, are the Arwacas; and beyond them the Canibals and to the South of them the Amazones.

To make mention of the severall beasts, birds, fishes, fruits, flowers, gummes, sweet woods, and of their severall religions and customes, would for the first require as many volumes as those of Gesnerus, and for the rest another bundle of Decades. The religion of the Epuremei is the same which the Ingas, Emperours of Peru used, which may be read in Cieza, and other Spanish stories, how they beleeve the immortalitie of the soule, worship the Sunne, and burie with them alive their best beloved wives and treasure, as they likewise doe in Pegu in the East Indies, and other places. The Orenoqueponi bury not their wives with them, but their jewels, hoping to injoy them againe. The Arwacas dry the bones of their Lords, and their wives and friends drinke them in powder. In the graves of the Peruvians the Spaniards found their greatest abundance of treasure: the like also is to be found among these people in every Province. They have all many wives, and the Lords five-fould to the common sort: their wives never eate with their husbands, nor among the men, but serve their husbands at meales, and afterwardes feede by themselves. Those that are past their younger yeeres, make all their bread and drinke, and worke their cotten beds, and doe all else of service and labour, for the men doe nothing but hunt, fish, play, and drinke, when they are out of the warres.

I will enter no further into discourse of their maners, lawes and customes: and because I have not my selfe seene the cities of Inga, I cannot avow on my credit what I have heard, although it be very likely, that the Emperour Inga hath built and erected as magnificent palaces in Guiana, as his ancestors did in Peru, which were for their riches and rarenesse most marvellous and exceeding all in Europe, and I thinke of the world, China excepted, which also the Spaniards (which I had) assured me to be true, as also the Nations of the borderers, who being but Salvages to those of the in-land, doe cause much treasure to be buried with them: for I was enformed of one of the Cassiques of the valley of Amariocapana which had buried with him a little before our arrivall, a chaire of golde most curiously wrought, which was made either in Macureguaray adjoyning, or in Manoa: but if we should have grieved them in their religion at the first, before they had bene taught better, and have digged up their graves, we had lost them all: and therefore I helde my first resolution, that her Majestie should either accept or refuse the enterprise, ere any thing should be done that might in any sort hinder the same. And if Peru had so many heapes of golde, whereof those Ingas were Princes, and that they delighted so much therin; no doubt but this which now liveth and reigneth in Manoa, hath the same honour, and I am assured hath more abundance of golde, within his territorie, then all Peru and the West Indies.

For the rest, which my selfe have seene, I will promise these things that follow, which I know to be true. Those that are desirous to discover and to see many nations, may be satisfied within this river, which bringeth foorth so many armes and branches leading to severall countries and provinces, above 2000 miles East and West, and 800 miles South and North, and of these, the most eyther rich in golde, or in other marchandizes. The common souldier shall here fight for golde, and pay himselfe in steede of pence, with plates of halfe a foote broad, whereas he breaketh his bones in other warres for provant and penury. Those commanders and chieftaines that shoot at honour and abundance, shall finde there more rich and beautifull cities, more temples adorned with golden images, more sepulchres filled with treasure, then either Cortez found in Mexico, or Pizarro in Peru: and the shining glory of this conquest will eclipse all those so farre extended beames of the Spanish nation. There is no countrey which yeeldeth more pleasure to the inhabitants, either for those common delights of hunting, hawking, fishing, fowling, or the rest, then Guiana doth. It hath so many plaines, cleere rivers, abundance of Phesants, Partriges, Quailes, Railes, Cranes, Herons, and all other fowle: Deere of all sorts, Porkes, Hares, Lions, Tygers, Leopards, and divers other sortes of beastes, either for chase, or food. It hath a kind of beast called Cama, or Anta, as bigge as an English beefe, and in great plentie.

To speake of the severall sorts of every kind, I feare would be troublesome to the Reader, and therefore I will omit them, and conclude that both for health, good ayre, pleasure, and riches I am resolved it cannot bee equalled by any region either in the East or West. Moreover the countrey is so healthfull, as of an hundred persons & more (which lay without shift most sluttishly, and were every day almost melted with heate in rowing and marching, and suddenly wet againe with great showers, and did eate of all sorts of corrupt fruits, and made meales of fresh fish without seasoning, of Tortugas, of Lagartos or Crocodiles, and of all sorts good and bad, without either order or measure, and besides lodged in the open aire every night) we lost not any one, nor had one ill disposed to my knowledge, nor found any Calentura, or other of those pestilent diseases which dwell in all hot regions, and so neere the Equinoctiall line.

Where there is store of gold, it is in effect needlesse to remember other commodities for trade: but it hath towards the South part of the river, great quantities of Brasil-wood, and diverse berries that die a most perfect crimson and carnation: And for painting, all France, Italy, or the East Indies yeelde none such: For the more the skin is washed, the fairer the colour appeareth, and with which, even those browne and tawnie women spot themselves, and colour their cheekes. All places yeeld abundance of cotton, of silke, of balsamum, and of those kindes most excellent, and never knowen in Europe, of all sortes of gummes, of Indian pepper: and what else the countries may afford within the land we knowe not, neither had we time to abide the triall, and search. The soile besides is so excellent and so full of rivers, as it will carrie sugar, ginger, and all those other commodities, which the West Indies have.

The navigation is short, for it may be sayled with an ordinarie winde in sixe weekes, and in the like time backe againe, and by the way neither lee shore, enemies coast, rockes, nor sandes, all which in the voyages to the West Indies, and all other places we are subject unto, as the chanell of Bahama, comming from the West Indies, cannot well be passed in the Winter, & when it is at the best, it is a perilous and a fearefull place. The rest of the Indies for calmes, and diseases very troublesome, and the sea about the Bermudas a hellish sea for thunder, lightning, and stormes. . . .

To conclude, Guiana is a countrey that hath yet her maydenhead, never sackt, turned, nor wrought, the face of the earth hath not bene torne, nor the vertue and salt of the soyle spent by manurance, the graves have not bene opened for golde, the mines not broken with sledges, nor their Images puld downe out of their temples. It hath never bene entered by any armie of strength, and never conquered or possessed by any christian Prince. It is besides so defensible, that if two forts be builded in one of the Provinces which I have seene, the flood setteth in so neere the banke, where the channell also lyeth, that no ship can passe up but within a Pikes length of the artillerie, first of the one, and afterwards of the other: Which two Forts will be a sufficient guarde both to the Empire of Inga, and to an hundred other severall kingdomes, lying within the said river, even to the citie of Quito in Peru.

There is therefore great difference betweene the easinesse of the conquest of Guiana, and the defence of it being conquered, and the West or East Indies: Guiana hath but one entrance by the sea (if it hath that) for any vessels of burden: so as whosoever shall first possesse it, it shall be found unaccessible for any enemie, except he come in Wherries, Barges, or Canoas, or else in flat bottomed boates, and if he doe offer to enter it in that manner, the woods are so thicke two hundred miles together upon the rivers of such entrance, as a mouse cannot sit in a boat unhit from the banke. By lande it is more impossible to approch, for it hath the strongest situation of any region under the sunne, and is so environed with impassable mountaines on every side, as it is impossible to victuall any company in the passage: which hath bene well prooved by the Spanish nation, who since the conquest of Peru have never left five yeeres free from attempting this Empire, or discovering some way into it, and yet of three and twentie severall Gentlemen, Knights, and Noble men, there was never any that knewe which way to leade an army by land, or to conduct shippes by sea, any thing neere the saide countrie. Orellana, of whom the river of Amazones taketh name, was the first, and Don Antonio de Berreo (whom we displanted) the last: and I doubt much, whether he himselfe or any of his yet know the best way into the sayde Empire. . . .

The West Indies were first offered her Majesties grandfather by Columbus a stranger, in whom there might be doubt of deceipt, and besides it was then thought incredible that there were such and so many lands & regions never written of before. This Empire is made knowen to her Majestie by her owne vassall, and by him that oweth to her more duetie then an ordinary subject, so that it shall ill sort with the many graces and benefites which I have received to abuse her Highnesse, either with fables or imaginations. The countrey is alreadie discovered, many nations wonne to her Majesties love and obedience, and those Spaniardes which have latest and longest laboured about the conquest, beaten out, discouraged and disgraced, which among these nations were thought invincible. Her Majestie may in this enterprize employ all those souldiers and gentlemen that are younger brethren, and all captaines and chieftaines that want employment, and the charge will be onely the first setting out in victualling and arming them: for after the first or second yeere I doubt not but to see in London a Contractation house of more receipt for Guiana, then there is now in Sivill for the West Indies.

And I farther remember that Berreo confessed to me and others (which I protest before the Majestie of God to be true) that there was found among prophesies in Peru (at such time as the Empire was reduced to the Spanish obedience) in their chiefest temples, amongst divers others which foreshewed the losse of the said Empire, that from Inglatierra those Ingas should be againe in time to come restored, and delivered from the servitude of the said Conquerours. And I hope, as we with these few hands have displanted the first garrison, and driven them out of the said countrey, so her Majestie will give order for the rest, and either defend it, and hold it as tributary, or conquere and keepe it as Empresse of the same. For whatsoever Prince shall possesse it, shall be greatest, and if the king of Spaine enjoy it, he will become unresistable. Her Majestie hereby shall confirme and strengthen the opinions of all nations, as touching her great and princely actions. And where the South border of Guiana reacheth to the Dominion and Empire of the Amazones, those women shall hereby heare the name of a virgin, which is not onely able to defend her owne territories and her neighbours, but also to invade and conquer so great Empires and so farre removed.

CHAPTER IX

Captain James Cook—1728–1779

Captain James Cook was already a navigator of great renown when he embarked on his last voyage, in which he met his tragic and untimely death in Hawaii. He was born in Yorkshire, England, and through his own industry acquired a thorough knowledge of mathematics and astronomy. His explorations were remarkable for their scientific contribution to the art of navigation and geography.

On his first voyage to the South Seas in 1768 he discovered, among other things, the Society Islands. He also established the fact that New Zealand was an island, and not part of a new continent, as previously assumed. He furnished complete surveys of all he found, which proved to be of inestimable value to all future explorers. On his second expedition, in 1772, he discovered several new islands in the South Pacific, among them New Caledonia and Georgia.

His third voyage in 1776 to Hawaii, called the Sandwich Islands, proved the most important in Cook's career. The task of the famous circumnavigator was to find the Northwest Passage, and the Admiralty's instructions covering this expedition follow. We take up Captain Cook's own journal from the point at which his astronomical purposes had been accomplished.

THIRD VOYAGE—JULY 14, 1776

The Admiralty's Instructions to Capt. Cook.

"Whereas, the Earl of Sandwich has signified to us his Majesty's pleasure, that an attempt should be made to find out a northern passage by sea from the Pacific to the Atlantic Ocean; and, whereas, we have in pursuance thereof caused his Majesty's sloops *Resolution* and *Discovery* to be fitted, in all respects, proper to proceed upon a voyage for the purpose above mentioned; and from the experience we have had of your abilities and good conduct in your late voyages, have thought fit to intrust you with the conduct of the present intended voyage, and with that view appointed you to command the first-mentioned sloop, and directed Captain Clerke, who commands the other, to follow your orders for his further proceedings; you are hereby required and directed to proceed with the said two sloops directly for the Cape of

227

Good Hope, unless you shall judge it necessary to stop at Madeira, the Cape de Verd, or Canary Islands, to take in wine for the use of their companies; in which case you are at liberty so to do, taking care to remain there no longer than may be necessary for that purpose; and on your arrival at the Cape of Good Hope, you are to refresh the sloops' companies with as much provision and water as can be conveniently stowed.

"If possible you are to leave the Cape of Good Hope by the end of October or beginning of November next, and proceed to the southward in search of some islands, said to have been lately seen by the French, in the latitude 48 deg. south, and under or near the meridian of Mauritius. In case you find those islands, you are to examine them thoroughly for a good harbor, and upon discovering one, make the necessary observations to facilitate the finding it again, as a good port in that situation may hereafter prove very useful, although it should afford nothing more than shelter, wood, and water. You are not, however, to spend too much time in looking out for those islands, or in the examination of them, if found, but to proceed to Otaheite, or the Society Isles (touching at New Zealand in your way thither if you should judge it necessary and convenient), and taking care to arrive there time enough to admit of your giving the sloops' companies the refreshment they may stand in need of before you prosecute the further object of these instructions. Upon your arrival at Otaheite, or the Society Isles, you are to land Omai at such of them as he may choose, and to leave him there.

"You are to distribute among the chiefs of those islands such part of the presents with which you have been supplied as you shall judge proper, reserving the remainder to distribute among the natives of the countries you may discover in the northern hemisphere; and having refreshed the people belonging to the sloops under your command, and taken on board such wood and water as they may respectively stand in need of, you are to leave those islands in the beginning of February, or sooner if you shall judge it necessary, and then to proceed in as direct a course as you can to the coast of New Albion, endeavoring to fall in with it in the latitude of 45 deg. north, and taking care in your way thither not to lose any time in search of new lands, or to stop at any you may fall in with, unless you find it necessary to recruit your wood and water.

"You are also in your way thither, strictly enjoined not to touch upon any part of the Spanish dominions on the western continent of America, unless driven thither by some unavoidable accident, in which case you are to stay no longer there than shall be absolutely necessary, and to be very careful not to give umbrage or offense to any of the inhabitants or subjects of his Catholic Majesty. And, if in your further progress to the northward, as hereafter directed, you find any subjects of any European prince or state upon any part of the coast you may think proper to visit, you are not to disturb them, or give them any just cause of offense, but, on the contrary, to treat them with civility and friendship.

"Upon your arrival on the coast of New Albion, you are to put into the first convenient port to recruit your wood and water and procure refreshments, and then to proceed northward along the coast as far as the latitude of 65°, or farther, if you are not obstructed by lands or ice; taking care not to lose any time in exploring rivers or inlets, or upon any other account until you get in the before-mentioned latitude of 65°, where we could wish you to arrive in the month of June next. When you get that length you are very carefully to search for and explore such rivers or inlets as may appear of considerable extent, and pointing towards Hudson's or Baffin's Bay, and if, from your own observations or from information from the natives (who, there is reason to believe, are the same race of people, and speak the same language—of which you are furnished with a vocabulary—as the Esquimaux), there shall appear to be a certainty, or even a probability, of a water passage into the afore-mentioned bays, or either of them, you are, in such case, to use your utmost endeavors to pass through with one or both of the sloops, unless you shall be of opinion that the passage may be effected with more certainty, or with greater probability, by smaller vessels; in which case you are to set up the frames of one or both of the small vessels with which you are provided, and when they are put together, and are properly fitted, stored, and victualed, you are to dispatch one or both of them, under the care of proper officers, with a sufficient number of petty officers, men, and boats, in order to attempt the said passage; with such instructions for rejoining you, if they should fail, or for their further proceedings, if they should succeed in the attempt, as you shall judge most proper. But, nevertheless, if you shall find it more eligible to pursue any other measures than those above pointed out, in order to make a discovery of the before-mentioned passage (if any such there be), you are at liberty; and we leave it to your discretion to pursue such measures accordingly.

"But, should you be satisfied that there is no passage through the bays, sufficient for the purposes of navigation, you are, at the proper season of the year, to repair to the port of St. Peter and St. Paul, in Kamtschatka, or wherever else you shall judge more proper, in order to refresh your people and pass the winter; and in the spring of the ensuing year, 1778, to proceed from thence to the northward, as far as in your prudence you may think proper, in further search of a Northeast or Northwest passage from the Pacific Ocean into the Atlantic, or North Sea; and if, from your own observation or any information you may receive, there shall appear to be a probability of such a passage, you are to proceed as above directed; and having discovered such a passage, or failed in the attempt, make the best of your way back to England, by such route as you may think best for the improvement of geography and navigation; repairing to Spithead with both sloops, where they are to remain till further orders.

"And at whatever places you may touch in the course of your voyage, where accurate observations of the nature hereafter mentioned have not been made, you are, as far as your time will allow, very carefully to observe the situation of such places, both in latitude and longitude; the variation of the needle; bearings of headlands; height, direction, and course of the tides and current; depth and soundings of the sea; shoals, rocks, etc.; and also to survey, make charts, and take views of such bays, harbors, and different parts of the coast, and to make such notations thereon as may be useful either to navigation or commerce. You are also carefully to observe the nature of the soil and the produce thereof; the animals or fowls that inhabit or frequent it; the fishes that are found in the rivers or upon the coast, and in what plenty; and in case there are any peculiar to such places, to describe them minutely, and to make as accurate drawings of them as you can; and if you find any metals, minerals, or valuable stones, or any extraneous fossils, you are to bring home specimens of each; as also the seeds of such trees, shrubs, plants, fruits, and grains, peculiar to those places, as you may be able to collect, and to transmit them to our secretary, that proper experiments and examinations may be made of them. You are likewise to examine the genius, temper, disposition, and number of the natives and inhabitants, where you find any; and to endeavor, by all proper means, to cultivate a friendship with them, making them presents of such trinkets as you may have on board, and they may like best; inviting them to traffic, and showing them every kind of civility and regard, but taking care, nevertheless, not to suffer yourselves to be surprised by them, but to be always on your guard against any accidents.

"You are also, with the consent of the natives, to take possession, in the name of the King of Great Britain, of convenient situations in such countries as you may discover, that have not already been discovered or visited by any other European power; and to distribute among the inhabitants such things as will remain as traces and testimonies of your having been there; but if you find the countries so discovered are uninhabited, you are to take possession of them for his Majesty, by setting up proper marks and inscriptions as first discoverers and possessors.

"But forasmuch as, in undertakings of this nature, several emergencies may arise not to be foreseen, and therefore not particularly to be provided for by instructions beforehand, you are, in such cases, to proceed as you shall judge most advantageous to the service on which you are employed; and you are, by all opportunities, to send to our secretary, for our information, accounts of your proceedings, and copies of the surveys and drawings you shall have made; and upon your arrival in England, you are immediately to repair to this office, in order to lay before us a full account of your proceedings in the whole course of your voyage, taking care, before you leave the sloop, to demand from the officers and petty officers the log-books and journals they may have kept, and to seal them up for our inspection, and enjoining them, and the whole crew, not to divulge where they have been, until they have permission so to do; and you are to direct Captain Clerke to do the same with respect to the officers, petty officers, and crew of the *Discovery*.

"Should any accident happen to the *Resolution* in the course of the voyage, so as to disable her from proceeding any further, you are in such case to remove yourself and her crew into the *Discovery*, and to prosecute your voyage in her, her commander being hereby strictly required to receive you on board, and to obey your orders, the same in every respect as when you were actually on board the *Resolution;* and in case of your inability by sickness, or otherwise, to carry these instructions into execution, you are to be careful to leave them with the next officer in command, who is hereby required to execute them in the best manner he can.

"The above instructions were given July 6th, 1776, under the hands of the Earl of Sandwich, Lord C. Spencer, Sir H. Palliser; and, by command of their lordships, signed, Philip Stephens, Secretary of the Admiralty."

CAPTAIN COOK'S THIRD VOYAGE, AS RELATED BY HIM IN HIS JOURNAL

Though seventeen months had now elapsed since our departure from England, during which we had not, upon the whole, been unprofitably employed, I was sensible that with regard to the principal object of my instructions, our voyage was, at this time, only beginning; and therefore my attention to every circumstance that might contribute towards our safety and our ultimate success, was now to be called forth anew. With this view I had examined into the state of our provisions at the last islands; and as soon as I had left them, and got beyond the extent of my former discoveries, I ordered a survey to be taken of all the boatswain's and carpenter's stores that were in the ships, that I might be fully informed of the quantity, state, and condition of every article, and by that means know how to use them to the greatest advantage.

In the night of the 22d we crossed the line in the longitude of 203° 15′ East, and on the 24th, about half an hour after daybreak, land was discovered bearing northeast. Upon a nearer approach, it was found to be one of those low islands so common in this ocean, that is, a narrow bank of land enclosing the sea within; a few cocoanut trees were seen in two or three places, but in general the land had a very barren appearance. . . .

At daybreak the next morning I sent two boats, one from each ship, to search more accurately for a landing-place, and at the same time two others to fish near the shore. These last returned about eight o'clock, with upwards of two hundred-weight of fish. Encouraged by this success, they were dispatched again after breakfast, and I then went in another boat to take a view of the coast and attempt landing, which, however, I found to be wholly impracticable. Towards noon, the two boats sent on the same search returned. In consequence of the report of the master, that about a league and a half to the north was a break in the land, and a channel into the lagoon, the ships weighed anchor and came to again in twenty fathoms of water, before a small island that lies at the entrance of the lagoon, and on each side of which there is a channel suitable for boats leading into it. The water in the lagoon itself is very shallow.

On the 28th I landed, in company with Mr. Bayley, on the island which lies between the two channels in the lagoon, to prepare the telescopes for observing an approaching eclipse of the sun, which was one great inducement to my anchoring here.

On the morning of the 30th, the day when the eclipse was to happen, Mr. King, Mr. Bayley, and myself, went ashore on the small island above mentioned, to attend the observation. The sky was overcast till past nine o'clock, when the clouds about the sun dispersed long enough to take its altitude to rectify the time by the watch we made use of. After this, it was again obscured till about thirty minutes past nine, and then we found that the eclipse had begun. We now fixed the micrometers to the telescopes, and observed or measured the uneclipsed part of the sun's disk. At these observations I continued about three-quarters of an hour before the end, when I left off, being, in fact, unable to continue them any longer, on account of the great heat of the sun, increased by the reflection from the sand.

In the afternoon, the boats and turtling party at the southeast part of the island all returned on board, except a seaman belonging to the *Discovery*, who had been missing two days. There were two of them at first who had lost their way, but disagreeing about the most probable track to bring them back to their companions, they had separated; one of them joined the party after having been absent twenty-four hours and been in great distress. Not a drop of fresh water could be had, for there is none upon the whole island, nor was there a single cocoanut tree on that part of it. In order to allay his thirst he had recourse to a singular expedient of killing turtles and drinking their blood. His mode of refreshing himself, when weary, of which he said he felt the good effects, was equally whimsical; he undressed himself and lay down for some time in the shallow water upon the beach. It was a matter of surprise to every one how these men could contrive to lose themselves. The land over which they had to travel, from the seacoast to the lagoon, where the boats lay, was not more than three miles across, nor was there anything to obstruct their view, for the country was flat, with a few shrubs scattered upon it, and from many parts of it the masts of the vessels could easily be seen.

As soon as Captain Clerke knew that one of the stragglers was still in this awkward situation, he sent a party in search of him; but neither the man nor the party having come back the next morning, I ordered two boats into the lagoon, to go different ways in prosecution of the search. Not long after, Captain Clerke's party returned with their lost companion, and my boats having now no object left, I called them back by signal. This poor fellow must have suffered far greater distress than the other straggler, not only as having been lost a longer time, but because he had been too squeamish to drink turtle's blood.

Having some cocoanuts and yams on board in a state of vegetation, I ordered them to be planted on the spot where we had observed the eclipse, and some melon seeds were sown in another place. I also left on the little island a bottle, containing the following inscription:—

Georgius Tertius, Rex, 31 December, 1777.

Naves { *Resolution*, Jac. Cook, Pr.
{ *Discovery*, Car. Clerke, Pr.

On the 1st of January, 1778, I sent boats to bring on board all our parties from the island, and the turtles they had caught. Before this was completed, it was too late in the afternoon, so that I did not think proper to sail till the next morning. We got at this island, for both ships, about 300 turtles, weighing, one with another, about ninety or a hundred pounds. This island has been produced by accessions from the sea, and is in a state of increase, for not only the broken pieces of coral, but many of the shells are too heavy and large to have been brought by any birds from the beach to the places where they now lie. Not a drop of fresh water was anywhere found, though frequently dug for, and there were not the smallest traces of any human being having ever been here before us. On the few cocoa-trees upon the island, the number of which did not exceed thirty, very little fruit was found, and, in general, what was found was either not fully grown or had the juice salt or brackish. A ship touching here must expect nothing but fish and turtles, but of these an abundant supply may be depended upon.

On some parts of the land were a few low trees, under which sat infinite numbers of a new species of tern, or egg-bird. These are black above and white below, with a white arch on the forehead, and are rather larger than the common noddy. Most of them had lately hatched their young, which lay under the old ones upon the bare ground. The rest had eggs, of which they only lay one, larger than that of a pigeon, bluish and speckled with black. There were also many common boobies, resembling a gannet, and a sooty or chocolate-colored one, with a white belly. To this list we may add men-of-war birds, tropic birds, curlews, sand-pipers, a small land bird like a hedge-sparrow, land crabs, small lizards, and rats.

As we kept our Christmas here, I called this discovery Christmas Island. I took it to be about fifteen or twenty leagues in circumference, and of a semicircular form—or like the moon in the last quarter, the two horns being the north and south points.

On the 2d of January, at daybreak, we weighed anchor and resumed our course to the north; and on the morning of the 18th discovered an island; and soon after more land, bearing north, and entirely sheltered from the former. Both had the appearance of being high land.

On the 19th, at sunrise, the island first seen bore east several leagues distant. This being directly to windward, which prevented our getting near it, I stood for the other, which we could reach, and not long after discovered a third island in the direction of west-northwest, as far distant as land could be seen. We steered for the second island, which at noon was about two leagues distant. At this time we were in some doubt whether or no the land before us was inhabited, but soon after saw some canoes coming off from the shore toward the ships. I immediately brought to, to give them time to join us. They had from three to six men each, and on their approach we were agreeably surprised to find that they spoke the language of Otaheite and of the other islands we had lately visited. It required very little address to get them to come alongside, but no entreaties could prevail upon any of them to come on board. I tied some brass medals to a rope, and gave them to those in one of the canoes; who, in return, tied some small mackerel to the rope as an equivalent. This was repeated, and some nails, or bits of iron, which they valued more than any other article, were given them. For these they exchanged more fish and a sweet potato; and having only some large gourd shells and a kind of fishing-net, one of them offered for sale the piece of stuff he wore round his waist. These people were of a brown color, and, though of the common size, were stoutly made. The hair of most of them was cropped pretty short; others had it flowing loose; and with a few, it was tied in a bunch on the crown of the head. In all it seemed naturally black; but most of them had stained it, as is the practice of the Friendly Islanders, with some stuff which gave it a brown or burnt color. In general they wore their beards. They had no ornaments about their persons, and the bits of cloth which they wore were curiously stained with red, black, and white colors. They seemed very mild, and had no arms of any kind, if we except some small stones, which they had evidently brought for their own defense; and these they threw overboard when they found that they were not wanted.

Seeing no signs of an anchoring place at the eastern extremity of the island, I bore away to leeward, and ranged along the southeast side, at a distance of half a league from the shore. As soon as we made sail the canoes left us; but others came off as we proceeded along the coast, bringing with them pigs and some very fine potatoes, which they exchanged as the others had done before, for whatever was offered to them. Several small pigs were purchased for a sixpenny nail, so that we again found ourselves in a land of plenty, and just at the time when the turtle, which we had so fortunately procured at Christmas Island, were nearly expended. We passed several villages; some near the sea, and others further up the country, the inhabitants of which crowded to the shore, and collected on the elevated places to view the ships.

We continued to sound, without striking ground, with a line of fifty fathoms. Night put a stop to further researches, when we stood off and on. The next morning we stood in for the land, and were met by several canoes, filled with people, some of whom took courage and ventured on board. In the course of my several voyages I never before met with the natives of any place so much astonished as these people were upon entering the ship. Their eyes were continually flying from object to object, the wildness of their looks and gestures fully expressing their entire ignorance about everything they saw, and denoting that, till now, they had never been visited by Europeans, nor been acquainted with any of our commodities, except iron, which, however, it was plain they had only heard of. They seemed only to understand that it was a substance much better adapted to the purposes of cutting or of boring holes, than anything their own country produced. They asked for it by the name of "hamaite," probably referring to some instrument, in the making of which iron could be usefully employed, as they applied that name to the blade of a knife, though we were certain that they had no idea of that particular instrument; nor could they handle it properly. For the same reason they frequently called iron by the name of "toe," which, in their language, signifies a hatchet, or rather, a kind of adze.

When we showed them some beads, they asked, first, what they were, and then whether they should eat them; but on their being told that they were to be hung in their ears, they returned them as useless. They were equally indifferent to a looking-glass which was offered them, and returned it for the same reason, but sufficiently expressed their desire for "hamaite" and "toe," which they wished might be very large. Plates of earthenware, china cups, and other such things, were so new to them that they asked if they were made of wood, but wished to have some, that they might carry them to be looked at on shore. They were, in some respects, naturally well-bred, or, at least, fearful of giving offense; asking whether they should sit down, and the like. Some of them repeated a long prayer before they came on board, and others afterwards sung and made motions with their hands, such as we had been accustomed to see in the dances of the islands we had lately visited. At first, on entering the ship, they endeavored to steal everything they came near, or rather, to take it openly, as what we either should not resent or not hinder. We soon convinced them of their mistake, and if they, after some time, became less active in appropriating to themselves whatever they took a fancy to, it was because they found that we kept a watchful eye over them.

At nine o'clock, being pretty near the shore, I sent three armed boats, under the command of Lieutenant Williamson, to look for a landing-place and for fresh water, with orders that if he should find it necessary to land in search of the latter, not to suffer more than one man to go with him out of the boats. Just as they were pulling off from the ship one of the natives, having stolen the butcher's cleaver, leaped overboard, got into his canoe, and hastened to the shore, the boats pursuing him in vain.

While the boats were occupied in examining the coast we stood on and off with the ships, waiting for their return. About noon Mr. Williamson came back, and reported that he had seen a large pond behind a beach, near one of the villages, which the natives told him contained fresh water, and that there was anchoring ground before it. He also reported that he had attempted to land in another place, but was prevented by the natives, who, coming down to the boats in great numbers, attempted to take away the oars, muskets, and in short everything that they could lay hold of, and pressed so thick upon him that he was obliged to fire, by which one man was killed. This unhappy circumstance I did not know till after we had left the island, so that all my measures were directed as if nothing of the kind had happened. Mr. Williamson told me that after the man fell his country-men took him up, carried him off, and then retired from the boat, but still made signals for our people to land, which he declined.

The ships being stationed, between three and four o'clock, I went ashore with three armed boats and twelve marines, to examine the water, and to try the disposition of the inhabitants, several hundreds of whom were assembled on a sandy beach before the villages, behind which was a narrow valley, having at the bottom the piece of water. The very instant I leaped on shore, the natives all fell flat on their faces, and remained in that humble position till, by expressive signs, I prevailed upon them to rise; they then brought a great many small pigs, which they presented to me, with a plan-tain tree, using much the same ceremonies that we had seen practiced on such occasions at the Society and other islands, a long prayer being also spoken by a single person, in which others of the assembly sometimes joined. I expressed my acceptance of their proffered friendship, by giving them in return such presents as I had brought with me from the ship for that pur-pose. When this introductory business was finished, I stationed a guard upon the beach, and got some of the natives to conduct me to the water, which proved to be very good, and in a proper situation for our purpose; it was so considerable that it may be called a lake, and it extended farther up the country than we could see. Having satisfied myself about this point, and about the peaceable disposition of the natives, I returned on board; and hav-ing given orders that everything should be in readiness for landing and filling our water-casks in the morning, I returned with the people employed in that service, and a guard of marines, who were stationed on the beach. As soon as we landed, a trade was set on foot for hogs and potatoes, which the people of this island gave us in exchange for nails and pieces of iron formed into something like chisels. We met with no obstruction in watering; on the contrary, the natives assisted our men in rolling the casks to and from the pool, and readily performed whatever we required.

Everything going on thus to my satisfaction, and considering my presence on the spot as unnecessary, I left the command to Mr. Williamson, who had landed with me, and made an excursion into the country. . . . A numerous train of natives followed us, and one of them, whom I had distinguished for his activity in keeping the rest in order, I made choice of as our guide; this man, from time to time, proclaimed our approach, when every one we met fell prostrate on the ground, and remained in that position till we had passed. This, as I afterwards understood, is the mode of paying their respect to their own great chiefs.

Among the articles which they brought to barter this day, we noticed a particular sort of cloak and cap, which, even in countries where dress is more particularly attended to, might be reckoned elegant. The first are nearly of the size and shape of the short cloaks worn by the women in Eng-land, and by the men in Spain, reaching to the middle of the back, and tied loosely before; the ground is a net-work, upon which the most beautiful red and yellow feathers are so closely fixed, that the surface might be compared to the thickest and richest velvet, which they resemble, both as to feel and glossy appearance. The manner of varying the mixture is very different; some having triangular spaces of red and yellow alternately, others a kind of crescent, and some that were entirely red, had a broad yellow border, which made them appear at some distance exactly like a scarlet cloak edged with gold lace. The brilliant colors of the feathers, in those that happened to be new, added not a little to their fine appearance; and we found that they were in high estimation with their owners, for they would not at first part with one of them for anything that we offered, asking no lesser price than a musket. However, some were afterwards purchased for very large nails.

The cap is made almost exactly like a helmet, with the middle part or crest sometimes of a hand's breadth, and it sits very close upon the head, having notches to admit the ears. It is a frame of twigs and osiers, covered with a net-work, into which are wrought feathers, in the same manner as upon the cloaks, though rather closer, and less diversified; the greater part being red, with some black, yellow, or green stripes on the side, following the curve direction of the crest. These, probably, complete the dress, with the cloaks; for the natives sometimes appeared in both together.

On the 22d the surf broke so high upon the shore that we could not land in our boats; but the natives ventured in their canoes, and bartered some hogs and roots. One of our visitors, on this occasion, who offered some fish-hooks for sale, was observed to have a very small parcel tied to the string of one of them, which he separated with great care, and reserved for himself when he parted with the hook. On seeing him so anxious to conceal the contents of this parcel, he was requested to open it, which he did with great reluctance and some difficulty, as it was wrapped up in many folds of cloth. We found that it contained a thin piece of human flesh, and that these people eat their enemies, using a small wooden instrument set with sharks' teeth, for the purpose of dissecting the bodies; indeed, one old man, upon being questioned as to whether they ate human flesh, answered in the affirmative, and laughed, seemingly at the simplicity of such a question. He also said it was excellent food, or, as he expressed it, "savory eating."

At seven o'clock in the evening the boats returned with two tons of water, a few hogs, a quantity of plantains, and some roots. Mr. King informed me that a great number of the inhabitants were at the watering or landing place, having come, as he supposed, from all parts of the island for the purpose of barter.

The ships quitted Atooi, as the natives called the island, on the 23d of January, but owing to the prevalence of light airs and calms, were forced on the 29th to anchor off a village on the neighboring island of Oneehow. . . .

On the 30th I sent Mr. Gore ashore with a guard of marines and a party to trade with the natives for provisions. I intended to have followed soon after, and went from the ship with that design. But the surf had increased so much by this time that I was fearful if I got ashore, I should not be able to get off again. This really happened to our people who had landed with Mr. Gore, the communication between them and the ships to our own boats being stopped. In the evening they made a signal for the boats, which were sent accordingly, and not long after they returned with a few yams and some salt. . . :

I sent a boat to the southeast point as soon as daylight returned, with an order to Mr. Gore that, if he could not embark his people from the spot where they now were, to march them up to the point. As the boat could not get to the beach, one of the crew swam ashore and carried the order. On the return of the boat, I went myself with the pinnace and launch up to the point, to bring the party on board; and being very desirous of benefiting these poor people by furnishing them with additional articles of food, took with me a ram and two ewes, a boar and sow of the English breed, and the seeds of melons, pumpkins, and onions. I landed with the greatest ease under the west side of the point, and found my party already there, with some of the natives in company. To one of them, whom Mr. Gore had observed assuming some command over the rest, I gave the goats, pigs, and seeds.

While the people were engaged in filling the water-casks from a small stream occasioned by the late rain, I walked a little way up the country, attended by the man above mentioned, and followed by two others, carrying the two pigs. As soon as we got on a rising ground, I stopped to look around me, and observed a woman, on the opposite side of the valley where I landed, calling to her countrymen who attended me. Upon this the chief began to mutter something, which I supposed was a prayer, and the two men who carried the pigs continued to walk round me all the time, making at least a dozen circuits before the other had finished his oration. . . .

After the water-casks had been filled and conveyed into the boats, and we had purchased from the natives a few roots, a little salt, and some salted fish, I returned on board with all the people, and on the 2d of February we stood away to the northward, in prosecution of our voyage. Thus, after spending more time about these islands than was necessary for all our purposes, we were obliged to leave them before we had completed our water. Our ship procured from them provisions sufficient to last for three weeks at least. And Captain Clerke, more fortunate than us, got a supply of vegetables that lasted his people upwards of two months.

It is worthy of observation that the islands in the Pacific Ocean which these voyages have added to the geography of the globe, have been generally found lying in groups or clusters, the single intermediate islands as yet discovered being few in proportion to the others, though, probably, there are many more of them still unknown, which serve as steps between the several clusters. Of what number this newly-discovered archipelago consists, must be left to future investigation. We saw five of them, whose names, as given to us by the natives, are Woahoo, Atooi, Oneeheow, Oreehoua, and Tahoora. I named the group the Sandwich Islands, in honor of the Earl of Sandwich. Atooi, which is the largest of these islands, is at least ten leagues in length from east to west.

The inhabitants are vigorous, active, and most expert swimmers; leaving their canoes upon the most trifling occasion, they dive under them and swim to others, though at a great distance. It was very amusing to see women with infants at the breast, when the surf was so high that they could not land in the canoes, leap overboard and, without endangering their little ones, swim to the shore through a heavy sea.

They seem to be blessed with a frank, cheerful disposition, and to live very sociably in their intercourse with one another, and, except the propensity to thieving, which seems innate in most of the people we have visited in this ocean, they were exceedingly friendly to us, and on all occasions appeared deeply impressed with a consciousness of their own inferiority. It was a pleasure to see with how much affection the women managed their infants, and how readily the men lent their assistance to such a tender office; thus sufficiently distinguishing themselves from those savages who esteem a wife and a child as things rather necessary than desirable, or worthy of their notice.

Both sexes adorn themselves with necklaces made of bunches of small black cord, or many strings of very small shells, or of the dried flowers of the Indian mallow; and sometimes a small human image of bone, about three inches long, neatly polished, is hung round the neck. The women also wear bracelets of a single shell, pieces of black wood, with bits of ivory interspersed, well polished, and fixed by a string drawn very closely through them; or others, of hogs' teeth laid parallel to each other, with the concave side outward and the points cut off, fastened together as the former, some of which, made only of large boars' tusks, being very elegant. The men sometimes wear plumes of the tropic-birds' feathers stuck in their heads; or those of cocks, fastened round neat polished sticks two feet long, commonly decorated at the lower part with oora; and for the same purpose the skin of a white dog's tail is sewed over a stick with its tuft at the end. They also frequently wear on the head a kind of ornament of a finger's thickness or more, covered with red and yellow feathers, curiously varied and tied behind, and on the arm above the elbow, a kind of broad shell-work grounded upon net-work.

Though they seemed to have adopted the mode of living in villages, there is no proportion as to the size of their houses, some being large and commodious, from forty to fifty feet long, and from twenty to thirty broad, while others of them are mere hovels. The entrance is made indifferently at the end or side, and is an oblong hole, so low that one must rather creep than walk in, and is often shut up by a board of planks fastened together, which serves as a door; no light enters the house but at this opening, and though such close habitations may afford a comfortable retreat in bad weather, they seem but ill-adapted to the warmth of the climate. They are, however, kept remarkably clean, and their floors are covered with a large quantity of dried grass, over which they spread mats to sit and sleep upon. At one end stands a bench about three feet high, on which their household utensils are placed. These consist of gourd-shells, which they convert into vessels that serve as bottles to hold water, and as baskets to contain their victuals and other things, with covers of the same, and a few wooden bowls and trenchers of different sizes.

The only musical instruments which we observed here were of an exceedingly rude kind. One of them does not produce a more melodious sound than a child's rattle; it consists of what may be called a conic cap inverted, but scarcely hollowed at the base, above a foot high, made of a coarse sedge-like plant, the upper part of which, and the edges, are ornamented with beautiful red feathers, and to the point or lower part is fixed a gourd-shell larger than the fist. Into this is put something to rattle, which is done by holding the instrument by the small part, and shaking or rather moving it from place to place briskly, either to different sides or backward or forward just before the face, striking the breast with the other hand at the same time. The other musical instrument (if either of them deserve the name) was a hollow vessel of wood, like a platter, combined with the use of the sticks, on which one of our gentlemen saw a man performing. He held one of the sticks, about two feet long, as we do a fiddle, with one hand, and struck it with the other, which was smaller and resembled a drum-stick, in a quicker or slower measure; at the same time beating with his foot upon the hollow vessel that lay inverted upon the ground, and thus producing a tune that was by no means disagreeable. The music was accompanied by the vocal performance of some women, whose song had a pleasing and tender effect.

In everything manufactured by these people, there appears to be an uncommon degree of neatness and ingenuity. Cloth is the principal manufacture, and they fabricate a great many white mats, with red stripes and other figures interwoven on one side. . . .

Their canoes in general are about twenty-four feet long, and have the bottom, for the most part, formed of a single piece or log of wood, hollowed out to the thickness of an inch, or an inch and a half, and brought to a point at each end. The sides consist of three boards, each about an inch thick, and neatly fitted and lashed to the bottom part. The extremities, both at head and stern, are a little raised, and both are made sharp, somewhat like a wedge, but they flatten more abruptly, so that the two side-boards join each other, side by side, for more than a foot. As they are not more than fifteen or eighteen inches broad, those that go single (for they sometimes join them as at the other islands), have out-riggers, which are shaped and fitted with more judgment than any I had before seen. They are rowed by paddles, such as we had generally met with, and some of them have a light triangular sail, like those of the Friendly Islands, extended to a mast and boom. The ropes used for their boats, and the smaller cord for their fishing-tackle, are strong and well made.

Though I did not see a chief of any note, there were, however, several, as the natives informed us, who reside upon Atooi, and to whom they prostrate themselves as a mark of submission. After I had left the island, one of these great men made his appearance, and paid a visit to Captain Clerke on board the *Discovery*. He came off in a double canoe, and like the king of the Friendly Islands, paid no regard to the small canoes that happened to lie in his way, but ran against or over them; and it was not possible for these poor people to avoid him, for they could not manage their canoes, it being a necessary mark of their submission that they should lie down when he passed. His attendants helped him into the ship, and placed him in the gangway. Their care of him did not cease there, for they stood round him, holding each other by the hands, nor would they suffer any one to come near him but Captain Clerke himself. He was a young man, clothed, from head to foot, and was accompanied by a young woman, supposed to be his wife. Captain Clerke made him some suitable presents, and received from him in return a large bowl, supported by two figures of men, the carving of which, both as to the design and the execution, showed some degree of skill.

On the 2d of February we stood away to the northward, and without meeting with anything memorable, on the 7th of March the long-looked-for coast of New Albion was seen, extending from northeast to southeast, distance ten or twelve leagues. The land appeared to be of moderate height, diversified with hills and valleys, and almost everywhere covered with wood.

After coasting along, and combating contrary winds, on the 29th we anchored in eighty-five fathoms of water, so near the shore as to reach it with a hawser. We no sooner drew near the inlet than we found the coast to be inhabited, and three canoes came off to the ship. In one of these were two men, in another six, and in the third ten. Having come pretty near us, a person in one of the two last stood up and made a long harangue, inviting us to land, as we guessed by his gestures; at the same time he kept strewing handfuls of feathers towards us, and some of his companions threw handfuls of a red dust powder in the same manner. The person who played the orator wore the skin of some animal, and held in each hand, something which rattled as he kept shaking it. After tiring himself with his repeated exhortations, of which we did not understand a word, he was quiet; and then others took it up, by turns, to say something; though they acted their part neither so long nor with so much vehemence as the other. We observed that two or three had their hair quite strewed over with small white feathers, and others had large ones stuck in different parts of the head. After the tumultuous noise had ceased, they lay at a little distance from the ship, and conversed with each other in a very easy manner; nor did they seem to show the least surprise or distrust. Some of them now and then got up, and said something after the manner of their first harangues; and one sang a very agreeable air, with a degree of softness and melody that we could not have expected. The breeze, which soon afterwards sprung up, bringing us nearer the shore, the canoes began to come off in greater numbers, and we had at one time thirty-two of them near the ship, carrying from three to seven or eight passengers each, both men and women. Several of these stood up in their canoes, haranguing and making gestures, after the manner of our first visitors. One canoe was remarkable for a singular head, which had a bird's eye and a bill of an enormous size painted on it; and a person in it, who seemed to be a chief, was no less remarkable for his uncommon appearance, having many feathers hanging from his head, and being painted in an extraordinary manner. He held in his hand a carved bird, of wood, as large as a pigeon, with which he rattled, as the person first mentioned had done; and was no less vociferous in his harangue, which was attended with some expressive gestures.

Though our visitors behaved very peaceably, and could not be suspected of any hostile intention, we could not prevail upon any of them to come on board. . . .

We employed the next day in hauling our ships into the cove, where they were moored head and stern, fastening our hawsers to the trees on shore. On heaving up the anchor of the *Resolution* we found, notwithstanding the great depth of water in which it was let go, that there were rocks at the bottom. These had done some considerable damage to the cable, and the hawsers that were carried out to warp the ship into the cove also got foul of rocks, from which it appeared that the whole bottom was strewed with them. The ship being again very leaky in her upperworks, I ordered the carpenter to caulk her, and to repair such other defects as on examination he might discover.

The fame of our arrival brought a great concourse of the natives to our ships in the course of this day. We counted above a hundred canoes at one time, which might be supposed to contain on an average five persons in each, for few of them had less than three on board, great numbers had seven, eight, or nine, and one was manned with no less than seventeen. Among these visitors many now favored us with their company for 1 e first time, which we could guess from their approaching the ships with their orations and other ceremonies. If they had any distrust or fear of us at first, they now appeared to have laid it aside, for they came on board and mixed with our people with the greatest freedom.

After a fortnight's bad weather, the 19th proving a fair day, we availed ourselves of it to get up the topmasts and yards, and to fix the rigging. Having now finished most of our heavy work, I set out the next morning to take a view of the Sound. I first went to the west point, where I found a large village, and before it a very snug harbor, in which was from four to nine fathoms of water over a bottom of fine sand. The people of this village, who were numerous, and to most of whom I was well known, received me very courteously, every one pressing me to go into his house, or rather his apartment, for several families live under the same roof. I did not decline the invitations; and my hospitable friends whom I visited spread a mat for me to sit down upon, and showed me every other mark of civility. In most of the houses were women at work, making dresses of plant or bark which they executed exactly in the same manner that the New Zealanders manufacture their cloth. Others were occupied in opening sardines, a large quantity of which I had seen brought on shore from canoes, and divided, by measure, amongst several people, who carried them up to their houses, where the operation of curing by smoke-drying is performed. They hang them on small rods; at first about a foot from the fire; afterwards they remove them higher and higher, to make room for others, till the rods, on which the fish hang, reach the top of the house. When they are completely dried they are taken down and packed close in bales, which they cover with mats. Thus they are kept till wanted, and are not a disagreeable article of food. Cod and other large fish are also cured in the same manner by them, though they sometimes dry them in the open air without fire.

*   *   *   *

On the 2d of October, at daybreak, we saw the island of Oonalashka, bearing southeast; and as all harbors were alike to me, provided they were equally safe and convenient, I hauled into a bay, but, finding very deep water, we were glad to get out again. The natives, many of whom lived here, visited us at different times, bringing with them dead salmon and other fish, which they exchanged with the seamen for tobacco. A few days before, every ounce of tobacco that was in the ships had been distributed among the crew, and the quantity was not half sufficient to answer their demands; notwithstanding this, so improvident a creature is an English sailor, that they were as profuse in making their bargains as if they were in a port of Virginia, so that in less than eight-and-forty hours the value of this article of barter was lowered above 1000 per cent.

At one o'clock in the afternoon of the 3d we anchored in Samganoodha harbor, and the next morning the carpenters of both ships were set to work to rip off the sheathing of and under the wale on the starboard side abaft. Many of the seams were found quite open, so that it was no wonder that so much water had found its way into the ship. While we lay here we cleared the fish and spirit rooms and the after-hold, disposing things in such a manner that, in case we should happen to have any more leaks of the same nature, the water might find its way to the pumps. And besides this work and completing our water, we cleared the fore-hold to the very bottom, and took in a quantity of ballast.

On the 14th, in the evening, while Mr. Webber and I were at a village a small distance from Samganoodha, a Russian landed there, who, I found, was the principal person among his countrymen in this and the neighboring islands. Ismyloff, as he was called, arrived in a canoe carrying three persons, attended by twenty or thirty other canoes, each conducted by one man. I took notice that the first thing they did after landing was to make a small tent for Ismyloff of materials which they brought with them, and then they made others for themselves of their canoes and paddles, which they covered with grass, so that the people of the village were at no trouble to find them lodgings. Ismyloff, having invited us into his tent, set before us some dried salmon and berries, which I was satisfied was the best cheer he had. He appeared to be a sensible, intelligent man, and I felt no small mortification in not being able to converse with him, unless by signs, assisted by figures and other characters, which, however, were a very great help. I desired to see him on board the next day, and accordingly he came, with all his attendants; indeed, he had moved into our neighborhood for the express purpose of waiting upon us.

I found that he was very well acquainted with the geography of these parts, and with all the recent discoveries of the Russians. On seeing the modern maps he at once pointed out their errors.

Both Ismyloff and the others affirmed that they knew nothing of the continent of America to the northward, and they called it by the same name which Mr. Stæhlin gives to his great island—that is, Alaschka. From what we could gather from Ismyloff and his countrymen, the Russians have made several attempts to get footing upon that part of this continent that lies contiguous to Oonalashka and the adjoining islands, but have always been repelled by the natives, whom they describe as a very treacherous people.

They mentioned two or three captains or chief men who had been murdered by them, and some of the Russians showed us wounds which they said they had received there.

In the following afternoon, M. Ismyloff, after dining with Captain Clerke, left us with all his retinue, promising to return in a few days. Accordingly, on the 19th he paid us another visit, and brought with him the charts, which he allowed me to copy. He remained with us till the evening of the 21st, when he took his final leave. To his care I entrusted a letter to the Lords Commissioners of the Admiralty, in which was enclosed a chart of all the northern coasts I had visited. He said there would be an opportunity of sending it to Kamtschatka or to Okotsk the ensuing spring, and that it would be at St. Petersburg the following winter. He gave me a letter to Major Behm, governor of Kamtschatka, and another to the commanding officer at Petropaulowska.

There are Russians settled upon all the principal islands between Oonalashka and Kamtschatka, for the sole purpose of collecting furs. Their great object is the sea-beaver, or otter. I never heard them inquire after any other animal, though those whose skins are of superior value also form part of their cargoes.

To all appearances the natives are the most peaceable, inoffensive people I ever met with, and as to honesty, they might serve as a pattern to the most civilized nation upon earth. The natives have their own chiefs in each island, and seem to enjoy liberty and property unmolested, but whether or not they are tributaries to the Russians we could never find out. These people are rather low of stature, but plump and well-shaped, with rather short necks, swarthy, chubby faces, black eyes, small beards, and long straight black hair, which the men wear loose behind and cut before, but the women tie it up in a bunch. Both sexes wear the same dresses in fashion, the only difference is in the materials. The women's frock is made of sealskin, and that of the men of the skins of birds, both reaching below the knee. This is the whole dress of the women, but the men wear over the frock another made of gut, which resists water, and has a hood to it, which draws over the head. Some of them wear boots, and all of them have a kind of cap made of wood, with a rim to admit the head. These caps are dyed with green and other colors, and round the upper part of the rim are stuck the long bristles of some sea animal, on which are strung glass beads, and on the front is a small image or two made of bone.

They make use of no paint, but the women puncture their faces slightly, and both men and women bore the under lips, to which they fix pieces of bone. Their food consists of flesh, sea animals, birds, roots, and berries, and even of seaweed. They dry large quantities of fish in summer, which they lay up in small huts for winter use. They eat everything raw. Boiling and broiling were the only methods of cookery that I saw them make use of, and the first was probably learnt from the Russians. Some have got little brass kettles, and those who have not, make one of a flat stone, with sides of clay. I was once present when the chief of Oonalashka made his dinner of the raw head of a large halibut, just caught. Before any was given to the chief, two of his servants ate the gills, without any other dressing than squeezing out the slime. This done, one of them cut off the head of the fish, took it to the sea and washed it, then came with it and sat down by the chief, first pulling up some grass, upon a part of which the head was laid, and the rest was strewed before the chief. He then cut large pieces off the cheeks, and laid them within the reach of the great man, who swallowed them with as much satisfaction as we should do raw oysters. When he had done, the remains of the head were cut in pieces and given to the attendants, who tore off the meat with their teeth, gnawing the bones like so many dogs.

They produce fire both by collision and by attrition. The former by striking two stones, one against another, on one of which a good deal of brimstone is first rubbed; the latter method is with two pieces of wood, one of which is a stick about eighteen inches in length, and the other a flat piece. The pointed end of the stick they press upon the other, whirling it nimbly round as a drill, thus producing fire in a few minutes. This method is common in many parts of the world. It is practiced by the Kamtschadales, by these people, by the Greenlanders, by the Brazilians, by the Otaheitans, by the New Hollanders, and probably by many other nations.

The canoes made use of by the natives are the smallest we had anywhere seen upon the American coast, though built after the same manner, with some little difference in the construction. The stern of these terminates a little abruptly, the head is forked, the upper point of the fork projecting without the under one, which is even with the surface of the water; the framing is of slender laths, and the covering of seal-skins. They are about twelve feet long, a foot and a half broad in the middle, and twelve or fourteen inches deep. Upon occasion, they can carry two persons, one of whom is stretched at full length in the canoe, and the other sits in the seat or round hole, which is nearly in the middle. Round this hole is a rim or hoop of wood, about which is sewed gut skin, that can be drawn together, or opened like a purse with leathern thongs fitted to the outer edge. The man seats himself in this place, draws the skin tight around his body over his gut-pouch, and brings the end of the thongs or purse-string over the shoulder to keep it in its place. The sleeves of his frock are tied tight round his wrists, and it being close round his neck, and the hood drawn over his head, where it is confined by his cap, water can scarcely penetrate either to his body or into the canoe. If any should, however, insinuate itself, the boatman carries a piece of sponge with which he dries it up. He uses the double-bladed paddle, which is held by both hands in the middle, striking the water with a quick regular motion, first on one side and then on the other. By this means the canoe is impelled at a great rate, and in a direction as straight as a line can be drawn.

The fishing and hunting implements lie ready upon the canoes, under straps fixed for the purpose. They are all made in great perfection, of wood and bone, and differ very little from those used by the Greenlanders, as they are described by Crantz. These people are very expert in striking fish both in the sea and in rivers. They also make use of hooks and lines, nets, and spears; the hooks are composed of bone, and the lines of sinews.

The people of Oonalashka bury their dead on summits of hills, and raise a little hillock over the grave. In a walk into the country, one of the natives who attended me pointed out several of these receptacles of the dead. There was one of them by the side of the road leading from the harbor to the village, over which was raised a heap of stones. It was observed that every one who passed it added one to it. I saw in the country several stone hillocks, that seemed to have been raised by art. Many of them were apparently of great antiquity.

* * * *

On the 1st of December, at eight in the morning, finding that we could fetch Owhyhee, I stood for it, and our visitors from Mowee, not choosing to accompany us, embarked in their canoe and went ashore. At seven in the evening we were close up with the north side of Owhyhee, where we spent the night standing off and on. In the morning of the 2d we were surprised to see the summits of the mountains on Owhyhee covered with snow. As we drew near the shore, some of the natives came off to us; they were a little shy at first, but we soon enticed some of them on board, and at last prevailed upon them to return to the island and bring off what we wanted. Soon after they had reached the shore, we had company enough, and few coming empty-handed, we got a tolerable supply of small pigs, fruit, and roots; we continued trading with them till the evening, when we made sail and stood off. We resumed trading with the natives on the 6th and 7th, and procured pork, fruit, and roots, sufficient for four or five days. We then made sail, and continued to work up to windward. Having procured a quantity of sugar-cane, and finding that a strong decoction of it produced a very palatable beer, I ordered some more to be brewed for our general use; but when the cask was now broached, not one of my crew would even so much as taste it. As I had no motive in preparing this beverage but to save our spirits for a colder climate, I gave myself no further trouble, either by exerting authority, or by having recourse to persuasion to prevail upon them to drink it, knowing that there was no danger of the scurvy, so long as we could get a plentiful supply of other vegetables. But, that I might not be thwarted in my views, I gave orders that no grog should be served in either ship. I myself, and the officers, continued to make use of the sugar-cane beer whenever we could get materials for brewing it. A few hops, of which we had some on board, improved it much. It has the taste of new malt beer, and I believe no one will doubt of its being very wholesome, yet my inconsiderate crew alleged that it was injurious to their health. They had no better reason to support a resolution which they took on our first arrival in King George's Sound, not to drink the spruce beer made there: but, whether from consideration that it was not the first time of their being required to use that liquor, or from some other reason, they did not attempt to carry their purpose into actual execution, and I had never heard of it until now, when they renewed their ignorant opposition to my best endeavors to serve them. Every innovation whatever on board a ship, though ever so much to the advantage of seamen, is sure to meet with their highest disapprobation. Both portable soup and sourkrout were at first condemned as stuff unfit for human beings. Few commanders have introduced into their ships more novelties, as useful varieties of food and drink, than I have done; indeed, few commanders have had the same opportunities of trying such experiments.

I kept at some distance from the coast till the 13th, when I stood in again six leagues farther to windward than we had as yet reached, and after having some trade with the natives who visited us, stood out to sea. I now determined to get round, or at least to get a sight of the southeast end of the island, but the wind was variable between the 14th and 18th, blowing sometimes in hard squalls, and at other times calm, with thunder, lightning, and rain. In the evening it shifted to east by south, and we stood to the southward, close-hauled under easy sail, as the *Discovery* was at some distance astern. At this time the southeast point of the island bore southwest by south, about five leagues distant, and I made no doubt that I should be able to weather it. But at one o'clock next morning it fell calm, and we were left to the mercy of a northeasterly swell, which impelled us fast towards the land, so that, long before daybreak, we saw lights and the shore, which was not more than a league distant. The night was dark, with thunder, lightning, and rain.

At three o'clock the calm was succeeded by a breeze, blowing in squalls, with rain, and at daybreak the coast was seen extending from north to southwest, a dreadful surf breaking upon the shore, which was not more than half a league distant. It was evident that we had been in the most imminent danger; nor were we yet in safety, the wind veering more easterly, so that for some time we did but just keep our distance from the coast. What made our situation more alarming was the leech-rope of the maintopsail giving way, which was the occasion of the sail being rent in two; and the two topgallant sails gave way in the same manner, though not half-worn out. By taking a favorable opportunity we soon bent others, and then we left the land astern. The *Discovery*, by being at some distance to the north, was never near the land, nor did we see her till eight o'clock.

As soon as daylight appeared, the natives ashore displayed a white flag, which we conceived to be a signal of peace and friendship. Some of them ventured out after us, but the wind freshening, and it not being safe to wait, they were soon left astern. In the afternoon, after making an attempt to weather the eastern extreme, which failed, I gave it up, and ran down to the *Discovery*. Indeed, it was of no consequence to get round the island, for we had seen its extent to the southeast, which was what I wanted; and according to the information we had gained from the natives, there is no other island to the windward of this. However, as we were so near the southeast end of it, and as the least shift of wind in our favor would serve to carry us round, I did not wholly give up the idea of weathering it, and therefore continued tacking the ship.

On the 20th, in the afternoon, some of the natives came off in their canoes, bringing with them a few pigs and plantains; but the supply being barely sufficient for one day, I stood in again the next morning, till within three or four miles of the land, where we were met by a number of canoes, laden with provisions. We brought to, and continued trading with the people till four in the afternoon, when, having got a pretty good supply, we made sail, and stretched off to the northward.

I had never met with a behavior so free from reserve and suspicion, in my intercourse with any tribes of savages, as we experienced in the people of this island. It was very common for them to send up into the ship the several articles they brought off for barter, after which they would come in themselves, and make their bargains on the quarter-deck. The people of Otaheite, even after our repeated visits, do not care to put so much confidence in us, whence I infer that those of Owhyhee must be more faithful in their dealings with one another than the inhabitants of Otaheite are; for, if little faith were observed among themselves, they would not be so ready to trust strangers. It is also to be observed, to their honor, that they had never once attempted to cheat us in exchanges, nor to commit a theft.

On the 22d, at four in the afternoon, after purchasing everything that the natives had brought off, we made sail, and stretched to the north; and at midnight we tacked and stood to the southeast. Supposing that the *Discovery* would see us tack, the signal was omitted, but she did not see us, as we afterwards found, and continued standing to the north, so that, at daylight next morning, she was not in sight. At this time, the weather being hazy, we could not see far, so that it was possible the *Discovery* might be following us; and being past the northeast part of the island I was tempted to stand on, till, by the wind veering to the northeast, we could not weather the land upon the other tack; consequently we could not stand to the north, to join or look for the *Discovery*. At six in the evening we had succeeded in getting to windward of the island, which we had aimed at with so much perseverance. The *Discovery*, however, was not yet to be seen; but the wind, as we had it, being very favorable for her to follow us, I concluded that it would not be long before she joined us; I therefore kept cruising off this southeast point of the island till I was satisfied that Captain Clerke would not join me here. I now conjectured that he had not been able to weather the northeast part of the island, and had gone to leeward, in order to meet me that way.

As I generally kept from five to ten leagues from the land, no canoes, except one, came off to us till the 28th, when we were visited by a dozen or fourteen.

We stood in again on the 30th, and brought to for the purposes of trade, but soon after our marketing was interrupted by a very hard rain, and besides, we were rather too far from the shore. Nor durst I go nearer, for

I could not depend upon the wind's remaining where it was for a moment, the swell also being high, and setting obliquely upon the shore, against which it broke in a frightful surf. In the evening the weather mended, but before daybreak the atmosphere was again loaded with heavy clouds, and the new year was ushered in with very hard rain, which continued at intervals, till past ten o'clock. Being about five miles from land, several canoes arrived with fruit and roots, and at last some hogs were brought off. We lay to trading with them till three o'clock in the afternoon, when, having a tolerable supply, we made sail with a view of proceeding to the northwest, or lee side of the island, to look for the *Discovery*. For several days past both wind and weather had been exceedingly unsettled, and there fell a great deal of rain. The three following days were spent in running down the southeast side of the island, for during the night we stood off and on, and part of each day was employed in lying to, in order to furnish an opportunity to the natives of trading with us. They sometimes came on board while we were five leagues from the shore, but whether from fear of losing their goods in the sea or from the uncertainty of a market, they never brought much with them. The principal article procured was salt, which was extremely good.

On the morning of the 5th of January, 1779, we passed the south point of the island, on which stands a pretty large village, the inhabitants of which thronged off to the ship with hogs. As I had now got a quantity of salt, I purchased no hogs but such as were fit for salting, refusing all that were under size; however, we could seldom get any above fifty or sixty pounds weight. It was fortunate for us that we had still some vegetables on board, for we now received few such productions; indeed, this part of the country, from its appearance, did not seem capable of affording them. Marks of its having been laid waste by the explosion of a volcano everywhere presented themselves, and though we had as yet seen nothing like one upon the island, the devastation that it had made in this neighborhood was visible to the naked eye.

The next morning the natives visited us again, bringing with them the same articles of commerce as before. Being now near the shore, I sent Mr. Bligh, the master, in a boat to sound the coast, with orders to land and to look for fresh water. Upon his return he reported that he found no running stream, but only rain water, deposited in holes upon the rocks, and even that was brackish from the spray of the sea, and that the surface of the country was entirely composed of slags and ashes, with a few plants interspersed. Between ten and eleven we saw with pleasure the *Discovery* coming round the south point of the island, and at one in the afternoon, she joined us. Captain Clerke, coming on board, informed me that he had cruised four or five days where we were separated, and then worked round the east side of the island, but that, meeting with unfavorable winds, he had been carried to some distance from the coast. He had one of the islanders on board all this time, who had remained there from choice, and had refused to quit the ship, though opportunities offered.

Having spent the night standing off and on, we stood in again the next morning, and when we were about a league from the shore, many of the natives visited us; at daybreak on the 8th we found that the currents had carried us back considerably to windward, so that we were now off the south-west point of the island. There we brought to, in order to give the natives an opportunity of trading with us. We spent the night as usual, standing off and on, and, at four in the morning of the 11th, the wind being at west, I stood in for the land, in order to get some supplies. We lay to or stood on and off during the next few days, trading with the natives, but got a very scanty supply.

At daybreak on the 16th, seeing the appearance of a bay, I sent Mr. Bligh with a boat from each ship to examine it, being at this time three leagues off. Canoes now began to arrive from all parts, so that before ten o'clock there were not fewer than a thousand about the two ships, most of them crowded with people, and well-laden with hogs and other productions of the island. We had the most satisfying proof of their friendly intentions, for we did not see a single person who had with him a weapon of any sort; trade and curiosity alone had brought them off. Among such numbers as we had at that time on board, it is no wonder that some should betray a thievish disposition. One of our visitors took out of the ship a boat's rudder, and was discovered, but too late to recover it. I thought this a good opportunity to show these people the use of firearms, and two or three muskets, and as many 4-pounders, were fired over the canoe which carried off the rudder; as it was not intended that any of the shot should take effect, the surrounding multitude of natives seemed rather more surprised than frightened. In the evening Mr. Bligh returned, and reported that he had found a bay in which was good anchorage and fresh water, in a situation tolerably easy of access. Into this bay I resolved to carry the ships, there to refit and supply ourselves with every refreshment that the place could afford. As night approached, the greater part of our visitors retired to the shore, but numbers of them requested our permission to sleep on board. Curiosity was not the only motive, at least with some, for the next morning several things were missing, which determined me not to entertain so many another night. At eleven o'clock in the forenoon we anchored in a bay which is called by the natives Karakakooa, in thirteen fathoms of water, and about a quarter of a mile from the northeast shore. The ships continued to be much crowded with natives, and were surrounded by a multitude of canoes. I had nowhere in the course of my voyages seen so numerous a body of people assembled at one place, for, besides those who had come off to us in canoes, all the shore of the bay was covered with spectators, and many hundreds were swimming round the ships like shoals of fish. We could not but be struck with the singularity of the scene, and perhaps there were few on board who now lamented our having failed in our endeavors to find a northern passage homeward last summer. In this disappointment we owed our having it in our power to revisit the Sandwich Islands, and to enrich our voyage with a discovery which, though the last, seemed in many respects to be the most

nportant that had hitherto been made by Europeans throughout the extent
f the Pacific Ocean.

*Captain Cook's narrative ends here. The circumstances surrounding his
·agic death are related by Capt. King.*

Karakakooa Bay is situated on the west side of the island of Owhyhee,
a a district called Akona. It is about a mile in depth, and bound by the low
oints of land distant half a league from each other. On the north point,
/hich is flat and barren, stands the village of Kowrowa, and in the bottom
f the bay, near a grove of tall cocoanut trees, there is another village of a
iore considerable size, called Kakooa; between them runs a high rocky
liff, inaccessible from the sea-shore. On the south side the coast, for about
mile inland, has a rugged appearance, beyond which the country rises with
gradual ascent, and is overspread with cultivated enclosures and groves of
ocoanut trees, where the habitations of the natives are scattered in great
umbers. The shore all round the bay is covered with a black coral rock,
/hich makes the landing very dangerous in rough weather, except at the
illage of Kakooa, where there is a fine sandy beach with a morai, or bury-
ig-place, at one extremity, and a small well of fresh water at the other. This
·ay appearing to Captain Cook a proper place to refit the ships and lay in an
dditional supply of water and provisions, we moored on the north side,
bout a quarter of a mile from the shore.

As soon as the inhabitants perceived our intention of anchoring in the bay,
hey came off from the shore in astonishing numbers, and expressed their
oy by singing and shouting, and exhibiting a variety of wild and extravagant
estures. The sides of the decks and rigging of both ships were soon com-
»letely covered with them, and a multitude of women and boys, who had
iot been able to get canoes, came swimming round us in shoals; many of
hem not finding room on board, remained the whole day playing in the
vater.

Among the chiefs who came on board the *Resolution* was a young man
:alled Pareea, whom we soon perceived to be a person of great authority.
)n presenting himself to Captain Cook he told him that he was a jackanee to
he king of the island, who was at that time engaged in a military expedition
.t Mowee, and was expected to return within three or four days. A few
oresents from Captain Cook attached him entirely to our interests, and he
·ecame exceedingly useful to us in the management of his countrymen, as
ve had soon occasion to experience; for we had not been long at anchor
vhen it was observed that the *Discovery* had such a number of people hang-
ng on one side, as occasioned her to heel considerably, and that the men
vere unable to keep off the crowds which continued pressing into her.
Captain Cook being apprehensive that she might suffer some injury, pointed
»ut the danger to Pareea, who immediately sent to their assistance, cleared
he ship of its incumbrance, and drove away the canoes that surrounded her.
The authority of the chief over the inferior people appeared from this in-
:ident to be of the most despotic kind. A similar instance of it happened

the same day on board the *Resolution*, when the crowd being so great as to impede the necessary duties of the ship, we were obliged to have recourse to the assistance of Kaneena, another of their chiefs, who had likewise attached himself to Captain Cook. The inconvenience we labored under being made known, he immediately ordered his countrymen to quit the vessel, and we were not a little surprised to see them jump overboard, without a moment's hesitation, all except one man, who, loitering behind and showing some unwillingness to obey, Kaneena took him up in his arms and threw him into the sea. Both these chiefs were men of strong and well-proportioned bodies, and of countenances remarkably pleasing. Kaneena especially, whose portrait was drawn by Mr. Webber, was one of the finest men I ever saw. He was about six feet high, had regular and expressive features, with lively, dark eyes, and his carriage was easy, firm, and graceful.

It has been already mentioned, that during our long cruise near this island the inhabitants had always behaved with fairness and honesty in their dealings, and had not shown the slightest propensity to theft, which appeared to us the more extraordinary because those with whom we had hitherto held any intercourse were of the lowest rank, either servants or fishermen. We now found the case exceedingly altered; the immense crowd of islanders, which blocked up every part of the ships, not only afforded frequent opportunity of pilfering, without risk of discovery, but our numerical inferiority held forth a prospect of escaping with impunity, in case of detection. Another circumstance, to which we attributed this alteration in their behavior, was the presence and encouragement of their chiefs; for, generally tracing the booty into the possession of some men of consequence, we had the strongest reason to suspect that these depredations were committed at their instigation.

Soon after the *Resolution* had got into her station, our two friends, Pareea and Kaneena, brought on board a third chief, named Koah, who, we were told, was a priest, and had been in his youth a distinguished warrior. He was a little old man, of an emaciated figure, his eyes exceedingly sore and red, and his body covered with a white leprous scurf, the effects of an immoderate use of the ava. Being led into the cabin, he approached Captain Cook with great veneration, and threw over his shoulders a piece of red cloth, which he had brought along with him; then, stepping a few paces back, made an offering of a small pig, which he held in his hand whilst he pronounced a discourse, that lasted for a considerable time. This ceremony was frequently repeated during our stay at Owhyhee, and appeared to us, from many circumstances, to be a sort of religious adoration. Their idols we found always arrayed with red cloth, in the same manner as was done to Captain Cook, and a small pig was their usual offering to the Eatooas. Their speeches, or prayers, were uttered, too, with a readiness and volubility that indicated them to be according to some formulary. When this ceremony was over, Koah dined with Captain Cook, eating plentifully of what was set before him, but like the rest of the inhabitants of the islands in these seas, could scarcely be prevailed on to taste, a second time, our wine or spirits. In the evening, Captain Cook, attended by Mr. Bayley and myself, accompanied him on shore. We landed at the beach, and were received by four men, who carried wands tipped with dogs' hair, and marched before us, pronouncing, with a loud voice, a short sentence, in which we could only distinguish the word "Orono." Captain Cook generally went by this name amongst the natives of Owhyhee, but we could never learn its precise meaning; sometimes they applied it to an invisible being, who, they said, lived in the heavens; and we also found that it was a title belonging to a personage of great rank or power in the island. The crowd which had been collected on the shore retired at our approach, and not a person was to be seen, except a few lying prostrate on the ground, near the huts of the adjoining village.

Before I proceed to relate the adoration that was paid to Captain Cook, and the peculiar ceremonies with which he was received on this fatal island, it will be necessary to describe the morai, situated, as I have already mentioned, at the south side of the beach at Kakooa. It was a square, solid pile of stone, about forty yards long, twenty broad, and fourteen in height; the top was flat and well paved, and surrounded by a wooden rail, on which were fixed the skulls of the captives sacrificed on the death of their chiefs. In the center of the area stood a ruinous old building of wood, connected with the rail on each side by a stone wall, which divided the whole space into two parts. On the side next the country were five poles, upwards of twenty feet high, supporting an irregular kind of scaffold; and on the opposite side, towards the sea, stood two small houses with a covered communication. We were conducted by Koah to the top of this pile by an easy ascent, leading from the beach to the northwest corner of the area. At the entrance we saw two large wooden images with features violently distorted, and a long piece of carved wood, of a conical form inverted, rising from the top of their heads; the rest were without form, and wrapped round with red cloth. We were here met by a tall young man with a long beard, who presented Captain Cook to the images, and after chanting a kind of hymn, in which he was joined by Koah, they led us to that end of the morai where the five poles were fixed. At the foot of them were twelve images ranged in a semicircular form, and before the middle figure stood a high stand or table, exactly resembling the "whatta" of Otaheite, on which lay a putrid hog, and under it pieces of sugar-cane, cocoanuts, bread-fruit, plantains, and sweet potatoes. Koah having placed the captain under this stand, took down the hog, and held it towards him; and after having a second time addressed him in a long speech, pronounced with much vehemence and rapidity, he let it fall to the ground, and led him to the scaffolding, which they began to climb together, not without great risk of falling. At this time we saw coming in solemn procession, at the entrance of the top of the morai, two men carrying a live hog and a large piece of red cloth; having advanced a few paces, they stopped and prostrated themselves, and Kaireekeea, the young man above mentioned, went to them and received the cloth, carried it to Koah, who wrapped it round the captain, and afterwards offered him the hog, which was brought by Kaireekeea with the same ceremony.

Whilst Captain Cook was aloft in this awkward situation, swathed roun
with red cloth, and with difficulty keeping his hold amongst the pieces o
rotten scaffolding, Kaireekeea, and Koah began their office, chanting some
times in concert, and sometimes alternately. This lasted a considerable tim
until at length Koah let the hog drop, when he and the captain descende
together. He then led him to the images before mentioned, and having sai
something to each in a sneering tone, snapping his fingers at them as h
passed, he brought him to that in the center, which, from its being covere
with red cloth, appeared to be held in greater estimation than the res
Before this figure he prostrated himself and kissed it, desiring Captain Coo
to do the same, who suffered himself to be directed by Koah throughou
the whole of this ceremony. We were now led back into the other divisio
of the morai, where there was a space, ten or twelve feet square, sunk abou
three feet below the level of the area; into this we descended, and Captai
Cook was seated between the wooden idols, Koah supporting one of hi
arms, whilst I was desired to support the other. At this time arrived a secon
procession of natives, carrying a baked hog and a pudding, some bread-frui
cocoanuts, and other vegetables. When they approached us, Kaireekeea pu
himself at their head, and presenting the pig to Captain Cook in the usua
manner, began the kind of chant as before, his companions making regula
responses. We observed that, after every response, their parts became grad
ually shorter, till, toward the close, Kaireekeea's consisted of only two o
three words, which the rest answered by the word Orono.

When this offering was concluded, which lasted a quarter of an hour, th
natives sat down fronting us, and began to cut up the baked hog, to peel th
vegetables, and break the cocoanuts; whilst others employed themselves i
brewing the ava, which is done by chewing it, in the same manner as at th
Friendly Islands. Kaireekeea then took part of the kernel of a cocoanut
which he chewed, and, wrapping it in a piece of cloth, rubbed with it th
captain's face, head, hands, arms, and shoulders. The ava was then hande
round, and after we had tasted it, Koah and Pareea began to pull the fles
of the hog in pieces, and to put it into our mouths. I had no great objectio
to being fed by Pareea, who was very cleanly in his person; but Captai
Cook, who was served by Koah, recollecting the putrid hog, could no
swallow a morsel, and his reluctance, as may be supposed, was not dimin
ished, when the old man, according to his own mode of civility, had chewe
it for him. When this last ceremony was finished, which Captain Cook pu
an end to as soon as he decently could, he quitted the morai, after distribut
ing amongst the people some pieces of iron and other trifles, with whicl
they seemed highly gratified. The men with wands conducted us to th
boats, repeating the same words as before; the people again retired, and th
few that remained prostrated themselves as we passed along the shore. W
immediately went on board, our minds full of what we had seen, and ex
tremely well satisfied with the good disposition of our new friends. Th
meaning of the various ceremonies with which we had been received, an
which, on account of their novelty and singularity, have been related a

length, can only be the subject of conjectures, and those uncertain and partial; they were, however, without doubt, expressive of high respect on the part of the natives, and, as far as related to the person of Captain Cook, they seemed approaching to adoration.

The next morning I went on shore, with a guard of eight marines, including the corporal and lieutenant, having orders to erect the observatory on the most suitable spot for superintending and protecting the waterers and the other working parties that were to be on shore. As we were viewing a spot conveniently situated for this purpose in the middle of the village, Pareea, who was always ready to show his power and his good-will, offered to pull down some houses that would have obstructed our observations; however, we thought it proper to decline this offer, and fixed on a field of sweet potatoes, adjoining the morai, which was readily granted to us; and the priests, to prevent the intrusion of the natives, immediately consecrated the place by fixing their wands round the wall by which it was enclosed. This sort of religious interdiction they call "taboo," a word we heard often repeated during our stay amongst these islanders, and found it to be of very powerful and extensive operation, and it procured us even more privacy than we desired. No canoes ever presumed to land near us; the natives sat on the wall but none offered to come within the tabooed space till he had obtained our permission.

But though the men, at our request, would come across the field with provisions, yet not all our endeavors could prevail on the women to approach us. Presents were tried, but without effect; and Pareea and Koah were tempted to bring them but in vain, as we were invariably answered that the Eatooa and Terreeoboo, which was the name of their king, would kill them. This circumstance afforded no small matter of amusement to our friends on board, where the crowds of people, and particularly of women, that continued to flock thither obliged them almost every hour to clear the vessel, in order to have room to do the necessary duties of the ship. On these occasions two or three hundred women were frequently made to jump into the water at once, where they continued swimming and playing about till they could again procure admittance.

From the 19th to the 24th, when Pareea and Koah left us to attend Terreeoboo, who had landed on some other part of the island, nothing very material happened on board. The caulkers were set to work on the sides of the ships, and the rigging was carefully overhauled and repaired. The salting of hogs for sea store was also one of the principal objects of Captain Cook's attention, and met with complete success.

We had not long been settled on the shore at the observatory before we discovered, in our neighborhood, the habitations of a society of priests, whose regular attendance at this morai had excited our curiosity. Their huts stood round a pond of water, and were surrounded by a grove of cocoanut trees, which separated them from the beach and the rest of the village, and gave the place an air of religious retirement. On my acquainting Captain Cook with these circumstances, he resolved to pay them a visit, and as he expected to be received in the same manner as before, he brought Mr. Webber with him to make a drawing of the ceremony. On his arrival at the beach, he was conducted to a sacred building called Harre-no-Orono, or the house of Orono, and seated before the entrance at the foot of a wooden idol, of the same kind as those in the morai. I was here again made to support one of his arms, and after wrapping him in red cloth, Kaireekeea, accompanied by twelve priests, made an offering of a pig with the usual solemnities. The pig was then strangled, and a fire being kindled, it was thrown into the embers, and after the hair was singed off, it was again presented with a repetition of the chanting, in the manner before described. The dead pig was then held for a short time under the captain's nose, after which it was laid with a cocoanut at his feet, and the performers sat down. The ava was then brewed and handed round; a fat hog, ready dressed, was brought in, and we here fed as before.

During the rest of the time we remained in the bay, whenever Captain Cook came on shore he was attended by one of these priests, who went before him, giving notice that the Orono had landed, and ordering the people to prostrate themselves. The same person also constantly accompanied him on the water, standing in the bow of the boat, with a wand in his hand, and giving notice of his approach to the natives, who were in canoes, on which they immediately left off paddling and lay down on their faces till he had passed. Whenever we stopped at the observatory, Kaireekeea and his brethren immediately made their appearance with hogs, cocoanuts, breadfruit, etc., and presented them with the usual solemnities. It was on these occasions that some of the inferior chiefs frequently requested to be permitted to make an offering to the Orono; when this was granted, they presented the hog themselves, generally with evident marks of fear in their countenances, whilst Kaireekeea and the priests chanted their accustomed hymns.

The civilities of this society were not, however, confined to mere ceremony and parade. Our party on shore received from them, every day, a constant supply of hogs and vegetables, more than sufficient for our subsistence, and several canoes, loaded with provisions, were sent to the ships with the same punctuality. No return was ever demanded or even hinted at in the most distant manner. Their presents were made with a regularity more like the discharge of a religious duty than the effort of mere liberality; and when we inquired at whose charge all this munificence was displayed, we were told it was at the expense of a great man called Kaoo, the chief of the priests, and grandfather of Kaireekeea, who was at that time absent, attending the king of the island.

As everything relating to the character and behavior of this people must be interesting to the reader, on account of the tragedy that was afterwards acted here, it will be proper to acquaint him that we had not always so much reason to be satisfied with the conduct of the warrior chiefs, or Earees, as with that of the priests. In all our dealings with the former we found them sufficiently attentive to their own interests; and besides their habit of stealing, which may admit of some excuse from the universality of the practice amongst the islanders of these seas, they made use of other artifices equally dishonorable.

Things continued in this state till the 24th, when we were a good deal surprised to find that no canoes were suffered to put off from the shore, and that the natives kept close to their houses. After several hours' suspense, we learned that the bay was tabooed, and all intercourse with us interdicted on account of the arrival of Terreeoboo. As we had not foreseen an accident of this sort, the crews of both ships were obliged to pass the day without their usual supply of vegetables. The next morning, therefore, they endeavored, both by threats and promises, to induce the natives to come alongside, and, as some of them were at last venturing to come off, a chief was observed attempting to drive them away. A musket was immediately fired over his head to make him desist, which had the desired effect, and supplies were soon after purchased as usual. In the afternoon, Terreeoboo arrived, and visited the ship in a private manner, attended only by one canoe, in which were his wife and children. He stayed on board till near ten o'clock, when he returned to the village of Kowrowa.

The next day, about noon, the king, in a large canoe, attended by two others, set out from the village, and paddled towards the ships in great state, presenting a striking appearance. In the first canoe was Terreeoboo and his chiefs, dressed in their rich feathered cloaks and helmets, and armed with long spears and daggers; in the second canoe the venerable Kaoo, the chief of the priests, and his brethren, with their idols displayed on red cloth. These idols were busts of a gigantic size, made of wicker-work, and curiously covered with small feathers of various colors, wrought in the same manner as their cloaks; their eyes were made of large pearl oysters, with a black nut fixed in the center, and their mouths were set with a double row of the fangs of dogs, and, together with the rest of their features, were strangely distorted. The third canoe was filled with hogs and various sorts of vegetables. As they went along, the priests in the center canoe sung their hymns with great solemnity, and, after paddling round the ships, instead of going on board, as was expected, they made towards the shore at the beach where we were stationed. As soon as I saw them approaching, I ordered out our little guard to receive the king; and Captain Cook, perceiving that he was going on shore, followed him, and arrived nearly at the same time. We conducted them into the tent, where they had scarcely been seated, when the king rose up, and, in a very graceful manner, threw over the captain's shoulders the cloak he himself wore, put a feathered helmet upon his head and a curious fan into his hand. He also spread at his feet five or six other cloaks, all exceedingly beautiful, and of the greatest value. His attendants then brought four very large hogs, with sugar-canes, cocoanuts, and bread-fruit; and this part of the ceremony was concluded by the king's exchanging names with Captain Cook, which, amongst all the islanders of the Pacific Ocean, is esteemed the strongest pledge of friendship. A procession of priests, with a venerable old personage at their head, now appeared, fol-

lowed by a long train of men leading large hogs, and other with plantains,
sweet potatoes, and other articles of food. By the looks and gestures of Kaireekeea, I immediately knew the old man to be the chief of the priests
before mentioned, on whose bounty we had so long subsisted. He had a piece
of red cloth in his hands, which he wrapped round Captain Cook's shoulders,
and afterwards presented him with a small pig in the usual form. A seat was
then made for him next to the king, after which Kaireekeea and his followers began their ceremonies, Kaoo and the chiefs joining in the responses.

I was surprised to see, in the person of this king, the same infirm and
emaciated old man that came on board the *Resolution* when we were off
the northeast side of the island of Mowee, and we soon discovered amongst
his attendants most of the persons who, at that time, had remained with us
all night. Of this number were the two younger sons of the king, the eldest
of whom was sixteen years of age, and his nephew Maiha-Maiha, whom at
first we had some difficulty in recollecting, his hair being plastered over with
a dirty brown paste and powder, which was no mean heightening to the
most savage face I ever beheld. As soon as the formalities of the meeting
were over, Captain Cook carried Terreeoboo, and as many chiefs as the pinnace would hold, on board the *Resolution*. They were received with every
mark of respect that could be shown them. And Captain Cook, in return for
the feathered cloaks, put a linen shirt on the king and girt his own hanger
round him. Kaoo and about half a dozen old chiefs remained on shore, and
took up their abode at the priests' houses. During all this time not a canoe
was seen in the bay, and the natives either kept within their huts, or lay
prostrate on the ground. Before the king left the *Resolution*, Captain Cook
obtained leave for the natives to come and trade with the ships as usual; but
the women, for what reason we could not learn, still continued under the
effects of the taboo.

The quiet and inoffensive behavior of the natives having taken away every
apprehension of danger, we did not hesitate to trust ourselves amongst them
at all times and in all situations. The officers of both ships went daily up the
country in small parties, or even singly, and frequently remained out the
whole night. It would be endless to recount all the instances of kindness and
civility which we received upon these occasions; wherever we went the
people flocked about us, eager to offer any assistance in their power, and
highly gratified if their services were accepted. Various little arts were practiced to attract our notice, or to delay our departure. The boys and girls ran
before us as we walked through the villages, and stopped us at every opening where there was room to form a group for dancing. At one time we
were wanted to accept a draught of cocoanut milk, or some other refreshment, under the shade of their huts; at another we were seated within a
circle of young women, who exerted their skill and agility to amuse us with
songs and dances.

The satisfaction we derived from their gentleness and hospitality was,
however, frequently interrupted by the propensity to stealing which they
have in common with all the other islanders of these seas. This circumstance

was the more distressing as it sometimes obliged us to have recourse to acts of severity, which we would willingly have avoided if the necessity of the case had not absolutely called for them. Some of their most expert swimmers were one day discovered under the ships, drawing out the filling-nails of the sheathing, which they performed very dexterously, by means of a short stick with a flint stone fixed in the end of it. To put a stop to this practice, which endangered the very existence of the vessels, we at first fired small shot at the offenders, but they easily got out of our reach by diving under the ship's bottom; it was therefore found necessary to make an example by flogging one of them on board the *Discovery*.

About this time a large party of gentlemen, from both ships, set out on an excursion into the interior of the country, with a view of examining its natural productions; and it afforded Kaoo a fresh opportunity of showing his attention and generosity, for as soon as he was informed of their departure he sent a large supply of provisions after them, together with orders that the inhabitants of the country through which they were to pass should give them every assistance in their power; and, to complete the delicacy and disinterestedness of his conduct, even the people we employed could not be prevailed on to accept the smallest present. After remaining out six days our officers returned, without having been able to penetrate above twenty miles into the land, partly from want of proper guides and partly from the impracticability of the country.

The head of the *Resolution's* rudder being found exceedingly shaken, and most of the pintles either loose or broken, it was unhung, and taken on shore the 27th to undergo a thorough repair. At the same time the carpenters were sent into the country, under conduct of some of Kaoo's people, to cut planks for the head rail-work, which was also entirely decayed and rotten. On the 28th Captain Clerke, whose ill-health confined him for the most part on board, paid Terreeoboo his first visit at his hut on shore. He was received with the same formalities as were observed towards Captain Cook; and on his coming away, though the visit was quite unexpected, he received a present of thirty large hogs, and as much fruit and roots as his crew could consume in a week.

As we had not seen anything of their sports or athletic exercises, the natives, at the request of some of our officers, entertained us this evening with a boxing match. Though these games were much inferior, as well in point of solemnity and magnificence as in the skill and prowess of the combatants, to what we had seen exhibited at the Friendly Islands, yet, as they differed in some particulars, it may not be improper to give a short account of them. We found a vast concourse of people assembled on a level spot of ground, at a little distance from our tents. A long space was left vacant in the midst of them, at the upper end of which sat the judges under three standards, from which hung slips of cloth of various colors, the skins of wild geese, a few small birds, and bunches of feathers. When the sports were ready to begin the signal was given by the judges, and immediately two combatants appeared. They came forward slowly, lifting up their feet very high behind, and drawing their hands along the soles. As they approached they frequently eyed each other from head to foot in a contemptuous manner, casting several arch looks at the spectators, straining their muscles, and using a variety of affected gestures. Being advanced within reach of each other, they stood with both arms held out straight before their faces, at which part all their blows were aimed. They struck in what appeared to our eyes an awkward manner, with a full swing of the arm; made no attempt to parry, but eluded their adversary's attack by an inclination of the body, or by retreating. The battle was quickly decided, for if either of them was knocked down, or even fell by accident, he was considered as vanquished, and the victor expressed his triumph by a variety of gestures, which usually excited, as was intended, a loud laugh among the spectators. He then waited for a second antagonist, and if again victorious, for a third, till he was at last in his turn defeated. A singular rule observed in these combats is, that whilst any two are preparing to fight, a third person may step in, and choose either of them for his antagonist, when the other is obliged to withdraw. Sometimes three or four followed each other in this manner before the match was settled. When the combat proved longer than usual, or appeared too unequal, one of the chiefs generally stepped in, and ended it by putting a stick between the combatants. The same good humor was preserved throughout which we before so much admired in the Friendly Islanders. As these games were given at our desire, we found it universally expected that we should have borne our part in them; but our people, though much pressed by the natives, turned a deaf ear to their challenge, remembering full well the blows they got at the Friendly Islands.

This day died William Watman, a seaman of the gunners' crew, an event which I mention the more particularly, as death had hitherto been very rare among us. He was an old man, and much respected on account of his attachment to Captain Cook. He had formerly served as a marine twenty-one years; after which he entered as a seaman on board the *Resolution* in 1772, and served with Captain Cook in his voyage towards the South Pole. On their return, he was admitted into Greenwich Hospital through the captain's interest, at the same time with himself; and being resolved to follow throughout the fortunes of his benefactor, he also quitted it along with him on his being appointed to the command of the present expedition.

At the request of the king of the island, he was buried on the morai, and the ceremony was performed with such solemnity as our situation permitted. Old Kaoo and his brethren were spectators, and preserved the most profound silence and attention whilst the service was reading. When we began to fill up the grave, they approached it with great reverence, threw in a dead pig, some cocoanuts, and plantains; and, for three nights afterwards, they surrounded it, sacrificing hogs, and performing their usual ceremonies of hymns and prayers, which continued till daybreak. At the head of the grave we erected a post, and nailed upon it a square piece of board, on which was inscribed the name of the deceased, his age, and the day of his death. This they promised not to remove; and we have no doubt but that it will be suffered to remain as long as the frail materials of which it is made will permit.

The ships being in great want of fuel, Captain Cook desired me, on the 2d of February, to treat with the priests for the purchase of the rail that surrounded the top of the morai. I must confess I had at first some doubt about the decency of this proposal, and was apprehensive that even the bare mention of it might be considered by them as a piece of shocking impiety.

In this, however, I found myself mistaken; not the smallest surprise was expressed at the application, and the wood was readily given, even without stipulating for anything in return. Whilst the sailors were taking it away, I observed one of them carrying off a carved image; and, on further inquiry, I found that they had conveyed to the boats the whole semicircle. Though this was done in the presence of the natives, who had not shown any mark of resentment at it, but had even assisted them in the removal, I thought it proper to speak to Kaoo on the subject, who appeared very indifferent about the matter, and only desired that we would restore the center image I have mentioned before, which he carried into one of the priests' houses.

Terreeoboo and his chiefs had for some days past been very inquisitive about the time of our departure. This circumstance had excited in me a great curiosity to know what opinion this people had formed of us, and what were their ideas respecting the cause and objects of our voyage. I took some pains to satisfy myself on these points, but could never learn anything further than that they imagined we came from some country where provisions had failed, and that our visit to them was merely for the purpose of filling our bellies; indeed, the meager appearance of some of our crew, the hearty appetites with which we sat down to their fresh provisions, and our great anxiety to purchase as much as we were able, led them naturally enough to such a conclusion. To these may be added a circumstance which puzzled them exceedingly, our having no women with us, together with our quiet conduct and unwarlike appearance. It was ridiculous enough to see them stroking the sides and patting the bellies of the sailors, who were certainly much improved in the sleekness of their looks during our short stay on the island, and telling them, partly by signs, and partly by words, that it was time for them to go; but if they would come again the next breadfruit season, they should be better able to supply their wants.

We had now been sixteen days in the bay; and if our enormous consumption of hogs and vegetables be considered, it need not be wondered that they should wish to see us take our leave. It is very probable, however, that Terreeoboo had no other view in his inquiries at present than a desire of making sufficient preparation for dismissing us with presents suitable to the respect and kindness with which he had received us; for, on our telling him we should leave the island on the next day but one, we observed that a sort of proclamation was immediately made through the villages to require the people to bring in their hogs and vegetables, for the king to present to the Orono on his departure.

We were this day much diverted, at the beach, by the buffooneries of one of the natives. His style of dancing was entirely burlesque, and accompanied with strange grimaces and pantomimical distortions of the face, which, though at times inexpressibly ridiculous, yet, on the whole, was without much meaning or expression. In the evening we were again entertained with wrestling and boxing matches, and we displayed in return the few fireworks we had left. Nothing could be better calculated to excite the admiration of these islanders, and to impress them with an idea of our great superiority, than an exhibition of this kind.

The carpenters from both ships having been sent up the country to cut planks for the head-railwork of the *Resolution*, this being the third day since their departure, we began to be very anxious for their safety. We now communicated our apprehensions to old Kaoo, who appeared as much concerned as ourselves, and were concerting measures with him for sending after them, when they arrived in safety. They had been obliged to go farther into the country than was expected, before they met with trees fit for their purpose; and it was this circumstance, together with the badness of the roads and the difficulty of bringing back the timber, which had detained them so long. They spoke in high terms of their guides, who both supplied them with provisions, and guarded their tools with the utmost fidelity. The next day being fixed for our departure, Terreeoboo invited Captain Cook and myself to attend him on the 3d to the place where Kaoo resided. On our arrival, we found the ground covered with parcels of cloth, a vast quantity of red and yellow feathers tied to the fibers of cocoanut husks, and a great number of hatchets and other pieces of ironware that had been got in barter from us. At a little distance from these lay an immense quantity of vegetables of every kind, and near them was a large herd of hogs. At first, we imagined the whole to be intended as a present for us, till Kaireekeea informed me that it was a gift or tribute from the people of that district to the king; and accordingly, as we were seated, they brought all the bundles and laid them severally at Terreeoboo's feet, spreading out the cloth and displaying the feathers and iron-ware before him. The king seemed much pleased with this mark of their duty; and having selected about a third part of the iron-ware, the same proportion of feathers, and a few pieces of cloth, these were set aside by themselves, and the remainder of the cloth, together with all the hogs and vegetables, was afterwards presented to Captain Cook and myself. We were astonished at the value and magnitude of this present, which exceeded everything of the kind we had seen either at the Friendly or Society Islands. Boats were immediately sent to carry them on board; the large hogs were picked out to be salted for sea store, and upwards of thirty smaller pigs and the vegetables were divided between the two crews.

The same day we quitted the morai and got the tents and astronomical instruments on board. The charm of the taboo was now removed, and we had no sooner left the place, than the natives rushed in and searched eagerly about, in expectation of finding something of value that we might have left behind. As I happened to remain the last on shore, and waited for the return of the boat, several came crowding round me, and having made me sit down by them, began to lament our separation.

It was, indeed, not without difficulty I was able to quit them. Having had the command of the party on shore during the whole time we were in the bay, I had an opportunity of becoming better acquainted with the natives, and of being better known to them, than those whose duty required them to be generally on board. As I had every reason to be satisfied with their kindness in general, so I cannot too often nor too particularly mention the unbounded and constant friendship of their priests. On my part I spared no endeavors to conciliate their affections and gain their esteem; and I had the good fortune to succeed so far, that, when the time of our departure was made known, I was strongly solicited to remain behind, not without offers of the most flattering kind. When I excused myself by saying that Captain Cook would not give his consent, they proposed that I should retire into the mountains, where they said they would conceal me till after the departure of the ships, and on my further assuring them that the captain would not leave the bay without me, Terreeoboo and Kaoo waited upon Captain Cook, whose son they supposed I was, with a formal request that I might be left behind. The captain, to avoid giving a positive refusal to an offer so kindly intended, told them that he could not part with me at that time, but that he should return to the island next year, and would then endeavor to settle the matter to their satisfaction.

Early in the morning of the 4th of February we unmoored and sailed out of the bay, with the *Discovery* in company, and were followed by a great number of canoes. Captain Cook's design was to finish the survey of Owhyhee before we visited the other islands, in hopes of meeting with a road better sheltered than the bay we had just left; and in case of not succeeding here, he proposed to take a view of the southeast part of Mowee, where the natives informed us we should find an excellent harbor. We had calm weather all this and the following day, which made our progress to the northward very slow. We were accompanied by a great number of these natives in their canoes, and Terreeoboo gave a fresh proof of his friendship to Captain Cook by a large present of hogs and vegetables that was sent after him.

In the night of the 5th, having a light breeze off the land, we made some way to the northward, and in the morning of the 6th, having passed the westernmost point of the island, we found ourselves abreast of a deep bay called by the natives Toe-yah-yah. We had great hopes that this bay would furnish us with a commodious harbor, as we saw several fine streams of water, and the whole had the appearance of being well sheltered. These observations agreeing with the accounts given us by Koah, who accompanied Captain Cook, and had changed his name, out of compliment to us, into Britannee, the pinnace was hoisted out, and the master, with Britannee for his guide, was sent to examine the bay, whilst the ships worked up after them. In the afternoon the weather became gloomy, and the gusts of wind that blew off the land were so violent as to make it necessary to take in all the sails, and bring to under the mizzen staysail. All the canoes left us at the beginning of the gale; and Mr. Bligh, on his return, had the satisfaction of saving an old woman and two men whose canoe had been upset by the violence of the wind, as they were endeavoring to gain the shore. Besides these distressed people, we had a great many women on board whom the natives had left behind in their hurry to shift for themselves.

In the evening, the weather being more moderate, we again made sail; but about midnight it blew so violently as to split both the fore and main-topsails. On the morning of the 7th we bent fresh sails, and had fair weather and a light breeze at noon. We were four or five leagues from the shore, and as the weather was very unsettled none of the canoes would venture out, so that our guests were obliged to remain with us, much indeed to their dissatisfaction, for they were all seasick, and many of them had left young children behind them.

In the afternoon, though the weather was still squally, we stood in for the land, and being about three leagues from it, saw a canoe, with two men paddling towards us, who we immediately conjectured had been driven off the shore by the late boisterous weather, and therefore stopped the ship's way in order to take them in. These poor wretches were so exhausted with fatigue that, had not one of the natives on board, observing their weakness, jumped into the canoe to their assistance, they would scarcely have been able to fasten it to the rope we had thrown out for that purpose. It was with difficulty we got them up the ship's side, together with a child about four years old, which they had lashed under the thwarts of the canoe, where it had lain with only its head above water. They told us they had left the shore the morning before, and had been from that time without food or water. The usual precautions were taken in giving them victuals, and the child being committed to the care of the women, soon perfectly recovered.

At midnight a gale of wind came on, which obliged us to double-reef the topsails and send down the topgallant yards. On the 8th, at daybreak, we found that the foremast had again given way, the fishes which were put on the head in King George's or Nootka Sound, on the coast of America, being sprung, and the parts so very defective as to make it absolutely necessary to replace them, and, of course, to unship the mast. In this difficulty Captain Cook was for some time in doubt whether he should run the chance of meeting with a harbor in the islands to leeward or return to Karakakooa. That bay was not so remarkably commodious, in any respect, but that a better might probably be expected, both for the purpose of repairing the masts and for procuring supplies, of which, it was imagined, the neighbor-hood of Karakakooa had been already pretty well drained. On the other hand, it was considered as too great a risk to leave a place that was tolerably sheltered, and which, once left, could not be regained, for the mere hope of meeting with a better, the failure of which might perhaps have left us without resource. We therefore continued standing on towards the land, in order to give the natives an opportunity of releasing their friends on board from their confinement; and at noon, being within a mile of the shore, a few canoes came off to us, but so crowded with people that there was not room in them for any of our guests; we therefore hoisted out the pinnace to carry them on shore, and the master, who went with them, had directions to examine the south coasts of the bay for water, but returned without finding any. The winds being variable, and a current setting to the northward, we made but little progress in our return; and at eight o'clock in the evening of the 9th it began to blow very hard from the southeast, which obliged us to close-reef the topsails. At two in the morning of the 10th, in a heavy squall, we found ourselves close in with the breakers that lie to the northward of the west point of Owhyhee; and we had just room to haul off and avoid them, and fired several guns to apprise the *Discovery* of the danger. In the forenoon the weather was more moderate, and a few canoes came off to us, from which we learnt that the late storms had done much mischief, and that several large canoes had been lost. During the remainder of the day we kept beating about to windward, and before night we were within a mile of the bay; but not choosing to run in while it was dark, we stood off and on till daylight next morning, when we dropped anchor nearly in the same place as before.

We were employed the whole of the 11th and part of the 12th, in getting out the foremast, and sending it with the carpenters on shore. Besides the damage which the head of the mast had sustained, we found the keel exceedingly rotten, having a large hole up the middle of it, capable of holding four or five cocoanuts. It was not, however, thought necessary to shorten it; and, fortunately, the logs of red toa-wood, which had been cut at Eimeo for anchor-stocks, were found fit to replace the sprung parts of the fishes. As these repairs were likely to take up several days, Mr. Bayley and myself got the astronomical apparatus on shore, and pitched our tents on the morai, having with us a guard of a corporal and six marines. We renewed our friendly correspondence with the priests, who, for the greater security of the workmen and their tools, tabooed the place where the mast lay, sticking their wands around it as before. The sailmakers were also sent on shore to repair the damages which had taken place in their department during the late gales; they were lodged in a house adjoining the morai, which was lent to us by the priests. Such were our arrangements on shore. Upon coming to anchor, we were surprised to find our reception very different from what it had been on our first arrival; no shouts, no bustle, no confusion, but a solitary bay, with only here and there a canoe stealing close along the shore. The impulse of curiosity, which had before operated to so great a degree, might now indeed be supposed to have ceased; but the hospitable treatment we had invariably met with, and the friendly footing on which we parted, gave us reason to expect that they would again have flocked about us with great joy on our return. We were forming various conjectures upon the cause of this extraordinary change, when our anxiety was at length relieved by the return of a boat which had been sent on shore, and brought us word that Terreeoboo was absent, and had left the bay under the taboo.

Towards the evening of the 13th, the officer who commanded the watering-party of the *Discovery* came to inform me that several chiefs had assembled at the well near the beach, driving away the natives, whom he had hired to assist the sailors in rolling down the casks to the shore. He told me at the same time that he thought their behavior extremely suspicious, and that they meant to cause a disturbance. At his request, therefore, I sent a marine along with him, but suffered him to take only his side-arms. In a short time the officer returned, and, on his acquainting me that the islanders had armed themselves with stones, and were grown very tumultuous, I went myself to the spot, attended by a marine with his musket. Seeing us approach, they threw away their stones, and on my speaking to some of the chiefs, the mob were driven away, and those who chose it were suffered to assist in filling the casks. Having left things quiet here, I went to meet Captain Cook, whom I saw coming on shore in the pinnace. I related to him what had just passed, and he ordered me, in case of their beginning to throw stones or behave insolently, immediately to fire a ball at the offenders. I accordingly gave orders to the corporal to have the pieces of the sentinels loaded with ball, instead of small shot.

Soon after our return to the tents we were alarmed by a continued fire of muskets from the *Discovery*, which we observed to be directed at a canoe that we saw paddling towards the shore in great haste, pursued by one of our small boats. We immediately concluded that the firing was in consequence of some theft, and Captain Cook ordered me to follow him with an armed marine, and to endeavor to seize the people as they came on shore. Accordingly we ran towards the place where we supposed the canoe would land, but were too late, the people having quitted it and made their escape into the country before our arrival. We were at this time ignorant that the goods had been already restored, and as we thought it probable, from the circumstance we had at first observed, that they might be of importance, were unwilling to relinquish our hopes of recovering them. Having therefore inquired of the natives which way the people had fled, we followed them till it was near dark, when, judging ourselves to be about three miles from the tents, and suspecting that the natives, who frequently encouraged us in the pursuit, were amusing us with false information, we thought it in vain to continue our search any longer, and returned to the beach. During our absence a difference of a more serious and unpleasant nature had happened. The officer who had been sent in the small boat, and was returning on board with the goods which had been restored, observing Captain Cook and me engaged in the pursuit of the offenders, thought it his duty to seize the canoe which was left drawn up on the shore. Unfortunately this canoe belonged to Pareea, who, arriving at the same moment from on board the *Discovery*, claimed his property, with many protestations of his innocence. The officer refusing to give it up, and being joined by the crew of the pinnace, which was waiting for Captain Cook, a scuffle ensued, in which Pareea was knocked down by a violent blow on the head with an oar. The natives who were collected about the spot, and had hitherto been peaceable spectators, immediately attacked our people with such a shower of stones, as forced them to retreat with great precipitation and swim off to a rock at some distance from the shore. The pinnace was immediately ransacked by the islanders, and but for the timely interposition of Pareea, who seemed to have recovered from the blow and forgotten it at the same instant, would soon have been entirely demolished. Having driven away the crowd, he made signs to our people that they might come and take possession of the pinnace, and that he would endeavor to get back the things which had been taken out of it. After their departure he followed them in his canoe, with a midshipman's cap and some other trifling articles of the plunder, and with much apparent concern at what had happened, asked if the Orono would kill him, and whether he would permit him to come on board the next day. On being assured that he would be well received, he joined noses (as their custom is) with the officers, in token of friendship, and paddled over to the village of Kowrowa.

When Captain Cook was informed of what had passed he expressed much uneasiness at it, and said, as we were returning on board, "I am afraid that these people will oblige me to use some violent measures; for they must not be left to imagine that they have gained an advantage over us." However, as it was too late to take any step this evening, he contented himself with giving orders that every man and woman on board should be immediately turned out of the ship. As soon as this order was executed I returned on shore; and our former confidence in the natives being now much abated by the events of the day, I posted a double guard on the morai, with orders to call me if they saw any man lurking about the beach. At about eleven o'clock five islanders were observed creeping round the bottom of the morai; they seemed very cautious in approaching us, and, at last, finding themselves discovered, retired out of sight. About midnight one of them ventured up close to the observatory, the sentinel fired over him, on which the man fled, and we passed the remainder of the night without further disturbance. Next morning at daylight I went on board the *Resolution* for the timekeeper, and on my way was hailed by the *Discovery*, and informed that their cutter had been stolen during the night from the buoy where it was moored.

When I arrived on board I found the marines arming, and Captain Cook loading his double-barreled gun. Whilst I was relating to him what had happened to us in the night he interrupted me with some eagerness, and acquainted me with the loss of the *Discovery's* cutter, and with the preparations he was making for its recovery. It had been his usual practice, whenever anything of consequence was lost at any of the islands in this ocean, to get the king, or some of the principal erees, on board, and to keep them as hostages till it was restored. This method, which had been always attended with success, he meant to pursue on the present occasion; and at the same time had given orders to stop all the canoes that should attempt to leave the bay, with an intention of seizing and destroying them if he could not recover the cutter by peaceful means. Accordingly the boats of both ships, well manned and armed, were stationed across the bay, and before I left the ship some great guns had been fired at two large canoes that were attempting to escape. It was between seven and eight o'clock when we quitted the ship together; Captain Cook in the pinnace, having Mr. Phillips and nine marines with him, and myself in the small boat. The last orders I received from him were to quiet the minds of the natives on our side of the bay, by assuring them that they should not be hurt, to keep my people together, and to be on my guard. We then parted; the captain went towards Kowrowa, where the king resided, and I proceeded to the beach. My first care, on going ashore, was to give strict orders to the marines to remain within the tent, to load their pieces with ball, and not to quit their arms. Afterwards I took a walk to the huts of old Kaoo and the priests, and explained to them, as well as I could, the hostile preparations, which had exceedingly alarmed them. I found that they had already heard of the cutter being stolen, and I assured them that though Captain Cook was resolved to recover it, and to punish the authors of the theft, yet that they, and the people of the village on our side, need not be under the smallest apprehension of suffering any evil from us. I desired the priests to explain this to the people, and to tell them not to be alarmed, but to continue peaceable and quiet. Kaoo asked me, with great earnestness, if Terreeoboo was to be hurt. I assured him he was not, and both he and the rest of his brethren seemed much satisfied with this assurance.

In the meantime Captain Cook, having called off the launch, which was stationed at the north point of the bay, and taken it along with him, proceeded to Kowrowa, and landed with the lieutenant and nine marines. He immediately marched into the village, where he was received with the usual marks of respect, the people prostrating themselves before him, and bringing their accustomed offerings of small hogs. Finding that there was no suspicion of his design, his next step was to inquire for Terreeoboo and the two boys, his sons, who had been his constant guests on board the *Resolution*. In a short time the boys returned along with the natives who had been in search of them, and immediately led Captain Cook to the house where the king had slept, and after a short conversation with him about the loss of the cutter, from which Captain Cook was convinced that he was in nowise privy to it, he invited him to return in the boat and spend the day on board the *Resolution*. To this proposal the king readily assented, and immediately got up to accompany him.

Things were in this prosperous train, the two boys being already in the pinnace, and the rest of the party having advanced near the water-side, when an elderly woman called Kanee-Kabareea, the mother of the boys, and one of the king's favorite wives, came after him, and, with many tears and entreaties, besought him not to go on board. At the same time, two chiefs who came along with her, laid hold of him and forced him to sit down. The natives, who were collecting in prodigious numbers along the shore, and had probably been alarmed by the firing of the great guns and appearance of hostility in the bay, began to throng round Captain Cook and their king. In this situation, the lieutenant of marines observing that his men were huddled close together in the crowd, and thus incapable of using their arms, if any occasion should require it, proposed to the captain to draw them up along the rocks close to the water's edge; and the crowd readily making way for them to pass, they were drawn up in a line, at the distance of about thirty yards from the place where the king was sitting. All this time the old king remained on the ground, with the strongest marks of terror and dejection in his countenance. Captain Cook, not willing to abandon the object for which he had come on shore, continued to urge him in the most pressing manner to proceed; whilst, on the other hand, whenever the king appeared inclined to follow him, the chiefs who stood round him interposed, at first with prayers and entreaties, but afterwards with force and violence, insisting on his staying where he was. Captain Cook, therefore, finding that the alarm had spread too generally, and that it was in vain to think any longer of getting the king off without bloodshed, at last gave up the point, observing to Mr. Phillips that it would be impossible to compel him to go on board without the risk of killing a great number of the inhabitants.

Though the enterprise which had carried Captain Cook on shore had now failed, and was abandoned, yet his person did not appear to have been in the least danger till an accident happened, which gave a fatal turn to the affair. The boats which had been stationed across the bay having fired at some canoes that were attempting to get out, unfortunately had killed a chief of the first rank. The news of his death arrived at the village where Captain Cook was, just as he had left the king and was walking slowly towards the shore. The ferment it made was very conspicuous; the women and children were immediately sent off, and the men put on their war-mats and armed themselves with spears and stones. One of the natives having in his hands a stone and a large iron spike, which they call a pahooa, came up to the captain, flourishing his weapon by way of defiance, and threatening to throw the stone. The captain desired him to desist, but the man persisting in his insolence, he was at length provoked to fire a load of small shot. The man having his mat on, which the shots were not able to penetrate, this had no other effect than to irritate and encourage them. Several stones were thrown at the marines, and one of the erees attempted to stab Mr. Phillips with his pahooa, but failed in the attempt, and received from him a blow with the butt-end of his musket. Captain Cook now fired his second barrel loaded with ball and killed one of the foremost of the natives. A general attack with stones immediately followed, which was answered by a discharge of musketry from the marines and the people in the boats. The islanders, contrary to the expectations of every one, stood the fire with great firmness, and before the marines had time to reload, they broke in upon them with dreadful shouts and yells. What followed was a scene of the utmost horror and confusion.

Four of the marines were cut off amongst the rocks in their retreat, and fell a sacrifice to the fury of the enemy; three more were dangerously wounded, and the lieutenant, who had received a stab between the shoulders with a pahooa, having fortunately reserved his fire, shot the man who had wounded him just as he was going to repeat the blow. Our unfortunate commander, the last time he was seen distinctly, was standing at the water's edge, and calling out to the boats to cease firing and to pull in. Whilst he faced the natives none of them had offered him any violence, but having turned about to give his orders to the boats he was stabbed in the back, and fell with his face into the water. On seeing him fall the islanders set up a great shout, and his body was immediately dragged on shore and surrounded by the enemy, who, snatching the dagger out of each other's hands, showed a savage eagerness to have a share in his destruction.

Thus fell our great and excellent commander! After a life of so much distinguished and successful enterprise, his death, as far as regards himself, cannot be reckoned premature, since he lived to finish the great work for which he seemed to have been designed; and was rather removed from the enjoyment than cut off from the acquisition of glory. How sincerely his loss was felt and lamented by those who had so long found their general security in his skill and conduct, and every consolation under their hardships in his tenderness and humanity, it is neither necessary nor possible for me to describe; much less shall I attempt to paint the horror with which we were struck, and the universal dejection and dismay which followed so dreadful and unexpected a calamity.

CHAPTER X

How Stanley Found Livingstone
November 10th, 1871

Henry M. Stanley was a journalist in the employ of James Gordon Bennett's New York Herald, when he was commissioned in 1869 to find Dr. Livingstone, missing somewhere in Central Africa.

David Livingstone, born in Scotland, was a famous explorer and missionary who was more responsible than anyone else for opening up the great interior of Africa to the world. After embarking on his third and last expedition in 1866, he was given up as lost by all the world.

Stanley's account of how he found Livingstone constitutes one of the more romantic episodes of our time. His famous "Mr. Livingstone, I presume," was a masterpiece of understatement that became a national by-word. The following extract from his book, How I Found Livingstone, *touches on that part of the long search which culminates in the famous meeting at Ujiji, on Lake Tanganyika.*

HOW I FOUND LIVINGSTONE

November 3rd.—What contention have we not been a witness to these last three days! What anxiety have we not suffered ever since our arrival in Uvinza! The Wavinza are worse than the Wagogo, and their greed is more insatiable. We got the donkey across with the aid of a mganga, or medicine man, who spat some chewed leaves of a tree which grows close to the stream over him. He informed me he could cross the river at any time, day or night, after rubbing his body with these chewed leaves, which he believed to be a most potent medicine.

About 10 A.M. appeared from the direction of Ujiji a caravan of eighty Waguhha, a tribe which occupies a tract of country on the south-western side of the Lake Tanganyika. We asked the news, and were told a white man had just arrived at Ujiji from Manyuema. This news startled us all.

"A white man?" we asked.

"Yes, a white man," they replied.

"How is he dressed?"

"Like the master," they answered, referring to me.

"Is he young, or old?"

"He is old. He has white hair on his face, and is sick."

"Where has he come from?"

"From a very far country away beyond Uguhha, called Manyuema."

"Indeed! and is he stopping at Ujiji now?"

"Yes, we saw him about eight days ago."

"Do you think he will stop there until we see him?"

"*Sigue*" (don't know).

"Was he ever at Ujiji before?"

"Yes, he went away a long time ago."

Hurrah! This is Livingstone! He must be Livingstone! He *can* be no other; but still,—he may be some one else—some one from the West Coast—or perhaps he is Baker! No; Baker has no white hair on his face. But we must now march quick, lest he hears we are coming, and runs away.

I addressed my men, and asked them if they were willing to march to Ujiji without a single halt, and then promised them, if they acceded to my wishes, two doti each man. All answered in the affirmative, almost as much rejoiced as I was myself. But I was madly rejoiced; intensely eager to resolve the burning question, "Is it Dr. David Livingstone?" God grant me patience, but I do wish there was a railroad, or, at least, horses in this country. With a horse I could reach Ujiji in about twelve hours.

* * * * * *

November 8th.—Long before dawn appeared, we were on the march, and, as daylight broke, we emerged from the bamboo jungle, and struck across the naked plain of Uhha, once more passing several large pools by the way—far-embracing prospects of undulating country, with here and there a characteristic clump of trees relieving the general nudity of the whole. Hour after hour we toiled on, across the rolling land waves, the sun shining with all its wonted African fervor, but with its heat slightly tempered by the welcome breezes, which came laden with the fragrance of young grass, and perfume of strange flowers of various hues, that flecked the otherwise pale-green sheet which extended so far around us.

We arrived at the Rugufu River—not the Ukawendi Rugufu, but the northern stream of that name, a tributary of the Malagarazi. It was a broad shallow stream, and sluggish, with an almost imperceptible flow south-west. While we halted in the deep shade afforded by a dense clump of jungle, close to the right bank, resting awhile before continuing our journey, I distinctly heard a sound as of distant thunder in the west. Upon asking if it were thunder, I was told it was Kabogo.

"Kabogo? what is that?"

"It is a great mountain on the other side of the Tanganyika, full of deep holes, into which the water rolls; and when there is wind on the Tanganyika, there is a sound like mvuha (thunder). Many boats have been lost there, and it is a custom with Arabs and natives to throw cloth—Merikani and Kaniki—and especially white (Merikani) beads, to appease the mulungu (god) of the lake. Those who throw beads generally get past without trouble, but those who do not throw beads into the lake get lost, and are drowned. Oh, it is a dreadful place!" This story was told me by the ever-smiling guide Asmani, and was corroborated by other former mariners of the lake whom I had with me.

At the least, this place where we halted for dinner, on the banks of the Rugufu River, is eighteen and a half hours, or forty-six miles, from Ujiji; and, as Kabogo is said to be near Uguhha, it must be over sixty miles from Ujiji; therefore the sound of the thundering surf, which is said to roll into the caves of Kabogo, was heard by us at a distance of over one hundred miles away from them.

Continuing our journey for three hours longer, through thin forests, over extensive beds of primitive rock, among fields of large boulders thickly strewn about, passing by numerous herds of buffalo, giraffe, and zebra, over a quaking quagmire which resembled peat, we arrived at the small stream of Sunuzzi, to a camping place only a mile removed from a large settlement of Wahha. But we were buried in the depths of a great forest—no road was in the vicinity, no noise was made, deep silence was preserved; nor were fires lit. We might therefore rest tranquilly secure, certain that we should not be disturbed. To-morrow morning the kirangozi has promised we shall be out of Uhha, and if we travel on to Niamtaga, in Ukaranga, the same day, the next day would see us in Ujiji. Patience, my soul! A few hours more, then the end of all this will be known! I shall be face to face with that white man with the white hairs on his face, whoever he is!

November 9th.—Two hours before dawn we left our camp on the Sunuzzi River, and struck through the forest in a north-by-west direction, having muzzled our goats previously, lest, by their bleating, they might betray us. This was a mistake which might have ended tragically, for just as the eastern sky began to assume a pale greyish tint, we emerged from the jungle on the high road. The guide thought we had passed Uhha, and set up a shout which was echoed by every member of the caravan, and marched onward with new vigor and increased energy, when plump we came to the outskirts of a village, the inhabitants of which were beginning to stir. Silence was called for at once, and the Expedition halted immediately. I walked forward to the front to advise with the guide. He did not know what to do. There was no time to consider, so I ordered the goats to be slaughtered and left on the road, and the guide to push on boldly through the village. The chickens also had their throats cut; after which the Expedition resumed the march quickly and silently, led by the guide, who had orders to plunge into the jungle south of the road. I staid until the last man had disappeared; then, after preparing my Winchester, brought up the rear, followed by my gunbearers with their stock of ammunition. As we were about disappearing beyond the last hut, a man darted out of his hut, and uttered an exclamation of alarm, and loud voices were heard as if in dispute. But in a short time we were in the depths of the jungle, hurrying away from the road in a southern direction, and edging slightly westward. Once I thought we were pursued, and I halted behind a tree to check our foes if they persisted in following us; but a few minutes proved to me that we were not pursued. After half-an-hour's march we again turned our faces westward. It was broad daylight now, and our eyes were delighted with most picturesque and sequestered little valleys, where wild fruit-trees grew, and rare flowers blossomed, and tiny brooks tumbled over polished pebbles—where all was bright and beautiful—until, finally, wading through one pretty pure streamlet, whose soft murmurs we took for a gentle welcome, we passed the boundary of wicked Uhha, and had entered Ukaranga!—an event that was hailed with extravagant shouts of joy.

Presently we found the smooth road, and we trod gaily with elastic steps, with limbs quickened for the march which we all knew to be drawing near its end. What cared we now for the difficulties we had encountered—for the rough and cruel forests, for the thorny thickets and hurtful grass, for the jangle of all savagedom, of which we had been the joyless audience! To-morrow! Ay, the great day draws nigh, and we may well laugh and sing while in this triumphant mood. We have been sorely tried; we have been angry with each other when vexed by troubles, but we forget all these now, and there is no face but is radiant with the happiness we have all deserved.

We made a short halt at noon, for rest and refreshment. I was shown the hills from which the Tanganyika could be seen, which bounded the valley of the Liuche on the east. I could not contain myself at the sight of them. Even with this short halt I was restless and unsatisfied. We resumed the march again. I spurred my men forward with the promise that to-morrow should see their reward. Fish and beer should be given them, as much as they could eat and drink.

We were in sight of the villages of the Wakaranga; the people caught sight of us, and manifested considerable excitement. I sent men ahead to reassure them, and they came forward to greet us. This was so new and welcome to us, so different from the turbulent Wavinza and the black-mailers of Uhha, that we were melted. But we had no time to loiter by the way to indulge our joy. I was impelled onward by my almost uncontrollable feelings. I wished to resolve my doubts and fears. Was HE still there? Had HE heard of my coming? Would HE fly?

How beautiful Ukaranga appears! The green hills are crowned by clusters of straw-thatched cones. The hills rise and fall; here denuded and cultivated, there in pasturage, here timbered, yonder swarming with huts. The country has somewhat the aspect of Maryland.

We cross the Mkuti, a glorious little river! We ascend the opposite bank, and stride through the forest like men who have done a deed of which they may be proud. We have already travelled nine hours, and the sun is sinking rapidly towards the west; yet, apparently, we are not fatigued.

We reach the outskirts of Niamtaga, and we hear drums beat. The people are flying into the woods; they desert their villages, for they take us to be Ruga-Ruga—the forest thieves of Mirambo, who, after conquering the Arabs of Unyanyembe, are coming to fight the Arabs of Ujiji. Even the King flies from his village, and every man, woman, and child, terror-stricken, follows him. We enter into it and quietly take possession, and my tent is set. Finally, the word is bruited about that we are Wangwana, from Unyanyembe.

"Well, then, is Mirambo dead?" they ask.

"No," we answer.

"Well, how did you come to Ukaranga?"

"By way of Ukonongo, Ukawendi, and Uhha."

"Oh—hi-le!" Then they laugh heartily at their fright, and begin to make excuses. The King is introduced to me, and he says he had only gone to the woods in order to attack us again—he meant to have come back and killed us all, if we had been Ruga-Ruga. But then we know the poor King was terribly frightened, and would never have dared to return, had we been Ruga-Ruga —not he. We are not, however, in a mood to quarrel with him about an idiomatic phrase peculiar to him, but rather take him by the hand and shake it well, and say we are so very glad to see him. And he shares in our pleasure, and immediately three of the fattest sheep, pots of beer, flour, and honey are brought to us as a gift, and I make him happier still with two of the finest cloths I have in my bales; and thus a friendly pact is entered into between us.

While I write my diary of this day's proceedings, I tell Selim to lay out my new flannel suit, to oil my boots, to chalk my helmet, and fold a new puggaree around it, that I may make as presentable an appearance as possible before the white man with the grey beard, and before the Arabs of Ujiji; for the clothes I have worn through jungle and forest are in tatters. Good-night; only let one day come again, and we shall see what we shall see.

November 10th. Friday.—The 236th day from Bagamoyo, and the 51st day from Unyanyembe. General direction to Ujiji, west-by-south. Time of march, six hours.

It is a happy, glorious morning. The air is fresh and cool. The sky lovingly smiles on the earth and her children. The deep woods are crowned in bright green leafage; the water of the Mkuti, rushing under the emerald shade afforded by the bearded banks, seems to challenge us for the race to Ujiji, with its continuous brawl.

We are all outside the village cane fence, every man of us looking as spruce, as neat, and happy as when we embarked on the dhows at Zanzibar, which seems to us to have been ages ago—we have witnessed and experienced so much.

"Forward!"

"Ay Wallah, ay Wallah, bana yango!" and the light-hearted braves stride away at a rate which must soon bring us within view of Ujiji. We ascend a hill overgrown with bamboo, descend into a ravine through which dashes an impetuous little torrent, ascend another short hill, then, along a smooth foot-path running across the slope of a long ridge, we push on as only eager, light-hearted men can do.

In two hours I am warned to prepare for a view of the Tanganyika, for, from the top of a steep mountain the kirangozi says I can see it. I almost vent the feelings of my heart in cries. But wait, we must behold it first. And we press forward and up the hill breathlessly, lest the grand scene hasten away.

We are at last on the summit. Ah! not yet can it be seen. A little further on—just yonder, oh! there it is—a silvery gleam. I merely catch sight of it between the trees, and—but here it is at last! True—THE TANGANYIKA! and there are the blue-black mountains of Ugoma and Ukaramba. An immense broad sheet, a burnished bed of silver—lucid canopy of blue above—lofty mountains are its valances, palm forests form its fringes! The Tanganyika!— Hurrah! and the men respond to the exultant cry of the Anglo-Saxon with the lungs of Stentors, and the great forests and the hills seem to share in our triumph.

"Was this the place where Burton and Speke stood, Bombay, when they saw the lake first?"

"I don't remember, master; it was somewhere about here, I think."

"Poor fellows! The one was half-paralyzed, the other half-blind," said Sir Roderick Murchison, when he described Burton and Speke's arrival in view of the Tanganyika.

And I? Well, I am so happy that, were I quite paralyzed and blinded, I think that at this supreme moment I could take up my bed and walk, and all blindness would cease at once. Fortunately, however, I am quite well; I have not suffered a day's sickness since the day I left Unyanyembe. How much would Shaw be willing to give to be in my place now? Who is happiest—he, revelling in the luxuries of Unyanyembe, or I, standing on the summit of this mountain, looking down with glad eyes and proud heart on the Tanganyika?

We are descending the western slope of the mountain, with the valley of the Liuche before us. Something like an hour before noon we have gained the thick matete brake, which grows on both banks of the river; we wade through the clear stream, arrive on the other side, emerge out of the brake, and the gardens of the Wajiji are around us—a perfect marvel of vegetable wealth. Details escape my hasty and partial observation. I am almost overpowered with my own emotions. I notice the graceful palms, neat plots, green with vegetable plants, and small villages surrounded with frail fences of the matete-cane.

We push on rapidly, lest the news of our coming might reach the people of Bunder Ujiji before we come in sight, and are ready for them. We halt at a little brook, then ascend the long slope of a naked ridge, the very last of the myriads we have crossed. This alone prevents us from seeing the lake in all its vastness. We arrive at the summit, travel across and arrive at its western rim, and—pause, reader—the port of Ujiji is below us, embowered in the palms, only five hundred yards from us! At this grand moment we do not think of the hundreds of miles we have marched, of the hundreds of hills that we have ascended and descended, of the many forests we have traversed, of the jungles and thickets that annoyed us, of the fervid salt plains that blistered our feet, of the hot suns that scorched us, nor the dangers and difficulties, now happily surmounted. At last the sublime hour has arrived!—our dreams, our hopes, and anticipations are now about to be realized! Our hearts and our feelings are with our eyes, as we peer into the palms and try to make out in which hut or house lives the white man with the grey beard we heard about on the Malagarazi.

"Unfurl the flags, and load your guns!"

"Ay Wallah, ay Wallah, bana!" respond the men, eagerly.

"One, two, three—fire!"

A volley from nearly fifty guns roars like a salute from a battery of artillery: we shall note its effect presently on the peaceful-looking village below.

"Now, kirangozi, hold the white man's flag up high, and let the Zanzibar flag bring up the rear. And you men keep close together, and keep firing until we halt in the market-place, or before the white man's house. You have said to me often that you could smell the fish of the Tanganyika—I can smell the fish of the Tanganyika now. There are fish, and beer, and a long rest waiting for you. MARCH!"

Before we had gone a hundred yards our repeated volleys had the effect desired. We had awakened Ujiji to the knowledge that a caravan was coming, and the people were witnessed rushing up in hundreds to meet us. The mere sight of the flags informed every one immediately that we were a caravan, but the American flag borne aloft by gigantic Asmani, whose face was one vast smile on this day, rather staggered them at first. However, many of the people who now approached us remembered the flag. They had seen it float above the American Consulate, and from the masthead of many a ship in the harbor of Zanzibar, and they were soon heard welcoming the beautiful flag with cries of "Bindera Kisungu!"—a white man's flag! "Bindera Merikani!"—the American flag!

Then we were surrounded by them: by Wajiji, Wanyamwezi, Wangwana, Warundi, Waguhha, Wamanyuema and Arabs, and were almost deafened with the shouts of "Yambo, yambo, bana! Yambo, bana! Yambo, bana!" To all and each of my men the welcome was given.

We were now about three hundred yards from the village of Ujiji, and the crowds are dense about me. Suddenly I hear a voice on my right say,

"Good morning, sir!"

Startled at hearing this greeting in the midst of such a crowd of black people, I turn sharply around in search of the man, and see him at my side, with the blackest of faces, but animated and joyous—a man dressed in a long white shirt, with a turban of American sheeting around his woolly head, and I ask:

"Who the mischief are you?"

"I am Susi, the servant of Dr. Livingstone," said he, smiling, and showing a gleaming row of teeth.

"What! Is Dr. Livingstone here?"

"Yes, sir."

"In this village?"

"Yes, sir."

"Are you sure?"

"Sure, sure, sir. Why, I leave him just now."

"Good morning, sir," said another voice.

"Hallo," said I, "is this another one?"

"Yes, sir."

"Well, what is your name?"

"My name is Chumah, sir."

"What! are you Chumah, the friend of Wekotani?"

"Yes, sir."

"And is the Doctor well?"

"Not very well, sir."

"Where has he been so long?"

"In Manyuema."

"Now, you Susi, run, and tell the Doctor I am coming."

"Yes, sir," and off he darted like a madman.

But by this time we were within two hundred yards of the village, and the multitude was getting denser, and almost preventing our march. Flags and streamers were out; Arabs and Wangwana were pushing their way through the natives in order to greet us, for, according to their account, we belonged to them. But the great wonder of all was, "How did you come from Unyanyembe?"

Soon Susi came running back, and asked me my name; he had told the Doctor that I was coming, but the Doctor was too surprised to believe him, and, when the Doctor asked him my name, Susi was rather staggered.

But, during Susi's absence, the news had been conveyed to the Doctor that it was surely a white man that was coming, whose guns were firing and whose flag could be seen; and the great Arab magnates of Ujiji—Mohammed bin Sali, Sayd bin Majid, Abid bin Suliman, Mohammed bin Gharib, and others—had gathered together before the Doctor's house, and the Doctor had come out from his veranda to discuss the matter and await my arrival.

In the meantime, the head of the Expedition had halted, and the kirangozi was out of the ranks, holding his flag aloft, and Selim said to me, "I see the Doctor, sir. Oh, what an old man! He has got a white beard." And I—— What would I not have given for a bit of friendly wilderness, where, unseen, I might vent my joy in some mad freak, such as idiotically biting my hand, turning a somersault, or slashing at trees, in order to allay those exciting feelings that were well-nigh uncontrollable. My heart beats fast, but I must not let my face betray my emotions, lest it shall detract from the dignity of a white man appearing under such extraordinary circumstances.

So I did that which I thought was most dignified. I pushed back the crowds, and, passing from the rear, walked down a living avenue of people, until I came in front of the semicircle of Arabs, in the front of which stood the white man with the grey beard. As I advanced slowly towards him I noticed he was pale, looked wearied, had a grey beard, wore a bluish cap with a faded gold band round it, had on a red-sleeved waistcoat, and a pair of grey tweed trousers. I would have run to him, only I was a coward in the presence of such a mob—would have embraced him, only, he being an Englishman, I did not know how he would receive me; so I did what cowardice and false pride suggested was the best thing—walked deliberately to him, took off my hat, and said:

"Dr. Livingstone, I presume?"

"YES," said he, with a kind smile lifting his cap slightly.

I replace my hat on my head, and he puts on his cap, and we both grasp hands, and I then say aloud:

"I thank God, Doctor, I have been permitted to see you."

He answered, "I feel thankful that I am here to welcome you."

I turn to the Arabs, take off my hat to them in response to the saluting chorus of "Yambos" I receive, and the Doctor introduces them to me by name. Then, oblivious of the crowds, oblivious of the men who shared with me my dangers, we—Livingstone and I—turn our faces towards his tembe. He points to the veranda, or, rather, mud platform, under the broad over-hanging eaves; he points to his own particular seat, which I see his age and experience in Africa has suggested, namely, a straw mat, with a goatskin over it, and another skin nailed against the wall to protect his back from contact with the cold mud. I protest against taking this seat, which so much more befits him than me, but the Doctor will not yield: I must take it.

We are seated—the Doctor and I—with our backs to the wall. The Arabs take seats on our left. More than a thousand natives are in our front, filling the whole square densely, indulging their curiosity and discussing the fact of two white men meeting at Ujiji—one just come from Manyuema, in the west, the other from Unyanyembe, in the east.

Conversation began. What about? I declare I have forgotten. Oh! we mutually asked questions of one another, such as:

"How did you come here?" and "Where have you been all this long time? —the world has believed you to be dead." Yes, that was the way it began; but whatever the Doctor informed me, and that which I communicated to him, I cannot correctly report, for I found myself gazing at him, conning the wonderful man at whose side I now sat in Central Africa. Every hair of his head and beard, every wrinkle of his face, the wanness of his features, and the slightly wearied look he wore, were all imparting intelligence to me —the knowledge I craved for so much ever since I heard the words, "Take what you want, but find Livingstone." What I saw was deeply interesting intelligence to me, and unvarnished truth. I was listening and reading at the same time. What did these dumb witnesses relate to me?

Oh, reader, had you been at my side on this day in Ujiji, how eloquently could be told the nature of this man's work! Had you been there but to see and hear! His lips gave me the details; lips that never lie. I cannot repeat what he said; I was too much engrossed to take my note-book out, and begin to stenograph his story. He had so much to say that he began at the end, seemingly oblivious of the fact that five or six years had to be accounted for. But his account was oozing out; it was growing fast into grand proportions —into a most marvellous history of deeds.

The Arabs rose up, with a delicacy I approved, as if they intuitively knew that we ought to be left to ourselves. I sent Bombay with them, to give them the news they also wanted so much to know about the affairs at Unyan-yembe. Sayd bin Majid was the father of the gallant young man whom I saw at Masange, and who fought with me at Zimbizo, and who soon afterwards was killed by Mirambo's Ruga-Ruga in the forest of Wilyankuru; and, know-ing that I had been there, he earnestly desired to hear the tale of the fight; but they had all friends at Unyanyembe, and it was but natural that they should be anxious to hear of what concerned them.

After giving orders to Bombay and Asmani for the provisioning of the men of the Expedition, I called "Kaif-Halek," or "How-do-ye-do," and in-troduced him to Dr. Livingstone as one of the soldiers in charge of certain goods left at Unyanyembe, whom I had compelled to accompany me to Ujiji, that he might deliver in person to his master the letter-bag he had been entrusted with by Dr. Kirk. This was that famous letter-bag marked "Nov. 1st, 1870," which was now delivered into the Doctor's hands 365 days after it left Zanzibar! How long, I wonder, had it remained at Unyanyembe had I not been despatched into Central Africa in search of the great traveller?

The Doctor kept the letter-bag on his knee, then, presently, opened it, looked at the letters contained there, and read one or two of his children's letters, his face in the meanwhile lighting up.

He asked me to tell him the news. "No, Doctor," said I, "read your letters first, which I am sure you must be impatient to read."

"Ah," said he, "I have waited years for letters, and I have been taught patience. I can surely afford to wait a few hours longer. No, tell me the general news: how is the world getting along?"

"You probably know much already. Do you know that the Suez Canal is a fact—is opened, and a regular trade carried on between Europe and India through it?"

"I did not hear about the opening of it. Well, that is grand news! What else?"

Shortly I found myself enacting the part of an annual periodical to him. There was no need of exaggeration—of any penny-a-line news, or of any sensationalism. The world had witnessed and experienced much the last few years. The Pacific Railroad had been completed; Grant had been elected President of the United States; Egypt had been flooded with savants; the Cretan rebellion had terminated; a Spanish revolution had driven Isabella from the throne of Spain, and a Regent had been appointed; General Prim was assassinated; a Castelar had electrified Europe with his advanced ideas upon the liberty of worship; Prussia had humbled Denmark, and annexed Schleswig-Holstein, and her armies were now around Paris; the "Man of Destiny" was a prisoner at Wilhelmshöhe; the Queen of Fashion and the Empress of the French was a fugitive; and the child born in the purple had lost for ever the Imperial crown intended for his head; the Napoleon dynasty was extinguished by the Prussians, Bismarck and Von Moltke; and France, the proud empire, was humbled to the dust.

What could a man have exaggerated of these facts? What a budget of news it was to one who had emerged from the depths of the primeval forests of Manyuema! The reflection of the dazzling light of civilization was cast on him while Livingstone was thus listening in wonder to one of the most exciting pages of history ever repeated. How the puny deeds of barbarism paled before these! Who could tell under what new phases of uneasy life Europe was laboring even then, while we, two of her lonely children, re-hearsed the tale of her late woes and glories? More worthily, perhaps, had the tongue of a lyric Demodocus recounted them; but, in the absence of the poet, the newspaper correspondent performed his part as well and truthfully as he could.

Not long after the Arabs had departed, a dishful of hot hashed-meat cakes was sent to us by Sayd bin Majid, and a curried chicken was received from Mohammed bin Sali, and Moeni Kheri sent a dishful of stewed goat-meat and rice; and thus presents of food came in succession, and as fast as they were brought we set to. I had a healthy, stubborn digestion—the exercise I had taken had put it in prime order; but Livingstone—he had been com-plaining that he had no appetite, that his stomach refused everything but a cup of tea now and then—he ate also—ate like a vigorous, hungry man; and, as he vied with me in demolishing the pancakes, he kept repeating, "You have brought me new life. You have brought me new life."

"Oh, by George!" I said, "I have forgotten something. Hasten, Selim, and bring that bottle; you know which; and bring me the silver goblets. I brought this bottle on purpose for this event, which I hoped would come to pass, though often it seemed useless to expect it."

Selim knew where the bottle was, and he soon returned with it—a bottle of Sillery champagne; and, handing the Doctor a silver goblet brimful of the exhilarating wine, and pouring a small quantity into my own, I said,

"Dr. Livingstone, to your very good health, sir."

"And to yours," he responded.

And the champagne I had treasured for this happy meeting was drunk with hearty good wishes to each other.

But we kept on talking and talking, and prepared food was being brought to us all that afternoon; and we kept on eating every time it was brought, until I had eaten even to repletion, and the Doctor was obliged to confess that he had eaten enough. Still, Halimah, the female cook of the Doctor's establishment, was in a state of the greatest excitement. She had been pro-truding her head out of the cookhouse to make sure that there were really two white men sitting down in the veranda, when there used to be only one, who would not, because he could not, eat anything; and she had been con-siderably exercised in her mind about this fact. She was afraid the Doctor did not properly appreciate her culinary abilities; but now she was amazed at the extraordinary quantity of food eaten, and she was in a state of de-lightful excitement. We could hear her tongue rolling off a tremendous volume of clatter to the wondering crowds who halted before the kitchen to hear the current of news with which she edified them. Poor, faithful soul! While we listened to the noise of her furious gossip, the Doctor related her faithful services, and the terrible anxiety she evinced when the guns first announced the arrival of another white man in Ujiji; how she had been flying about in a state of the utmost excitement, from the kitchen into his presence, and out again into the square, asking all sorts of questions; how she was in despair at the scantiness of the general larder and treasury of the strange household; how she was anxious to make up for their poverty by a grand appearance—to make up a sort of Barmecide feast to welcome the white man. "Why," said she, "is he not one of us? Does he not bring plenty of cloth and beads? Talk about the Arabs! Who are they that they should be compared to white men? Arabs, indeed!"

The Doctor and I conversed upon many things, especially upon his own immediate troubles, and his disappointment, upon his arrival in Ujiji, when told that all his goods had been sold, and he was reduced to poverty. He had but twenty cloths or so left of the stock he had deposited with the man called Sherif, the half-caste drunken tailor, who was sent by the British Consul in charge of the goods. Besides which he had been suffering from an attack of dysentery, and his condition was most deplorable. He was but little improved on this day, though he had eaten well, and already began to feel stronger and better.

This day, like all others, though big with happiness to me, at last was fading away. We, sitting with our faces looking to the east, as Livingstone had been sitting for days preceding my arrival, noted the dark shadows which crept up above the grove of palms beyond the village, and above the rampart of mountains which we had crossed that day, now looming through the fast approaching darkness; and we listened, with our hearts full of gratitude to the great Giver of Good and Dispenser of all Happiness, to the sonorous thunder of the surf of the Tanganyika, and to the chorus which the night insects sang. Hours passed, and we were still sitting there with our minds busy upon the day's remarkable events, when I remembered that the traveller had not yet read his letters.

"Doctor," I said, "you had better read your letters. I will not keep you up any longer."

"Yes," he answered, "it is getting late; and I will go and read my friends' letters. Good-night, and God bless you."

"Good-night, my dear Doctor; and let me hope that your news will be such as you desire."

And now, dear reader, having related succinctly "How I found Livingstone," I bid you also "Good-night."